D0418494

THE CLIMB

ANATOLI BOUKREEV was one of the world's foremost high-altitude mountaineers. Twenty-one times he went to the summit of the world's highest mountains. For his heroic actions on Mount Everest in May 1996 he was awarded the American Alpine Club's highest honour, the David A. Sowles Memorial Award. He died in an avalanche in 1997 while attempting a winter assault on Annapurna in Nepal.

G. WESTON DEWALT is a writer and documentary filmmaker who lives in Pasedena, California.

THE CLIMB

*Tragic
Ambitions
on Everest*

ANATOLI BOUKREEV
AND
G. WESTON DEWALT

PAN BOOKS

First published 1998 by St Martin's Press, New York

First published in Great Britain 2001 by Macmillan

This edition published 2002 by Pan Books
an imprint of Pan Macmillan Ltd,
Pan Macmillan, 20 Wharf Road, London N1 9RR
Basingstoke and Oxford
Associated companies throughout the world
www.panmacmillan.com

ISBN 978-0-330-48896-9

A CIP catalogue record for this book is available from
the British Library.

Printed and bound in Great Britain by
Mackays of Chatham plc, Chatham, Kent

Visit **www.panmacmillan.com** to read more about all our books and to buy
them. You will also find features, author interviews and news of any author
events, and you can sign up for e-newsletters so that you're always first to hear
about our new releases.

THIS EDITION OF *THE CLIMB*
IS DEDICATED TO THE MEMORY OF

ANATOLI NIKOLIAVICH BOUKREEV

DIMITRI SOBOLEV

VLADIMIR BASHKIROV

BRUCE HERROD

LOPSANG JANGBU SHERPA

SCOTT FISCHER

YASUKO NAMBA

ROB HALL

ANDY HARRIS

DOUG HANSEN

NGAWANG TOPCHE SHERPA

CHEN YU-NAN

Mountains have the power to call us into their realms and there, left forever, are our friends whose great souls were longing for the heights. Do not forget the mountaineers who have not returned from the summits.

—ANATOLI BOUKREEV

WITH EVERLASTING THANKS TO

LINDA WYLIE

BETH WALD

TERRY LeMONCHECK

ALEX DAVIS

SIMONE MORO

ERVAND ILINSKI

RINAT KHAIBULLIN

GENE AND SHIRLEY FISCHER

JEANNIE FISCHER-PRICE

BOB PALAIS

DYANNA TAYLOR

GARY NEPTUNE

ACKNOWLEDGMENTS

The authors would like to offer their thanks to those individuals who contributed to this effort, some of whom, for reasons of privacy, have asked not to be publicly identified. To the members of the 1996 Mountain Madness expedition to Mount Everest we are most grateful.

Many contributed to the weave and texture of the moments and events that led to this book. We extend our appreciation to: Reina Attias, Kevin Cooney, Charles Ramsburg, Michele Zackheim, Bob Palais, Charlie Mace, Perry Williamson, Gary Neptune, Laurie Brown, Michael DiLorenzo, Todd Skinner, Jack Robbins, David Shenk, Alex Beers, Elliot Robinson, Fleur Green, Christian Beckwith, Anne Krchik, Dr. Roger Miller, Beth Wald, Sue Fearon, and Greg Glade.

To Jed Williamson, former president of the American Alpine Club and current editor of the annual *Accidents in North American Mountaineering*, Weston DeWalt owes a special thanks. His encouragement of this effort was a consistent source of support.

Two translators/interpreters, Natalya Lagovskaya and Barbara Poston, saw us through the entire project, and the final shape of the words on these pages are due largely to their untiring efforts.

Our primary researcher, sometimes interviewer, was Terry LeMoncheck, whose commitment to this effort was a true gift. It could not have been done without her.

For her belief in our project and her enduring efforts, we extend our thanks to Kathleen Anderson of Scovil, Chichak and Galen.

To our editor at St. Martin's, George White, we offer our

sincerest gratitude for his efforts in guiding us on the mountain that was this book.

To a special friend, Linda Wylie, we both owe our deepest of thanks. Her hospitality, graciousness, level-headedness, and commitment to the human spirit brought us, more than once, out of the clouds and down to the issues.

Climbing today is not only mainstream, it is business, and with that comes the rising tendency for climbing decisions—objectives as well as tactical decisions on a climb—to be business decisions as well. The up side to that is that now climbers—like skiers and sailors before them—can make a living from what they love to do. The down side can be seen in increased crowds at the crags, the proliferation of new regulations aimed at climbers, and today and forevermore, the "circus" at Everest Base Camp.

—CHRISTIAN BECKWITH,

"PREFACE," *AMERICAN ALPINE JOURNAL*, 1997

The mountain doesn't play games. It sits there unmoved.

—BRUCE BARCOTT,

"CLIFFHANGERS," *HARPER'S MAGAZINE*, AUGUST 1996

CONTENTS

AUTHORS' NOTE

Five days after the Everest tragedy of May 10, 1996, nine climbers sat in a circle at the Mountain Madness Everest Base Camp and recorded their thoughts and memories. Many of the details and some of the quotes in this book are drawn from those recorded recollections. Anatoli Boukreev, a participant in the taped "debriefing," has drawn upon that source and wishes to thank everyone who participated. Their attempts at truth-telling and self-reflection have added considerably to the historical record. Quotes, when taken from the debriefing tapes, have been noted with this symbol:❖

PROLOGUE

In ancient Buddhist scriptures the Himalaya are referred to as the "storehouse of snow," and in 1996 the storehouse was filled again and again as unusual amounts of snow fell in the mountains.

In the early evening of May 10, 1996, a particularly vicious storm blew into Mount Everest and lingered at its highest elevations for more than ten hours. Twenty-three men and women, mountaineers who had climbed the mountain that day from its southern side in Nepal, could not make it to the safety of their highest-altitude camp. In a virtual white-out, battered by hurricane-force winds strong enough to blow over a semi-trailer truck, the climbers fought for their lives.

The mountaineers had been caught in the Death Zone, the elevations above 8,000 meters where extended exposure to sub-zero temperatures and oxygen deprivation combine and kill, quickly.

As the climbers fought for survival, they were often blind but for an arm's length. Sometimes there were ropes to secure and guide them. The pressure gauges on their oxygen tanks fell to zero, and the raging confusion of hypoxia began to conquer most rational figurings. The foretelling numbness of frostbite pushed the possibilities of amputations from remote to probable. In the dark and the screaming howl of the storm the climbers began to bargain. My fingers for my life? Fair enough; just let me *live.*

Below the descending climbers, in the high-altitude camp they were struggling to reach, a Russian mountaineer and climbing guide was fighting his own battle: yelling, cajoling, and pleading with other climbers to assist him in an effort to rescue those who were above, lost in the storm.

Anatoli Nikoliavich Boukreev made a decision, one that some would later call suicidal. He decided to attempt a rescue, to go into the storm solo, into a pelting blow of snow, into a lacerated darkness, into the roar of what one climber described as "a hundred freight trains passing over your head." Boukreev's efforts resulted in what the mountaineer and writer Galen Rowell would later call "one of the most amazing rescues in mountaineering history."

Two weeks after the disaster on Mount Everest, Boukreev flew from Kathmandu, Nepal, to Denver, Colorado, where he was met by friends and driven to Santa Fe, New Mexico, to recuperate from his ordeal. Upon arriving, he asked to meet me, because a few months earlier, at a mutual friend's request, I had arranged for him the purchase of a camera and its delivery to the Everest Base Camp. On May 28, 1996, we met for the first time.

I had seen photographs of Boukreev that had been taken prior to the events on Mount Everest. Lean, taut, with a confident smile, is how I imagined him. As I walked into our mutual friend's house, he rose slowly from a chair to greet me. His eyes were sunken, tired. The tip of his nose and places on his lips were crusted in black, the telltale dead skin that comes with severe frostbite. He was distant; he looked as if he'd moved out of his body and into a place that had no address.

Something about him was familiar—the hollowness, the emptiness behind the eyes. As he took a step forward to shake my hand, I made the connection: a Russian soldier I'd encountered in Mozambique during the war there, sitting in the back of a canvas-topped troop transport, an AK-47 cradled in his lap. He'd looked at me with those same eyes and warned away my attempts to record him on motion-picture film. It had been a disturbing moment, not so much for the casualness with which he pointed his weapon, but for the blankness he wore on his face.

Over dinner we talked. My attempts to revive my college Russian were useless, so Boukreev spoke in English, fluid and understandable enough, but simple in its constructions. He wanted to talk about Everest, not to tell his story, but to inquire out loud about what had happened. He was trying to understand what he had just been through.

The next day we met again, and then the next, and we talked. Our mutual friend told me that Boukreev was having dreams at night, troubling dreams about being on Mount Everest, knowing that he had to get oxygen to stranded climbers whom he could never find. He never told me about the dreams, but he told me about what had happened on Everest, how he had come to the mountain, how he had left it in the last days of May. His stories were dramatically told, not embellished. A brewed pot of tea had the same rhetorical weight as being lost in a blizzard. I came to appreciate his forthrightness, his responses to my questions that with my growing curiosity became harder and more detailed. We began to tape our conversations.

On June 3, 1996, Boukreev and I agreed to collaborate on this book. We would cooperate, yes, but I explained I would want to range beyond his experiences, to ask my own questions. The idea appealed to Boukreev. He knew some pieces, but was missing others. For his own reasons he was as curious as I about where the trail would take us.

On January 3, 1997, after getting a contract from St. Martin's Press, our interviewing and writing efforts began. Boukreev contributed his personal journals, letters, expedition logs, and memories. He regained the twenty pounds he'd lost on Mount Everest; the smiles returned to his face. I traveled, met those who had climbed with him and the friends and associates of those who had not returned. With the help of translators, interpreters, and friends, and through intervening tragedies and between the moments of our ongoing lives, we assembled this story of the climb.

—G. Weston DeWalt, Santa Fe, New Mexico

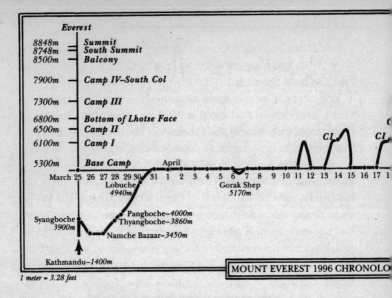

Everest

8848m	—	**Summit**
8748m	—	**South Summit**
8500m	—	**Balcony**
7900m	—	**Camp IV–South Col**
7300m	—	**Camp III**
6800m	—	**Bottom of Lhotse Face**
6500m	—	**Camp II**
6100m	—	**Camp I**
5300m	—	**Base Camp**

March 25 26 27 28 29 30 31 April 1 2 3 4 5 6 7 8 9 10 11 12 13 14 15 16 17 1

CI *CI*

Lobuche
4940m

Gorak Shep
5170m

Syangboche
3900m

Pangboche–4000m
Thyangboche–3860m
Namche Bazaar–3450m

Kathmandu–1400m

1 meter = 3.28 feet

MOUNT EVEREST 1996 CHRONOLO

Kathmandu to Syangboche to Namche Bazaar
Namche Bazaar
Namche Bazaar to Thyangboche
Thyangboche to Pangboche
Pangboche to Lobuche
Lobuche to Everest Base Camp
Base Camp
Base Camp
Base Camp
Base Camp
Base Camp
Base Camp
Base Camp to Gorak Shep to Base Camp
Base Camp
Base Camp (Expedition Members Arrive)
Base Camp
Base Camp
Base Camp through Khumbu Icefall to Camp I to Base Camp
Base Camp
Base Camp to Camp I
Camp I to Camp II to Base Camp
Base Camp
Base Camp
Base Camp to Camp I
Camp I to Camp II
Camp II (Fix Ropes to 7,100m) to Base Camp
Base Camp
Base Camp
Base Camp

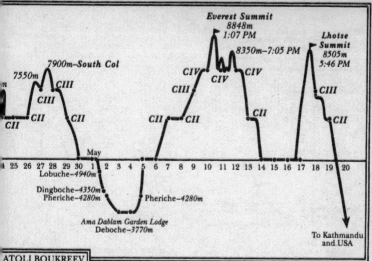

Everest Summit
8848m
1:07 PM

8350m–7:05 PM

Lhotse
Summit
8505m
5:46 PM

7900m–South Col

7550m

CIV   CIV   CIV

CIII   CIII

CII   CII   CII   CII   CII   CII   CIII   CII

May

4 25 26 27 28 29 30 1 2 3 4 5 6 7 8 9 10 11 12 13 14 15 16 17 18 19 20

Lobuche–4940m

Dingboche–4350m
Pheriche–4280m   Pheriche–4280m

Ama Dablam Garden Lodge
Deboche–3770m

To Kathmandu
and USA

ATOLI BOUKREEV

April 23	Base Camp to Camp II
April 24	Camp II to 7,300m–Return to Camp II
April 25	Camp II (Rest)
April 26	Camp II to Camp III to 7,550m–Return to Camp III
April 27	Camp III to Camp IV–South Col to Camp III
April 28	Camp III to Camp II (Assisting Fischer with Kruse)
April 29	Camp II to base Camp (With Kruse and Gammelgaard)
April 30	Base Camp
May 1	Base Camp to Dingboche
May 2	Dingboche to Pheriche to Ama Dablam Garden Lodge–Deboche
May 3	Deboche
May 4	Deboche to Base Camp
May 5	Base Camp
May 6	Base Camp to Camp II
May 7	Camp II
May 8	Camp II to Camp III
May 9	Camp III to Camp IV–South Col
May 10	Camp IV to Summit–Return to Camp IV (Rescue)
May 11	Camp IV to 8,350m (Fischer Rescue Attempt)
May 12	Camp IV to Camp II
May 13	Camp II to Base Camp
May 14	Base Camp
May 15	Base Camp (Taped Debriefing)
May 16	Base Camp–Begin Ascent of Lhotse 8.30 PM
May 17	To Summit of Lhotse to Camp III
May 18	Camp III to Camp II
May 19	Camp II to Base Camp–Descend to Syangboche through Night
May 20	Syangboche to Kathmandu by Helicopter

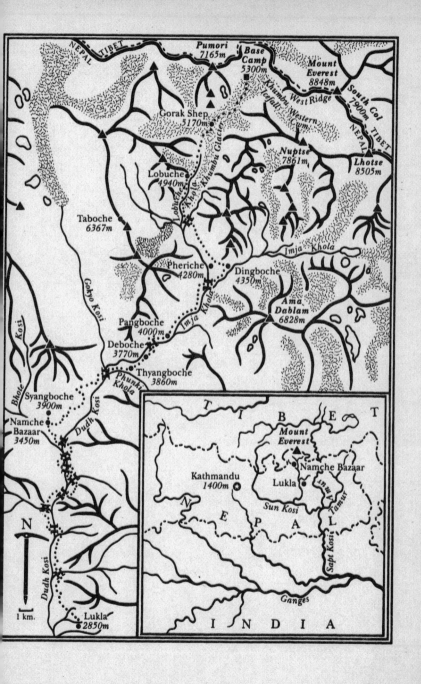

Everest Summit–8848m
Hillary Step
South Summit–8748m
The Balcony–8500m

North Ridge

S. E. Ridge

Lhotse
8505m

Nuptse
7861m

South Col
7900m
Camp IV

Camp III
7300m

Lhotse Face

Western Cwm

Camp II
6500m

Camp I
6100m

Khumbu Icefall

Base Camp
5300m

THE CLIMB

CHAPTER 1

MOUNTAIN MADNESS

A star, one that didn't belong, appeared in the night sky over the Himalaya in March 1996. For several consecutive days the star had been moving over the mountains, its trailing tail fanning into the darkness. The "star" was the comet Hyakutake. It was the beginning of the spring season on Mount Everest (8,848 m), that interval of time between the decline of winter and the coming of the summer monsoons when, historically, expeditions to Everest have been most successful, and Hyakutake's stellar trespass was considered an ominous sign by the Sherpas in whose villages the cosmic smear was a matter of concern and conversation.

The Sherpas, an ethnic group indigenous to Tibet, many of whom now live primarily in the highland valleys of Nepal, derive a substantial part of their family incomes from the mountaineering expeditions that come to the Himalaya. Some work as porters, cooks, and yak drivers; others take on the more dangerous and more lucrative roles as high-altitude support personnel, joining foreign expeditions in their ultimate wager: skill and endurance pitted against a physical environment that precludes prolonged human existence.

By 1996, in the seventy-five years that had passed since the first attempt was made on its summit in 1921, more than 140 climbers had died on Mount Everest. Almost 40 percent of those fatalities had been Sherpas. So, when the natural orders were disturbed, the Sherpas took notice.

Kami Noru Sherpa is in his midthirties, married, and the father of three children. He is one of the new generation of Sherpas who have, since the 1950s, exchanged their traditional dress for Gore-Tex parkas and embraced the cash economy of mountaineering. In 1996, as he had been for the past several years, Kami Noru Sherpa was hired by Himalayan Guides, a commercial adventure company based in Edinburgh, Scotland, to serve as a sirdar (manager) for an Everest expedition.

Headed by the bearded and burly Englishman Henry Todd, a fifty-one-year-old former rugby player turned expedition packager, Himalayan Guides had the distinction of never having lost a client. Todd's practicality and good luck in the mountains and his cooperative relationship with Kami Noru Sherpa had brought them both a measure of success in the Himalaya.

In the spring of 1995, Todd had offered a commercial expedition to Mount Everest, taking his client climbers to the mountain from the north side, from Tibet. The expedition had been an unqualified success. Eight climbers from his expedition had made it to the top. After such success, Todd and Kami Noru Sherpa were riding high, but not to the point of overconfidence. In fact, in March 1996, they were both anxious about the season ahead.

Kami Noru Sherpa had pointed out the errant "star" to Todd, and Todd recalls that Kami was disturbed by its presence. When Todd asked Kami Noru Sherpa what it meant to him and the other Sherpas, Kami said simply, "We don't know. We're not liking it."

"It [the comet] had been there for some time," said Todd, "and for the Sherpas it presaged things not going terribly well." A superstition, yes, thought Todd, but a matter of serious concern, because the people who knew the mountain best said it mattered.

To the uncertain meaning of the stellar disruption Todd could add his own problem. As of late March the winter snows had yet to melt to the point where his yak caravan could safely travel the trekking trail that led to the Mount Everest Base Camp (5,300 m). Some Sherpa porters were getting through on a narrow snow-packed trail, but hardly anyone else. Since the quantity of supplies required by expeditions requires the carrying power and capacity of yak teams, the pace of his supply effort had been slowed considerably. It was a headache, not yet a nightmare, but a problem that could grow to that proportion if the trails remained impassable for much longer. The weather window for attempts on the Everest summit stays open only for a brief period and closes abruptly with the coming of the monsoon season. If expeditions are not adequately provisioned when the time for their summit bid arrives, they might as well have never traveled to the mountain.

As almost everyone does in the face of an uncertainty, Todd and Kami Noru Sherpa took actions that might forestall or minimize the problems that each of them faced. In Kathmandu, Nepal (1,400 m), where he was addressing an accumulation of logistical problems and waiting for snows north of him to further melt, Todd took delivery of several cases of J & B Scotch, a gift from one of his climbers who had been sponsored, in part, by the distillery. Giving careful packing instructions to his Sherpas who would be freighting the spirits to his Base Camp, Todd more than half-anticipated some nights when the libation might serve to take off the edge. Kami Noru Sherpa, not a Scotch drinker, prepared for what was ahead in his own way.

On March 29, in his slate-roofed stone house in Pangboche (4,000 m), a village niched into a series of terraces overlooking the trekking trail that winds to the base of Mount Everest, Kami Noru Sherpa held a *puja*, a ritual thanks to the mountains and a prayer of blessing. At sunrise, in a large, second-floor room above a grain storage area, five Buddhist monks in maroon and saffron robes seated themselves in a circle. Encircling them were Kami Noru Sherpa and several other of the Sherpas from Pangboche who had been hired to work on Everest. A wavering, pale yellow glow from yak-butter lamps and a few stray beams of morning sun offered the only light, nicking here and there the weave of reds and blues in the Tibetan rugs on the hand-sawn plank floors. Spirals of smoke drifted from a cooking fire, and the rich, sweet smell of juniper branches escaped as they were burnt in offering.

The chants of the monks played off the walls and echoed back into their repetition, and with every redoubling came a calm and peace, an assurance that, if the Sherpas honored it, the mountain would protect them and deliver them home. As the *puja* ended, the monks gave each of the Sherpas a protective amulet, a knotted loop of red string. With quiet reverence and a bow of thanks, each of them accepted the gift and placed the string around their necks.

Over the next few days, as the snows continued to melt, Kami Noru Sherpa and the Sherpas would leave their homes and trek to the Everest Base Camp, where they would join the expeditions that had hired them. Working for anywhere from $2.50 to $50 a day, they would help establish camps, carry loads up the mountain, and cook for and serve the climbers who were coming to Everest in ever greater numbers.

In the early 1980s the number of climbers and expedition support personnel who would gather in the Everest Base Camp during the spring season could have fit into one Paris metro car. In 1996, more than four hundred people would eventually come up the trail and pitch their tents, giving the camp the appearance of a rock concert encampment. One climber described the 1996 Everest Base Camp as having all the appearances of "a circus, except there were more clowns in our tents." By many accounts, there were some real "punters" on the mountain in 1996.

A Taiwanese expedition headed by Makalu Gau was the source of endless jokes, which thinly veiled serious concerns about his team's qualifications and their ability to get off the mountain alive. One climber said, "I'd as soon have been on the mountain with the Jamaican bobsled team." And then there was the Johannesburg *Sunday Times* Expedition, which had publicly been embraced by Nelson Mandela. Stories about the relative inexperience of many of their climbers and questions about the veracity of their wiry and short-tempered leader, Ian Woodall, were roundly exchanged over Henry Todd's Scotch.

American climber and Everest veteran Ed Viesturs was heard to say, "A lot of people are up here who shouldn't be." Viesturs, thirty-seven, was working as a guide and doubling as an on-camera talent for the MacGillivray Freeman IMAX/IWERKS Expedition, headed by the American climber and filmmaker David Breashears. The film production, with one of the largest budgets ever committed to a documentary about Everest, was to result in a large-format film to be released in 1998. Designed to be projected in theaters outfitted with wraparound screens and state-of-the-art sound systems, the film would offer virtual, armchair Everest.

Breashears, in his early forties, was something of a legend in the Himalaya. More than any other climber, except for perhaps Sir Edmund Hillary, who with Tenzing Norgay summited Mount Everest for the first time in 1953, Breashears had been successful in making Everest a cash cow, deriving over the years a substantial portion of his income from his activities on the mountain. In 1985, he had the distinction of having guided Texas businessman and millionaire Dick Bass to the summit. Bass, at fifty-five, became the oldest climber to date to make the top. This accomplishment is seen by many as the pivotal point in the history of attempts to climb Everest. The adventuresome and the well-to-do took notice. If a fifty-five-year-old with motivation and discretionary income could do it, anybody could! Commercial expedition companies were spawned to address the demand that was stimulated and to service customers who could pay big dollars for big mountains.*

---

*Everest expeditions changed. Expedition organizers who had previously focused on national and corporate sponsorship were increasingly looking toward individuals with decent climbing experience and money who could be *(cont.)*

As Breashears and his IMAX/IWERKS expeditionary force trekked toward the Everest Base Camp, they made an impression. Not far from Kami Noru Sherpa's house in Pangboche, several members of the expedition had stopped at a teahouse and occupied some of its tables. They ordered tea, but refused the offer of local food, preferring instead home-bought goodies pulled from expedition bags. One veteran at the Everest Base Camp who found the team a little too coiffed and cool referred to them as the "Gucci guys."

Tenting nearby the IMAX/IWERKS Expedition at the Everest Base Camp were Henry Todd's Himalayan Guides expedition and several other commercial expeditions that, like Todd's, had brought paying clients to the mountain. Among the "dollar dogs," as one Everest chronicler has privately labeled commercial expedition members, was the Adventure Consultants Guided Expedition, headed by New Zealander Rob Hall.

Hall, black bearded and imposing with a "Lincolnesque" appearance, had an intensity and quiet reserve that made many think he was much older than his thirty-five years. Since 1990, when his company began taking expeditions to Everest, Hall had taken a record thirty-nine climbers (clients and expedition personnel combined) to the top of Everest. His company's "adverts" that ran in international climbing magazines were large, alluring, and not immodest. One that appeared in early 1995 read: "100% Success! Send for Our Free Color Brochure." One hundred percent that is until May 1995, when he turned all of his clients back from their bid to the summit as deep snows at higher elevations had slowed their progress. No clients had made the summit.

In 1996, Rob Hall was back, ready to go again, determined, if he could, to get back into the win column. The pressure was on. Success, not turnarounds, brought in new business, and

---

pooled to "buy" an expedition. Out of this reality came the marriage of the extreme alpinist and the serious amateur, both looking for a way to the top of the world's highest peaks.

there was an additional challenge in 1996: a new competitor in the game.

Scott Fischer from West Seattle, Washington, was coming to the mountain. Six foot four with a chiseled, symmetrical face and long, flowing blond hair, he ran his West Seattle, Washington–based adventure company, Mountain Madness, as an extension of his personal ambition: to climb mountains around the world and to have a hell of a time doing it.*

With his talent, good looks, and charm, he was a prime candidate for mountaineering's poster boy. He had a charismatic personality with the drawing power of an industrial magnet. He could attract clients, motivate them, get them to commit, to write their checks and pack their rucksacks. He was a contender, but new to the business of guiding a commercial expedition to Mount Everest.

His motivation for becoming an Everest "dollar dog," one of his business associates has said, was fairly simple: "I think that he looked at Rob Hall's success and thought . . . 'If he can do it, I can do it.' And not in a competitive macho way, but just saying, 'Hey, I'm a really great climber. Why can't I do it, too? . . . I'll get clients and I'll go, too.' " Go, too, and make the money, too.

Mountain Madness's former general manager, Karen Dickinson, described the company's decision to package expeditions to Everest as "kind of the ultimate in high-altitude mountaineering. There was a demand from our clients that we wanted to service or else lose them to the competition. If it goes well, it could be very lucrative, so there was a financial motivation. Of course, I can't stress enough that you're equally as likely to lose your shirt. . . . It's just a high-stakes game financially."

---

*Fischer had paid his dues. He came from a solid experiential background, having begun his climbing education at the age of fourteen. A student of the National Outdoor Leadership School in Wyoming, he had developed a reputation as a teacher of rock climbing and mountaineering, and was known as a highly qualified mountain guide with many successful and safe expeditions to his credit.

Fischer was focused on the potential of the big rewards that could come from running a successful expedition. He had been thinking about changing his life. Karen Dickinson said, "He had turned forty the year before; his business had finally gotten to where he wanted. . . . He'd climbed K2 [8,611 m]; he'd climbed Everest; he was established as a successful guide. . . . He was talking about maybe he wouldn't go back to the summit of Everest again, that he would hire people to do that."

The plan had been loosely sketched, little more than casual conversations between Fischer and Dickinson, but those who knew him best said Fischer was giving more consideration to shaking things up. His personal life, his role in the company, his public persona, everything was up for midlife review.

Fischer had worked at developing the Mountain Madness business since the early 1980s, but it had never consistently provided him a good, steady income. Climbing had been his thing; the business had enabled that, but he'd never been a headliner, had never played in the big tent. A commercial success on Everest, he knew, could considerably alter the picture. If he could draw enough clients at $65,000 apiece (Hall's asking price), and if he could build a successful big-mountain expedition schedule, he could solve a lot of problems, finance a lot of change.

Part of the challenge in his birthing a new direction was his lack of international visibility. He didn't have the reputation of many of the other players in high-altitude mountaineering who graced the covers and pages of climbing magazines and equipment catalogs. As his efforts as an expedition leader had progressed, his personal climbing career had taken a back seat. He had come to feel, as one friend put it, "that he wasn't getting his due in the media . . . the press didn't treat him fairly, that he wasn't respected; his name wasn't really brought up much; he wanted to be recognized."

His difficulty, as some of those around him saw it, was his image: accomplished climber, instructor, guide, and photographer, yes, but also swashbuckling, devil-may-care, good-time guy. These characterizations made for a certain kind of notoriety, but it wasn't the kind of image that made the big-dollar clients comfortable or drew the lucrative Fortune 500 sponsorships. He was, for that league, perhaps too "dicey." A successful Everest expedition, one with a lot of visibility, could "skew the do."

Working the phones from their West Seattle office, Dickinson, Fischer, and their staff massaged the client list to promote their expedition, and they mailed out hundreds of promotional brochures, two-color productions that had the graphic allure of a lawn-mower operator's manual. They didn't have the luster or panache of Rob Hall's advertising, but they were on the street with the word: "Climbers on the 1996 team will get a crack at the highest mountain in the world. . . . We'll build a pyramid of camps, each stocked from the one below. The guides and high-altitude Sherpa staff will fix rope, establish and stock camps, and provide leadership for all summit attempts. Climbers will carry light loads, saving their strength for the summit."

For Fischer's competitors in the Everest game, it was not good news to hear that he'd decided to move into the market. Fischer's easygoing style and his efforts in packaging expeditions to the remotest destinations in Africa, South America, and Asia had attracted a lot of customers from around the world, and his success, if it came, would be especially problematic for Rob Hall, who had been incredibly successful in recruiting American clients for his Everest expeditions.

━━━━■━━━━

In an effort to generate more press for both Mountain Madness and himself, Fischer and his staff trolled for media attention as aggressively as they did for client climbers, and early on in their efforts they had a bite, one that promised a serious opportunity.

Outside, the leading outdoor-recreation magazine in the United States, wanted to sponsor a climber-writer, Jon Krakauer, a Seattle-based journalist and best-selling author whom they were commissioning to write a feature article on the boom in commercial expeditions to Mount Everest. They wanted to buy a slot on Fischer's team for Krakauer, but they wanted a deal, a good deal.

Keen to the opportunity that having such an accomplished journalist on their roster could bring, Mountain Madness aggressively worked the executives of *Outside*. They explored a variety of trades and exchanges that would work to each organization's advantage and kept the heat turned up. A business associate of Fischer's recalled, "Karen [Dickinson] was just lighting a fire right and left underneath *Outside*, saying, 'Yeah!' "

Negotiations went well, and Fischer was excited about the potential relationship. In exchange for a discounted price to *Outside*, Mountain Madness was lobbying for advertising space *and* a feature story, replete with color photos, that they hoped would contain precious promotional prose. Krakauer was enthusiastic, too, telling one of Fischer's associates that he wanted to climb with Scott's team because Scott's team actually had better climbers and that Scott was a local guy and an interesting character.

This, Fischer thought, could be the press he was looking for, coverage in a major, mass-market magazine whose demographics had the clusters of "Beemers" and backpackers who could afford big-mountain prices. Dickinson remembered, "There was a long period where we really thought that Jon was going to be on our trip. . . . And we sort of held open a slot for him, thinking that was his, and we were negotiating heavily with *Outside* about how the payment might look . . . a combination of advertising and just writing us a check."

But, a Mountain Madness associate recalled, "They were nickel-and-diming her [Dickinson] and basically wanted, I think, Mountain Madness to pick up the whole tab, not just have him go for cost, but less than cost, so Mountain Madness would be going out-of-pocket to have somebody on the climb. You know, come on, get real! . . . So, at a certain point, *Outside* went to Rob [Hall] and said, 'Okay, what will you give it to us for?' and Rob said, 'Less than that.' Bingo!" At the eleventh hour

Outside bought Krakauer's ticket from Adventure Consultants.

A spokesperson for *Outside*, recalling the magazine's decision to take Hall's offer, said they did not select Adventure Consultants "solely for financial reasons" but had also taken into consideration that Rob Hall had "consistently more experience guiding on Everest, more of a track record in terms of safety, and according to Jon Krakauer, a better oxygen system."

Fischer was enraged by *Outside*'s decision, saying, "God, it's typical of the media. Typical bullshit." A friend of his remembered Fischer's "paint-peeling" response: "He just thought it was really screwed of *Outside* to take this idea and run with it, and . . . getting all this information from Karen [Dickinson] and then just for a difference of maybe a thousand bucks—I don't know what it was, but it probably wasn't a huge amount—and going with Rob."

Exit one opportunity, enter another, perhaps a better one. Mountain Madness was able to sign on Sandy Hill Pittman, forty, a Contributing Editor to *Allure* and to *Cònde Nast Traveler*. Already Pittman had climbed the highest mountain on six of seven continents, but Everest had eluded her. On two previous climbs, one of them with David Breashears of the IMAX/IWERKS team, she had turned back before the summit.

Pittman was a prize. She had more high-altitude experience than Krakauer, and she had an agreement with NBC Interactive Media to do a daily feed to a World Wide Web site (www.nbc.com/everest),* and if Fischer could get her to the top, he would have publicity that a Pope in the pulpit couldn't buy. But, he had to get her to the top, and Fischer knew that.

"I think that first Scott saw her as somebody, kind of a plum," said a friend of Fischer's. "If he gets her to the top, whew! . . . She'll write about him; she'll talk about him; she'll carry him on the wave of good fortune she's had." But, if he didn't, he could have a publicity fiasco. An associate has said

---

*As this book went to press, the archive for this site was consulted, and its files had been removed.

she could imagine Pittman saying, "It was Scott Fischer; it was Scott Fischer. He wouldn't let me climb; I could have climbed."

———■———

To get his clients to the top, Fischer had secured the services of three guides and promoted their commitment to his potential clients. In his promotional literature he identified the expedition guides as Nazir Sabir of Pakistan, a veteran guide and expedition packager who had climbed several 8,000-meter peaks; Neal Beidleman, an aerospace engineer, a climber, and ultra-marathon runner from Aspen, Colorado; and Anatoli Boukreev.

Boukreev, thirty-eight, a native of Russia and resident of Almaty, Kazakhstan, was considered one of the world's foremost high-altitude mountain climbers. By spring 1996 he had climbed seven of the most challenging of the globe's 8,000ers (some of them more than once), and all of those he had climbed without the use of supplementary oxygen.*

---

*There are fourteen 8,000-meter peaks in the world. Eight of those are within Nepal or extend into its territory.

CHAPTER 2

THE EVEREST INVITATION

Scott Fischer and Anatoli Boukreev had been on some of the same mountains in their careers, but their climbing routes had never crossed. Through a mutual friend, the highly respected Russian mountaineer Vladimir Balyberdin, they had heard about each other; Boukreev about the gregarious, intrepid American who in 1992 had climbed the "savage mountain" K2 as a member of a Russian-American expedition; Fischer about a maverick climber who had dodged the draft for the Afghan war to climb mountains and was quickly becoming legendary for his endurance and the speed of his high-altitude ascents. Finally, in May 1994, they met for the first time.

We met at a party being thrown at a restaurant in Kathmandu where Rob Hall was celebrating the success of his most recent expedition to Mount Everest. There were about sixty of us: climbers, Sherpas, and friends, all of whom had been invited to celebrate the end of the spring 1994 climbing season in Nepal. It is a small world, that of high-altitude mountaineers, and many of us knew each other from previous expeditions, but it was the first time I was to meet both Scott and Rob Hall.

I had just come from the first commercial expedition to Makalu (8,463 m), led by my friend Thor Kieser of Colorado. Our results had not been very good. Only three of us, including Neal Beidleman from Aspen, Colorado, and myself, had made the summit. Scott, like Neal and me, was celebrating his own success. Finally, after three attempts, he had made the summit of Mount Everest. It was a great achievement for Scott, especially since he had successfully summited Everest without the use of supplementary oxygen.

For me Scott was a Russian's classical idea of an American. He looked like he was from the movies, tall and handsome. His benevolent, open smile just drew people to him.

I thought Scott had great potential as a high-altitude climber. I have had the good fortune to climb with many of the world's finest alpinists, and Scott could stand with the best of them. Although he was less well known, I had for him a respect like I had for the American Ed Viesturs, whom I had met in 1989. Ed, who has summited nine of the world's fourteen 8,000ers without the use of oxygen, is in my estimation America's finest high-altitude climber.

———■———

Chance brought Boukreev and Fischer together a second time in October 1995; again they were both in Kathmandu, Boukreev struggling to keep his mountaineering career going, Fischer to negotiate with Nepal's Ministry of Tourism for a permit to take an expedition onto Everest.

Boukreev had earlier in the year been invited by a Kazakh team to go to Nepal and join their expedition to Manaslu (8,162 m) scheduled for fall 1995. The expedition was to be made in memory of several Kazakh climbers who had perished in a 1990 attempt on the mountain. Boukreev, who had an ambition to climb all of the world's 8,000ers and had not climbed Manaslu, had readily accepted the offer and trained religiously.

Like other states that had once been members of the USSR, Kazakhstan had been struggling to find the monies to keep their mountaineering programs alive. It was hardly a surprise to Boukreev when Ervand Ilinski, who was to lead the expedition, announced that the team had not found the funds necessary to support the expedition, that they would have to delay their attempt on Manaslu until spring 1996.

I found out about the expedition being canceled just prior to my departure for Nepal. I thought, "What is the use to stay in Almaty?" My opportunities as a high-altitude climber were in the Himalaya, and I needed to go there. If I waited for opportunity to find me in Kazakhstan, my career could be finished. So, I flew to Kathmandu in the hope that I could find some work as a guide or that I could find an expedition to an 8,000er that I could join.

By the time I arrived in Kathmandu there were no guiding jobs to be found, but I did run into some Georgian friends with whom I had previously climbed in the Pamir and Tien Shan ranges of Asia.

The Georgians, unlike the Kazakhs, had been able to find and hold on to the monies for a planned attempt on Dhaulagiri (8,167 m), and recognizing Boukreev's experience and potential contributions to their effort, they invited him to join on the condition that he pay his own expenses and his proportionate share of the permit fee being charged by the Nepalese government. The no-free-lunch realities that had come with the breakup of the Soviet Union were slowly supplanting the generosity more common in the days of state support, and despite his limited personal resources Boukreev accepted the offer.

Because the Georgians thought Boukreev's presence on the climb could be misunderstood and dilute the potential public impact of whatever success they realized as a team, it was agreed that Boukreev would climb with them until it was time to make the final push to the summit; then they would go their separate ways. If they achieved the summit, the Georgians didn't want to seem dependent upon the expertise of a Russian, especially one who lived in Kazakhstan. The issue was not so much competitiveness between climbers (a prevailing condition in high-altitude mountaineering), but a matter of national pride and politics.

On October 8, 1995, Boukreev, alone and without the use of supplementary oxygen, made a push to the summit of Dhaulagiri. Without intending to, Boukreev set a speed record for the time of his ascent: seventeen hours and fifteen minutes.

———■———

Returning to Kathmandu on October 20, Boukreev went immediately to work, looking for opportunities and planning to continue conversations with Henry Todd of Himalayan Guides, who had made him a verbal offer of a job. In May of 1995, it had been Boukreev who had guided Todd's successful expedition on the north side of Everest while Todd was in Base Camp recovering from a back injury. Given Boukreev's success, Todd was eager to secure his services for the 1996 season when Todd was planning an Everest expedition from the south side, via the Southeast Ridge route, the most popular route to the top.

I had just finished breakfast and was walking in a narrow side street of the Thamel district where traffic had come to a complete standstill. In a confusion of jammed-up rickshaws, pedicabs, trucks, and cars, I heard someone yelling my name, and from one of the cars arms were waving and beckoning me into the street. Looking closely, I recognized several of my climber friends from Almaty, and I went to their car. They had just come in from the airport, and they were ecstatic. Somehow, the expedition to Manaslu had been moved up; someone had scavenged the necessary money, and now the plan was to make the ascent in December of '95, instead of spring 1996. This was good news on two counts. First, there was going to be an expedition! Second, I would have more flexibility in my efforts to find guiding work in the spring. It was a few days later that I ran into Scott.

I was walking down a narrow side street when I saw him browsing in the market stalls near the Skala, a Sherpa-owned guesthouse, where I was staying. I thought maybe he wouldn't remember me, so I tapped him on the shoulder and asked him what was happening in America. Immediately he recognized me and broke into a smile.

"Hi, Anatoli. How's it going? You have time for a beer?"

We found a restaurant close to the Ministry of Tourism, where he had a meeting later that afternoon, and we began to catch up on what each of us had been doing since we'd last met. Scott told me that he had successfully guided from Pakistan an expedition to Broad Peak (8,047 m), and that now he was in the middle of permit discussions for Everest. Permit politics, he said, were incredible, and the price they were asking! "Fifty thousand for five climbers; ten thousand for each additional climber. Unbelievable." He said he already had some clients signed up and that it looked like a "go" if he could just get the permit.

Fischer was playing the Everest shell game. He'd been promoting his Everest expedition without a permit in hand, not an uncommon practice among commercial expedition packagers. Karen Dickinson said, "We were all sweating bullets. The year before, we were going to run a trip [to Everest] and we didn't get the permit. And so we decided to bail on the trip. And so of course they gave us the permit, like late January, and we're like, 'Hey, it's too late now,' and our competitors had all lied and said they had the permit when they didn't, and their trips ran. So in '96, we just said, 'Oh yeah, we have a permit,' . . . but we didn't get it in hand until February."

Scott asked me what I was doing in Kathmandu, and I told him that I'd just come off Dhaulagiri, the second time I had climbed it. "Doing some guiding work?" he asked me. "No, just for the sport of it," I told him. "I had the opportunity to tag on to a Georgian expedition and made a speed ascent." Scott was, I think, surprised. "You weren't guiding any paying clients?" he asked me, laughing. My pockets then were almost empty, and his question seemed reasonable. Scott knew the situation in the former Soviet Union where support for climbers had all but disappeared. Like me, he had heard the news; our mutual friend Vladimir Balyberdin had been killed in St. Petersburg while operating his personal car as a gypsy cab.

I didn't want so much to talk about hard times, so I told Scott, "I'm going to do Manaslu with a team from Kazakhstan next month. You want to come along?" At first he was silent, and then he realized I was serious, and he began to laugh again, saying how much he envied me and my extreme adventures.

Scott knew, as I did, that no American had ever summited Manaslu. "You could be the first," I told him. His eyebrows went up and his eyes brightened. "Oh, Anatoli, man, I would love to make that one, but I am so incredibly busy. I'm trying to put together this Everest package for May; I've got some stuff working in Kilimanjaro. Man, I'd love to do it, but I'm just too damn busy."

Fischer's itinerary for Mountain Madness took him all over the world and away from the family he loved. His house in West Seattle was where he had clothes in the closet and where his wife, Jeannie, and his two children lived, but more and more often he was living out of a suitcase or an expedition duffel, suffering the hassles of humorless, palms-open border functionaries. He'd "had problems getting completely strip-searched at airports," Karen Dickinson said, "because, of course, he's coming through with his ponytail and his little gold earring, and [his] travel itinerary that makes no sense at all. You know, like . . . he went to Thailand; he went to Nepal; now he's going to Africa, so the customs people always are like, 'Oh, yeah, what are you up to?' "

I tried to get him off his schedule, to do something for himself, to climb. I told him, "I don't doubt that we'll have success. We have a truly strong team, and you would make it even stronger. Join us!" I could see it was hard for him not to accept my invitation. Clearly his business was pulling him one way, his love of the mountains in another. He told me, "I'm not as free as you are. I've got obligations, a business, family commitments." His dilemma I understood. It is extremely difficult for high-altitude climbers to support their climbing careers without going commercial in some way or another. But, still, it was with disappointment that I heard him say no.

As Boukreev and Fischer talked, Fischer kept glancing at his watch, mindful of his upcoming meeting at the Ministry of Tourism, wanting to be punctual and properly respectful to the authorities. Good relations with the bureaucracy were mandatory. Nobody climbs without a ticket.

When Scott got up to go, he asked me if I would meet him at his hotel, the Manang, the next day and join him for breakfast. He had some things, he said, he wanted to talk to me about.

Boukreev was eager to see Fischer again because he knew Fischer was expanding his operations, looking for new markets, and Boukreev was hungry for opportunities. The years since the collapse of the Soviet Union had been more difficult for Boukreev than Fischer could have imagined. Soviet mountaineering had been decimated. Many of the climbers of Boukreev's generation, some of the finest mountaineers in the world, were now near paupers. With families to feed, their ambitions went on the shelf when they took jobs running mountain hostels, or teaching skiing to the children of Mafia bosses—whatever would put bread on the table.

Boukreev knew the despair and humiliation that came with the loss of state support. After his successful 1994 ascent of Makalu, while Neal Beidleman and the other American members of the expedition were jetting back to the States, he was holed up in Kathmandu's cheapest hotel and selling off his climbing gear to purchase a ticket home to Almaty. Looking into a mirror one day, he realized that after the rigors and challenges of Makalu he had actually gained weight on the expedition food, much better than what he could buy at home. All of his American counterparts had lost weight, some of them as much as nine kilograms (20 pounds). That was the near bottom of his career, and he wasn't far above that now.

I wanted to introduce Scott to the potentials of the mountains in Kazakhstan. The opportunities were there just waiting to be tapped. Long the training ground for climbers from the former Soviet Union, the mountains presented some interesting challenges. The infrastructure was poor; there were few hotels, but capital was starting to flow into the country, and someone with Scott's skills, I thought, could make something happen.

The next morning, over second and third cups of coffee, Fischer and Boukreev looked over maps of Kazakhstan and some brochures about the Tien Shan and Pamir ranges that Boukreev had brought to the meeting. Fischer was intrigued, asked a number of pointed questions, and then abruptly turned the conversation toward Everest. He wanted to talk about Boukreev's experience there. Like all high-altitude climbers who stay wired to news of the Himalaya, Fischer knew about Boukreev's success with Henry Todd's Himalayan Guides the year before. Among the seven climbers whom Boukreev had guided on Everest, three were firsts: the first Welshman, the first Dane, and the first Brazilian.

Scott talked a lot about Everest, and then we began to discuss high-altitude guiding and how it was different from his experiences at lower altitudes. He said he was interested in more than just Everest; he had big plans for the future, for all the 8,000ers. He was giving serious thought to a commercial K2 expedition. A lot of Americans were interested, he said. "I would need some good guides, maybe six, maybe Russians who were willing to take the risk, because there aren't many Americans who could do it."

K2, though it is "only" the second-highest mountain in the world, is generally regarded as the most dangerous of the 8,000ers. Because of its pyramidal mass, the hardest climbing is done on its flanks at the highest elevations; it is one of the great high-altitude challenges. The difficulties of its routes and the dramatic stories, too many of them tragic, about the attempts to make its summit were well-known by Fischer. In fact, as Bou-kreev knew, Fischer had been a player in one of the most dramatic of those stories.

In August 1992, after having successfully made the summit of K2, Fischer, exhausted and suffering from a shoulder injury, descended the mountain at night in a snowstorm, lowering below him the dead weight of a climber rigged to his climbing harness. The climber, Gary Ball from New Zealand and a business partner of Rob Hall's, had been stricken with a pulmonary ailment and was unable to move under his own power. Fischer's heroic actions helped save Ball's life.*

I told Scott, "What is true for Everest is true for K2. You know. You've been there. There is no room for mistakes. You need good weather and very good luck. You need qualified guides, professional climbers who know high altitude and the mountain. And clients? You need to screen them carefully; you need people who can carry the responsibilities and challenges of high altitude. This is not Mount Rainier. Climbing at high altitude requires a different set of rules. You have to develop self-reliance in your climbers because you cannot hold their hands all the time. It is dangerous to say that Everest can be guided in the same sense that Mount McKinley can be guided." Scott listened carefully, then surprised me.

"I need a lead climber," he said, "somebody with your kind of experience. Come with me to Everest, and after Everest, hey, we'll look at K2 with a Russian guiding team and the Tien Shan. What do you say?"

I had to tell Scott that I had already been made a tentative offer by Henry Todd of Himalayan Guides, who, like him, was planning a commercial expedition from the Nepal side of the mountain if he got a permit and enough clients. I told him we have an expression in Russia, "You don't change ponies at the ford of the stream." Scott laughed and asked me what Henry Todd was paying. When I told him, he said, "Look, you're a free agent. You don't have a signed

---

*A few months after his rescue on K2, Gary Ball died on Dhaulagiri from an ailment similar to the one he had suffered on K2.

contract." And then he offered to pay me almost twice what Henry had offered.

For Boukreev it was a welcome invitation, and the offer of prospects beyond was promising. Boukreev had a great deal of confidence in Fischer's ability to handle the complexities of fielding an expedition and appreciated him as a climber. Also, Beidleman was a friend. Boukreev had assisted him in his effort to climb Makalu in 1994, Beidleman's first 8,000er, and had a lot of respect for the determination Beidleman had shown in his exhaustive effort. His endurance was extraordinary, Boukreev noted, because he was an ultra-marathon runner. But the demands of high-altitude climbing are very different from those of long-distance running and Beidleman had no Everest experience.

I didn't want to say no, but didn't feel that I could say yes at that moment, so, instead, I asked for $5,000 more than what Scott was offering, thinking if he agreed, Henry would more readily understand my acceptance. Scott put his coffee down and looked at me as if he couldn't believe what I'd said, and responded, "No way. No way."

I said, "Okay, no problem." Honestly, I thought that was the end of our conversation, that I'd be working for Henry Todd as I had the year before, but then Scott said, "Think about it, what I'm offering you," and he got up to leave for another appointment at the Ministry of Tourism. As he was leaving, he said, "Let's have breakfast again in the morning at Mike's. Nine? Think about it."

The next morning Boukreev arrived earlier than the appointed 9:00 A.M. at Mike's Breakfast, a restaurant in the Durbar Marg area that is popular with American climbers and the expatriates of Kathmandu because of its coffee and pancakes, a conscious pandering to home-away-from-home comfort food desires. Finding a table, Boukreev rehearsed the English for what he was going to say to Fischer, that he would agree to the terms as Fischer had offered them the day before. Boukreev was not going to hold out for the additional dollars. The relationship with Mountain Madness, he thought, could be a productive one, and if it had no beginning, it might not have a future. Thirty minutes went by; then an hour was gone. Boukreev ordered breakfast, suspecting Fischer had changed his mind, that the opportunity was lost.

I had already finished breakfast and had paid the waiter when I noticed Scott walking into the restaurant with his agent, P. B. Thapa of HimTreks, the Kathmandu company that would be organizing logistics for the Mountain Madness expedition in Nepal. Scott came to my table, smiling as always, said, "Good morning," and immediately, before I could even respond, said, "Are you ready to go to Everest with me?" And I said, joking with him, "Are you ready to pay me my price?" Without hesitation he said, "Yes."

The decision made, P. B. Thapa, Fischer, and Boukreev began to discuss details of expedition planning. Of immediate concern to Fischer was the oxygen he needed to order for his climbers. He'd heard about a new Russian source, Poisk (meaning "quest" in English) in St. Petersburg. They were supplying a lightweight, titanium canister that was at least one-half kilogram (1.1 pounds) lighter than the usual three-liter canister used on the mountain, and Fischer was interested in keeping the weight down for his clients. Boukreev had contacts in the St. Petersburg factory, and it was agreed that as soon as he came back from Manaslu, Boukreev would begin negotiations with Poisk.

A few days later I met with Scott at the hotel where my Georgian friends were staying, and I showed him some high-altitude tents made in the Urals that the Georgians had used in their ascent of Dhaulagiri. Good quality, and proven in the raging winds at high altitude. Scott bought one of them and said he would like for me to have another manufactured to his specifications, and it was agreed that, like the oxygen, I would tend to getting it ordered.

Boukreev and Fischer parted, both pleased with their agreement. For the first time in years, Boukreev could see real possibilities ahead, and this year, because Fischer agreed to advance him some money on his contract, he wouldn't have to sell his ice ax or any other gear to get a ticket home. Similarly, Fischer was satisfied. For his expedition and his clients he had been able to secure the services of one of the Himalaya's strongest climbers. Boukreev, he told friends later, was hired for a very specific purpose. "If we get our butts into trouble, Anatoli will be there to pull us off the mountain."

Karen Dickinson recalled Fischer's excitement over having recruited Boukreev. "I heard Scott say, 'You couldn't ask for a stronger climber than Anatoli to be up there with you. Who knows what might happen up there?'"

CHAPTER 3

DOING THE DEALS

For Scott's invitation to join his Everest expedition, I was grateful, and I was very eager to develop a close working relationship with him. I thought about my friends, mountaineers like me, who would never have such an opportunity. Their dreams smashed by the financial realities that came with the breakup of the Soviet Union, many of them would never go to the mountains again. I thought of the climbers who had died in their attempts to advance Soviet mountaineering, attempts that in the history of high-altitude climbing had become legendary. It was an insult, I thought, that what many of them had died for was now suffering its own slow death.

In early November, Boukreev and the members of the Kazakh team continued their preparations for the Manaslu climb. Still tired, both psychologically and physically, from his ascent on Dhaulagiri little more than a month earlier, Boukreev was committed to the Kazakh effort and focused on the challenge. Like all high-altitude attempts, this one would have its risks, and to them could be added that it was a winter ascent and that some of the team's members were young and relatively inexperienced. In combination—the vagaries of winter weather and untested talent—these elements didn't improve the odds, but Boukreev, encouraged by the strength of the more senior climbers, some of whom had summited Kanchenjunga (8,586 m) with him in 1989, was not overly concerned. Later, he would say, "The end of every road is only the beginning of a new one, even longer and more difficult." The road to Manaslu almost proved fatal.

Fischer, who had flown to Denmark after hiring Boukreev, was at the beginning of his own road, building the team he would take to Everest. He had gone to Copenhagen to spend some time with Lene Gammelgaard, thirty-four, a lawyer-therapist-adventurer whom he'd met in the Himalaya in 1991 and with whom he'd been conducting a personal correspondence since then. In their exchanges they had been open and revealing, Fischer about career and personal issues, Gammelgaard about life, ambition, and her interests in climbing, both of them about their futures.

Gammelgaard recalled, "When we met in 1991, we kept on writing, thinking maybe we could meet up and climb something in Europe, or I could go to Alaska and we could climb something. Then, finally in 1995, everything sort of got together."

Fischer had encouraged Gammelgaard to join his 1995 expedition to Broad Peak, to climb her first 8,000er, but in the years that had intervened since their first meeting, Gammelgaard had made a decision. She wasn't going to climb the big ones. She had new priorities, and she took them to Pakistan to personally discuss them with Fischer.

"I went knowing I was going to leave mountaineering behind," she said. "I wanted a family; I wanted kids; I wanted to settle down, sort of keep my drive, but I didn't want to be out there climbing mountains."

With the expedition team, Fischer and Gammelgaard hiked the trekking trail to the Broad Peak Base Camp, and Gammelgaard clearly laid out her decision to Fischer. "It was kind of a turnaround point for me, where I decided, 'Okay . . . I'm going to be satisfied with the trek and see if I feel happy about that.' So that was a very conscious decision. 'Okay, I'm grown up now. I'm making the wise decision.' "

Gammelgaard was resolute, firm, decided. "Then Scott asked me if I wanted to go to Everest in spring 1996." Without hesitation, without a moment of reflection, Gammelgaard immediately answered, "Yes!" No Scandinavian woman had ever summited Everest; she had held it as a dream for years. She had one more mountain to climb.

"I went back to Denmark [thinking], 'I'm going to take it easy and see if this guy survives Broad Peak, because if he doesn't, there's not going to be an Everest expedition.' So I sort of hold the horses for a while, until I got the message that he was safe down. Then I started working to get sponsors together."

Fischer wanted Gammelgaard on the expedition and had offered to assist in her fund-raising efforts. Gammelgaard remembered, "[It was] hard work, eight, ten hours a day, continuously calling, writing, promoting, using the press to create some public image and attract sponsors. So that was sort of a strategically planned, media-using job, to get money together."

Fischer had raised his share of money in the past and was helpful to Gammelgaard, but he was not his usual self. "He was going on a huge expedition to Kilimanjaro in January 1996," she recalled. "He had a very, very tough schedule from January until he was going to Everest. . . . I was shocked about how exhausted he was. He was totally exhausted. And he kept on being exhausted. He kept on being sick. . . . Here's a friend, and . . . so I tried whatever you can do to a grown-up man [suggesting] . . . you have to rest, you have to really, really rest, maybe you have to rest for half a year, maybe you have to rest for a whole year. Because his whole life he has been pushing himself, and so far being able to cope with it, because he was a very, very strong physical personality."

Fischer, Gammelgaard knew, was struggling with his personal limits. After his 1995 Broad Peak expedition and its challenges, he had written to Gammelgaard and said that he "had to get humble; I [have] to learn to be humble, because I don't want to die in the mountains."

One of the problems, as Gammelgaard saw it, was the image that people had of him, one he felt he had to maintain. "It was really shocking to see in Pakistan that the people who were on the support trek, the only thing they could see was their image of a hero. They just couldn't see the human being. They just absolutely were totally blind to the reality. They had that picture of what a hero should be, and they addressed him like that, but they couldn't see him, and I thought, 'Is that an American symptom? How can they be so blind?' And I think maybe the people in Mountain Madness . . . the business partners . . . they might also have been . . . not dragging him back, saying now you have to . . . settle down and find the ground. They needed him for creating the money, and he was playing the game, too, so he's to blame; there's nobody else to blame; he's a grown-up man."

——■——

By December 6, the Kazakhs and I, ten of us altogether, had advanced to 6,800 meters on Manaslu, where we spent an incredibly cold night. The outside temperature got as low as minus forty degrees centigrade. The next day we advanced to 7,400 meters and, on a platform of hard-packed snow, set up what would be our highest-altitude camp, Camp IV, the place from which we would make our bid for the summit. Into each of our two four-person tents we crammed five climbers, and we weathered the night where winds blew at close to sixty miles an hour. Looking at a temperature gauge periodically, I noted that the temperature hardly ever got above minus twenty degrees centigrade.

The next morning at 4:00 A.M., hoping to leave at the same hour, the ten climbers began their preparations for the final assault, but in the crowded tents it was impossible for everyone to ready themselves at the same time, and the decision was made to stagger the departures. At 6:00 A.M. the first climbers began their ascent along the gradual slope of hard snow and ice that lead to the corniced ridge of the summit. Between 10:00

and 11:30 A.M., eight of the ten climbers summited. Two others, Michael Mikhaelov and Demetri Grekov, who had tired early in the climb, had turned back before making the summit.

By 2:00 P.M. all the eight climbers who had summited made it back to Camp IV, where Michael Mikhaelov and Demetri Grekov, who had previously descended, were waiting. We took a brief moment to warm ourselves and then began our descent. While descending toward Camp III, I noticed that many of the climbers were moving slowly and having a difficult time because of their prolonged exposure to the cold and altitude. By 6:00 P.M., in the darkness, eight of us had made it to Camp III, but somewhere above something had happened to Mikhaelov and Grekov. At Camp IV they had appeared fine, prepared to descend with us, but now they were missing. A radio message from Base Camp gave us some information, but no answers.

From the base camp the two missing climbers had been seen through binoculars and telephoto lenses not long after we started our descent sitting in the snow on a steep face just below Camp IV. I could only imagine that they had misjudged their strength and had spent all their power.

With the message about the missing two, Shafkat Gataullin, a young Kazakh climber, and myself, without having had an opportunity to warm ourselves or to take a hot drink, started back up the mountain. Our ascent was hampered by the night, and because we were afraid that the batteries in our headlamps would fail at a critical moment we turned our lamps on and off as we needed them. Finally, after three hours, we found the climbers, down on the ice. One of them had somehow come out of his crampons* and didn't have the strength to fasten them again to his boots. Getting the climbers to their feet, I tethered them to my climbing harness, and with Gataullin's assistance we descended through a night fog and temperatures that were almost as cold as the night before our summit bid.

---

*Fastened to the bottoms of a climber's boots, these devices, ovals of sharpened points fashioned from chrome-molybdenum steel or similar metal, have become standard gear when climbing on snow and ice faces.

Just above Camp III a couple of the Kazakh team members, having seen the descending climbers' headlamps, climbed up to meet Boukreev and the others and to give them hot tea. Mikhaelov and Grekov relaxed at the sight of the illuminated tents below them and began to eagerly drink down the hot tea. Distracted by the tea and relieved by the proximity of the warm tents, one of the climbers lost his balance and slipped on the ice. Tumbling as he fell, he pulled the other climber and Boukreev behind him over a fifteen-meter ice wall and onto the face of Manaslu.

With a jerk, I was torn from my ice ax, which I had used in belaying* the pair. Sliding down the mountain and falling more than twenty meters, we were stopped by a rope that I had fixed to an anchor† just a moment after we had stopped for tea. No one was seriously injured, but somehow I lost my gloves in the fall. In the fifteen minutes it took to get to our tents at Camp III, my hands were frostbitten, but fortunately, my exposure was for a short time and I did not suffer any lasting damage.

Boukreev would later say, "There is not enough luck in the world. That night I got somebody's share."

———————■———————

Returning to Kathmandu with the Kazakh team, his fellow climbers safe and without frostbite, Boukreev checked into the offices of P. B. Thapa of HimTreks, Fischer's agent. In the several weeks that Boukreev had been on Manaslu, a number of faxes had arrived for him from the offices of Mountain Madness. Fischer wanted Boukreev, as soon as he could, to begin negotiations with Poisk in St. Petersburg for the purchase of the expedition's oxygen supply and to arrange with the tent makers

---

*A belay is a technique of climbing safety that provides for one climber to rely upon another by roping together and having one climber stand by to provide friction on the rope to stop a fall.

†The point to which a belay rope is attached. It can be a natural rock feature or a manufactured device such as an ice screw, piton, or snow stake.

in the Urals to manufacture the tent he'd talked to Boukreev about in Kathmandu.

Depleted from his back-to-back climbs of two 8,000-meter peaks and eager to see his mother, who had been widowed the year before, Boukreev returned to Kazakhstan for a brief rest; then, after a New Year's celebration with friends, he headed to Russia to do his deals.

Traveling to St. Petersburg on a gray, freezing day to visit the Poisk oxygen factory, Boukreev considered how fortunate he was to have signed on with Fischer. He knew the "joke" that during the winter it was the Kazakhs, Georgians, Ukrainians, and other "outsiders" who stood on the street corners to peddle shish kebabs while the Russians got the jobs next to the furnaces in the foundries. While he is a native of Russia, Boukreev strongly identifies with the Kazakhs of his adopted country, and being a high-altitude mountaineer he laughingly jokes that he qualifies for his own minority status. He was glad not to be standing on the street, stoking a brazier.

Boukreev worked diligently, but by January 29, there was still not an oxygen deal. There had been complications. Boukreev's negotiations with Poisk had hit a wall. In his conversations with factory representatives he was told that Henry Todd of Himalayan Guides, with whom Boukreev had gone to Everest in 1995, had cornered the market on oxygen, that he had made an advance purchase agreement on the condition that he be the sole supplier for Everest, effectively making him the exclusive distributor of Poisk. Boukreev, who had introduced Todd to factory personnel at Poisk the year before, was nonplussed.

Boukreev and Karen Dickinson, who was handling Mountain Madness business while Fischer was in Africa leading an expedition on Kilimanjaro, had a problem. In late March the clients who were signing on for Everest were to depart for Kathmandu, and by as early as the first week in May they could be making their bid for the summit. They needed oxygen to climb; Mountain Madness didn't have any.

Miffed by Todd's attempt to corner the Poisk oxygen supply, Boukreev suggested to Dickinson that Mountain Madness consider another supplier, Zvesda in Moscow, where he knew he could get a better price than what Todd was charging.

In his Edinburgh apartment office Henry Todd got a phone call from Poisk. "Henry, what's going on here? We've been threatened by Anatoli that if he doesn't get a deal through us he's going to Zvesda." Todd, like the winter coal fire that burned in his living room, began to smolder: "I'm very bad with people trying to get an upper hand. I like to have the drop. I'm not going to shoot, but I like to have the drop."

Boukreev opened discussions with Zvesda but continued to pursue his conversations with Poisk. If Poisk relented and did a deal with him, he could save Mountain Madness almost a third of the price Todd was asking and perhaps even make a small commission for himself. In West Seattle, Dickinson scurried around to get her passport renewed, because if Mountain Madness was going to get the Poisk deal, Boukreev told her, they were going to want cash up front, on the table. She had to be ready to fly with a suitcase full of dollars.

Fischer had been clear in his preference. He wanted to keep the carry weight of the oxygen canisters low. At high altitude, weight matters, and he wanted to maximize his clients' shot at the summit, so Mountain Madness came up with a compromise plan. They would purchase their Poisk canisters from Todd, just enough to supply their clients for the summit push. The balance of the oxygen, what they calculated the clients would need at lower elevations and what the Sherpas would need in their climbing efforts, they would order from Zvesda. Zvesda's canisters, while they carried four liters as opposed to Poisk's three liters, were proportionally heavier.

The compromise proposal was transmitted to Todd, and he deliberated: "Because I knew Scott was a vacillator, I didn't know exactly how it was going to work out." Poisk called again, wanting to know, "Do you have a deal with Mountain Madness or don't you have a deal?" Todd assured them, "Don't worry: it's all okay; the deal's on." Todd had seemingly been boxed into a corner. Poisk was nervous about losing the business, and

Boukreev was continuing to play the Zvesda card. Todd gambled and took a hard-line position. He called Karen Dickinson and forced her hand.

"I asked her, 'What's going on?' and she says, 'Well, we're only looking for the . . . ' I said, 'Look, I'm dealing with Poisk. I sell Poisk. They're not going to sell to anyone else; they're not going to deal with anyone else. The deal is with me or it's not with me, and there's a whole set of masks and regulators and they're all in the deal. You either have it all or I just—I don't need the money that badly. I'm switching the plug on this.' " Dickinson, doing her job, parried, "But Anatoli says he can get us a better deal." Todd, growing increasingly impatient, but remaining characteristically cool under extreme circumstances, responded, "Look, this is the deal; take it or leave it. You sign this fax that I'm sending to you . . . or you forget it. I don't care."

Mountain Madness capitulated. The order was written. The deal was made. Dickinson canceled her plans for flying to Russia. "Anatoli did everything he could, and he tried really hard to bring this around for us. . . . But, I think we . . . just got things started a little bit too late, and I think Henry Todd simply outmaneuvered us. You know all is fair in love and war. I mean, he won this round."

While maddening to those negotiating the deal, there was nothing particularly unusual about what had transpired. Expedition commerce, the behind-the-scenes dollar mechanics of putting climbers on the mountain, has no less drama than buying a used car in Trenton or Manchester or Osaka. Sharks swim in all the waters; everybody wants the best price; the invoice tells the ultimate story.

In a confirmation memo to Boukreev, Karen Dickinson summarized the order: "Regarding Os—We have purchased from Henry Todd the following: 55 Poisk 3 litre bottles, 54 Zvesda 4 litre cylinders, 14 regulators, 14 masks." Numbers on a page, numbers that would later come under close scrutiny, numbers about which endless, painful questions would later be asked.

On February 9, Fischer, finally back in his Mountain Madness office, faxed a personal note to Boukreev. He reinforced his enthusiasm for Anatoli's role in the expedition, telling him, "I am very excited we are guiding Everest with you. We have the potential to do amazing things. I really expect to have a smashingly successful expedition. If we do well on this one, we will be able to climb, guide many peaks. Yes?" That was his lead, gracious and solicitous, but in a few more sentences, he got to a troubling matter. "Perhaps the rumor is wrong, but I heard from friends in Denmark that you might be guiding Michael Joergensen on Lhotse. Anatoli, I am not paying you big bucks to have you moonlighting off on Lhotse. You are under contract for the duration of the Everest season. If you guide Lhotse, it will be for Mountain Madness."

Michael Joergensen had been a member of Henry Todd's Himalayan Guides Everest expedition in 1995, which Boukreev had guided, and had made the summit, becoming the first Dane to make the top. He and Boukreev had talked about doing Lhotse together, but no definite plans had been made. Boukreev had no intention of committing to Joergensen until he had cleared it with Fischer, but because Fischer had been traveling, Boukreev had not had an opportunity to raise the subject with him. Knowing that Fischer was planning to climb Manaslu with Rob Hall, Ed Viesturs, and some other climbers immediately after Everest, Boukreev assumed he, too, would be on his own, but that's not the way Fischer saw it.

Fischer, good as he was at trying to make it work for everybody, proposed a deal to Boukreev. He thought some of the clients he was recruiting for Everest could be interested in an attempt on Lhotse following his Everest expedition. "How about this for an offer?" he faxed. "You guide Lhotse for the few clients that we have interested and we will pay for your permit costs and give you an additional $3,000.00. If Michael wants you to guide him he will have to deal directly with Mountain Madness." Never intending to create a problem, Boukreev accepted the offer by return fax and sent Fischer the names of two climbers he might solicit for the Lhotse bid. Boukreev, fresh to capitalist waters, felt as if he were swimming upstream. When he got to the mountains, he thought, he'd be in his medium: ice and altitude. There he had a reputation for making fewer mistakes.

CHAPTER 4

THE CLIENTS

By February 29, 1996, Mountain Madness had been successful in signing up eight climbers. In a personal letter to each of them Fischer said, "This is shaping up to be a great climbing team and I am really psyched. Not only are we a strong bunch, but personalities seem compatible as well."

Lene Gammelgaard was still committed to the climb even though her fund-raising efforts, which had continued after Fischer left Denmark, had not yet reached the target of the fee Fischer had asked from her. Eager to have Gammelgaard along, Fischer reassured her, telling her not to worry, that "I want you to come, so we'll figure it out."

Not one of the clients who Mountain Madness had signed on, except for Sandy Hill Pittman, had paid the full asking price of $65,000. Dickinson recalled, "Sandy paid for her father to accompany her on the trek and a lot of other stuff. She paid for extra Sherpas to bring in her gear . . . other miscellaneous things, so her [cost] ended up . . . quite a bit higher than sixty-five thousand dollars actually."

As for the other six clients, the prices of their tickets varied as much as their qualifications to climb at high altitude. The client list was a mixed bag of talent and experience.

For Fischer, one of his most satisfying recruits was Pete Schoening of Bothell, Washington. At sixty-eight, if he was successful, Schoening would be the oldest person ever to summit Everest. Lionized in the annals of high-altitude climbing, Pete Schoening was something of a hero to Scott Fischer.

On August 10, 1953, Schoening and seven other Americans turned around on their summit bid on K2, which at that time had yet to be conquered. They had given up their effort for the most honorable of purposes, an attempt to save the life of a fellow climber who had developed a blood clot in one of his legs, a condition that unless treated was likely to cause his death. During their descent in a driving snowstorm, Schoening was providing a belay to the stricken climber, as five other roped team members below him were making their way down an ice slope. One of the climbers, who was suffering from severely frostbitten hands, lost his balance and fell. One by one, four of the other climbers between him and Schoening were pulled off the mountain. Schoening, his end of the connecting rope tied to his ice ax, which he'd wedged behind a boulder, felt the rope play out over his shoulders. The friction of that play and his skill at anchoring the rope arrested the fall, and the five climbers came to a dangling stop, one of them more than 150 feet below Schoening. It was a textbook save, one of the greatest mountain rescues of all time, and Fischer, who had personally felt the cruelty and danger of K2, had nothing but the highest respect for him. As Fischer characterized him, Schoening was "an incredibly strong, strong person, strong climber . . . so, I'm really confident in his ability to climb Everest."

Joining Pete Schoening on the expedition was his nephew Klev Schoening, thirty-eight, of Seattle, Washington. Klev, not nearly as experienced a climber as his uncle, had never summited an 8,000er. Formerly a nationally ranked downhill ski racer, he was a superb athlete who maintained his conditioning by frequently climbing in the Cascades. A "big, strong young buck" Fischer called him.

Then there was the Colorado trio: Martin Adams, Charlotte Fox, and Tim Madsen, all of whom had been recruited by Neal Beidleman, the Aspen, Colorado, climber whom Fischer had signed on as a guide. Beidleman, according to Dickinson, was untested and "had not climbed Everest or any real big mountains as a guide before," so in lieu of a salary, he was "paid" by having his expenses for the climb covered and by offering him a commission on the fees paid by any clients he could recruit.*

Beidleman was aggressive in his recruiting efforts, Martin Adams remembered, saying that Beidleman pitched the climb to him several times.

Adams, forty-seven, who had retired after a successful career selling and trading bonds on Wall Street, had climbed some of the classics in the Alps and the Rockies, and had climbed Aconcagua, Mount McKinley, and Kilimanjaro, but he'd never summited an 8,000er. In May 1993, he had attempted Broad Peak, but had turned around at 7,000 meters. In 1994, on the same expedition that Beidleman had made to Makalu with Boukreev, Adams had climbed to 7,400 meters before turning back.

If he was going to climb Everest, Adams wanted the best advice his money could buy. When he heard that Boukreev was one of the guides with whom Mountain Madness had contracted, he made the decision to go and negotiated a price of $52,000 for his slot. "I like the way Toli operates. He doesn't bother you. . . . He tells you something, he tells it straight up. . . . Hey, Toli is himself . . . he's not out there trying to schmooze everybody." Adams was not looking for a Club Med excursion to the top of a hill. He knew the dangers of high-altitude climbing, and he trusted Boukreev's judgment and experience. "That's what I bet on when I mailed in my check. I knew my chances of summiting were infinitely greater with Toli on the team."

---

*This is a typical way to allow a novice guide to win his stripes. It is the way Boukreev began his own career as a guide.

Charlotte Fox, thirty-eight, an Aspen resident and friend of Beidleman's, was a highly qualified find for the Mountain Madness expedition. She had summited two 8,000ers in her climbing career and had climbed all fifty-four of the 14,000-foot peaks in Colorado. Unassuming and secure, she was a team player, and Fischer regarded her as a true asset, somebody who could perform with a minimum of maintenance. She knew how to take care of herself in the mountains.

Fox signed on with her friend Tim Madsen, thirty-three, who, like her, was a ski patroller in the Snowmass Ski Area. Madsen, while inexperienced as a high-altitude climber, was in excellent physical condition and had good climbing experience on lower elevation peaks. Realizing that they both needed to be prepared for Everest, Madsen and Fox both committed to training extensively in the Canadian Rockies before taking on the mountain.

The eighth client on the roster was Dale Kruse, forty-five, a dentist from Craig, Colorado, who had been the first to sign on and had gotten the best price. A good friend of Fischer's for more than twenty years, Kruse (aka Cruiser) had been the financial fuel that had enabled Fischer's launch of the Mountain Madness expedition to Everest, according to Karen Dickinson. "Dale Kruse was what you'd call the 'seed' client. . . . He paid all of his money like eighteen months in advance and said, 'Here, take this cash; go do what it takes.' And, so, he got a substantial discount, because he was almost like a partner in getting it off the ground."

■

With eight climbers signed on, Fischer and his staff had done a commendable job in their first effort to package a commercial Everest expedition, but Fischer wanted more. In his February 29 letter to his clients, he asked them, "If you know of any eleventh hour candidates, please have him or her call ASAP."

Outside's decision to sign Krakauer with Rob Hall had created an open slot, and Mountain Madness was scrambling to fill the vacancy. A last-minute, full-price sign-on, if they got lucky, could

mean an additional $65,000, and that would make a substantial
dent in expedition overhead; it might even make the difference,
ultimately, in Fischer's ability to turn a profit. As the departure
date for Everest approached, the bills were piling up on Karen
Dickinson's desk. Henry Todd's oxygen tab alone came to more
than $30,000. But neither Fischer nor Dickinson was particu-
larly optimistic. They knew the odds of signing on another cus-
tomer with less than a month to go before the expedition was
improbable; the chances of selling a full-price ticket, ridicu-
lously small. They would do better to take the company's bank
balance and bet that on the next Saturday it would be a sunny
day in West Seattle.

Among the clients there was a general sense that the recruiting had gone well. Adams had been impressed. "The people
on this team were as qualified and as strong as the average
person on the other two teams with which I had gone to the
Himalaya." And Gammelgaard, with one exception, had been
enthusiastic about the job Mountain Madness had done. In fact,
she wondered if she could hold her own against most of them.
"My first impression: 'How am I going to deal with this? They
are so strong; they are so experienced.' "

The exception to Gammelgaard's enthusiasm was Dale Kruse,
who Gammelgaard thought was a questionable candidate for
Everest. "He had been on Fischer's 1995 expedition to Broad
Peak and had failed to make the summit. I knew that Dale
couldn't cope with altitude. He's a very strong man, but he
cannot cope with altitude. He gets sick very early on. . . . So
there was no reason for him, if he had been very honest toward
himself, that he should try to attempt to climb a high mountain,
because above four thousand meters he just gets sick all the
time." Reflecting on why Fischer accepted him as a client and
what she would have done instead, Gammelgaard said, "It was
about being Scott Fischer, being a nice guy and giving people
what they want and also wanting to have the money. . . . If it was
me, I wouldn't have taken him. . . . I would really have taken

care of [Dale] and said, 'You're not going. I will risk our friend-
ship to save your life.' "*

Some expedition leaders, according to Henry Todd of Himalayan Guides, are not above suspicion for taking on marginal
clients, pocketing their money and dreams while all the time
strongly suspecting that they didn't have a prayer of making the
top. Considering one of his archrivals on Everest, an American
packager of Everest expeditions, he's said, "That's his stock-in-
trade. He hasn't had anyone up [Everest] for two years!"

But, on the subject of Fischer's decision to accept Kruse's
money and to invite him on the expedition, Todd has been
more generous. "What happens is this: you don't know who's
going to come good and who's going to go bad. You can get
the best climbers not perform, and you can get other people
who are very marginal who are just utterly determined and will
be successful. I've had this happen to me again and again. I've
taken someone whom I thought, if anyone fails, it will be him,
and he's just waltzed up. And someone whom I've taken thinking, 'Hey, here's a "cert," put a tick by his name before we go,'
and he hasn't done it. This happened . . . on the trip I was on with
Anatoli in 1995. The strongest climber that I had with me . . .
didn't make it, and someone whom I thought was marginal but
okay, he got to the summit before Anatoli." But Todd adds, "Making those wrong calls, those calls we make before we go, those calls
can kill you and other people. You've got to make them right.
You've absolutely got to make them right. You cannot get them
wrong!"

---

*Fischer, whose personal philosophy was that it was the experience that
counted, was more relaxed in his consideration of Kruse. Fischer felt that
wherever you got on the mountain was an achievement. The summit wasn't
everything.

CHAPTER 5

THE TRAIL
TO EVEREST

On March 13, Boukreev flew from Almaty to Delhi, then connected to Kathmandu, arriving on March 15. For Boukreev, arrival in Kathmandu was a mixed blessing. It inspired grateful emotions as the beginning point of an expedition, but over the years Boukreev had seen the city move from a relatively isolated enclave to a city of a half million people, and with that boom came problems.

In Kathmandu the air on most days is polluted with a suspension of heavy metals from the exhaust of diesel engines and airborne particles of human waste, which irritate the lungs and can cause respiratory illnesses. Also, a scatter of bacteria are found in some restaurants and market foods that can lead to gastrointestinal problems. Either of these maladies, if a climber falls to them, can seriously impact his or her potential to perform, so for those who come to Nepal to climb Everest, one of the first challenges is to leave Kathmandu healthy.

———■———

Shortly after arriving in Kathmandu, Boukreev met with Henry Todd to arrange delivery of the oxygen he was providing for the Mountain Madness expedition, but to Todd's chagrin he couldn't deliver. Several weeks earlier the oxygen had been loaded onto a truck in St. Petersburg, and from there it was to go to Amsterdam to be loaded on a jet that would bring it to Kathmandu. But, according to Todd, "The truck was halted [in Russia] because one of the items in the truck belonging to somebody else, nothing to do with us, did not have the proper customs paper, so rather than take that item out of the container . . . they left them all together."

All Todd knew was the oxygen he'd ordered for Fischer and several other expeditions was likely parked beside the road at some Russian border crossing. He had been promised, he said, that the shipment would proceed any day, someday, but not on a known day. Boukreev was not sympathetic to Todd's problem. O's weren't something you could pick up at the corner store in Kathmandu. The oxygen problem wouldn't go away. It would get worse.

Todd reassured Boukreev. He had made a deal and he would deliver. In the worst case, if the oxygen didn't make it, he would give them his expedition's supply, which had already arrived in Kathmandu.

On March 22, Fischer arrived in Kathmandu to meet with Boukreev and P. B. Thapa. Immediately he was hit with the oxygen news, but was reassured by Todd's promise to make good on the order. Then, Boukreev had to break some more bad news. The high-altitude tent he'd ordered made to his specifications in the Urals was, like the oxygen, still in Russia. It was supposed to have come in on a charter flight that was carrying a Russian expedition to the Himalaya, but the charter had been delayed. The Mountain Madness clients were supposed to arrive in four days!

That night Scott invited me to dinner, and we were joined by P. B. Thapa and two of the Sherpas that Scott had hired for the expedition,

Ngima Kale Sherpa and Lopsang Jangbu Sherpa. Ngima (Neema) was going to be our Base Camp sirdar and would be responsible for porters, kitchen staff, supplies, and general operations. Lopsang had been hired to work as the climbing sirdar and would manage the high-altitude Sherpas who would work and climb with us as we made our bid for the summit.

Boukreev was pleased with Fischer's choice of Ngima, a veteran of eight previous expeditions to Everest. Only twenty-six years old, he seemed mature beyond his years, and he had a sense of humor that Boukreev thought would help hold things together when the logistical nightmares that inevitably develop descended upon the expedition. About Lopsang, Boukreev was less certain. Lopsang, twenty-three, had summited with Fischer in his successful 1994 ascent of Everest, and had summited Broad Peak with him in 1995.* It was not Lopsang's experience at high altitude, but his youthfulness that made Boukreev anxious.

Henry Todd, commenting on Fischer's choice of Lopsang, said, "To reach the position of sirdar takes quite a long time and you have to prove yourself again and again, leading as well as climbing. . . . [Lopsang's] climbing no one could question. But, his leading, I don't know." Todd's intuition about a young sirdar who hadn't much leadership experience: "That he's going to make all sorts of mistakes and could well blow it big time."

Over dinner we discussed the outstanding problems of oxygen and the missing high-altitude tent and divided up responsibilities for making sure that all the necessary provisions would get to Base Camp. I needed to buy some extra polypropylene climbing rope. P. B. Thapa was given the responsibility of packing the supplies and getting them

---

*Fischer had embraced Lopsang as a friend and as his protegé. He was strong, with a natural aptitude for high-altitude climbing, and Fischer was devoted to him. Lopsang regarded Fischer as a personal friend and hero, and worked for Fischer although he offered Lopsang less money than his competitors.

to the airport on March 25 when Ngima and I were scheduled to fly with our provisions to Syangboche (3,900 m), where we would connect with porters and yak teams, who would ferry our supplies to the Everest Base Camp.

Quickly, I was able to do my jobs, and then I had some spare time before I was to depart. I spent most of my days with friends from Russia: Vladamir Bashkirov, a highly regarded alpinist, and Sergei Danilovi, a helicopter pilot who was flying under contract to Asian Airlines. Danilovi is a fun-loving character and a champion pilot. I think his job, flying into the mountains almost every day, is as dangerous as being a high-altitude guide, and I have great admiration for him.

Boukreev's time with his Russian friends was a way to stay connected to home and language. For at least two months, at the Everest Base Camp and going up and down the mountain, he would live and work almost exclusively in the company of Americans and Sherpas for whom English would be the lingua franca. He'd been practicing his English fairly religiously for the past two years and had come a long way from his earliest expeditions with Americans and climbers from the U.K., when he had relied almost exclusively on hand signals and the fundamentals of *yes* and *no*. Still, subtleties of jokes, gossip, and social conversation were often lost on him. But, as he once told a friend, "I think it is not so necessary that a guide chat good, but that he can climb good." As the expedition wore on, he would see that precept called into question.

On the Sunday night before Ngima and I were to leave Kathmandu for Everest, I had dinner with Scott again, and this time we were joined by Lene Gammelgaard, who had flown in from Denmark, arriving a few days before the rest of the clients were due from the States. When we were introduced, she explained we had met before, in the spring of 1991 at the Dhaulagiri Base Camp. Frankly, I did not remember, because in our Base Camp several trekkers from Denmark had come to visit. I didn't want to offend, so I pretended to remember. Scott, who was listening to our conversation, knew I was not telling her the truth, and he smiled broadly and said to me quietly, "Anatoli, you are amazing." I think he thought it would be impossible to forget someone as dramatic as Lene.

Excusing myself and leaving Lene and Scott to finish their conversation, I headed back to my hotel to make ready for my departure for Everest the next day, because Scott wanted me to go ahead of him and the clients to supervise the Sherpas in preparing our Base Camp and to coordinate efforts for establishing higher camps.

———■———

Just after lunch on March 25, Boukreev's friend Sergei, flying a Russian transport helicopter, took on the Mountain Madness cargo, Boukreev, and Ngima Sherpa and lifted off. For the passengers: no tea, no coffee, no cocktails, no emergency-exit drills, just cotton for their ears to protect against the deafening noise of the rotating blades.

In less than an hour, after dodging gathering clouds and hunting his way up the Khumbu Valley, Sergei found the Syangboche landing area and put down in a gathering fog.

The fog did not allow Sergei to return to Kathmandu, so he decided to overnight at a local lodge while Ngima and I descended to Namche Bazaar (3,450 m), where I had planned to spend the night and then depart the next morning for the Everest Base Camp. But on March 26, rain fell throughout the day. The steep trails leading from Namche Bazaar to Thyangboche (3,860 m) were slick, a serious problem for yak teams and porters.

There were still a lot of problems even further up the trekking trail to Everest Base Camp. Snow was still lingering on many of its sections, and in places it was still several feet deep. Expedition porters and yak drivers who had shunted off the trail were holding in lodges and campsites until they could get a clearer passage.

The trek to Base Camp, weather permitting, I planned to make in five days, a shorter time than would normally be required, because I had trained rigorously for this season. In Almaty I had been doing two speed ascents of 4,000-meter peaks in a week; in the past year I had spent more than five months in the Himalayas and climbed three 8,000ers, including Everest in 1995. Had I not spent that much time at altitude in the previous months, I would have allowed ten to twelve days, the number of days Scott and I had planned for our clients to take. Some of them were coming from sea level and would need at least that many days to make their adjustments.

Finally, at noon on March 27, Boukreev was able to resume his trek and left Namche Bazaar, descending to the Dudh Kosi River (3,250 m) and from there ascending again to Thyangboche. It was a grueling workout for most trekkers, and Boukreev arrived tired, but without feeling any effects from the gain in altitude he'd made from Kathmandu.

The next day, back on the trail, I came upon Ed Viesturs and David Breashears with their IMAX crew at a waterfall on the Dudh Kosi and had to maneuver myself out of their panoramic view to avoid spoiling their shot. That evening I arrived in Pangboche (4,000 m) in the upper reaches of the forested zone, and at the lodge in Pangboche was able to take in the sun setting on Everest and visit with Ed Viesturs and his beautiful wife.

On March 29, I gained a kilometer of altitude, and as I climbed, I would occasionally come upon yak teams that had boldly ventured into the melting snow and mud that continued to frustrate the Sherpas who were driving them on the trail. It was slow and dangerous going for these teams, because often the yaks would break through the crust of snow and stand frozen in place until they were unloaded and pulled from the snow and back onto more solid ground.

Boukreev spent his last night on the trail at Lobuche (4,940 m) in a Sherpa-owned guesthouse where he bunked with the IMAX crew. The unheated rooms, where everyone slept together on a sleeping platform, offered little privacy, but provided some shelter from the below-freezing temperatures that were still prevailing.

On March 30, about 11:00 A.M., I arrived at the Mount Everest Base Camp. Advance teams like ours had come ahead of expedition members to stake out sites, choosing parcels of the rocky terrain to accommodate their camps. Several tents had already been pitched to house the Sherpas who were responsible for building the camps and to mark the perimeters of each expedition's territory. Usually the pitching of tents is enough to establish a site, but this year one team had gone a bit further. The advance team for Rob Hall's Adventure Consultants expedition in a prime location had spray-painted several boulders with *NZ* (for New Zealand) to mark a large area they wanted to claim for their camp. I had heard about this situation before leaving Kathmandu, and there had been jokes about the reaction that David Breashears, a dedicated environmentalist, would have when he saw the mess. Rob Hall had a good reputation for his concerns and care about the mountains, and everyone believed it must have been done, without his approval, by an overzealous Sherpa. Whoever had done it, I thought, they had a big job ahead to clean it up.

At the site of the Mountain Madness camp Tashi Sherpa, a young man from Pangboche and a friend of Ngima, had already been at work for almost a week. He had been sent ahead with a small crew to construct platforms for tents from rock rubble, so that our tents would be above the pools of ice water that would form on warm days. Also, he and his crew had busied themselves with erecting the stone walls for what would be our kitchen and fashioning pathways that would interconnect our tents and prevent the occasional broken ankle that occurs.

That afternoon I threw myself into physical labor with the Sherpas and worked steadily with them every day until our clients arrived. I would rise around 8:00 A.M. when the sun would hit the tents, have some steaming-hot, milky black tea, and go immediately to work. Around 10:00 A.M. we would break and have breakfast, chapatis with eggs, oatmeal, or tsampa, a barley-flour porridge. Then, in the evenings, a large meal: rice, lentils, garlic soup, and whatever fresh vegetables had been brought in by porters in previous days. For many Westerners I think it would be considered a monotonous diet, but I had become accustomed to it in my years in the Himalaya, and I've always preferred it over the packaged and exotic foods that many expeditions bring onto the mountain. Heavy on carbohydrates and always with a lot of hot liquid, it is perfectly suited to the physical demands of high altitude.

Our work was strenuous at that altitude, but for me the work is part of my adjustment to altitude. Pushing the body, keeping it exercised and active at those elevations, is, I think, important and contributes to acclimatization. I enjoyed the measured, regular schedule and the rhythms of the work, and every evening the physical fatigue was so great that sleep came easily.

CHAPTER 6

DOING THE DETAILS

As Boukreev and the Sherpas made Base Camp ready, Gammelgaard, Fischer, and his publicity agent, Jane Bromet, waited in Kathmandu for the arrival of the rest of their team. Bromet, a climbing partner and close friend of Fischer's, who was also from Seattle, had accompanied Fischer to Kathmandu and was planning to trek to Base Camp with him, the clients, and Dr. Ingrid Hunt.* In the months immediately preceding her arrival in Kathmandu, Bromet had been aggressively pursuing public relations work on Fischer's behalf and had been successful in negotiating a job as correspondent for Outside Online, a Seattle-based provider of on-line news and features packaged for computer consumers of recreation and adventure news. Not a division of *Outside*, the magazine, Outside Online did have a co-operative relationship with *Outside* that allowed them to use the magazine's logo and selected content for distribution.

---

*Dr. Hunt, thirty, a physician from New England, had been recruited by Fischer. Her job, as Fischer had outlined it, would be to serve both as team doctor and Base Camp manager.

For Fischer and for Bromet, who was eager to establish herself in the adventure media industry, her successful negotiation of the Outside Online arrangement provided both opportunity and insurance. There was no guarantee of how Pittman would cover the expedition on the NBC Internet site to which she was reporting, no control over content. Bromet, loyal and devoted to Fischer's objectives, could be counted upon to maintain the company line. There was one slight problem. Without Pittman's resources, which included a satellite telephone, Bromet could hardly compete. Once she left Kathmandu and the hardwired telephone in her hotel room, she was off the grid, out of luck. So, prior to departing Seattle, according to Bromet, she struck a deal that would allow her to use Pittman's satellite phone. "The agreement was that I could use the sat phone that Sandy was provided by NBC. . . . I had talked with Jane, her secretary, saying, 'I need to use these sat phones. Is there a problem?' " According to Bromet, she was assured that her use of the phone would not be an issue. She was in business.

One of Bromet's first reports filed for Outside Online (http:/ outside.starwave.com) from Kathmandu was an on-line interview with Fischer in which he described his clients and climbing guides, Beidleman and Boukreev.* In his responses to Bromet's questions Fischer emphasized the "good mix" of his choice of guides, saying that their combination was "very good for safety." Beidleman, he said, was "hungry to step on top of the world" and that he [Fischer] would feel comfortable, if problems arose with some of his clients on summit day, "to take somebody down [and] let Neal continue up with other climbers to get to the summit so everybody can sort of satisfy their goals."

Boukreev, Fischer introduced as his "head climbing guide" and extolled his achievements as a high-altitude climber who had summited several 8,000-meter peaks without oxygen. He

---

*Nazir Sabir, who had been advertised as a guide, had withdrawn just before the expedition, citing family obligations. Fischer, who had wanted four guides on the expedition, now had only three: himself, Beidleman, and Boukreev.

went on to say about Boukreev's role on his expedition, "Anatoli I know will not be using oxygen. Anatoli is an animal, a monster, that's great."*

Introductions made, Bromet, before leaving Kathmandu, filed a number of dispatches that detailed some of the challenges immediately in front of Fischer's expedition, including the possibility of delays on the trekking trail that Boukreev and the Sherpa team had already encountered.

"From Kathmandu we've learned that yaks can't get to Everest Base Camp. All expeditions have been delayed. There are now ten expeditions waiting to get to Base Camp.

"Because of this, the porters have basically doubled their rates from 150 rupees to 300 rupees for the trip. The porters are asking for more because they have to work much harder and need more equipment under these conditions, and due to the demand for their services."

That problem, the oxygen delivery problem, the missing tent problem, were standard fare in the launching days of an expedition, and, according to Bromet, Fischer was "doing the details" as soon as their plane landed. "The moment Scott arrived in Kathmandu his telephone started to ring. The logistics of this whole effort boggle the mind."

One of the details that Fischer had to handle was professionally and personally problematic. Karen Dickinson contacted him from West Seattle to tell him that Gammelgaard, according to her books, still owed Mountain Madness somewhere around $20,000. "I sent Scott the paperwork while he was in Kathmandu. I said, 'Either she signs this . . . what our deal is, or she doesn't go. Don't let her out of Kathmandu unless she signs this.' "†

Confrontation, especially with friends, was not something

---

*Fischer went on to explain that, as a safety precaution, an emergency reserve of oxygen would be provided on summit day in the event Boukreev chose to draw upon it.

†Fischer was, by many accounts, used to making up the shortfall for friends with whom he wanted to climb. His loyalty to friends and generosity toward them was legendary.

with which Fischer was comfortable. Bromet said of him, "He didn't want to make people upset and wanted everybody to be comfy-cozy. . . . He hated, hated confrontation. He would just avoid it." Fischer's strength was elsewhere, according to Bromet. It was in his ability to take his expertise and natural abilities to perform in the mountains and to share that with his clients, to enable their own ambitions. And sometimes, he would promote those ambitions over his own. "He wanted them [the clients] to have their glory," Bromet said. "He wanted them to feel the excitement and to feel the inner power and strength of what it's like to stand on the top of Mount Everest and accomplish a goal like that. I mean, in a very kind, wonderful, almost tender way he wanted to impart that enthusiasm of the mountains and climbing to these people, as phony baloney as some of them were. To Scott it really didn't matter what the reason was behind the clients' drive. He just saw himself as being there to provide what motivation he could, a psychic motivation if you will. He was like a boat cruising full speed ahead, making a wake, and his clients would get caught up in the wake of this very positive, dynamic energy. . . . He was able to spread the good word and the excitement about climbing . . . even if you're somebody that can barely tie your shoelaces. . . . 'You can do it. We can do it,' he would say. That's who Scott Fischer was."

———■———

The itinerary that had been prepared for the Mountain Madness clients coming from the United States called for them to depart Los Angeles on March 23, to spend some time in Kathmandu, and then on March 28 to fly to Lukla (2,850 m). It was a prudent and conservative itinerary, designed specifically to help the clients avoid acute mountain sickness (AMS),* more

---

*Acute mountain sickness (AMS) in its moderate form causes headache, nausea, disturbed sleep, fatigue, shortness of breath, malaise, dizziness, loss of appetite, and poor sleep patterns. It has two more serious and often deadly manifestations: HACE, high-altitude cerebral edema, and HAPE, high-altitude pulmonary edema.

commonly referred to as altitude sickness, which is brought on by going too high too fast, making large increases in elevation before properly allowing the body to adjust to the lower levels of oxygen that are available as one gains altitude.

By planning to go initially to Lukla at 2,850 meters, Fischer was honoring a commonly held maxim: start below 3,040 meters and walk up, slowly. This routine is widely recommended by high-altitude specialists and has been incorporated in most of the more popular trekking and climbing guides for the Himalaya.*

But, Fischer, just before the expedition began, announced a change of plans. Instead of helicoptering the clients to Lukla, he announced he was going to fly them with the expedition gear that had not gone with Boukreev and Ngima Sherpa to Syangboche on March 29.

Syangboche was the same village to which Boukreev and Ngima Sherpa had flown four days earlier. For them the increase in altitude from Kathmandu had not been at all troublesome, but for the clients, the dramatic jump to Syangboche was felt almost immediately. Pittman reported to her NBC World Wide Web site, "Almost everyone on the team is feeling the effects of our sudden jump in elevation. We're out of breath just walking around." Additionally, she reported, two people were in bed with upset stomachs, possible Kathmandu casualties. One of the stricken was Lene Gammelgaard. She had left Kathmandu with the team. Dickinson, in West Seattle, never got her signature on the agreement papers.

From Syangboche, as Boukreev and Ngima had done, the Mountain Madness team trekked to Namche Bazaar, where they spent the next two days resting and taking short hikes, trying to acclimatize. For some, AMS symptoms continued to linger, normal enough for the first day or two, but indicative of problems if the symptoms persist.

Many of the team members resorted to taking Diamox, a

---

*Rob Hall's Adventure Consultants expedition flew from Kathmandu to Lukla to begin their trek to Everest Base Camp.

sulfa-drug derivative that helped them metabolize more oxygen. Used by climbers for more than twenty years, the drug has a proven record, and knowledgeable physicians, like Dr. Charles Houston, one of the world's authorities on high altitude medicine, recommend Diamox as a preventive. However, the drug's manufacturer warns in literature it distributes, "Gradual ascent is desirable to try to avoid acute mountain sickness. If rapid ascent is undertaken and Diamox is used, it should be noted that such use does not obviate the need for prompt descent if severe forms of high altitude sickness occur."

———■———

Internet trekkers, thanks to Pittman, were kept informed almost every day of the Mountain Madness team's progress as it headed toward Base Camp. Curiously, for those who had been keyboarding into Bromet's dispatches, they noted her Outside Online site had been quiet since shortly after leaving Kathmandu. What they didn't know about was the Lobuche showdown. "So, we get to Lobuche, the armpit of Nepal, and Sandy is very, very uptight with me . . . and then she says, 'You can't use that sat phone anymore. . . . NBC's . . . going to pull all the money, and they said that it's too much competition.' "

———■———

Neal had sent word through the Khumbu Grapevine (by means of Sherpas) that the expedition would be arriving in Gorak Shep (5,170 m) on April 6, and I was eager to meet all the clients and see how the trek had gone. Seeing that most of the work on the camp was done, I trekked for two hours over the Khumbu Glacier, circumventing huge lakes and ice extrusions caused by the warming weather. On my route I encountered members of Henry Todd's expedition who told me that our oxygen supply had finally arrived in Kathmandu and that it was now on a yak caravan somewhere outside of Namche Bazaar. Arriving in Gorak Shep, I reported to Scott Fischer about the work that had been accomplished. I warmly greeted Neal, whom I have known since 1990 when I first visited America, and then in generous terms Scott introduced me to everyone else. This experience was important to me because, while I had already heard something of their backgrounds, I learn a lot more from observing the physical appearance and demeanor of people. For me, even in my own country, it is not so much what people say, but how they behave. There was much I had to learn about the clients who, I knew, had been training hard.

This was not the first time, I knew, that Sandy Pittman had tried to climb Everest. Her healthy appearance at this altitude gave me no doubt about her well-being.

Lene Gammelgaard looked as good as she had in Kathmandu, and I thought she was in a great frame of mind to be the first woman from Denmark to climb Everest. I was mildly alarmed, however, when she declared her intention to climb without supplementary oxygen. Her lack of experience at high altitude, I thought, made that a not so very wise thing to consider.

The third woman mountain climber in our expedition, Charlotte Fox, had experience in successfully ascending the 8,000-meter peaks of Cho Oyu (8,153 m) and Gasherbrum II (8,035 m), and she had also ascended Aconcagua and McKinley. Her friend Tim Madsen, a highly qualified mountain skier, I understood did not have high-altitude experience, but he had extensive experience in summiting lower-elevation peaks in the western mountains of America and as a mountain skier.

Another athlete having past experience with mountain skiing was Klev Schoening, who had extensive preparatory experience on lower-elevation peaks such as Kilimanjaro and Aconcagua. His uncle Pete Schoening I respected as a mountaineer. I sympathized with his wish to be the oldest person to summit Everest and admired his ambition, but his age did provoke some guarded feelings in me.

For Dale Kruse, I understood, his greatest achievement was an ascent on Baruntse, a 7,000er in Nepal. Baruntse is an uncomplicated peak neighboring Makalu and is located in the Everest region, but Baruntse's level of difficulty is significantly lower than what was ahead of us, and it does not pose the same altitude challenge as Everest.

The last of the participants in our expedition, Martin Adams, I knew from our experiences on our Makalu expedition. A determined climber, I knew he was highly motivated to climb Everest, and I assured him of my best help and advice.

After meeting with all the participants, I returned to Base Camp that same day. Along the way I analyzed all the participants. I was most concerned about the people who had no high-altitude assault experience: Tim Madsen, Klev Schoening, Lene Gammelgaard, and Dale Kruse. Above 5,000 meters the participants' good form was reassuring. They had a fighting spirit and, from their external appearances, didn't look as if they had any serious problems with their health or *samochuvstvie*.* However, I knew I could draw a final conclusion on their preparedness only by observing all the participants while at Base Camp and during their attempts to attain higher altitudes.

About the team's overall level of readiness and ability I had concerns. I could only count on the professional flair of Scott Fischer, whose success on his first, large-scale commercial expedition to Everest was very important. I understood that he had worked hard to establish himself and had put much effort into bringing a good team to Everest. In a short time it is very difficult to successfully select a uniformly strong group of clients and to find qualified guides. I felt that Scott should be given his due for his sincere aspiration.

With Scott's, Lopsang's, and my Everest experiences I felt we had a good reservoir of talent to offer the clients on this expedition who, for the most part, were reasonably conditioned. But, for me, on a commercial expedition there was always a critical adjustment to make. I had trained in the tradition of the Russian High-Altitude Mountaineering School, where a collective effort and teamwork were always emphasized and personal ambitions had a second-level place. Our practice in training and developing climbers was to build their experience and confidence over a long time, starting with lower-level mountains and graduating them to 8,000ers when they were prepared. Here, I understood, as had been the situation on other commercial expeditions, I had been hired to prepare the mountain for the people instead of the other way around.

---

*A Russian concept. An impression of a person's state of being, the combined and observable aspects of a person's mental, physical, and emotional state.

CHAPTER 7

BASE CAMP

The Mountain Madness team continued to hold in Gorak Shep when Boukreev returned to Base Camp on the evening of Saturday, April 6. They were waiting for the expedition's yak caravan to complete its supply runs. To that point the majority of the supplies necessary for Base Camp had come in on the backs of Sherpa porters, and their efforts had been sufficient to keep Boukreev and the advance team of Sherpas supplied, but not until the yaks could move ahead with the balance of their supplies could the clients move into Base Camp.

Progress of all the expeditions' yak caravans had been excruciatingly slow. On the day before their arrival in Gorak Shep, the Mountain Madness team had departed Lobuche after lunch and shortly thereafter had encountered a few of their yaks up to their necks in snow, their Sherpa drivers furiously at work trying to dig them out.

To kill time in Gorak Shep and to promote their acclimatization, Fischer's team took a day trip and summited Kala Pattar (5,554 m), a "subsidiary feature" from which the climbers had an unobstructed and dramatic view of the Khumbu Icefall, the first serious obstacle they would encounter in their effort to summit Mount Everest. On the top of Kala Pattar, several of the climbers experienced a transition from the "going there" to the "being there" and the simultaneous sinking and soaring that many climbers feel when they encounter the physical presence of the objective ahead. This was what they had written their checks for.

Finally, on Monday, April 8, Fischer's team made their push. A few hundred meters north of the sandy flats of Gorak Shep, they picked up a trail that took them down a moraine wall and onto the Khumbu Glacier. In about three hours, following the trail that had been packed down by the porters and the yak teams that had finally begun to move, the team reached the Everest Base Camp.

Working their way over the lunarscape of strewn rubble, stepping carefully from rock to rock to avoid broken ankles, they found the site of their camp. Pitching a tent that for the next month would be their home was the first priority of many of the climbers, and with the help of the Sherpas they set about clearing sites and establishing what would be their home for the next six weeks.

The Sherpas who had been my coworkers were transformed when the clients arrived. In the morning the Sherpas would go to the clients' tents and wake them with tea and coffee, and a cheerful "Good morning!" In the mess tent there were always thermoses of Starbucks coffee, sports drinks, PowerBars, beef jerky. The meals were often rich, things like pizzas and stews. I much preferred the Sherpas' food—maybe more boring, but easier to digest and more appropriate I thought for high altitude. There was a hot shower and mail service. We even had a communications tent outfitted with Sandy Pittman's gear, satellite telephones, computers, solar panels for power. Base Camp had more services than many of the hotels in Kathmandu, certainly more than the Skala, where I often stayed.

The creature comforts, though, didn't take all the edges off. Several of the clients were struggling with their adjustments to

altitude, and many of the climbers, especially the first-timers to
Everest, began to seriously obsess about every bodily function.
One base-camper remarked, "People became totally self-
absorbed, monitoring their bodies, whether they're peeing or
not, what their urine looks like, whether they're pooping every
day, whether they're nauseous, whether they have a headache
or not." Nobody was without concerns about the status of his
or her health. Something as simple as a gastrointestinal problem or a respiratory infection could keep you off the mountain,
and that was not an indignity any of the climbers had come to
suffer. As one climber said, "Even hypochondriacs get sick."

Neal Beidleman was an early concern at Base Camp. Shortly after arriving he developed a "Khumbu cough,"* and according to
one Base Camp resident, "Neal was coughing his brains out. He
would cough all night long, so he couldn't sleep. Dr. Hunt
treated him with everything, steroids to stop the inflammation,
bronchodilators to make the muscles relax. Nothing was helping." While other members of the team such as Pittman developed a similar problem, Beidleman's difficulties were more of a
worry. Beidleman had responsibilities to get clients to the top. Already the expedition had one less guide than had originally been
planned. It was doubtful, if Beidleman didn't recover, that Fischer, Boukreev, and the climbing Sherpas could carry the load.

As there were people issues, there were equipment issues,
and one concern that arose early was that of the two-way radios
Fischer had brought for use by the expedition. A critical item
in an expedition inventory, a radio creates a link between Base
Camp and climbers as they wend their way to the summit and
provides a conduit for information on developing problems,
emergencies, equipment needs, the weather, and medical matters. An experienced climber considers the state of his expedition's communications capabilities, and Martin Adams did.

_____

*At high altitude the dryness and coldness of the air can irritate the lungs,
which, all things considered, would prefer the damp and humidity of a Carib-
bean beach. And the lungs, when they get irritated, get inflamed, and a serous
fluid drains into your lungs causing you to cough, and cough and cough.

"These days you have these great little radios that weigh next to nothing that every one of the climbers should have, because the cost of carrying them is zero. They're easy to use—two buttons—it's black-and-white. And Scott pulls out a few of these old radios with ten channels, and I said, 'These are the radios we're using?!' And he says to me, 'Yeah, this is all I got.' The radios, in my opinion, were a joke. It was a major misstep for him to go over there with those antiquated models."

———■———

One of my first priorities in Base Camp was to formalize an acclimatization plan. The demands of properly acclimatizing required that team members stay in Base Camp for at least a few days until their bodies had adjusted to that altitude, and then we would begin a series of excursions that would take our climbers higher onto the mountain, climbing from Base Camp to successively higher camps that our Sherpas would establish. The idea is that you gradually allow your body to adjust to higher and higher elevations, so that on the day of the summit bid you can dash to the highest altitude and then retreat to an altitude to which you have acclimated.

The plan Scott and I worked out called for four acclimatization excursions. Our first would be to 6,100 meters, which is where we would establish our Camp I, but on the first excursion we would not overnight there. On this excursion, and on all those that followed, the clients would carry only their personal belongings and personal equipment, so that they could save their strength. Our climbing Sherpas, working under Lopsang Jangbu Sherpa, would carry rope and whatever supplies we might need.

After the first excursion to 6,100 meters, we would return to Base Camp on the same day and not push the clients. Afterward we would rest to allow the team to recover and give us an opportunity to observe their conditions.

On our second excursion we planned to again reach the height of Camp I, spend the night there, and then, on the next day, do a training excursion to the altitude of 6,500 meters, where our Sherpas would be working to establish Camp II, our Advance Base Camp. This camp would be a smaller version of our Base Camp and would be completely outfitted with mess tent,* facilities for cooking, and tents that climbers would share when we overnighted there. On this excursion we would not overnight at the Camp II elevation, but descend and again take a multiday rest during which time our climbers could restore their strength and we could again see our climbers up close, to observe them for potential problems and to discuss with them their conditions and preparedness.

Our hope was that after their rest the clients would then be ready to do a third excursion, which would take us first to Camp I, where we would spend the night, and then on to Camp II, where we would overnight for the first time. On the third day we would try to reach an altitude of 6,800 meters, the elevation at which we would eventually be moving onto the face of Lhotse, where we would be establishing our Camp III at 7,300 meters. On that same day it was planned that we would descend through Camp II and return to Base Camp.

Before the fourth and final acclimatization excursion we planned three days of rest. After this we would attempt to go from Base Camp straight through to Camp II. After spending the night there and assessing the team members' *samochuvstvie,* we would continue to Camp III and spend our final night, then the next day attempt to go a few hundred meters higher before descending. This excursion, we agreed, would be mandatory for all members, because this would be the highest we would climb before our summit bid, and it was necessary that all our team members make their adjustments to those altitudes before subjecting themselves to the ultimate challenge.†

Boukreev took the acclimatization excursions very seriously, and he felt that the routines that had been established should be strictly followed. Fischer had hired him, he understood, to bring his experience to bear and was relying upon him to help insure client safety. Boukreev shared his thoughts about the expedition's potential for success with Fischer.

---

*This tent, a smaller version of the Base Camp mess tent made in the Urals, finally made it to Nepal and had been delivered to Base Camp.

†Acclimatization is unique to each climber and, even though Boukreev and Fischer hoped to move the clients through it together, they understood there

I said if the clients use oxygen, and if we are lucky in getting a successful confluence of circumstances, our clients can have success, but it is critical that we adhere to our acclimatization plan and allow the opportunities for our clients to get sufficient rest. We cannot make up now for lack of training or experience, but we can maximize the opportunity of our clients if we do these things.

Our job is to get our clients the necessary acclimatization with a minimal number of nights at high-altitude camps. From my experience I know that by staying at high altitude strength quickly disappears and that it will not be possible to restore it during the short rest intervals at Base Camp. Sometimes you can be deceived; you begin to have less serious problems with the increases, and you feel relatively good, but, then, on summit day you do not have the strength for the final assault. So, my opinion was that after our excursion to 7,300 meters we should descend and rest for at least a week at an elevation lower than Base Camp, somewhere in the forest zone around 3,800 m. There we will have more oxygen and relaxing distractions away from our Base Camp routine, which can help with the psychology of our clients.

Fischer had no problems with the plans for the acclimatization excursions, but he was not receptive to Boukreev's plan for a deep descent and rest before the summit bid. Why he opposed the idea Boukreev was not certain.

---

would be a varying response to their recommended routine and tried to build some flexibility into the regimen.

CHAPTER 8

KHUMBU TO CAMP II

Before first light on the morning of April 11, the Mountain Madness clients crawled from their tents and began preparations for their excursion into the Khumbu Icefall. The day Fischer had chosen for his expedition's first trip through, Boukreev recalled, was clear and promising. It would have been an ideal day for a summit bid, because the weather had been stable for several days and the winds moderate.

What the conditions would be on the mountain when Fischer's clients were finally acclimatized was anybody's guess. Weather on the mountain, like the people with the hubris to climb it, cannot be predicted with any reasonable degree of accuracy. It was possible that when the climbers were ready, the mountain wouldn't be, and if that was the case, there would be no ticket refunds. They would go home without the summit in their pockets.

◆■◆

Most of the Mountain Madness expedition members had not reacted dramatically to the slight increase in elevation they had made from Gorak Shep to Base Camp. Their resting respiratory rates had returned to normal, but any exertion caused a rapid and disconcerting shortness of breath for most team members. One of the members has said that at Base Camp, with only half the oxygen available to her at sea level, she felt as if she were working on one lung and walking around in a two-martini fog.

A few of the team members were still struggling with nausea and headaches, but none were complaining too loudly, wanting to put the best picture on their condition, not wanting to "talk about the fact that they felt like shit," as one base-camper described the situation.

Fischer, who was often heard to say to his team members, "It's attitude, not altitude," seemed to most of them to be strong, without any apparent difficulties. But according to Jane Bromet, there was a considerable difference between those perceptions and Fischer's physical reality. "He'd get up in the morning and . . . it would take him about five minutes to finally stand up. . . . Scott was exhausted." And, she said, he was taking Diamox, 125 mg every other day, which suggests he was addressing the challenge of acclimatization.*

———■———

For Beidleman, and all of the clients except Sandy Hill Pittman, this would be their first trip into the Icefall. As casual and relaxed as everyone tried to appear, most of them knew the history of the obstacle ahead. Since people had begun keeping score, nineteen people had died in the Icefall.

A perilous, jagged mass of blue ice set on an incline that slants toward the Everest Base Camp, the Icefall is constantly being transformed. Its descending mass, perpetually pulled upon by gravity, fractures and separates like ice cubes cracked from a tray into freestanding towers called seracs, some of them more than ten stories high. Interconnecting the seracs is a net-

---

*Some climbers, despite evidence to the contrary, still believe that prophylactic use of Diamox will prevent severe forms of altitude sickness.

work of fissures, or crevasses, that can be more than three hundred feet deep.

To cross the Icefall to make it to Camp I at 6,100 meters, one has to climb two thousand vertical feet over the distance of slightly more than a mile. To assist climbers in their negotiation of the route, the Icefall is "threaded" before each climbing season by a team of Sherpas. In March 1996, that team was coordinated by the efforts of Henry Todd and Mal Duff from the United Kingdom, a leader, like Todd, of a commercial expedition.

The "Icefall Doctor," as the lead Sherpa of the effort is known around Base Camp, oversees the extremely dangerous job of putting into place aluminum ladders (in 1996 more than seventy), some of which provide the means for climbers to ascend vertically and the others to span the crevasses. Given the distances that have to be covered over the yawning fissures, sometimes more than three or four ladders are overlapped at their ends and lashed together with climbing rope in order to cover a span. The challenge is to cross the ladders while clipped to fixed ropes, literally rope handrails, that are installed for the season. The "clipping on" is most usually done with a carabiner attached to a short length of rope affixed to a climbing harness. An aluminum alloy oval or D-shaped link (something like a large chain link), a carabiner can be snapped open and closed to allow a climber to attach or remove himself from a run of rope. Less often, and usually in a vertical ascent, climbers might use a jumar (sometimes referred to as a mechanical ascender), a handheld, metallic device with a self-braking mechanism. The jumar is fastened to the fixed rope and the rope feeds through the device as you hold it in your hand and push it ahead of you. If you pull the jumar toward your body (or fall backward), a cam grips the rope and holds you in position. So, in a push-pull rhythm called jugging, you advance along the ropes.

Moving through the course you hear creaks, splinters, and moans, because the landscape, just as it is at Base Camp, is always on the move. Your prayer is that none of the sounds is announcing a catastrophic shift, one that could cause a crevasse to suddenly gape under a spanning ladder or to topple a crystalline bank building onto the route.

Fischer had told his clients that to qualify to climb higher on the mountain they had to be able to clear the Icefall, bottom to top, in under four hours. The stakes were high, and Klev Schoening said, "The hors d'oeuvres are over, and we're into the meat and potatoes big time!"

The instructions to the Mountain Madness clients on how to navigate the Icefall, one client remembers, were brief and succinct. "But as far as 'Watch out for this!' or 'Watch out for that!' it was more like 'Watch out for yourself!,' and that was it."

For most of the climbers the most unsettling moments were not the hand-over-hand moves up the vertical ladders, but the crossings of the crevasses on the ladders that had been lashed together. Advancing, stepping on one rung, then onto another, their crampons clunking and occasionally snagging, the climbers often found themselves bouncing over a maw of ice that, in a misstep, if they were not properly clipped on, could swallow them down. If they could be found and reached after a fall, they could imagine a rag-doll extraction, a slack, cold body being raised in its climbing harness.

According to Martin Adams, "Some people would walk across the ladders; some people would crawl. And, quite frankly, Sandy and Lene probably crossed the ladders as well if not better than anybody else. . . . They were very well-balanced, and they weren't intimidated." Charlotte Fox, according to one of Pittman's Internet dispatches, found that "butt scooching"—pulling herself across on her butt—was sometimes considerably less terrifying than teetering on her crampons and peering down into an ice vault with the capacity of a municipal parking garage. On May 10, Fox would turn thirty-nine, and she was keen on seeing that day.

All of the climbers made it through in less than the four hours Scott had required, and I was generally pleased, but I was surprised by the number of clients who did not have the self-reliance to move through it without being almost constantly monitored by a guide. Some of them, I was afraid, had the idea that a guide should control all the situations they might encounter. I would just wonder, "What is going to happen when there is nobody to hold their hands?"

Boukreev had begun to consider the Mountain Madness Everest equation. They were all factors: the guides, the clients, and the Sherpas. If they went up healthy and properly acclimatized and they made good decisions and their efforts were added and multiplied correctly and the weather gave them grace, he knew everyone could come back alive. But to what extent could he rely upon the clients' abilities to look after themselves, to take appropriate action in critical situations when the guides weren't looking over their shoulders?

What Boukreev brought to the calculations were his training and experience at high altitude, the attributes Henry Todd had hired him for the year before. "When I used him in '95, it was perfect. He was absolutely super. He did exactly what he was supposed to do. I knew who he was; I knew what he was capable of. . . . If anything went wrong, I wanted a rope bullet up that hill—a rope gun." In Todd's mind, Boukreev's value was in his power and the margin of safety he could bring to a climb. If clients got into trouble, he could "get them, bring them down." In Todd's opinion Boukreev was not a hand-holder. To hire him with that in mind, Todd thought, would be a gross misappropriation of his talents. "It's not what he's designed for. It's like using a racing car for taking children to school."

Our return through the Icefall was uneventful, and everyone returned to Base Camp with a little more assurance, pleased with their success. As had been planned, the clients looked forward to two days of rest while the Sherpas erected tents at Camp I and supplied it in preparation for our next excursion, when clients would overnight there for the first time.

During this rest period, Boukreev began to openly question the readiness of some of the clients who had been signed on.

Boukreev, while generally satisfied with client performance, had some concerns about Dale Kruse and Pete Schoening and their capacities for the climb ahead, but Fischer, Boukreev remembered, reassured him, "Pete will listen to me. He's got the experience; he doesn't get ambition and reality mixed up." And, about Kruse: "Dale is an old friend; it'll be easy for me to turn him around. For him it's not that big a deal. He'll have had some good food, drink a little beer in Base Camp. No big deal."

Privately, to a member of his support team, Fischer was expressing both concern for Kruse and a frustration. Kruse on the trek in and in the early days at Base Camp had been distancing himself from the group, being somewhat "antisocial" and going to "his own beat." Fischer knew Kruse was struggling, but "early on it was bugging Scott. And Scott was just saying, 'He's just going to have to deal with it himself.'" Fischer thought that Kruse needed to power through the problem. As one observer saw it, "I think Dale was suffering the whole time. . . . As a team player, in his emotional state, for sure he was the weakest link, and not in an offensive way. He just was very, very, very quiet, and I think he was being screwed up by the altitude. . . . I think he was hypoxic from probably sixteen, seventeen thousand, but he was so quiet. It was really hard to get a read on him."

As the clients were making their adjustments to altitude, so were they having to adjust to each other. "Look, many of us, before we got to Kathmandu, didn't know each other that well," one of the clients said. "Think of it as a blind date. All you initially have in common at the bottom is the reason you're there, the top of the mountain. So, there's this feeling-out period, getting to know one another. At altitude you want to know who you're climbing with. If things get strange, you can't call a cab and go home. . . . Surprisingly, given the randomness of our jumble, we were, with few exceptions, a relatively homogeneous group."

By several accounts, Tim Madsen was quiet, something of a loner, "as quiet as they come," a member of the Mountain

Madness team described him. "He was just as quiet as Dale . . . like a closed book, totally." Although Madsen and Kruse were "odd fits," they got on well with everybody. In fact, as one Mountain Madness staffer recalled, everybody except Sandy Pittman and Lene Gammelgaard seemed to get along "pretty darned well."

"What I noticed," said one of the Base Camp residents, "was that after a while [there] was a kind of competition going on between Sandy and Lene. . . . Lene looked at Sandy as a big showoff. . . . Sandy is this multimillionairess throwing around Ivana Trump's name and Tom Brokaw's . . . dropping names and what she's written and what she's doing and how powerful she is. . . . Lene, on the other hand, was [talking about] a life of detachment and how you don't need anybody. . . . I think that their drive came less from the innate love of climbing, but more from trying to establish . . . identity. . . . Neal just about came unglued with both of them . . . not uptight, but like he was really going to have to just grit his teeth to make it through these two female personalities. . . . Neal started getting really disgruntled."

Compounding Beidleman's difficulties with Pittman, according to the same source, were the problems she was having with her communications gear. "She did not know her equipment. . . . I bet he [Beidleman] put well over twenty-five hours into her equipment, and I said, 'Neal, before you put any more time in, call NBC, man, and get your hourly rate. This is NBC for Christ sakes!' They didn't send up a technician to help her out. 'Bill them for it,' I told him. He said, 'No, no . . .' I thought, 'God, if you're that dumb . . . !' "

Through all this, said one of Fischer's confidants, "Scott was trying to keep his cool. He just didn't want to get sucked into their [Pittman's and Gammelgaard's] shenanigans at all." Privately, Fischer admitted that perhaps he'd made a mistake by bringing Pittman. "She was a big piece of work. . . . If she doesn't make it to the top, she'll blame it on him. . . . If she gets to the top, she won't mention him. . . . We both talked about this pretty extensively."

My relationship with the team members was formed as the expedition progressed and it was different with each person. Before this expedition I had become pretty well acquainted with Neal Beidleman and Martin Adams through our Makalu expedition in the spring of 1994. Lene Gammelgaard looked at me with a great deal of respect. She had heard about me from Michael Joergensen, the first Danish mountain climber to reach the summit of Everest in the spring of last year when he took part in Henry Todd's expedition. Lene, like me, wasn't from the USA, and this made her distinctly different from the other expedition members. Moreover, she was not especially wealthy and was able to pay for only a part of the cost of this expedition herself. These things together, I think, isolated her a little from the other members of the expedition. My relationship with Charlotte Fox and Tim Madsen more or less took shape. We were very close in spirit because of our devotion to the mountains. The other expedition members acted cautiously toward me. Pete Schoening and his nephew Klev stuck together, isolated from the others. For them there wasn't much difference between a Russian mountain climber hired for the expedition and the Sherpa high-altitude porters. Perhaps some of their reactions could possibly be explained by the not so distant memory of the Cold War. On top of that, my English left much to be desired and I couldn't always freely answer their questions and vice versa. I couldn't take the initiative and advise something practical like a guide is supposed to and to explain the importance of my advice.

———■———

On Saturday, April 13, the Mountain Madness climbers went again into the Khumbu Icefall and, without incident, climbed through it and into the Western Cwm (pronounced coom), a panorama that no matter where the climbers stood their wide-angle camera lenses couldn't contain the scene.

The Western Cwm is a glacial hollow, an undulating sweep of snow and ice about four kilometers long that tilts gradually upward and is enclosed on three sides by the peaks and con-

necting ridges of Mount Everest, Lhotse, and Nuptse, the major
peaks of the Mount Everest Massif. It offers from its vantage a
view that is obstructed in Base Camp: the looming, magnificent,
and daunting summit of Mount Everest.

Gammelgaard, whose "can-do" personality and stoic style
some found overpromoted, was overtaken by the beauty in front
of her. "I consider myself being pretty tough . . . so not all that
many things touch me . . . that deeply." Encountering the
sweeping, slowly rising plateau of the Western Cwm and the
mountain she'd come to climb, Gammelgaard stood apart from
the other climbers and silently wept.

A half hour from the terminus of the Icefall, on the snow and ice of
the Western Cwm, we had sited our Camp I in a place a little higher
than we would normally have placed our tents because many expeditions had already clustered their camps in the location we would
have preferred. But, the location we chose we felt was safe, placed
in a position so that it would not be seriously threatened by ava-
lanches.

Mindful of their need to rehydrate and to warm themselves
as soon as they arrived at Camp I, the Mountain Madness climbers began to melt snow on their high-altitude stoves suspended
over their sleeping bags from the struts of their tents. Pittman,
who reported on her experience of Camp I to the NBC Internet
site, said that being at that altitude addled her mind to the
point that watching snow melt became an entertaining experience, something like "watching TV." She also thanked Gammelgaard, who had shared a tent with her, dug into her
rucksack, and for dinner pulled out one tasty morsel after another, courtesy of one of her Danish sponsors. While in the
neighboring tents the climbers ate just-add-hot-water specialties,
the two shamelessly dug into dried fruits and nuts and spooned
down something Pittman referred to as an "exotic Middle Eastern nomadic dish." Climbing to high altitude can inhibit appetite, but the problem wasn't registered in Pittman's Internet
dispatch. Whatever the personal differences between Gammel-

gaard and Pittman, they were both struggling to meet the same objective. Friends or not, they were in it together up to their glacier glasses and cooperating in their effort.

———■———

The next morning Boukreev and some of the other expedition members advanced up the Western Cwm to where Camp II (6,500 m) would be sited, while the others descended to Base Camp straight away, but by the time dinner went down on the table in the Base Camp mess tent, everyone had returned safely.

———■———

On April 15 and 16, the climbers curbed their crampons and luxuriated in the mandatory rest. Breakfast spreads of pancakes and yak-cheese omelettes accompanied by Starbucks coffee, hot showers, sunbathing, reading a favorite book, watching a movie on a Sony Watchman—these were the challenges of the Mountain Madness acclimatization routine. On April 17, they were back at it.

All the team members except Sandy and Tim left early for our third excursion through the Khumbu Icefall. Scott and I felt the clients were capable of making their passage without close supervision. Sandy lingered behind to do some work in her communications tent. Tim, who was suffering acute symptoms of AMS, had the day before descended to Pheriche with our team doctor, Ingrid, who was also experiencing problems. . . . I wasn't too surprised by their difficulties because neither of them had been to high altitude before and the challenge was new to their bodies.

Despite Bromet's concern about how Pittman would eventually handle Fischer in the media, he continued to participate in her NBC World Wide Web site, and on the morning of their third excursion he spent more than an hour in her communications tent and participated in an on-line Internet chat with Pittman and Sir Edmund Hillary, who was then in Kathmandu.

Hillary, despite his well-known criticism of commercial expeditions to Mount Everest and his expressed feeling that they denigrated the mountain, had agreed to the conversation and offered some sage advice: "For any expedition you must treat the mountain with considerable respect. If you're an athlete and are affected by the altitude, go lower in altitude and recover. In the ultimate, success on Everest demands a certain degree of physical fitness."

While Pittman was signing off and tending to other communications chores, Fischer and Boukreev left Base Camp to play "sweep," to push on and assist any stragglers.

———■———

Boukreev has estimated that more than one hundred climbers went through the Icefall that day. Sherpas from various expeditions with packs and haul bags full of gear and supplies were working their way up the mountain to establish higher camps. Like Fischer's clients, climbers from other expeditions were also on the move, making their acclimatization excursions.

Scott and I, as we were on our way to Camp I, took notice of the climbers from some of the other commercial expeditions. We agreed that our climbers in comparison looked far better, although I noted to myself that the overall level of ability and preparedness of all the commercial clients, including ours, seemed lower than those who had climbed from the Tibetan side the year before.

If we got lucky, I thought, we would make it. Scott, Neal, and I would have to plan our ascent so that all of the team members who qualified for the summit would find themselves at Camp IV at just the right time for an attempt. Even then, if we got it right, we would still be dependent upon the weather. Against this we had no insurance. No one of us could protect against the dangers of high winds or other dramatic shifts in the weather. Perhaps, if we were unlucky in our timing, we could descend and reconsider. If there was the desire, the time, and the strength, maybe we could wait for a more favorable situation and try again. But then, what would be the condition of our clients and our oxygen supply? I had my doubts that many of the clients would be strong enough to stay at high altitude until the weather became more favorable, and I didn't know if, when the time came, we would have enough oxygen to make a second attempt. Ultimately, I knew, the mountain would make many of the decisions for us.

If there was for Boukreev a transitional day on the expedition, this was probably it. As Fischer fell behind in the line of travel to check on Pittman, who was still climbing behind them, Boukreev found himself alone, thinking about the decision he'd made to sign on to the Mountain Madness expedition. He'd never seen anything quite like this: the electronic fussiness, the publicity-mongering, the pampering and politics.

Reflecting on my past experience and the variability of weather above 8,000 meters, I mused on the possibilities ahead. I thought, what on earth would happen if we found ourselves in a critical situation at high altitude? Would my strength and that of Scott, Neal, and the Sherpas be enough to handle the situations that might develop?

Wisely our clients had left early in the morning for Camp I, because as the day wore on, the weather began to deteriorate, and by nightfall the snow had begun to fall in large flakes. Only Sandy was out in it for any length of time, but because of her previous experience on Everest I don't think she was ever in any real danger.

By daybreak on April 18, more than six inches of snow had fallen on the Mountain Madness encampment as the climbers had slept at Camp I, but the snow had stopped by sunrise, and it was decided to proceed to Camp II and overnight there. Boukreev took a look at the clients, and to his eye, everyone was exhibiting a good *samochuvstvie*.

The guides, each of us carrying a small load, moved at a steady pace with the clients through the fresh snow. Charlotte and Lene on this day were slower than the other climbers, but Sandy was robust and cheerful. Her only problem was her continuing cough, which, like Neal's, was aggravated by the dry mountain air.

After passing through the line of advancing clients, Boukreev, in just under three hours, made it to the location where the Mountain Madness Sherpas climbing ahead of them had already brought up supplies for Camp II. Tucked in at the base of Everest, their camp was sited on a flat of scree, fragments of rock distributed by the grinding of glacial action. Protected somewhat from the wind by their location, the tents in the camp would be warmed by the sun in the mornings, but toasted in the afternoons.

When there is stationary air in calm weather and the sun is shining, the site for Camp II is soaked by solar radiation, and the heat at midday can become intense and cause dehydration and lethargy, so, when I arrived at Camp II, I began to help the Sherpas, who hadn't yet gotten our mess tent erected. As I worked, the clients began to arrive, the first of them arriving in a cluster, then a last knot of them who had been trailing the first by about three hundred meters.

As the clients arrived, Boukreev continued his efforts with the Sherpas, and when the mess tent was erected, the Sherpas dispersed to assist some of the clients who were setting up their tents. Having spent several days working with some of the same Sherpas at Base Camp before the arrival of the clients, Boukreev was surprised at the zeal with which the Sherpas threw themselves into the job, eager to demonstrate "good work" and to curry favor with clients, who, if they felt they'd gotten good service, would often tip them at the conclusion of a climb.

Not wanting to appear a "competitor who was laying claim to their piece of bread," and because he was tired from his earlier advance through the pack of climbers, Boukreev poured himself some hot tea and sat down on a rock to rest.

CHAPTER 9

CAMP II

As the sun settled behind Everest and the temperatures began to drop precipitously in the last hours of the day, the climbers in the narrow confines of their tents pulled on their high-altitude clothing. Hours earlier it had been shirtsleeve weather; now the Mountain Madness clients and guides were contorting themselves like circus acrobats, wedging themselves into goose down and Gore-Tex, preparing for their exposure to the evening cold, a dash to the mess tent, and their first night at Camp II.

From this point on there would be no more overnights at Camp I. Most of the tents had been struck, though a few remained for gear and supply storage, a depository that the Sherpas could use in their relays to supply higher camps. But now, only in the case of emergency would the tents be occupied.

In the evening, as the Sherpas prepared a dinner of rice and dal in the nearby kitchen tent, Neal and I and all of the clients except Pete Schoening, who had gone down to Base Camp earlier in the day with Scott Fischer, gathered around the mess tent table, hungry and satisfied with the day's excursion. Everyone had an "arctic" look, dressed in their bulky clothes. Martin Adams, with whom I felt comfortable making jokes because we knew each other from earlier days, came to the table in a new, green climbing suit, and I greeted him with, "Hey, crocodile!" As my English was still not so good, I hoped that I didn't offend, and Martin and some of the other clients laughed in good spirit.

Seeing everyone's good mood and that they were all feeling well, I turned to Neal and asked, "What's the plan for tomorrow?" and suggested that after an early breakfast we consider an outing to 6,800 meters, to the face of Lhotse, where a run of fixed ropes began.

Beidleman and Boukreev discussed the idea with the clients, and among them they put together a plan that would get them out early in the morning, so they could return to Camp II in time for lunch, rest, and then depart for a return to Base Camp before dark.

The plan agreed upon, Boukreev made another suggestion to Beidleman. "As we were coming into Camp II yesterday, I noticed Sherpas fixing ropes to Camp III. Why don't we go even a little higher and take some of our ropes up to them?" Beidleman agreed with the idea, offering that he felt great enough to go all the way to Camp IV if he had to.

With our clients we discussed again the necessity of proper acclimatization, and we reminded them that they needed to carefully monitor the condition of their bodies, being constantly aware that at high altitude their sensations and reactions would not be altogether familiar. We could do our jobs as guides and monitor them, but only they would know the interior truth. Between us we needed to be clear and communicate. The earliest symptoms of HACE and HAPE, for even the most experienced climber, can be confused with the usual discomforts of acclimatization, and a misunderstanding can be fatal. We reinforced the importance of always maintaining a reserve, not allowing yourself to get totally depleted, being careful to understand that "I can't" usually means exactly that. You can't and you shouldn't. Stop, turn around, and save your life.

After dinner, Fischer—who was still in Base Camp with Pete Schoening—was raised by radio, and the acclimatization excursion for the next day was discussed and approved. With a radio link established, Pittman dictated her NBC "journal entry" to Fischer, who patched it by satellite phone to the NBC offices in New York, where Pittman's voice was "nearly inaudible," but Fischer's was "loud and clear." In New York the message was keyboarded, digitized, and then fed to the NBC World Wide Web site. Instantaneously, thousands of electric Everest fans could catch the latest news: "We are set up here with food, supplies, and our trusty Sherpa staff." A bwana couldn't have said it better.

The next morning most of the climbers didn't have their enthusiasm of the day before, and at breakfast in the mess tent, the conversations didn't have the animation or jokes of the night before. The increase in altitude from Camp I to Camp II was having its impact, but seeing nothing in their lethargy except the body's usual struggle to adjust to altitude, Neal and I felt they were fit for our excursion.

Boukreev and Beidleman both put a coil of rope into their packs and with the clients picked up the trail. Boukreev led and maintained a slow pace, keeping watch for narrow crevasses along the route, some of which were barely visible because they had been dusted with a light snow that had fallen the night before. About two hours into the excursion the slope of the trail began to increase, and Boukreev deviated left off the marked path, choosing a lower-angle slope over which they could travel the three hundred meters that remained between them and the start of the fixed ropes on the Lhotse Face.

After about thirty meters on this new route I noticed something unusual ahead, something dark protruding from the snow. At first I thought it was a piece of equipment that had fallen down from a higher camp during a previous expedition, but as I moved closer, I noticed a pair of crampons attached to boots, and to the boots the lower half of a human body. Immediately there were questions: Who is this? What tragedy had befallen this person? I could only guess that this was a climber who several years earlier had fallen to his death from Lhotse, and whose body, drawn by gravity over a torturous trail, had been ravaged, broken apart, and brought finally to this place.

Boukreev pulled off his pack and stood quietly, looking down at the body as the other climbers, unaware of his discovery, moved toward him.

The eternity and power of the mountains penetrated me. I remembered from school a story about a custom of the Romans. After a victorious battle, they would have a banquet of fine food and perpetual music, but at the height of the banquet, at the peak of their revelry, the doors to the banquet hall would be thrown open and the bodies of their dead comrades would be brought in and laid before them. In that somber moment they understood the price of the battle they had won.

Were those coming up behind me honestly evaluating their preparedness for the upcoming ascent? Just a few hours before, thanks to the Sherpas who had carried the loads to Camp II, all of us had been enjoying a level of well-being that many people on the earth would consider luxurious. By whatever means we had gotten there, we were privileged, but not secure. In a few weeks, if all went well, we would be climbing again past this point on our way to the summit. Climbing above eight thousand meters, where any mistake is amplified in the rarefied air, where a swallow of hot tea from a thermos is the difference between life and death, no amount of money that had been paid would guarantee success.

Of course, each one of us has an ambition to reach the summit, to overcome obstacles and to do something that many consider impossible. But maybe, I thought, the price of climbing Everest is now being calculated in a different way. More and more people, it seems, are willing to pay a cash price for the opportunity, but not a physical price for preparedness: the gradual development of body and spirit as you climb lower-level peaks, moving from the simple to the complex and finally to the 8,000ers. Isn't there accomplishment to be felt in such a process, I wondered, or has high-altitude climbing forever been changed by the use of oxygen, advances in technologies, and the proliferation of services that allow the marginally prepared to climb higher and higher?

As Beidleman and the clients advanced and encountered the body, Boukreev recalled, "Very little was said. Everyone considered it in his or her way. The quiet seemed to me respectful, maybe instructional."

As a guide on the Mountain Madness expedition, Boukreev was a player in a game that he had increasingly begun to question. He was with climbers considerably less qualified than himself, and he understood that their safety was his primary responsibility, but some things were out of his control. He was worried about Pete Schoening and his condition. His problems at altitude were starting to pull at the hem of full-dress effort. His health could be at serious risk, Boukreev thought, and there was the problem of O's. At the beginning of the expedition Mountain Madness had what Boukreev thought was a sufficient supply of oxygen, even a surplus for unforeseen circumstances, but Pete Schoening had begun to sleep on oxygen at Base Camp, not a common circumstance. If he continued to use it, the expedition's margin of safety could be reduced. The elder Schoening was stoic, determined and focused Boukreev thought, and Boukreev's respect for his effort continued, but his concerns for Schoening's well-being wouldn't go away. Boukreev had hopes that his having to descend would be enough to convince Fischer to suggest to Schoening that he make no further ascents.

In little more than fifty to one hundred meters after we encountered the body, we found ourselves at the start of the fixed ropes where the route became steeper on the icy Lhotse Face. Neal suggested that we leave our ropes at this place and return to Camp II, because the clients didn't have crampons or ice tools with them and couldn't safely go onto the ropes, but I looked at my watch and said that I would prefer to continue up the fixed ropes and work at putting in more of the route that would take us to Camp III.

From my pack I took my crampons, a climbing harness, and a jumar, and then from Neal I took the coil of rope he carried. As I clipped onto the fixed rope to begin my ascent, Neal turned around to escort the clients down. Everyone had come alive after the slowness of the morning, and I was comfortable they would be safe with Neal in good weather and on the clearly marked trail. I envied a bit their lunch at Camp II on the way down, but I was also glad to have the opportunity to burden my system a bit more with work at a slightly higher altitude. In my experience the harder I work at a new altitude before I descend to rest, the better suited I am to that altitude when I return to it.

In just less than an hour Boukreev climbed to around 6,900 meters, where the work of the Sherpas who'd been ahead had stopped, and he pulled a coil of rope from his pack. Over the next hour and a half, working at a steady pace, Boukreev continued to thread the route, putting down both the ropes that he and Beidleman had brought up the mountain and stringing more than two hundred meters of rope to an altitude of 7,100 meters. Somewhere around 4:00 P.M., still with some power but wanting to make it through the Khumbu Icefall before dark, Boukreev began his descent, pleased with the advance he'd made in the route. In just a few days, after the clients had rested from their first excursion to Camp II, they would be moving onto the fixed ropes and heading toward Camp III, and Boukreev didn't want any delays. The window for the summit, when it appeared, could last for a day; it could last for a week; but an open window would be of no value to the clients if they weren't prepared to climb through it. They needed to maintain their acclimatization routine and to advance they needed the fixed ropes.

It was an easy descent for me and I covered the distance from 7,100 to 6,500 meters in about an hour. As I had expected, Neal and the clients had already departed, but there was still activity among the tents as the Sherpas continued their work to secure the camp. Our cook, Gyalzen Sherpa, greeted me and kindly offered me some food and hot tea, and after a few minutes of rest I continued my descent and arrived in Base Camp before dark. Joining the rest of the expedition members in the mess tent, I exchanged a few words with Scott and Neal and then went to my tent, because after a full day's work at altitude I was extremely tired and looked forward to the days of rest ahead.

That same evening Sandy Hill Pittman transmitted her April 19 journal entry to NBC. Reporting on her encounter with the torso discovered by Boukreev, she said, "The discovery was a macabre ending to an otherwise successful climb."

On the morning of April 20, Boukreev had "no particular wish" to climb out of his sleeping bag as the sun hit his tent around 8:00 A.M. Even after he'd downed a cup of coffee brought to him by one of the Sherpas, he lingered, savoring the opportunity to rest after the excursion and work of the day before. Finally, in one of those off-to-work, propulsive bursts, he zipped out of his bag, got into his clothes, and headed for the mess tent.

Most of the expedition members had already eaten and were sitting on their chairs outside the mess tent, some sunning themselves, others conversing. After a quick breakfast, as I was myself warming in the sun, I noticed Scott getting ready to go up with Pete Schoening, who wanted to attempt Camp II again and to try an overnight. Scott appeared tired, and I know he could not have been enthusiastic about having to climb, because it was my impression that he was worn out from the logistical problems with which he had been dealing and because he had taken little rest after his previous acclimatization excursion.

Scott approached me and greeted me in a friendly way, then totally surprised me by saying, "Anatoli, you did your work poorly on the last excursion."

Boukreev was taken aback, caught totally off guard, because he had been pleased with his work and efforts of the previous few days, and asked Fischer, "What is this about my work?"

Fischer responded in a friendly but firm way, "I've been told you've not been very attentive to the clients. You didn't help them set up their tents at Camp II." Not having a clue that his actions had been a problem, Boukreev explained to Fischer that upon arriving at Camp II, before the clients had arrived, he had begun working with the Sherpas who were setting up the mess tent, that he'd busied himself with that and then rested. True, he'd not assisted the clients, because they didn't seem to be needing help and because he felt that some work on the route would contribute to their acclimatization. Fischer didn't see it that way.

I began to understand that there was a difference in understanding about why I had been hired or that somehow the expectations of me had shifted. It had been my impression that Scott's primary interests were in my experience and what I could bring to ensure client safety and success on summit day, and I had been working with that in mind, focusing primarily on details that I thought would bring success and attempting to anticipate the problems that would prevent us from making a bid on the summit. It was not clear to me that equally if not more important was chatting and keeping the clients pleased by focusing on their personal happiness. For this role, I knew several guides in America, guides with less high-altitude experience perhaps, but guides who were much better qualified.

Boukreev, who took great pride in his capacities as a climber, was in a quandary. Where should his focus go? Could he reasonably do what he thought had been expected of him *and* fulfill Fischer's expectations? For some advice he spoke with Beidleman.

I shared this problem with Neal and explained my concerns about what Scott had said. When I asked him what he thought, Neal said, "Anatoli, many of our members are at high altitude for the first time, and they don't understand many of the simple things. They want us to hold their hands through everything." I replied simply, saying that was an absurd position. I repeated again my concerns that we had to encourage self-reliance, and that our contributions to fixing ropes, getting the route ready, were just as important. About this Neal disagreed, saying that we had enough Sherpas to do this job. I told Neal that I thought, judging by our current situation, we were going to fall behind in the establishment of our high-altitude camps and our acclimatization routines could be compromised.

Neal, who almost always had a quiet and peaceful disposition, assured me, "Anatoli, everything will be okay. On the last excursion we felt okay, and that's the most important thing. Half of the clients don't have a chance for success. For many the ascent will end on the South Col (7,900 m). I don't have a doubt that at the crucial moment above eight thousand meters you will be able to show your work and everyone will understand and appreciate it."

CHAPTER 10

THE FIRST DELAYS

On our second rest day, April 21, we got a radio report from Scott, who had spent the previous night with Pete Schoening at Camp II, and he said the winds had raged throughout the night, sometimes blowing at over sixty miles an hour. With the help of Sherpas they'd collapsed some of our tents to keep them from being shredded and blown off the mountain. The storm, I think, must have been fierce all the way down the mountain as my tent at Base Camp was buffeted throughout the night.

During this rest period the expedition physician, Dr. Ingrid Hunt, utilizing a pulse oximeter, performed for some of the clients and guides, as she had on previous occasions, an "O_2 SAT" test to determine the maximum amount of oxygen that could be carried in the blood under the prevailing environmental conditions. As he always had, Boukreev tested in the low 90s, a result that at sea level would be considered normal, a result that according to Dr. Hunt made him and Fischer, who had also tested in this range, exceptional in their capacities to adjust to altitude. In contrast, Dr. Hunt, who had administered the test to herself, scored in the mid-70s; one of the clients, about whom she was particularly concerned, had tested in the 60s, a result that she considered "low even for up there."*

Boukreev, who had scientific training in college, has recalled the testing and said he was not convinced. "These readings meant little to me. I didn't believe too much in the procedure. You can receive a lot more information by observing the clients' . . . external appearances." However they came to their readings of the situation, Boukreev and Hunt shared a similar concern. Some of the clients could be at high risk if they made a summit bid.

While the clients rested, there was much discussion about our acclimatization routine, and we scheduled an excursion to Camp III for April 23, by which time, as had previously been planned, the Sherpas should have established and stocked the camp. This excursion, as was understood, was mandatory in the plan that had been devised for acclimatization. I stressed to the clients the importance of spending time at this altitude and suggested that after a night at Camp III they consider trying to gain another two hundred to three hundred meters before descending, telling them that, based upon my experience, success with such a routine—and a proper recovery afterwards—would contribute significantly to the possibility of their success above eight thousand meters.

The goal, Boukreev kept reinforcing, was not only proper acclimatization, but also the maintenance of a reserve of energy.

---

*Subsequently, a medical authority questioned about this reading agreed that Dr. Hunt was right to be concerned about a client who had exhibited symptoms of AMS and was testing in the 60s, but cautioned that pulse oximeters are notoriously inaccurate. One authority went so far as to say that a client who was obviously having difficulties and was continuously testing in the 60s could, if he or she persisted in efforts to ascend, be headed for a "dirt nap."

Boukreev reminded the clients that while they were going through the routine, they were also losing strength, strength that even during the rest periods they wouldn't totally recover, that "full compensation does not happen even during a long rest at Base Camp." In Boukreev's opinion, the message was not getting across. "Many of the clients were not attentive to their rest and recuperation. Their focus of attention was displaced, and they only understood acclimatization as gaining altitude from excursion to excursion." An exception, Boukreev thought, was Martin Adams.

During one of our rest days, sometime before dinner, Martin and I had a conversation, and he asked me if in my opinion he had a chance to complete the expedition with success. He told me, "Last time, when we were on Makalu, I had no problems at high altitude, but after my night on the Makalu-La Pass and descent to Base Camp, my strength was gone. Even after resting I felt empty, without any desire to try a summit assault."

Boukreev, recalling Adams's experiences on Makalu, reminded him that he'd made several acclimatization excursions in quick succession, and, in Boukreev's opinion, Adams hadn't properly rested between them.

I told him, "Your job is to get sufficient acclimatization with a minimal number of nights spent at high altitude. . . . During the period of rest prior to our assault bid, you need to rest, eat properly, and totally relax. For a much better recovery I recommend that you descend lower than Base Camp, to the forest zone where there is a lot more oxygen. . . . The recovery processes in the body happen much more completely and quickly when there is a large amount of oxygen in the air. Also, a walk down and back promotes muscle tone. Active rest will be far more beneficial than lying around Base Camp."

Martin Adams recalled the advice and remembers thinking, "I really didn't want to do it, because it was a lot of work to walk back down that valley and then walk back up."

If any doubt about the perils of AMS remained in any of the clients' minds, a tragedy nailed the warning to the wall. On Monday, April 22, altitude took its first victim in the Fischer expedition. A team of Sherpas was climbing from Camp I to Camp II, ferrying supplies to advance the route, and among them was Ngawang Topche Sherpa, the uncle of Lopsang Jangbu Sherpa. As Fischer was descending from Camp II, the riotous storm behind him and the tents restored, he came upon Ngawang Topche Sherpa, who appeared somewhat confused, not well. Fischer, who had a reputation on the mountain for his attentiveness to Sherpas and a concern for their well-being, told him to descend. Expecting him to comply, Fischer continued his own descent, eager for some rest after his stint at Camp II, but Ngawang Topche Sherpa didn't follow him down. For whatever reason—personal pride, a misunderstanding of Fischer's order, or confusion brought on by his condition—he had instead continued up the mountain.

A radio transmission from Camp II to Base Camp alerted the expedition members to the problem above. Like a drunken sailor headed for his ship, Ngawang Topche Sherpa had somehow navigated the route and was found disoriented and coughing up a froth of sputum and blood. Given the symptoms, the diagnosis came quickly: high-altitude pulmonary edema or HAPE. While the appropriate drug therapy for HAPE is still being debated, it is generally agreed that an immediate descent of 610–1,220 meters is a necessary lifesaving measure, but Camp II was only four hundred meters above Camp I. To get Ngawang Topche Sherpa to an elevation where the symptoms might abate, they would have to take him into the Khumbu Icefall.

Coordinating the rescue effort at Camp II were Klev Schoening and Tim Madsen, who had gone to Camp II to further their acclimatization. The job fell to them because there were no Mountain Madness guides at Camp II. Fischer had left Camp II that morning, and Boukreev and Beidleman were in Base Camp resting from their previous acclimatization excursion. When consulted, Boukreev knew that the first action taken in a rescue situation is often the most important one and advised, "Get him down as quickly as possible; give him oxygen."*

My surprise in this situation was that Sherpas who were in Base Camp didn't go up immediately upon hearing the news of Ngawang Topche Sherpa's distress. I expected that because, like Lopsang Jangbu Sherpa and many of our other Sherpas, Ngawang Topche Sherpa was from the Rolwaling Valley, but as it turned out, they didn't go up until later in the day. The exact reason for this I am not sure, but it made me consider what we might expect from our Sherpas in an emergency. I hold the Sherpas' capacities for physically demanding work in the highest regard, but you shouldn't automatically assume that in a critical situation the Sherpas will perform to your expectations. It is not that they are not capable, far from it, because their history of efforts and their ability to assist and give good advice and direction on 8,000ers is well established. Instead, it is the matter of risk, asking them to do something dangerous that falls outside their assigned jobs *and* the responsibilities they are paid to assume.

Because Ngawang Topche Sherpa was not responding to treatment, Klev Schoening and Tim Madsen rigged a makeshift sled to lower the stricken Sherpa. As they moved down the mountain, Neal Beidleman and several of the Mountain Madness Sherpas left Base Camp and headed through the Icefall to connect with the descending climbers. Just before dark, Beidleman and the Sherpas took over from Madsen and Klev Schoening, who stayed on the mountain so they could continue their acclimatization efforts.

On the morning of April 23 the acclimatization excursion that had previously been planned was kept on the schedule. It was decided, Boukreev recalls, that Beidleman, who had been

---

*The advice from Base Camp, however, was to intervene with drugs, because Ngwang's symptoms suggested he wouldn't be able to descend on his feet, but the drugs that were administered seemed to have no effect. Next they attempted to place him in a Gamow bag, a bag that can be inflated around a stricken climber and filled with air. This procedure increases the concentration of oxygen molecules and simulates a descent to a lower altitude.

hailed for his efforts in maneuvering Ngawang Topche Sherpa through the Icefall at night, would delay his departure until that afternoon or perhaps the next day, depending upon how quickly he recovered from the ordeal of the day before.

That morning, before breakfast, Fischer began work in the tent that held Pittman's communication gear. Fischer, in addition to maintaining a connection with the Mountain Madness office in West Seattle, being honcho in absentia, was also doing regular phone feeds to Jane Bromet, his publicist, who was still serving as a correspondent for Outside Online* despite the fact that she had departed the Everest Base Camp and had returned home to the Capitol Hill neighborhood of Seattle.

Fischer, when he wasn't giving Bromet the printable news, was giving her his behind-the-scenes impressions, Everest naked, the stuff that the armchair climber in Milwaukee, tapped into the Internet during television commercial breaks, was never going to see on the computer monitor. One of his recurring themes was money, how it was evaporating at high altitude.

A business associate of Fischer's said, "I think it was a really major stress on him, and especially after Ngawang . . . and he thought, 'Man, this guy's going to be in a hospital for two years in a coma, and who's going to be paying the tab for that?' So . . . oh, yeah, I think the whole money issue was a huge stress. I think he tried to just . . . keep it out of his mind, but it really became a substantial problem for him. . . . He thought, 'Man, I'm going to climb this mountain, and I'm going to come home with ten thousand bucks if I'm lucky, and that's just not okay.' "

Gammelgaard, according to Karen Dickinson, still owed Mountain Madness more than $20,000; the oxygen supply, given that Pete Schoening and some of the other clients had been drawing it down at $325 a bottle, was dwindling; Fischer was facing the possibility of having to evacuate Ngawang Topche

---

*Bromet had been able to report for a while from Base Camp after arranging to use a satellite phone that was kept in an "ice-box of a tent" in Mal Duff's Everest Base Camp.

Sherpa by helicopter to Kathmandu (a formidable expense); he
was physically tired beyond the normal condition of being at
altitude; his team physician and Base Camp manager was suffering from recurring altitude sickness; Camp III had yet to be
established; the fixed ropes were still not in place between
Camp III and Camp IV. He was behind schedule, thrashed by
his physical efforts, wondering how he was going to pull it off.
He was dancing toward a precipice as precarious as any in the
Khumbu Icefall, but, almost always, powering through it, smiling and positive.

Most of the clients, without any of the guides, departed for the Icefall
around 6:00 A.M., wanting to avoid the heat of the day and the blinding glare off the ice that, as it absorbed the heat of the sun, became
more unstable and threatening. Prior to their departure, Scott and I
had agreed that, as we had in the past, we would tail them at a
distance. Our continuing practice of letting the clients move through
some situations without us drew the attention of other expedition
guides and clients who, I know, disagreed with the practice. But, on
this point, Scott and I were much in agreement.

Personally, I looked with concern upon the closely regimented
expeditions where the clients performed as tin soldiers. Given my
history as a trainer and coach in cross-country skiing and mountaineering, I felt it was important to encourage independent action.

It was not only the guiding styles of Mountain Madness that
many of the other expedition members thought strange; it was
also one of their guides, Boukreev. Up and down the mountain,
during his forays with clients or at work above Base Camp, he
was often noticed wearing track shoes with spiked cleats. This
was "normal dress" for Boukreev when he wasn't high on the
mountain. Some of those who made his footwear a matter of
concern began to call him Sneakers behind his back, a moniker
that he initially overheard as "Snickers." Boukreev couldn't
make out what possible connection he had with the candy bars
he'd seen the clients putting down in the mess tent. Finally,

when he understood, he was offended by the pettiness of it all and thought, "You don't drag an unnecessary four kilograms up the mountain. The energy I save in these lightweight shoes I will have above eight thousand meters, and there will be no more jokes."

Boukreev, dedicated to his own formulas, had the discipline of an Olympic athlete and the intense focus of a test pilot. He kept his attention on his body's controls and paid heed to what was going on outside the cockpit. He stayed focused on what he considered important, what kept you alive. Seen by some as detached, by others as self-absorbed and aloof, he was in his Himalayan head, a place that for Lene Gammelgaard was an okay place to live. "I would have liked to have been on an expedition with only Anatolis, but there is only one Anatoli in the whole world, and then there are the Scotts."

Coming into Camp I, I saw many of our clients resting in the sun, relaxing after their crossing of the Icefall. Given what had happened with Ngawang Topche Sherpa the day before and because several of the Sherpas were helping to bring him down, we were shorthanded on April 23, and a lot of supplies still needed to be taken from Camp I to Camp II where they could be staged in preparation for establishing Camp III. I filled my pack with several expedition sleeping bags and set off immediately for Camp II, and along the route I passed four of our Sherpas also carrying loads. Like me, it was their plan to spend that night at Camp II, and then, the next day, they would ferry all the supplies to Camp III that would be required to establish it for the clients.

Climbing in the clear, windless day, Boukreev was thankful for the warm temperature. As they moved higher, they would no longer be climbing in fleece jackets. The cold that was coming could find your bones.

I arrived as the Sherpas were putting down a lunch for the clients advancing behind me, and I quickly got something to eat before I went to my tent. Tired from my carry and lulled by the heat and stillness, I fell almost immediately to sleep.

Sharing Boukreev's tent at Camp II was Martin Adams, who was growing increasingly dismayed at the way the expedition was being managed, where logging on seemed to have a higher priority than logistics. He wanted the summit, and he was never going to get there at the speed things were moving. He was particularly upset that Camp III had yet to be established and that he was not going to be able to advance to spend the next night at Camp III in order to maintain his acclimatization routine.

Like me, Martin slept for a few hours before dinner, and as it started to get dark, he changed into his "crocodile" costume, and I got into my down suit. In the mess tent there was much discussion about the progress on our route. And because Camp III had yet to be established, we devised a compromise plan that would allow the clients to advance to the fixed ropes and climb to an altitude of 7,000 meters, a position on the fixed ropes with which I was familiar because I had fixed the ropes to that point. Then we planned that Scott and I would climb higher to 7,300 meters, where we would choose the location for Camp III and supervise the preparation of the site and the setting up of tents.

That night a storm came in, bringing with it a heavy cover of clouds and some snow, but thankfully not the wind that Fischer had suffered through a few nights earlier. In the morning, before first light, a group of Sherpas loaded with supplies and gear for Camp III departed Camp II, leaving behind them a boot-marked trail that the clients, who arose around 6:00 A.M., would later follow to the fixed ropes. After breakfast, Fischer decided to return to Base Camp with Tim Madsen, who had not been recovering well after helping with the rescue of Ngawang Topche Sherpa. Needing to get Camp III established, Fischer instructed Boukreev to catch up to the Sherpas who had left earlier and go to 7,300 meters as planned, while the clients, at their own speed, would climb on the fixed ropes to 7,000 meters and return in time for lunch.

I started out slowly, carrying in my pack my high-altitude clothing and a high-altitude tent. As I reached 6,800 meters and clipped onto the fixed ropes on the Lhotse Face, the weather, which had been cloudy but not particularly threatening at first light, began to deteriorate. The wind picked up; a drizzle of snow began; and a fog settled around the fixed ropes as I continued to move ahead. As I advanced, I realized I had made a mistake that morning by not changing out of my "Snickers," and I was upset at having made such a blunder. I was not in a dangerous situation because I was on fixed ropes, but in a not-so-good place. The traction I had with my cleats on the hard ice covered in fresh snow was not good, and I had to be deliberate when I placed my feet.

At times the visibility was down to one to two meters, but the force of the wind would sometimes sculpt a hole in the weather. In one of those holes, just below the proposed site of Camp III, Boukreev saw the Mountain Madness Sherpas descending. Surprised to see them coming down, he asked if they had prepared the Camp III site and put up tents. To both questions they answered no, saying that the winds were too high and that the weather was not good.

I was upset with the Sherpas' abandonment of the work schedule for Camp III, because we were already behind in our acclimatization schedule and we'd yet to overnight there, but it was not within my power to order them to stay. Only Scott, who had descended, or Lopsang, who had accompanied his stricken uncle to Base Camp, could give that kind of order. Frustrated with this reversal, I continued up the fixed ropes to their end, and as if endorsing the Sherpas' decision, the weather turned from bad to terrible. A steady snow began to fall; the wind began to gust in threatening bursts; and visibility went almost to zero. Removing the high-altitude tent from my pack, I stashed it where the porters had left their loads, there at the terminus of the fixed ropes. Shivering from the rapid drop in temperature and feeling my way because of the mistake of my shoes, I made it off the face of Lhotse. In less than a hour from my turnaround I made it to the tents, where I joined the other members of the expedition, who were having dinner.

Wisely, although they had not made the target altitude of their excursion, the clients had turned back to the tents when the weather had abruptly changed.

That night (April 24) I spoke by radio to Scott, who, along with Neal, was still at Base Camp, and we discussed the problems we had. Camp III was still not in place, and our Sherpas were bordering on exhaustion after having worked several days straight. I suggested that the next day four of our Sherpas go to the site of Camp III and set up our tents, then descend to Base Camp for a much needed rest. Sending them down meant they would not be able to work on April 26, and that complicated our situation.

An agreement had been reached between Fischer, Rob Hall of Adventure Consultants, Todd Burleson of Alpine Ascents, Ian Woodall of the Johannesburg *Sunday Times* Expedition, and Makalu Gau of the Taiwanese National Expedition to cooperate in lacing the ropes between Camps III and IV on April 26. As the other expeditions had planned, Mountain Madness was not going to use any of its guides for this effort, but to instead dispatch several Sherpas to the job. Boukreev's and Fischer's problem: if Mountain Madness directed their Sherpas' efforts to establishing Camp III on April 25 and then sent them to Base Camp to rest on April 26, they would have no Sherpas to contribute to the effort. So, a decision was made to send Boukreev in the Sherpas' stead.

We could have refrained from contributing, but we would have lost our privilege to be among some of the first expeditions to make our bid. May 10 was circulating as a proposed summit date, and we didn't want to lose our position.

The fixing of ropes from Camp III to Camp IV is one of the most laborious and time-consuming jobs that has to be done when laying siege to Everest on the Southeast Ridge Route, and Boukreev was pleased to get the assignment. He wanted to know that the route was ready and safe prior to the summit bid. But, to contribute to that effort he needed a day of rest, and it was agreed that he would spend the following day at Camp II, resting and collecting from each of the other expeditions their contribution of supplies that would be necessary for the job.

Meanwhile, a few of the clients were becoming increasingly restless, frustrated by the delays and the seeming lack of focus of their guides. One of the clients, who has asked to remain anonymous, said that on several occasions when walking with two other Mountain Madness climbers between camps, they would talk among themselves about their situation. They "would raise comments about the fact that Neal, Scott, and Anatoli didn't seem to be paying attention to details. Neal and Scott would go zipping by everybody like they were racing each other between camps, or they'd hang out and take photographs or something." The "hired help," as one of the clients referred to the guides, were not making a favorable impression.

CHAPTER 11

TOWARD THE PUSH

On April 25 the weather stabilized, and our clients, as was planned, began their excursion that would take them onto the fixed ropes. As Scott and I had agreed, I stayed at Camp II, resting for the work ahead, gathering the supplies we would need in the effort to fix ropes between Camps III and IV, and meeting with Ang Dorje Sherpa, Rob Hall's climbing sirdar, to discuss how we would divide up the work the next day.

Because Fischer was still in Base Camp and Beidleman had yet to make it to Camp II, the clients were left to maneuver their own way to the fixed ropes. Some of them made it to the target of 7,000 meters; others didn't. Thanks to eager street vendors in Kathmandu, as one climber has since mused, the only people that were getting high were in Base Camp.*

---

*As one of Fischer's clients has put it: "There is a romantic notion about Base Camp, that somehow the people there are in some kind of suspended animation, members of a spartan cult. But, who you are at home, that's who you are in Base Camp. You smoke at home; you smoke at Base Camp. You have a cocktail before dinner; you have one at Base Camp."

Very early in the morning, somewhere around 4:00 A.M., I started my climb from Camp II, barely awake and not too cheerful. Even strong coffee at that time in the morning is not much help! A full sky of stars suggested a good day, and as I squeaked along on firm-packed snow, I could see ahead of me by about 150 to 250 meters the headlamps of the Sherpas from Hall's expedition, and behind me, trailing at about the same distance, I could see the bobbing lights of the Taiwanese Sherpas. Traveling in tandem at a steady pace, we made it to the site of Camp III in about three and one-half hours, arriving at about 7:30 A.M. as the first rays of sun began to edge toward two tents the Sherpas had set up the day before.

Camp III, located at the end of the fixed ropes where Boukreev had stashed his carry two days previously, had been notched into the sloping face of Lhotse. Given the angle of the slope, about that of a ladder going to a second-story window, platforms for the two standing tents had been cut into a natural ice shelf, but another platform for a third tent still needed to be carved from the oblique ice, so Boukreev and the Sherpas went to work with the adze and pick ends of their ice ax heads. Using small arcing swings that pivoted from their wrists, they took the ice down in a steady rhythm.

I left some of my things in the tents and advanced above Camp III where Ang Dorje and some other Sherpas from the Rob Hall expedition were already at work threading the fixed ropes. After one run of rope I changed positions with Ang Dorje, who had been in the lead, and for the rest of the day I worked in the lead as Ang Dorje belayed me, and the other Sherpas passed the ropes up the mountain. We went in this way for almost five hours, working at an even pace, until we reached 7,550 meters, a place just below the Yellow Band.*

Having put in a full day, Boukreev decided to descend to Camp III to spend the night and further his acclimatization,

---

*This is a band of overlapping, yellowish slabs of limestone.

while Ang Dorje and the other Sherpas who had been working on the fixed ropes returned to Camp II. Looking toward Camp II as he descended the fixed ropes, Boukreev expected to see activity around the tents or some of the Mountain Madness clients advancing toward the camp, but no one was in sight.

The Mountain Madness clients at Camp II had spent most of the day in their tents resting because bad weather had pinned them down. Reporting on the day to NBC, Pittman groped for some "human interest" to flesh out her dispatch and devoted most of her coverage to the music the Mountain Madness climbers liked to listen to on the Base Camp boom-box or on their personal CD or cassette players. Neal Beidleman, Pittman reported, preferred the Chipmunks' "Lollipop, Lollipop." Lene Gammelgaard, she said, preferred Nick Cave's "Murder Ballads." As they were in music, they were on the mountain. Different.

Beidleman, soft-spoken, measured, and solicitous, was a tall, forest pine for Gammelgaard's lightning personality. Opinionated, strong-willed, determined to climb the mountain on her own terms and with a taste for the bold "out theres" of the world, she felt that Beidleman's limited experience at high altitude made him overeager to prove himself, that he needed to be "worshiped" and "respected" as a guide. "And there's no way I did that. . . . 'I don't need a guide, especially not you.'. . . And when he doesn't get that, then he has to find another way, which doesn't work . . . so, 'Grow up. . . . Stay away from me or I'll kill you.' . . . So, I think he had a hard time with me."

Like Boukreev and Fischer, Beidleman had a few critics among the clients, but he kept a professional edge to his encounters, only rarely slipping from character to offer a public parry.

That evening I had our tents at Camp III to myself and enjoyed the solitude and quiet on the Lhotse Face away from the activity of Base Camp. Using one of our high-altitude stoves, I prepared tea and some food. Often, as you advance in altitude, you lose your appetite, but because of the day's work I was particularly hungry and devoured my dinner. Later, as the temperature fell and the cold began to return to my body, I made a radio call to Base Camp asking that the Sherpas bring more rope up the next day, and then I zipped into my sleeping bag and fell almost immediately to sleep.

Boukreev's first night above seven thousand meters was more fitful than those he'd spent at Camp II, and he woke with a lethargy not unusual as one advances to a higher altitude in the acclimatization routine. Somewhere between 7:00 and 8:00 A.M., as he continued to rest in the warmth of his sleeping bag, a few Sherpas passed his tent in conversation as they carried a supply of rope up to the Yellow Band. Still not fully restored after his day of work and fighting for about thirty minutes the desire to stay nestled in the warmth of his bag, Boukreev finally wriggled out of his tent and clipped onto the fixed rope that was little more than a stride from the zippered flap of his tent.

As I advanced up the ropes, I checked the work we had done in the days before, making certain the anchors that had been placed were not creeping and that our tie-offs were secure. Also, I was removing some lengths of old rope that still remained attached to anchors we were using, wanting to prevent a climber from mistakenly clipping on to an old rope that was either weak or not properly anchored. I could see Ang Dorje working in the lead. In cooperation, we advanced the route further above the Yellow Band, and then stopped for rest and lunch.

As Boukreev drank hot tea from his thermos, he watched as Sherpas above him pulled old fixed ropes out of the snow and examined their condition. Sorting through them, they chose the ropes that appeared still sound and then climbed higher, fixing those ropes and new rope to anchors as they went, advancing the route. After a brief rest, Boukreev followed behind the Sherpas, examining the fixed ropes as he went, making his way to the South Col.

At about 7,800 meters, at a place where the rise to the South Col was becoming more gentle, I saw the Sherpas who had been ahead now descending. I asked how they were doing, and they reported "good" but that they were hurrying to return to Camp II before darkness fell. Because I was planning to spend another night at Camp III, I had not such a long descent ahead and I continued on to find a site for our Camp IV and to leave a high-altitude tent that I had been ferrying. The wind, as I came to the South Col, was high and steady, but I had not observed any threatening weather during the day, nor did there seem to be any immediate possibility of a storm, so I took the time to locate a place from which we would launch our summit bid.

Descending to Camp III after locating a site for Mountain Madness's Camp IV, Boukreev, to his relief, found that five of Fischer's eight clients, Lene Gammelgaard, Klev Schoening, Martin Adams, Sandy Hill Pittman, and Dale Kruse, had arrived during his absence. To Boukreev the climbers seemed to be doing well, and were strong after their climb from II to III, but he recalled his own first night up and considered that things have a way of changing at altitude.

The next morning (April 28) we all arose somewhere around 8:00 A.M. as the sun began to warm our tents. By radio we were informed that Scott and Neal had advanced to Camp II and were planning that day to climb to Camp III for their acclimatization. My condition, I think because of my work, was much improved, though I was still tired, and all of the clients except for Lene and Dale seemed to be adjusting well. Lene's eyes were red and inflamed and she was somewhat lethargic. Like me the day before, she seemed to be having some minor, but not threatening problems. Dale Kruse was altogether a different matter.

Continuing to be concerned about Kruse, Boukreev was monitoring him closely and noticed that, unlike the other clients, he seemed "apathetic, withdrawn and distant." To Boukreev's trained eye, Kruse looked to be in trouble. Around 10:00 A.M.,

Martin Adams, who'd finally had his night at Camp III, started to gather his gear and said he was going down as soon as he was together. Boukreev, particularly eager to get Kruse to a lower altitude, was encouraging all of the climbers to follow Adams's lead.

One night at that altitude for a person who has come there for the first time in his or her life was, I thought, enough, and I was discouraging both Lene and Sandy, who were expressing a desire to spend yet another night at Camp III. I thought that their ambitions were misplaced, that they needed rest, so I proposed that they consider climbing that morning to 7,500 to 7,600 meters and then descend to Camp II, but neither appeared to have any desire to climb higher.

As I talked with the clients about their intentions, I noticed that Dale's situation seemed to be getting worse, and I began to encourage him to prepare for a descent, and I was joined in my efforts by some of the clients who were also becoming concerned about his deteriorating condition.

Finally, Kruse was convinced, and he began to pack his gear and get dressed for the descent. As Boukreev watched Kruse moving about, his concern turned to alarm. Kruse, according to Boukreev, was "wobbly, having trouble standing," and now, Boukreev thought, he had a potential disaster on his hands. Kruse was a big man, much larger than Boukreev, and he was not in total control of his movements. If Kruse fell, Boukreev wasn't at all certain that he could get him up and safely to Camp II.

I got Dale onto the fixed ropes with some difficulty. Whether it was his condition or my problem of making myself understood, I don't know, but it took a lot for me to explain how he should clip on and move with me to descend. Fortunately, as we were beginning our descent, Scott and Neal came into view, and Scott, immediately upon seeing Dale's condition, began to assist.

We decided that the two of us would take Dale down, while Neal stayed behind at Camp III, because he needed to get an overnight for his acclimatization.

Securing Kruse with a rope attached to his climbing harness, Fischer led the descent. He, in turn, was secured to Boukreev, who trailed the two of them. Behind Kruse, Fischer, and Boukreev, Lene Gammelgaard followed, but Sandy Hill Pittman, despite Boukreev's encouragement and advice, had elected to remain behind.

Somewhere around 6,900 meters Kruse began to rouse, to come to his senses, and he seemed much more in control of his movements. Finally, around 5:00 P.M., as we made it to the bottom of the slopes of Lhotse and onto the Western Cwm that would take us to Camp II, Kruse seemed back to normal, and we removed our connecting ropes to move independently.

As Kruse moved down the glacier in front of them, Fischer and Boukreev talked about the events of the past several days, Boukreev about the progress that had been made on the climbing route, Fischer about the problems with which he'd been dealing at Base Camp.

Scott was sharing with me the situation with Ngawang Topche Sherpa, telling me that Lopsang Jangbu Sherpa had flown with his uncle and Ingrid to Kathmandu and that the rescue costs were maybe going to be as much as $10,000. This expense, Ngawang Topche's condition, his use of oxygen from our dwindling supply, and the fact that our Sherpas had still not prepared Camp IV or taken our oxygen supplies to that altitude were of the greatest concern to Scott. Seeing his openness, I talked with him about our Sherpa team, saying I felt it had not been strong from the beginning and that, when compared to Rob Hall's team headed by Ang Dorje, ours was not as strong or as well led. In discussing this we agreed that after the expedition we should evaluate how our Sherpas had performed and consider who among them should join future expeditions.

Safely in Camp II by dark, Fischer checked in with both Base Camp and Camp III, and while there were no encouraging reports on Ngawang Topche Sherpa's condition, no other immediate problems needed Scott's attention, so he decided to ascend the next day with Pete Schoening to Camp III in the hope that the elder Schoening could further acclimatize and continue his bid for the summit.

On the morning of April 29, Scott and Pete began their ascent to Camp III, and I continued my descent to Base Camp, climbing with both Dale and Lene. For much of the route I was constantly securing and controlling the movements of Dale, because, while he was much improved from the day before, I was concerned that he could make a mistake, especially in the Icefall, and I wanted to avoid a problem there. Arrival in Base Camp was a relief and the warm temperatures a welcome pleasure. After six continuous nights above Base Camp and the work that I had been doing on the fixed ropes, I was much in need of a rest.

On April 30, I made use of the quiet and good weather in Base Camp and took some simple pleasures: a shower and the time to read a book in the sun. I understood from my body that I had acclimatized well, and I made plans to descend to the forest zone for an extended rest and again encouraged Martin Adams to do the same.

We were now strewn up and down the mountain from Pheriche, where Tim and Charlotte had gone to recover from AMS symptoms, to Camp III where Scott had spent the previous night with Pete. This geographical spread was not of particular concern to me as the art of acclimatizing is not something that can be held to a rigid schedule, dependent as it is upon events, circumstances, and personal physiologies, but what did concern me was the spread of readiness between the Mountain Madness climbers. Of growing concern to me was Scott, whose routine had repeatedly been broken in his efforts going up and down the mountain.

By May 1, every one of the guides and clients, except for Charlotte Fox and Tim Madsen, had returned to Base Camp.

Fischer, longing for some rest, decided to take a shower before dinner. As Boukreev rested in his tent, he heard Lene Gammelgaard call to Fischer as he emerged from his shower.

They began to talk about the plans for summit day, and Scott told Lene that in a few days we would all ascend to Camp III, and then, from there, the clients would go onto oxygen and make the summit bid with supplementary O's. This plan upset Lene, who was still holding to her plan to climb without oxygen, and the conversation became loud and heated.

Gammelgaard had been counting on extra days to continue her acclimatization excursions because the delays in establishing higher-altitude camps had not given her enough time at higher altitudes to test her physiology. Now, Fischer was announcing to her that everyone would be climbing with oxygen, and she was furious. "I was saying [to him], 'There's no chance I can acclimatize enough to climb without oxygen. . . . For half a year you've been supporting me in this, knowing the conditions on your expedition. . . . I've been creating my own expectations, training for this. . . . You're not together in your head.' "

Fischer told Gammelgaard that she had no chance to ascend without oxygen, and like everyone else, she would fall into line and go on the bottle. Holding tenaciously to her position, Gammelgaard continued to harangue Fischer for his pushing her to "fit in." "I got mad. . . . It's not something that enforces my respect for a grown-up expedition leader. . . . I got fucking mad."

The issue unresolved, Fischer and Gammelgaard ended their conversation. Boukreev, sensing that he might be able to help settle their dispute, left his tent and caught up to Fischer as he headed toward the quiet and privacy of his own tent.

We had much to catch up on, and I asked him how it had gone with Pete Schoening. Scott told me that it had gone well enough, but that Pete was still unable to sleep without using oxygen. About Dale, he said he felt that Dale had been lucky, that if he had descended any later from Camp III, he could have been at serious risk for HACE. But about Dale or Pete Schoening, he was not at that moment prepared to say no. Instead, he felt that we should keep them under observation, that on our "final push" we could turn them around at Camp II or III if they proved not to be fit.

Boukreev was concerned with Fischer's decision, and Martin Adams, though not in a position to directly intervene, was also concerned. "Scott's got everybody going. He's got Dale going; he's got [Pete] Schoening going. It's obvious that these people are sick; they can't do it, but for whatever reason they want to go, and Scott says fine. . . . I mean Scott desperately wanted to get people up the mountain for advertisement's sake. . . . I told Neal at Base Camp . . . 'Look, these guys have no business going up there. You get somebody killed and you're going to get more publicity than if you get them up the mountain, so you better consider what their life is worth before you take them up there.' "

Scott was totally frustrated with Lene. When I asked about her intentions to climb without oxygen, he just threw up his hands and shook his head, so I offered to intervene and speak with her, because, like him, I thought that for her to climb without oxygen would be dangerous. She had neither the experience to properly judge her physiology nor the proper acclimatization.

Just before dinner I went to Lene's tent and asked her if I might speak to her about her intentions, and she welcomed me and my thoughts. I explained that when I had climbed Everest without oxygen for the first time in 1991, I had gone as far as to spend a night at the South Col before descending to Base Camp in order to push my acclimatization. Because she had been no higher than 7,300 meters on the expedition, and because she had no experience upon which to calculate the probability of success, I suggested that she give up the idea, promising that if she was successful in climbing with oxygen, I would repeat the climb with her and assist her in her effort to climb without O's. I confess now that I knew she probably would not have the energy, but I was serious in my offer and would have made the effort if she had decided to take me up on it.

That evening in the mess tent Fischer addressed the Mountain Madness clients, excepting Charlotte Fox and Tim Madsen, who had yet to return, and Martin Adams, who had headed down to the forest zone, and told them that on May 5, after a prolonged rest and weather permitting, the expedition would begin its final push to the summit. Joking about Boukreev's and Adams's decision to descend lower than Base Camp for their final resting period, he said he suspected they were motivated primarily by their interest in meeting women trekkers and in drinking beer.

On the heels of the joke, Lene entered the mess tent and came up behind me, putting her arms around my chest and giving me a kiss on the cheek. In a voice that everyone could hear, she said, "Thank you very much, Anatoli," and then she went to an empty seat at the table. Everyone in the tent, not understanding her purpose in saying this, grinned and looked from me to Lene. Scott, though, understood. He knew the oxygen problem had been solved.

CHAPTER 12

THE COUNTDOWN

Saying good-bye to everyone that evening, I switched on my head-lamp and began my descent, but within an hour the night was brilliant as a nearly full moon rose and illuminated the Khumbu Glacier. To my right the silhouette of Pumori was for a while my companion, and then, as it fell behind me, I was alone on the trail, thinking about the richness of the air and the warmth into which I would be descending. My body felt properly acclimatized and healthy, but because of my activities in the past several weeks my reserves of energy were low and I needed to replenish my strength.

For several hours Boukreev continued his descent. Passing through Lobuche, the scene of the Bromet-Pittman satellite-phone showdown, he took a left fork of the trail that took him toward Dingboche (4,350 m), where he hoped to connect with Martin Adams. At 1:00 A.M., still thirty minutes out of the village, he bivouacked under the stars.

The next morning I went to the lodge where I thought Martin would be staying, but the Sherpani who was managing things said that no one had arrived the day before, so I had breakfast and then continued my trek, arriving less than an hour later in Pheriche (4,280 m), where I found not Martin but Ingrid, our expedition doctor, who had just returned from Kathmandu.

Dr. Hunt didn't have good news to report. Ngawang Topche Sherpa, who six days earlier had been airlifted from Pheriche to Kathmandu, had lapsed into a coma and appeared to have suffered brain damage. If he survived his ordeal, Ngawang Topche Sherpa, as Fischer had suspected, was probably going to require extended medical care.

After hearing of our high-altitude Sherpa and his tragedy and visiting with Ingrid and some of my acquaintances from Himalayan Guides who had come down from Base Camp for a rest, I continued my descent, arriving finally around dinnertime at the Ama Dablam Garden Lodge in Deboche (3,770 m), a small village in the last stand of forest as you ascend toward Everest Base Camp.

For two days in Deboche, Boukreev followed a simple routine: rest and moderate exercise, enjoying "the fatigue of the organism" and the "saturation of the air."

I was sure that my plan of rest and rehabilitation would allow me to gather my strength and provide me the reserve I would need to get our clients to the summit, and I committed to protecting and strengthening my body for that purpose. I regretted that Scott had not endorsed my plan for himself, Neal, and our clients, and I hoped that the rest they would get at Base Camp would be sufficient.

At 4:00 P.M. on the afternoon of May 4, feeling "remarkable" and "restored," Boukreev began his trek back to Base Camp. Stopping only briefly in Pheriche at a Sherpa teahouse for some tea and fried potatoes, he hiked steadily and arrived at around midnight. Weaving through the tents of the various expeditions, he could hear the errant sounds of late-night conversations and see in the moonlight an occasional figure moving about, but in the cluster of Mountain Madness tents all was quiet. All the lights in the tents of the guides and clients had been extinguished; even Sandy Hill Pittman's communications tent was dark. In the mess tent Boukreev found a thermos of hot tea and poured himself a cup. From Deboche to the Everest Base Camp, the temperature had fallen by at least forty degrees.

Awakening on the morning of May 5, Boukreev could hear the familiar voices of the clients as they moved around the camp, but absent was the unmistakable voice and Khumbu cough of Sandy Hill Pittman, who, Boukreev later discovered, had descended while he was in Deboche.

On Saturday, May 4, a Sherpa runner had brought to Base Camp news that three friends of Pittman's had trekked to Pheriche and were eager to see her, so she and three Sherpas, one of them packing her satellite phone, trekked down to meet them.

I was surprised that someone with her experience had acted in that way. She was an experienced climber, yes, but I thought her rapid descent was not a particularly smart thing to do just prior to a summit bid. An extended rest would have been beneficial, but the quick up and down, I suspected, had cost her a great deal of energy.

Except for Pittman, all the clients were in Base Camp on the morning of May 5. She had not returned because, before her departure, Fischer had announced that May 6 was the day the expedition would begin its final push. Adams, who had descended to Pheriche but missed Boukreev when he was in the village, looked strong and rested. Fox and Madsen looked reasonably good after their rest, but Boukreev was extremely concerned about their acclimatization. Only higher on the mountain would the truth of their situation become apparent. The other clients were no better, no worse than he would have expected, but Fischer, he learned, was having problems.

Scott, I heard, had gone with Neal during the rest period onto Pumori to take photographs. That was an expense of energy, especially given the schedule Scott had been maintaining, that I found troubling; even more so when I heard that Scott had not been feeling well and was taking antibiotics. While there is no evidence of which I am aware that antibiotics are particularly dangerous if taken before a high-altitude summit bid, I have always been wary of taking them—or any drugs for that matter—before such an effort. I like to know what my body is doing, and I don't want drugs covering any of my body's signals.

Pittman had returned to Base Camp the night before, and on the morning of Monday, May 6, at 5:00 A.M., she was back at work. In her communications tent she powered up for a satellite connection to NBC, and for the world of Internet cruisers she detailed the events of her past few days down the mountain. Her news was upbeat, enthusiastic, and strangely focused.

"We had a great yak steak and french fries at my favorite restaurant. . . . I had only the day to visit with my friends, and on Sunday, we walked up to Lobuche, where we had lunch. I then scampered back to Base Camp Sunday night."

A remote report from the scene of a plane crash that detailed what the victims were wearing would not have appeared less strange to anyone who knew what she was looking at, what was ahead. In less than two hours she would be leaving to attempt the summit of Mount Everest. As Lene Gammelgaard would later say, "I just couldn't get her climbing history to fit with the way she behaved in the mountains."

While Pittman dictated her adventures, the rest of the Mountain Madness climbers made their way to the mess tent for the last of their big-table spreads. The banter was mostly practical: matters of gear, what to take, what to leave behind, but it was not all matter-of-fact; some of it was deadly serious.

Martin Adams remembered coming into the mess tent and seeing Scott Fischer and Dr. Ingrid Hunt in a conversation that he characterized as "tense and strained." Whatever they'd been talking about, it appeared they didn't want to share it with others. Adams suspected it may have had something to do with the conversation he had had with Dr. Hunt the day before when she had expressed concern about the health of some of the team members and their fitness to make a summit bid. Adams, seeing her concern, advised her to ask for a release of liability from Fischer, absolving her of responsibility.

Dr. Hunt never got her release. In the early morning hours of May 6—with Mountain Madness clients in tow—Beidleman strode away from Base Camp, headed for the Camp II.

As Boukreev sat in the mess tent eating his breakfast, the climbers headed into the Icefall for what they hoped would be their second-to-last trip through its fractured hazards. The last trip through, if they were lucky, would be in a mood of celebration and thanks. They would have made the summit and would be headed home.

I met with Scott after breakfast because he had stayed behind to get everyone off, and I asked him if I needed to be with the clients, because I preferred to save my strength and move at my own speed to Camp II. Scott asked me when I wanted to go out, and I told him that I would like to shower, rest a little more, and then start later in the morning. We agreed to this plan and shortly afterward Scott left camp.

Then, the Mountain Madness compound at Base Camp was virtually deserted. In the quiet, without the distractions of day-to-day operations and routines, Boukreev had some time to consider what he'd seen of the climbers before they departed. To his relief, Beidleman's severe bout of coughing had stopped, and he looked fit and ready, but Boukreev's concerns about Fox and Madsen continued.

I now understood that Scott intended to let Charlotte Fox and Tim Madsen ascend even though they had broken the acclimatization routine, had not yet spent a night at Camp III. At Camp II, I could only assume, Scott would look more closely at them and the other climbers. By Camp II, on the final summit push, climbers are usually experiencing something—a cough, headaches, intestinal problems—and because it is the final push, climbers are not always their most objective. If they are hiding a problem, they can put themselves and the other climbers at great risk.

Boukreev did not know that Madsen and Fox had their own concerns about making the bid without proper acclimatization. A few days before the push they confided in another member of the expedition their concerns about the projected May 10 summit day. "We sat around and talked about the time line. I said, 'You've just got to tell Scott that you don't want to go, that you want to wait and try your attempt after you've acclimated.' Which they did. And Scott said, 'Well, we're not set up to make two attempts. We're only going to make one attempt.' Which was a big surprise for everybody, because we paid all this money and we only get one shot at it!' . . . I thought that's not what the advertising said."*

Shortly after 11:00 A.M. Boukreev went to the mess tent to eat some lunch. He estimated it would take him four hours to reach Camp II, that he would be in well before dark and could sweep anyone who was straggling. After his meal, as he was preparing to leave Base Camp and head into the Icefall, Boukreev met three trekkers, women who introduced themselves as Pittman's friends, the ones with whom she had spent the previous weekend. As Anatoli politely made the small talk he was loath to make as he was gathering his focus, he considered again Pittman's french-fry folly: "Not so very smart."

Impatient, eager to get up the mountain, Boukreev excused himself and headed toward the Icefall. He had tarried too long. Martin Adams, above him at Camp I, had come upon a disturbing scene.

"I came up on Kruse and he was in one of the tents at Camp

---

*Mountain Madness advertising had said they would provide leadership "for all summit attempts," implying there could be more than one attempt made.

I. Well, we weren't supposed to stop at Camp I, so I said, 'What's with you? What's wrong?' He said he wasn't doing well, feeling pretty bad, that he was going to rest up, maybe spend the night and catch up tomorrow. 'That's not the plan,' I'm thinking, and right behind me are Tim and Charlotte, and I say to them, 'Hey, go check on Kruse. I don't think it looks too good.' So they went into the tent and talked to him, and they thought he was a little out of it, too. When I got to Camp II, Scott and Neal were already there drinking some tea. So I told them Kruse was in trouble. They said they'd suspected he'd have a problem, and Scott said, 'Okay, he's out of here.' So I said, 'Hey, look, just wait until Tim and Charlotte get here and get their take on the situation; just hang on.' So Tim and Charlotte came up and they had seen it the way I did. So Scott and Neal went down to tell Kruse he had to go down."

Not knowing where Boukreev was on the route and not having supplied him with a radio so the two could communicate, Fischer headed down, irked. Another trip down! He could have climbed the mountain three times for all the distance he'd covered in the past several weeks.

Just as I came out of the Icefall and was moving onto the plateau of the Western Cwm, I saw Scott and Dale Kruse coming toward me [Beidleman had returned to Camp II], and Dale was not in good shape. Scott seemed tense, a little upset. Seeing that he was stressed and feeling he should be with the team, I offered to take Kruse down, but Scott said he would prefer to do it himself.

In their brief meeting Boukreev considered Fischer's condition. Whatever the reason for his taking antibiotics, the trouble seemed to have passed, and Scott didn't in any way seem to be struggling. As they parted to head in their separate directions, Boukreev looked up the Western Cwm and noticed that the sky had changed dramatically and was ablaze, full of purples and crimsons, a possible sign of unstable weather. He feared a re-peat of Scott's earlier Camp II experience: high winds of a velocity that could destroy their advance base camp. That would mean a retreat to Base Camp and a wait until the Sherpas could rebuild Camp II, another delay.

At around five-thirty in the evening Boukreev reached Camp II, where the other climbers were already having dinner. Below, at Base Camp, Fischer had safely returned with Kruse. According to Pete Schoening, who had decided to take himself out of the bid for the summit, Fischer was "joking around, had a beer, wanted Dale to have a beer."❖ Dr. Hunt didn't see anything that gave her any concerns about Fischer's health. "He was Scott. I had no indication that he was sick."❖

———————■———————

To Boukreev's surprise and relief, the weather on May 7 was calm, without wind, and the temperature, although it had been as low as minus fifteen degrees centigrade during the night, began to rise steadily and warm the climbers' tents. As the climbers luxuriated in the relative warmth, Fischer was, yet again, moving through the Icefall. Whatever his condition had been in Base Camp the day before, he was now, according to one source, in serious decline.

Somewhere near the upper terminus of the Icefall, he encountered Henry Todd of Himalayan Guides on the fixed ropes. Ten years older than Fischer and by his own admission, a much slower climber, Todd was surprised to see they were moving at the same speed as they moved up the mountain. "Normally," Todd said, "he just flashed up these things."

"Bloody hell," Todd said to Fischer. "What are you doing down here? Your people are going up to Camp III. You're not going up to III?" Fischer, Todd said, didn't respond immediately, but began to cough, "seriously cough."

"He said he had had to take Dale [Kruse] down. I said, 'But, Dale was already ill. Why didn't you send him down with somebody else?' And he said to me, 'The man was in tears, and I couldn't send him with anyone else. . . . I didn't want Anatoli or Neal or one of the Sherpas [to do it]. He's my friend.' "

Todd recalled, "He [Fischer] was just burning himself up. I

knew he wasn't well." That observation was troubling enough to Todd, but what concerned him even more was one of Fischer's parting comments. "I'm worried about these people. I'm worried about the situation."

That evening Scott rejoined us, and in the mess tent he expressed relief that Dale had made it down safely. The climb, he said, was over for Dale. That problem was solved, but Scott had some concerns about our oxygen situation and some of the clients, so we spent some time discussing those matters. I asked him if arrangements had been made for me to climb with oxygen if I made that decision, and he said that I seemed to be doing okay, that probably I would not need it. Not wanting to commit until summit day when I could read my condition clearly, I explained that I was not 100 percent certain and wanted the same amount of oxygen that was being supplied for the clients.

About Sandy, Scott was more optimistic than he had been earlier in the expedition. He said he thought she had a chance to summit. I agreed, but I remained concerned about how she had spent the past weekend in Pheriche instead of resting. About Charlotte and Tim we had a joint concern, but Scott thought Charlotte's successful experiences on her two previous expeditions to 8,000ers and Tim's athletic ability would prevail.

Like me, Scott was not sure if he was going to climb without oxygen. He said that he had already summited Everest without it and that he would see how he felt on summit day. About Neal, Scott said he was uncertain, and that he thought Neal should probably climb with it, but it would be Neal's decision to make.

The next morning, after a brief delay due to high winds, the Mountain Madness expedition headed toward Camp III. Because the weather was clear and the route from Camp II to Camp III could continuously be kept in view, Boukreev and Fischer decided to depart later than the clients, while Beidleman stayed with the pack ahead. As Boukreev and Fischer clipped on to the fixed ropes, they continued their conversation of the night before, again reviewing the clients and talking about oxygen. Fischer expressed his appreciation that Boukreev had been able to convince Lene to climb with oxygen. Some-how, where Fischer had come to a dead-end, Boukreev had been successful in making a case. But even on oxygen, they agreed, she was an unknown. She was a well-conditioned ath-lete, but altitude was a leveler; she could go down at any time. And the same was true for Klev Schoening, who had looked aggressive in his efforts, perhaps a little too aggressive. Boukreev had been telling the climbers, "You have to pace yourself. It's not who gets up first; it's who gets up." But to a competitive athlete who likes to lead, to be first, Boukreev thought, that's a hard lesson to get across. He wasn't sure that Klev Schoening had understood him when he would say, "Save yourself."

Martin Adams remembered Boukreev saying the same thing to him on their previous climb on Makalu. "Toli would say 'Martin, save yourself. Save yourself,' because I would try to keep up with him. And I never understood until later what he meant. I thought he was saying don't fall in a crevasse, don't screw up, but what he was trying to tell me was, 'Save your energy.' "

As Scott and I climbed, although we had departed late, we passed almost all of Rob Hall's clients, and Scott observed that his clients were not nearly as well conditioned as ours. Overall, we had a younger team and they were outperforming Rob's climbers in every respect. I shared his opinion, but where he saw something good, I saw a potential problem.

Fischer had previously announced to his team that he and Rob Hall had decided to join forces on summit day, and Bou-kreev had expressed concern. Hall's climbers could slow them up, he had told Fischer. Now, on this stretch of the route, not as difficult or dangerous as it would be above Camp IV on sum-mit day, the evidence—specifically, the Hall team's butts—had been in their faces.

Boukreev's concerns about Hall's climbers were shared by several other members of the Mountain Madness expedition. One said, "It was kind of like, 'Why are we getting in with these

guys? They're weaker than we are; what good's it going to do?'
But I think Fischer was tailing Rob Hall; . . . he went to Nepal
and said, 'I'm going to do it just like Rob Hall does it.' That's
the impression I had."

Climbing ahead of Fischer as he dropped back, Boukreev
continued to pass climbers as he moved toward Camp III. Ascending, he saw some climbers above him coming down the
fixed rope. Stopping as they approached in order to unclip and
let the descenders navigate a passing, Boukreev recognized
among the climbers an old acquaintance, Ed Viesturs from the
IMAX/IWERKS team. Hardly winded, Viesturs was his usual
calm self. Boukreev, leaning into a ski pole that he used for
balance on the snow and ice, talked with Viesturs about conditions above.

"We're coming down," Ed told me. He said they didn't like the
weather, that it was too unstable and they were going to hang back
for a few days and see if the weather would stabilize.

Viesturs recalled the meeting and the events leading to the
IMAX/IWERKS team's decision to descend. "For our filming
purposes we wanted to have a lonely summit ridge, and for
safety's sake we didn't want to be with forty other people on
the summit ridge . . . so we decided we'd go a day before them."

While the Fischer and Hall teams were spending the night of
May 7 at Camp II, the IMAX/IWERKS team was above them at
Camp III, preparing to make a bid for the summit on May 9,
but Viesturs said that when they awoke, they had a change of
mind. "We spent a windy, windy night at Camp III and got up,
and it was still windy up high. . . . And David [Breashears] and
I both knew that it wasn't the window we were waiting for. . . .
So, we said, 'What the hell! We'll go down; we have time; we
have patience; let these guys [below us] do their climb and we'll
come back up when the weather is more stable and better.' "

Encountering Boukreev, Viesturs remembers that he and
some of his fellow expedition members were a little embarrassed. "We shook hands and said hello, have a good time; it

was very cordial. . . . We felt a bit sheepish coming down. Everybody is going up and we thought, 'God, are we making the right decision?' But, we just said, 'Well, this is our decision.' Here this whole group is going up, smiley, happy faces, and we're going down, deciding that it wasn't time yet for us to go to the summit.''

It was fair weather as Viesturs and Boukreev stood and talked. Viesturs wished Boukreev good luck, maneuvered around him on the fixed rope, and headed down. As Boukreev looked after him and the other IMAX/IWERKS climbers, he could see the Hall and Fischer teams in motion, set on the summit, two days away.

CHAPTER 13

INTO THE DEATH ZONE

Like Ed Viesturs, I was not happy with conditions on the mountain. After more than two decades of climbing I had developed certain intuitions, and my feeling was that things were not right. For several days the weather had not been stable, and high winds had been blowing at higher elevations. I wanted very much for my feelings to be heard, but it had become increasingly clear to me that Scott did not look upon my advice in the same way as he did Rob Hall's. I thought about my attempt to convince Scott to take our clients down to the forest zone to rest prior to our summit bid and his unwillingness to consider the proposal. My voice was not as authoritative as I would have liked, so I tried not to be argumentative, choosing instead to downplay my intuitions.

At Camp III, on the ice ledges that Boukreev and the Sherpas had cut into the face of Lhotse, the clients and the guides settled into three tents. Fox, Madsen, and Klev Schoening shared one; Fischer, Beidleman, and Pittman shared another; Boukreev, Gammelgaard, and Adams were in the third. According to Boukreev, all the climbers seemed to be doing well and, in fact, were "joking and jovial."

Pittman, who wanted to file reports from Camps III and IV and then from the summit if she made it, had had one of the seven climbing Sherpas advancing with the team carry up a satellite phone she had been using at Base Camp. After a macaroni and cheese dinner with Fischer and Beidleman, she phoned in her dispatch to NBC. Barely able to talk because of her continuing Khumbu cough, she kept it short, letting anyone who wanted to know that she was melting water and eating red licorice and that the IMAX/IWERKS expedition had turned back, having failed to reach the summit. If she or any of the other climbers in her tent were concerned that Ed Viesturs and David Breashears, two of the world's most highly regarded Everest veterans, had thought it prudent to go down and wait for a better window, she didn't mention it.

The next morning, May 9, we were awakened by the conversations of some Sherpas who were ferrying oxygen canisters from Camp II to Camp IV from where we would make our summit bid. As we were preparing our breakfasts on our high-altitude stoves, some of our Sherpas approached our tents and told us with great concern that one of the members of the Taiwanese expedition had earlier that morning stepped out of his tent to go the bathroom and, because he was not wearing crampons, slipped and fell into a crevasse. They were, they said, going to assist the Sherpas climbing with the Taiwanese in their efforts to extricate the climber, Chen Yu-Nan.

As the Sherpas went to offer their assistance, Fischer and his guides hurried their clients through breakfast, eager to get them back onto the fixed ropes and to Camp IV, where they could rest in preparation for the next day's summit bid. Most of the clients had changed into full-body down suits to protect against the serious cold they would encounter at Camp IV. All of them had placed a full canister of Poisk in their rucksacks and had draped their masks and connecting hoses over their shoulders, preparing to go on oxygen as they departed camp.

As Henry Todd explained, Camp III is the point at which most climbers, if they're going to climb with oxygen, strap on. "From III to IV you have got a little bit of climbing to do; you have to climb over the Yellow Band. This is the first time you're doing something which is fairly strenuous. So . . . you don't want to knack yourself, so you have a cylinder and you use it."

Boukreev was one of the last climbers to leave Camp III. Ahead of him on the route were the Mountain Madness climbers and climbers from two other expeditions that had also overnighted at Camp III: Rob Hall's Adventure Consultants and the American Commercial Pumori/Lhotse Expedition headed by the Americans Daniel Mazur and Jonathan Pratt. With more than fifty climbers ahead of him, Boukreev's progress on the fixed ropes was slowed as he had to maneuver around one after another. At about 7,500 meters Boukreev encountered Fischer, who, like him, was climbing without oxygen.

I said to him that I thought I should move to the head of the pack and to arrive first at the South Col, the site of Camp IV, before our clients to make certain that everything was ready for them. Scott agreed and said that he would drop back and do a "sweep" behind our clients. We then wondered where Neal was. Scott said that he was not ahead, and because I had passed a number of climbers whose faces were covered with oxygen masks, I couldn't be certain where he was in the line of climbers. We thought he seemed to be ascending slowly, perhaps adjusting to the challenge of the altitude.

Climbing steadily, Boukreev passed most of the climbers from Rob Hall's expedition and those from Mazur and Pratt's, and somewhere just above the top of the Yellow Band he passed the last of the Mountain Madness clients, Klev Schoening, who was going strong.

He was ascending with a good speed, almost like mine, and I had to strain a little to keep ahead at the pace he was maintaining. This put

me on notice, because I knew that tomorrow it would be necessary
for me to maintain at least the pace of our fastest client. So, I kept
the oxygen question open, thinking I would decide to use it or not
to use it at the point we made our summit bid.

When Boukreev arrived at the South Col around 2:00 P.M. he
encountered a refrigerated pandemonium. Blowing across the
South Col at more than 60 mph, the wind was tearing across
the exposed, trapezoidal plateau. In freezing temperatures,
amid a scatter of hundreds of depleted oxygen canisters jettisoned by previous expeditions, the Mountain Madness Sherpas
had already set up one tent and were struggling to erect another. Gripping the edges of the tent in gloved hands, the Sherpas were wrestling the flapping, snapping construction to the
ground, trying to anchor it to the mountain. For Boukreev, it
was not a heartening scene.

For me, one of the most difficult things during an ascent of Everest is
a squall that tries to rip you off the mountain. It is one of my greatest
enemies at high altitude. Almost always, if I can choose, I would
prefer foul, calm weather over any day during which the wind is
blowing as fiercely as it was at the South Col that afternoon.

Afraid they could lose the tent in their efforts, Boukreev
pulled off his rucksack and grabbed for a loose, flying corner
and tried to wrestle it to the ground. He'd seen more than one
expedition foiled when a high-altitude shelter was lost and
forced a descent to the safety of a lower camp. He was not going
to see that story written on his watch. While Boukreev muscled
the tent, the Sherpas threaded the struts and threw their own
weight into the effort. As they fought against the wind, Klev
Schoening, who had come up behind Boukreev, offered to
help, and Boukreev asked him to climb into the tent, to pin it
to the ground while Boukreev and the Sherpas finished securing it.

I felt that for Klev it would be better for him to get some rest and to get ready for the assault. I thought his strength on oxygen might deceive him into thinking that his energy was without limits.

The initial plan had been to erect three tents for the clients and guides, but because the wind was not dying, in fact was increasing in velocity, Boukreev thought it would be smarter to settle in only two. By distributing the climbers into fewer tents, he thought, they could trap more body heat for the cold night ahead, and if the worst should happen, if they lost a tent, they would have a reserve shelter to protect the climbers.

Standing slightly hunched with his back to the wind that threatened to pitch him over, Boukreev conferred with one Sherpa and then another, putting his mouth a few inches from their ears and yelling to be heard. In the cacophony they found consensus, and the third tent was left in its stuff bag.

Working steadily to secure the tents and protect them from the ripping forces of the wind, Boukreev saw Gammelgaard and Adams arrive, looking tired but not complaining of any serious problems, and steered them into the tent with Schoening. Beidleman took shelter in the other tent when he arrived. According to Boukreev, it "seemed as if he was feeling the altitude," which made Boukreev think that Beidleman's decision to climb with oxygen was a "right one."

As the wind continued to pick up through the afternoon, Boukreev's concerns increased exponentially. The weather variable in the Everest equation was threatening a summit bid, and some of the Mountain Madness factors hadn't yet shown up to figure into the calculations. By 5:00 P.M., according to Boukreev, Fischer and Pittman had yet to arrive at Camp IV.

Wondering how we were going to proceed, I decided to speak with Rob Hall, whom I had seen supervising the construction of his own camp, and when I approached him near one of his tents, we had to scream to be heard over the constant roar of the wind. "What are we going to do? I'm sure that the weather is clearly not good enough for assaulting the summit." To this Rob Hall said: "My experience is that often it is calm after a squall like this, and if it clears in the night, we will make our bid tomorrow. If the weather doesn't change by midnight, then my group will wait another twenty-four hours. If the weather is still bad on the second day, then we will descend."

For some reason I cannot explain I did not share Rob Hall's optimism, and I thought it highly unlikely the weather would stabilize. My intuitions continued to bother me, and I fully expected that we would not climb the next day.

Finishing his conversation with Hall and concerned that Fischer had yet to arrive in camp, Boukreev walked away from Camp IV and began to backtrack toward Camp III. About forty meters from the tents, through a wind-driven snow that had begun, Boukreev saw Fischer moving in his direction with some other climbers in tow. Among them Boukreev recognized Sandy Hill Pittman.

Scott, yelling to be heard, asked me in what tents everyone should go, and I explained to him that instead of the three tents we had struck only two. When he suggested that we pitch another one, I explained the circumstances and the rationale for my decision, and he agreed with what had been done. Then we had a discussion about the weather, and as I had told Rob, I told Scott, "I don't think conditions are so very good, and I think we should consider descending." Then, I told Scott that I had spoken with Rob about the weather, and I told him of Rob's intentions to wait to see if the storm cleared. After our conversation it was clear to me that Scott agreed with Rob. If the weather cleared, we would climb.

Somewhere around 5:30 P.M. Boukreev joined Gammelgaard, Adams, and Schoening in their tent; Fischer settled into the other tent with Beidleman, Pittman, Fox, and Madsen. The wind persisted, and everyone hunkered down, wondering what the next few hours would bring.

The original plan, agreed upon in Base Camp before the last

push began, was that the Mountain Madness climbers would depart Camp IV at midnight on May 9 and head for the summit. But in Boukreev's tent, according to Martin Adams, the general feeling was that the climb wasn't going to happen on the magic day. "The wind was blowing hard enough that you didn't want to mess around with climbing. And generally, we felt like we'd blown it." Gammelgaard, too, had her concerns. "The night we arrived at the South Col, it was blowing heavily and it kept on blowing. . . . And I had doubts in me, and I know there were some people in our tent talking about it. 'Are we going to climb or are we not going to climb?' Because I don't personally think it's a wise thing to start out climbing after a big storm because it's not a good sign."❖

In another tent at Camp IV, there were similar doubts and conversations. Lou Kasischke, fifty-three, an attorney from Bloomfield Hills, Michigan, and a client-climber in Rob Hall's expedition, was sharing a tent with three other climbers: Andy Harris, Beck Weathers, and Doug Hansen. Everyone except Andy Harris, a Rob Hall guide, thought a summit bid the next day was a bad idea.

Kasischke recalled, "It was a roaring storm out there at high camp, and I remember in our tent we were arguing . . . and it was three to one that we ought to be waiting. We were concerned that we really hadn't had a full day of good weather, a full twenty-four hours of good weather, and we just . . . thought it would be smart to wait a day. . . . I mean, if it were this way twenty-four hours later, we were going to have a problem trying to get down."

Two tents. Two different expeditions. Eight climbers. Six votes: bad idea.

Boukreev knew the call was out of his hands. Fischer would decide, and if the decision was made to go, he would need to be rested. Wanting to warm himself and the other climbers in his tent, he and Martin Adams scrounged for a pan in which to melt some snow over the high-altitude stove they had in their tent. But, as Adams recalled, they couldn't find one. "Just another foul-up, but, hey, I had resigned myself to the fact that things were fouled up, and I just decided to do the best I could and not get too rattled about it."

Fortunately, the Sherpas thought to look in on the climbers in Boukreev's tent and brought all of them some hot tea through the howl and blow of the storm, but Adams can't recall that they had anything to eat. "Lene had good food with her, but we didn't have a pot to cook it in."

After drinking some hot tea, I decided the best way of waiting was to sleep, so zipping into my bag, I fell almost immediately to sleep.

As Boukreev slept, Gammelgaard and Adams tried, but they had a small problem: Klev Schoening was threatening to leave the tent and sleep outside in the storm! Adams remembered, "When we were trying to sleep, Klev, who I think was suffering symptoms of AMS, started yelling at everybody to move over, which was a little strange, because Lene, Toli, and I were already squeezed into one-half of the tent while Klev was in the other half with our packs." Gammelgaard and Adams exchanged smiles and quizzical looks, but didn't respond, because, as Adams said, "Klev is a nice guy. We didn't take it personally. It wasn't his attitude; it was the altitude."

For Schoening it was a jumpy, quirky night. Boukreev, however, slept solidly, only to be awakened just before 10:00 P.M. by something that at first puzzled him, the absence of the howling wind.

There was no fluttering of the tent fabrics; the wind had totally died. All I could hear around me was the sound of the Sherpas firing up high-altitude stoves, bits and pieces of their conversation, and the clattering of equipment. Ahead, I figured, was the summit assault, and I didn't have any wish to do it. For some reason my internal voice was quiet, and I didn't have the usual pre-assault high when every muscle is ready and poised for the first command.

In Fischer's tent, too, Beidleman recalled, the climbers began to stir at 10:00 P.M. "Ten o'clock exactly is when I heard the first Sherpas rumbling around, and approximately fifteen minutes or so after that we had a pot of tea from the Sherpas. We spent the next hour and fifteen minutes organizing ourselves, and at approximately eleven-thirty we piled out of the tents."❖

As the clients and guides came out of their tents and looked into the night sky, they saw an inverted bowl of lacquered black jammed with stars. The rages of the wind had died to a whisper of breeze. Boukreev said, "It was as if the mountain was beckoning with a finger and speaking softly, 'Come on. Come on.' "

Outside, with enough light from the moon to illuminate their movements, Boukreev and Beidleman saw that the clients were properly strapped into their crampons and did a global check of their conditions and equipment. As they worked, according to Boukreev, Fischer began to distribute oxygen to the clients. Adams has recalled that Boukreev gave him two canisters and told him to check their pressures, a precaution against getting a partially filled bottle.

In total, the Mountain Madness climbers had sixty-two canisters at Camp IV, nine Zvesda canisters and fifty-three of the lighter Poisk canisters. Fifty-one percent (by volume) of the oxygen purchased from Henry Todd was on hand for the summit bid. Most of the rest had been consumed (the largest amounts by Pete Schoening and by Ngawang Topche Sherpa); a small amount remained at Base Camp for emergency medical purposes.

Given how they intended to use it, the quantity of oxygen available to the Mountain Madness expedition at Camp IV was minimal. The nine Zvesda canisters, because they were heavier, had been reserved for sleeping on the night before the summit bid. The fifty-three Poisk canisters had been set aside for the May 10 climb.

Six Sherpas were climbing with the expedition; five of them were planning to climb with oxygen; the climbing sirdar, Lopsang Jangbu Sherpa, was climbing without. Lopsang Jangbu Sherpa did carry one canister for emergency purposes; the remaining five each carried two canisters for their own use on the climb and an additional two canisters for use by the clients and guides. So, total, the Sherpas took twenty-one bottles from Camp IV to carry up the mountain.

The six climbing clients, Fischer, and Beidleman carried two bottles each, and Boukreev carried one. Guides and clients, total, carried seventeen bottles.

Combined, all climbers carried thirty-eight Poisk canisters, which left fifteen full Poisk canisters and whatever little was left over from the Zvesdas from the night before at Camp IV. It was a slim margin of safety, certainly not enough to allow the climbers to overnight if they ran into complications on their summit bid and wanted to make a second bid on May 11. It was May 10 or not at all, which was not a surprise to Fox and Madsen, who had already been told, one shot, no more.

———■———

The oxygen consumption/use calculations Fischer based his oxygen plan upon were, in part, based upon advice from his supplier Henry Todd. Todd estimated that each of his Poisk canisters, if consumed at his suggested flow rate of two to two and one-half liters per minute, would last for six hours. "Two should last you for twelve hours, and that twelve hours should take you to the summit [from Camp IV] and back down to pick up a third bottle at the South Summit." On paper, the plan looked bulletproof.

The Mountain Madness climbers leaving at midnight, if the weather held and there were no complications, could reasonably expect to be on the summit in ten to eleven hours. If they stayed at Todd's recommended flow rate, they would be sitting on top of Everest with one or two hours of oxygen left in their canisters. From the summit, again assuming favorable weather and no surprises, it would take individual climbers anywhere from three-quarters of an hour to an hour to descend to the South Summit. At the South Summit, as had been planned, each descending climber would pick up a third canister that the Sherpas were to cache there. With an additional six hours of O's, assuming all went well, every climber could make it back to Camp IV on the bottle.

————————————■————————————

As the climbers loaded their two tanks of oxygen into their rucksacks, Fischer asked, "Is anybody ready? Because Lopsang is, and if anybody is ready, they should go with him." Pittman stepped forward. Lopsang Jangbu Sherpa approached Pittman and, with what one climber referred to as a girth hitch, fastened a short length of rope around Pittman and hooked the rope to his climbing harness with a carabiner. Somewhere around midnight, Lopsang Jangbu Sherpa took off for the summit, Pittman on a towline behind him. Shortly after her, at Beidleman's urging, Charlotte Fox strode away from Camp IV, ten minutes into her thirty-ninth birthday.

At the South Col the temperature was severely cold, and there was a fresh dust of snow. As for me, after I'd slept, I felt a new wave of strength, but I still had not decided whether I would climb with oxygen or without, so I put a canister and a mask into my rucksack just in case. Somewhere near the back of our pack I departed camp with Martin Adams.

The last of the clients and guides to leave Camp IV was Fischer, who, as had been agreed, would be the sweep. Climbing just ahead of him, the next-to-last climber to depart was Lene Gammelgaard. When she noticed that Fischer was not trailing her closely, Gammelgaard doubled back to check on him. "I was very happy to see that he was using oxygen. Because I'd tried to do whatever I could to say, 'Use oxygen or stay at camp and guide the expedition from there,' which is what he should have done. But, at least, okay, he was using oxygen, and I was very happy about it. Then I went off and stuck to the group. . . . It was very, very clear to me when I

started out from the South Col that there was no way I
wanted to be alone on summit day. I'd been climbing very
much on my own up and down the Icefall and things like
that. But, then it became obvious to me the power that psychologically comes to you by being in a group."

CHAPTER 14

TO THE SOUTH SUMMIT

As the Mountain Madness climbers moved away from Camp IV, they could see an undulating chain of lights, the headlamps of Rob Hall's climbers, who had left camp thirty minutes ahead of them. Hall was taking fifteen climbers onto the mountain: himself, two other guides, eight clients, and four Sherpas, including Ang Dorje, his climbing sirdar, with whom Boukreev had worked in putting down fixed ropes.

Trailing Rob Hall's expedition did not make Gammelgaard happy. "It was a really good team, but they were old and they were slow. They were the strongest you can be when you're forty-five or fifty, but it does mean you're very, very slow." Another Mountain Madness climber said, "In my mind, starting behind Rob Hall, then comingling with his group on the fixed ropes, probably cost our teams a couple of hours on the ascent."

Within two to three hours after leaving the South Col, the Mountain Madness climbers began to overtake Rob Hall's climbers, and by 4:00 A.M. they were thoroughly comingled—Fischer's team with Hall's, Hall's with Fischer's, and both of them with three members of the Taiwanese National Expedition: Makalu Gau, the expedition leader, and two Sherpas. The Taiwanese, to the surprise of both Hall and Fischer, had decided to tag in behind the two teams in their bid for the summit, most likely for the purpose of slipstreaming, climbing in the wake of stronger climbers, who would break trail and fix ropes.

For a couple of hours Boukreev climbed with Adams and then began to drop back after they had passed several other climbers, some from Rob Hall's expedition and others from their own. Adams recalled that as they left Camp IV, he had told Boukreev that he felt lethargic, without much energy, but as they climbed, Adams found his stride. His acclimatization efforts and his use of oxygen were fueling what he considered "a great day."

Alternating the lead of the snake dance in the hours of breaking dawn were three climbers from Rob Hall's expedition, Ang Dorje Sherpa, Mike Groom, one of Hall's guides, and Jon Krakauer, the journalist-climber-client who had signed on with Hall in February after *Outside* decided not to buy his slot from Mountain Madness. At several places along the climbing route, according to Krakauer, the three climbers had come to a dead stop, not because of any difficulties or problems, but because Hall had instructed his climbers "for the first half of the summit day" not to put any more than one hundred meters between themselves "until" they reached the Balcony, a cleft at the base of the Southeast Ridge at about 8,500 meters. Krakauer, accustomed to independence of action as a climber, has said that he was frustrated at having his decisions tied to the lowest common denominators of the climb, but he felt his position as a client had "forced" him to give up his personal commitment to self-reliance and independent decision-making, to become a tin soldier.

■

The differences between Hall's and Fischer's philosophies of guiding were emblematic of an ongoing debate between practitioners in the adventure travel industry. The camps of belief can be roughly divided between the "situationalists" and the "legalists." The situationalists argue that in leading a risky adventure no system of rules can adequately cover every situation that might arise, and they argue that rules on some occasions should be subordinated to unique demands that present themselves. The legalist, believing that rules can substantially reduce the possibility of bad decisions being made, ask that personal freedom take a backseat.

Critics of the legalist philosophy argue that an omniscient, rule-based position that minimizes independent action is being promulgated largely out of fear of bad publicity or lawsuits that might result from a lack of demonstrable "responsibility." These critics find it confoundingly odd that an industry that promotes the values of personal freedom and initiative would expound a philosophy that minimizes the pursuit of these very values.

———■———

According to Krakauer, at 5:30 A.M. he and Ang Dorje, after a stop-and-go progress that had cost them more than an hour, reached the Balcony at 8,500 meters, but stopped there and sat down on their backpacks, not advancing any higher.

At about 8,400 meters I began to encounter deep snow, but my progress was not as slow as it might have been because members of Rob Hall's expedition had broken trail ahead of me. I arrived at the Balcony somewhere around 6:00 A.M. just as the sky was breaking into light with fantastic, beautiful colors. Looking at the sky and to the summit of Lhotse at exactly our altitude, I judged we had no immediate weather problems to worry about.

At the Balcony the climbers from the three ascending expeditions began to bunch. At this natural resting place about the size of a franchise-motel room, climbers used the panting pause to switch from their first oxygen canister to their second, to drink some liquids to rehydrate, and, if they had the energy and coordination, to take some photographs. Adams said that at that altitude he and the other climbers were moving from a place "where you could hardly think to where you couldn't think at all." They were parked in "the Death Zone," that stretch of vertical real estate between Camp IV and the summit of Everest where prolonged exposures to the cold and oxygen deprivation conspire to cut you down. Lingering above Camp IV has all the pleasurable possibilities of picnicking in a minefield.

—■—

The Mountain Madness clients understood that the ropes that needed to be fixed between Camp IV and the summit were to have been fixed by the time they reached the Balcony. Pittman recalled, "I . . . heard that the lines were all to be fixed by our Sherpa and Rob Hall's Sherpa in advance, and that they were going to leave at ten o'clock; we were going to leave at midnight."❖ Klev Schoening agreed, "That was my understanding of what was supposed to transpire."❖ And, Gammelgaard concurred, "I heard specifically that Scott said that the lines would be fixed in advance so that the members should at no point wait."❖

Most of the members of both the Fischer and Hall expeditions agree about what was supposed to have happened. They were told that Ang Dorje, Hall's climbing sirdar, and Lopsang Jangbu Sherpa, Fischer's climbing sirdar, were supposed to leave Camp IV well ahead of the clients and fix ropes so that as the clients and guides advanced, they would not have to wait. But that's not what happened. Neither Lopsang Jangbu Sherpa nor Ang Dorje Sherpa nor any other Sherpas had departed early to fix ropes.

When he was debriefed after the climb, Lopsang Jangbu Sherpa said that a member of a Montenegrin expedition that had made a failed bid on the summit on May 9 had told him, "Already fix rope, you no need anything."❖ Subsequently, when Jon Krakauer wrote about the climb for publication, he cast suspicion on the explanation, saying that guides from Fischer's and Hall's expeditions who should have been told there had been a change in plans were not *and* that Lopsang Jangbu Sherpa and Ang Dorje Sherpa both left Camp IV with their expedition members carrying three hundred feet of rope in their packs, an action "for which there would have been no reason" if fixed ropes were in place.

Krakauer's "evidence" has been troubling to some, who have found it circumstantial. Fischer did not arrive at Camp IV until five-thirty on the evening of May 9, and by several accounts was, at best, extremely tired. In the gale that was blowing, with the security of the camp and climbers on his mind and struggling with his own well-being, it seems entirely within reason that he had gotten a report from Lopsang and felt he had one less thing to worry about. To not consider that scenario—and a similar one for Rob Hall—is to suggest the possibility that both Fischer *and* Hall made a purposeful decision to hold their Sherpas back or not to inform their guides, when they started the climb, of their Sherpas' failure to perform. Either action would have seriously compromised their guides and clients; it could have contributed to their deaths. Whatever their philosophical differences and personal styles, that was not the kind of men they were.

As for the rope that Lopsang Jangbu Sherpa and Ang Dorje Sherpa carried onto the mountain, many experienced high-altitude climbers have wondered, why not? A climbing sirdar would take rope onto the mountain for the same reason you keep an extra pair of shoelaces in your dresser drawer. Things happen. A rising storm can bury ropes. You can find ropes improperly fixed. An alternative route might have to be established. An accident might necessitate additional ropes. Your information might not be 100 percent reliable.

At 8,600 meters a series of rock steps better suited for mythical, claw-footed creatures than mortals in cumbersome down climbing suits needed to be negotiated, and fixed ropes were required from that point to the South Summit at 8,748 meters.

Beidleman, after more than an hour of waiting, spoke with Boukreev and said he intended to go ahead of the numbing climbers and see to the fixing of ropes ahead.

I agreed with Neal and said I thought it was a reasonable decision,
and I offered him the canister of oxygen I was carrying. I was feeling
well acclimatized and strong, and I knew I would be okay to go
ahead. My original intention had been to leave the oxygen and retrieve it on my descent, but when I considered we were running a
little late and Neal was going to be doing hard work, I offered it to
him and he accepted it.

With Klev Schoening tailing behind, Beidleman followed
Lopsang and Ang Dorje over a bulge and broke through some
fresh snow to a ledge, where he found Lopsang bent over, vomiting. Realizing that Lopsang was in no position to take on the
labor of fixing ropes, Beidleman took some rope from Lopsang's pack and with Ang Dorje's assistance began to thread the
rope toward the South Summit. In some places they found old
ropes in place that could be trusted; in others they had to
thread with new ropes, which was arduous work. As Beidleman
and Ang Dorje advanced, Boukreev began to motivate clients,
to get them onto their feet.

I started to hurry them up, because we had already been on the
Balcony more than an hour and we were falling behind schedule.
On the fixed ropes I stopped to let a few clients pass me, and I fell
back in the hope that I might see Scott, but I couldn't see him. I had
wanted to talk with him about our clients, because since leaving
Camp IV we had had no discussions and I was unsure about many
details. About the general plan, yes, I understood, but things were
changing. Should I now be going up or falling back? Should I be
moving aggressively toward the summit or rendering help?

Finally, after not seeing him after waiting, I decided to continue
my ascent, thinking that because he had slept on oxygen the night
before and was climbing on oxygen, he would soon catch up to me

and we could have our talk. Moving up I could see that the clients were in good condition, but not going too cheerfully.

At 9:58 A.M. Beidleman made it to the South Summit, and thirty minutes later, by his recollection, he was followed by Martin Adams. Beidleman remembered thinking they were getting late and said, "I was very antsy."❖ For an hour and a half to two hours, Adams recalled, he and Beidleman sat at the South Summit alone. "Basically, the problem was that everybody behind us was jammed up on the fixed ropes. Somehow, I think, some of Rob Hall's slower clients had gotten in front of our group and they couldn't pass."

One of Hall's clients, Frank Fischbeck, fifty-three, a Hong Kong publisher, had turned back within hours after leaving Camp IV, the first of the ascending clients on May 10 to return. As of 10:30 A.M., Hall's seven other clients were staggered between the Balcony and just below the South Summit, jumbled among all of Fischer's clients—except Martin Adams—and the Taiwanese climbers. If each climber had been using oxygen at the flow rate suggested by Henry Todd, they were on their second canister and had one to two hours of oxygen left. Their third and last canister (six more hours of oxygen at the recommended flow rate) had yet to arrive on the South Summit. The Sherpas carrying the extra oxygen, like the clients, were also strung between the South Summit and the Balcony. It was, said one of Fischer's clients, "a jungle fuck."

Three of Hall's clients, John Taske, fifty-six, Lou Kasischke, and Stuart Hutchison, thirty-four, were near the back of the logjam, moving up the ropes Beidleman and Ang Dorje had fixed to the South Summit and climbing behind the Taiwanese, who were moving slowly and impeding their progress. Climbing separately, each was in his own hypoxic consideration of the scene developing in front of them. Each of them had begun to consider turning back.

Lou Kasischke remembered, "I moved past John, and then Stu, who had been right ahead of me, was coming back, and

Stu and I had a conversation. The only thing I can remember about my conversation with Stu was that he was convinced of two things. One was that Rob was going to be turning everybody around because it was too late. He said he didn't see any way that, given the logjam . . . that we were going to be able to make it back by . . . one o'clock. We had a one o'clock turnaround time. And Stu was convinced of that. And what I remember about my conversation with Stu was, well, I'm not ready yet. . . . I remember saying that and moving on, but I didn't get very far.

"It was about eleven-thirty and I was near the back of the logjam. I've been at this for a long time, and I'm pretty good at managing fatigue and hardship. I've just learned how to do it—I'm a long-distance runner. I really think of myself as an endurance athlete. And I had been pretty much tuning everything out of my existence and just kind of bumping along. Now that isn't necessarily a compliment, because that's a dangerous thing to do. . . . I'm just moving along, one step at a time. And as I was then backed up in the logjam—I remember this was just below the South Summit—I dropped down to my knees and just clipped into the rope, just resting. I was very, very dehydrated, and I took off one of my gloves to scoop up some snow, which isn't necessarily the smart thing, but it was the only thing that I had to work with. My water was a block of ice in my backpack. I realized that all of my fingers were frostbitten. And I took off the other glove—same thing. But actually that was really no surprise to me, I already knew that. But I guess I just didn't care because summiting Everest was so important to me, that I was just going to go no matter what. But as I was waiting, I started—kind of a wake-up call in a sense, and I started to now think about what was really happening to me. And as I was kneeling there, I now started to look inside of myself and really to see my state of fatigue. Also, you know, these breathtaking views that we were able to see at the Balcony, as we made the turn—the most spectacular sights I've ever seen—really, now you couldn't see them anymore. You looked back, down the mountain, and there was very poor visibility.

Now I'm not saying there was horrendous weather—it was not horrendous weather. But it was changing weather. And when I asked Lhakpa, who was one of our Sherpas—I asked him how much longer—I knew I was pretty close—he told me two hours. I asked him where he thought we were, and he said eighty-seven hundred meters. I wasn't even capable—my brain wasn't capable of—I usually think in terms of feet—and I wasn't even capable at that point of translating that into feet, which was kind of how my brain was functioning. But when he told me two hours, I think my heart just sunk to my feet. I think at that moment it was sort of like lightning striking me. I knew that I had a problem. And it was never a question as to whether I could go another two hours, that was never the question. And I could get to the top. But I started to have serious questions about my ability to get down. And I thought I was either going to die coming down or—I'd get down somehow. I mean, I've been in tough spots before and I've always kind of toughed it out, but . . . And there were two voices talking to me. I mean, I still remember this, probably some moments that I will never forget. People have always warned me about the inability to reason at that high altitude, but I'll never forget these moments because I had these two voices struggling away, that one voice just telling me to go for it, 'Do it, you can do it, what's the big deal, another two hours.' But that other voice was saying, 'Lou, you're going to die coming down, or even if you can tough it out, you're going to lose these fingers.' To this day, I'm just amazed that I actually turned around. I told Lhakpa, I said, 'Lhakpa, you go and tell Rob I've decided to go back.' But that took place over about four or five minutes.

"I suspect Stu's comments were also influential, on a lower level. But I remember when I made my decision, it was based on simply me and my inability at that point to get there and back alive. Or at least in one piece.

"I would have to sum it up just by saying that I didn't think that I could get there and back alive or, best case, I'd lose some fingers and toes. And the other thing, too, is, I'm a little different from, I think, a number of the other people in that I wasn't really subject to a lot of the same pressures. I mean, I wanted to go to the summit of Everest. I mean, God, I wouldn't have been there beating my brains out if I didn't. But . . . I live in Detroit. I'd come back to Detroit and say, 'I just climbed Mount Everest.' People round here would look at me and say, 'Yeah, and did you hear about the Detroit Redwings?' . . . I mean, nobody here cares, or for that matter even knows where Mount Everest is. 'Oh, yeah, that's that highest in the world, isn't it?' In fact, a number of people said, 'I thought you already climbed that.' So to me, in my perspective of things, it wasn't life-and-death to me, it wasn't the most important thing in the world, and I wasn't going to have newspapers writing stories about me. And media, fame and fortune, world records, and all that kind of stuff, which were kind of the stakes for . . . some of the others in our expedition. It meant a lot to me, I don't want to suggest that it didn't. But it just didn't—my ambition to get there just wasn't suffocating every other thought that I had in my mind.''

At about 11:40, Lou Kasischke made his move and headed down, and Stuart Hutchison and John Taske also turned back. For them, Everest was over. Somewhere around noon, Kasischke has remembered, he ran into Scott Fischer.

''We had a conversation, and I said to Scott, 'Scott, I think it's smart for me to go back.' And one of the ironic things of my experience is that I really didn't think too much of this at the time, but Scott looked right at me and said, 'Good decision, Lou.'

''He was the same old Scott—I mean, twinkle in his eye, snow in his hair—that look of his, that all-American look, that blond hair with the snow in it. . . . We just kind of hung out for maybe thirty seconds, and then he moved one way and I moved another.''

CHAPTER 15

THE LAST HUNDRED

At the South Summit, one hundred meters below the peak of Everest, Martin Adams encountered a not very happy Beidleman. "I don't know why, but he wasn't saying much, seemed to be in a bad mood. I sat down, removed my pack, and got out some water because I was thirsty, and I offered some to Neal, who took it because his was frozen solid."

For a while, maybe twenty minutes, Adams recollected, they just sat there, saying little, and then Beidleman got up and descended to a natural alcove just below the South Summit where he was a little better protected from the wind. Adams followed, and as they resettled, according to Adams, Beidleman asked him, "How much oxygen do you have?" Adams took off his pack, because his pressure gauge, like all the climbers', was affixed to the top of his canister. " 'I read five pounds on my gauge,' and then I asked him, 'How much have you got?' and he said, 'Me, too, five pounds, but I got a full bottle from Toli, too.' "

Adams's impatience with the progress of the climb began to chafe against his natural inclination to take action. He was not the type to sit around. Even in his mildly hypoxic state he understood clearly that he was sucking the last of his oxygen from his second canister.

"So, I knew it would have been pushing my luck, but I said to Neal, 'Let's go! Give me the full bottle of oxygen and let's go.' But, he said, 'No, I'm not giving you this bottle.' So, I said, 'Okay, I've got five pounds, give me your five and let's get out of here.' And he agreed to that, but then we never went anywhere."

Adams developed a healthy preoccupation. He kept looking over his shoulder, looking for any one of the Mountain Madness Sherpas who were carrying the extra canisters of oxygen, and he remembers thinking about little else except his consideration of the question "When are things going to start going right?" It would be a while.

Just before I reached the South Summit, I let Tim Madsen come around me on the fixed ropes, and I was encouraged to see him moving briskly under the power of oxygen. When I reached the South Summit, I saw there Martin, Neal, Ang Dorje, Tim, and a few others, but nobody was moving. It seemed they had no desire to move ahead. It was bright and sunny, and in our down suits, even though the wind was beginning to pick up, everyone was becoming warm. Our strength, because we had been climbing for so long, had begun to diminish, and no one seemed to be in a hurry.

More than a hour after he had reached the South Summit, Adams recognized the first of the Mountain Madness Sherpas to arrive and went to him to get his third and last bottle. Discarding his almost empty canister and the one Beidleman had given him, Adams screwed his hose onto the full one and began to breath a little more easily. He had at least six more hours of O's, more than enough, he thought, to summit and get back to Camp IV. Adams, a normally sagacious individual, made an assumption, fashioned it literally out of thin air. He was wrong.

As I was resting, I was looking around, and I noticed that Ang Dorje looked tired. The other Sherpas, too, didn't seem ready to go ahead, although I had understood from before the summit push that the Sherpas would be fixing the ropes on the Hillary Step.

Also, there on the South Summit, I began to wonder again where Scott was. Here, I thought, maybe it would be necessary to turn some clients around, but there was no Scott to do it. I felt I did not have the right to make this decision. The clients had paid big money and had given Scott that authority, not me.

Adams, who probably knew Boukreev better than any other client, has said that probably Boukreev couldn't have turned climbers around, but speculates that Beidleman "might" have been able to do so. "I mean, it would have been a tough call, but I think if he'd exercised the leadership, they would have turned around. . . . But, hey, it's conceivable that some of them might not have."

And, probably, some wouldn't have. Gammelgaard has said that on summit day her state-of-mind would likely have over-ruled an attempt to turn her back. "You know, it's a risky game when you're out there. When you push for the summit, you know you risk dying. It's a fucking dangerous bit of climbing . . . but you're a risk taker; you're an adventurer; you're fucked-up somewhat or otherwise you wouldn't be doing it." But, Gammelgaard added, if there had been rules laid down in advance, she would have followed them. "Okay, we're an expedition. If we'd agreed to rules, no matter what I would have played by those rules. No matter what." However, Gammelgaard has said, "I never heard anything whatsoever about a turnaround time on summit day. The only time I heard that we had a turnaround point was the first day going through the Icefall, and everybody played by that rule."

◼

In a feature story about Fischer that appeared in the *Seattle Weekly* six weeks before summit day, the journalist Bruce Barcott commented upon Fischer's philosophy about turnaround times. "Every climber has a set of personal guidelines he or she follows, little Stay Alive Rules. One of Fischer's is the Two O'Clock Rule. If you aren't on top by two, it's time to turn around. Darkness is not your friend."

Fischer never set a definite turnaround time for his climbers on summit day. He never said, "If you're not at X by whatever o'clock, you should turn around." Instead, he had worked out with Beidleman and Boukreev a simple strategy, an adaptation of the tactic he'd been using throughout the expedition. His climbing sirdar, Lopsang Jangbu Sherpa, and his guides, Boukreev and Beidleman, would alternatingly lead; he would bring up the rear, and as he overtook stragglers, he would turn them around. If problems arose, he would establish radio contact with Lopsang Jangbu Sherpa, who, it was assumed, would always be at or near the front of the pack. Neither Beidleman nor Boukreev was issued a radio.

Hall had hedged around setting a specific turnaround time. Some of his climbers understood it was one o'clock; some understood it was two; others thought it could be either one or two and that the call would be made on the mountain.

After waiting almost an hour on the South Summit I began to understand that nobody was going to take any action, so I spoke with Neal, and we decided that we would work together to fix the ropes to the summit. Back on the ridge, I took out a few lengths of old rope from the snow, but then, to speed up the ascent, decided to move on to the Hillary Step and leave that section of the route to guides and Sherpas behind me.

The Hillary Step is an upward thrust of the Southeast Ridge, a rocky tower about ten meters high, prominent enough that with a telephoto lens some of the Mountain Madness climbers had been able to survey it from Thyangboche. At its base, after twelve hours of climbing, it presents climbers with a formidable physical and psychological challenge. Exhausted, sucking in three or four breaths for every step you take, its in-your-face presence is intimidating and disheartening. It is a common turnaround point for climbers.

I was familiar with this obstacle because in 1991 I had climbed Everest by this same route and had gone up the Hillary Step solo without fixed ropes, but good mountaineering skills are necessary on this pitch, and to secure our clients it was necessary to do this job. Neal stood below and played out the rope that he had gotten from one of the Sherpas, and, while Neal belayed me, I tied on to existing anchors that had been placed by earlier expeditions.

Shortly after I reached the top of the Hillary Step and tied on, Neal came up, and he was followed by one of Rob Hall's guides, Andy Harris, and one of Hall's stronger clients, Jon Krakauer.

Below the Hillary step, because he wanted to push the route forward, Boukreev had left a stretch of the route for those coming behind to fix for the clients, but Harris had advanced with Krakauer and not fixed any additional rope, leaving what Martin Adams would later call "the most exposed part of the climb where the climbers had to perform a pretty precarious solo traverse where a slip could be fatal."

At the top of the Hillary Step, Krakauer produced a coil of rope that he'd gotten from Ang Dorje at the South Summit, and it was discussed how to proceed. Above the Hillary Step the angle of the Southeast Ridge takes climbers over a gently undulating run of snow, and, because the wind had continued to rise as the climbers had moved up the mountain, the decision was made to fix one more rope. Seeing plenty of hands to do the job, Boukreev decided, as he had earlier, to lead and advance the route breaking trail.

As Boukreev led off, Krakauer, who had become increasingly worried about his oxygen supply, explained his "concern" to Beidleman and asked if it would be a problem if he "hurried ahead" to the summit and left the fixing of the rope to him. Beidleman agreed. "I said fine. I uncoiled the rope. . . . Martin [Adams] was below me. I asked Martin if he would help me pay out the rope and tie the end to [an] anchor, which he did. I started up. I made it maybe twenty or thirty feet, until the rope caught in the rocks. . . . Martin finally helped me untangle the rope from the rock. I continued up to a snow stake, tied off the rope. There, the remaining forty or fifty meters, I walked up further to fix. I didn't find another anchor."❖

Beidleman couldn't find an anchor to tie into. Not wanting to leave the unanchored length of rope on the surface of the snow because a climber might clip on thinking it was anchored above him, Beidleman tossed the rope toward Tibet. Less than half of the intended route to be fixed had been covered.

At 1:07 P.M., Boukreev reached the summit of Mount Everest, more with a sense of relief than of celebration. The goal had been to summit as early as possible so as to get the clients back to Camp IV under oxygen, and while 1:07 was considerably later than he would liked to have arrived, he understood that if the clients followed quickly, they would be able to make it. The margin was close, but they could do it. And, even if some of them ran out of oxygen just above Camp IV, that wouldn't necessarily foretell a disaster, because on the descent you can make some distance without oxygen. But it's a crapshoot as to how far you can go.

At 1:12 P.M., having followed Boukreev's trail, Krakauer reached the summit, and Harris followed shortly thereafter. Beidleman, climbing behind Harris, "was moving a little slow," according to Adams. "He asked me to turn up his oxygen bottle, so I turned it up, and we headed for the summit. When we were almost to the summit, he asked me to turn it up again, so I turned it up all the way."

At about 1:25, Beidleman and Adams made the summit after passing Krakauer and Harris on their descent. Concerned about his oxygen supply, Krakauer had decided to descend quickly. Unlike Beidleman, he was still on his second bottle, and his supply and his luck were being stretched.

At about 1:45, Klev Schoening came up over the last rise leading to the summit of Everest, and Boukreev took his photograph. His hands raised over his head in celebration, he approached the aluminum tripod that marks the true summit and was soon in tears.

After Schoening's summit the traffic to the top stopped. By 2:00 P.M., no more heads had bobbed over the last ridge on the summit approach, and Boukreev was becoming concerned.

Every one of our team that I saw on the summit looked good, in no danger, and I had little concern about them, but I began to wonder, "Where are the other clients?" More than fifteen minutes had passed since Klev had summited, and no one was coming.

But, they were coming, and down the mountain in Camp II where various expeditions were staging for their own assault bids in the days to come, there was a rising concern. Ed Viesturs of the IMAX/IWERKS expedition and some others had been monitoring the climbers' progress through a telescope, scanning the climbing route from the South Summit to the Hillary Step, and they could see climbers still going up at 2:00 P.M. "We just saw them standing there and moving very slow. . . . And we could see streamer clouds going over the top, and I'm going, 'God, it's way too late. . . . They're really pushing it.' Not only was it late in the day, but I mean you . . . only have eighteen hours of oxygen. You have to assume that you get to the summit in twelve hours; that gives you six hours to get back down. So, kind of in my mind, I was thinking they're going to run out of oxygen—not only daylight, but they're going to run out of oxygen."

Also at Camp II observing the climbers above the South Summit was Henry Todd of Himalayan Guides, some of his staff, Mal Duff, and several others, probably more than twenty people, Todd has recalled. As they were watching, and like Ed Viesturs discussing the lateness of the hour, the Sherpas became excited and, according to Todd, "freaked out about the star." Todd didn't at first see what they were talking about, and then they pointed it out to him, a star in the middle of the day above the South Summit. "We're not talking about me being a little nutty. I saw it."*

"This is not good. This is not good," the Sherpas kept repeating, and Todd agreed. Retrieving a radio, Todd called down to Rob Hall's Base Camp and asked, "What is your turnaround time?" They responded, "The turnaround time was two o'clock." Two o'clock had come and passed.

Todd, with his experience of running expeditions, knew something of the psychology that must have been prevailing. "You're absolutely knackered. . . . You stop being logical. . . . You think you can hack it."

———■———

Adams, like Krakauer, understood he was on borrowed air and didn't hang out on the summit. "I sat on the summit, as I recollect, ten or fifteen minutes. I took some pictures with Toli's camera, and Neal took a picture of the two of us with the national flag of Kazakhstan spread out between us. And then I said, 'Hey, guys, I'm outta here.' And I just got up and started down." Shortly after Adams, Boukreev, then Schoening, followed.

I was on the summit about an hour. I had no radio, nor did Neal, so neither of us knew what was going on below. I suspected there might be trouble at the Hillary Step, and I felt I should go down. At about 2:00 P.M., maybe slightly later, I moved away from the summit, and I stooped to collect some rocks as a souvenir. As I did, something caught my eye, a five-rupee Indian coin, and I put it into my pocket, thinking, "For good luck."

---

*Astronomers consulted about the appearance of this "star" say no heavenly body was in that quadrant of the sky on that day at that time. The comet Hyakutake had long ago disappeared from view.

CHAPTER 16

DECISION AND DESCENT

As Adams descended toward the top of the Hillary Step, a chain of climbers passed him, some of Hall's clients, all the remaining Mountain Madness clients—Charlotte Fox, Lene Gammelgaard, Sandy Hill Pittman, Tim Madsen—and four of the Mountain Madness Sherpas, including Lopsang Jangbu Sherpa. Adams recalled they said little as they passed. The climbers were on automatic, minutes away from their goal.

A few minutes after I started my descent, I saw a group of climbers in close rank moving toward the summit, and somewhat separated from them were two climbers, and one of them I thought I recognized as Scott. Because I was eager to understand our situation and discuss our plan, I approached him and began to speak, then realized that I had made a mistake and that I was speaking with Rob Hall, who was going to the summit with one of his clients. I asked about how he was, if he needed any help because I was thinking to go down, and he said that everybody was doing okay, that no one needed any help, and he thanked me for my work on the fixed ropes.

After I left Rob, I saw that our climbers were coming in a dense grouping, but my relief at seeing them was shadowed by my understanding that most of them had been climbing now for fourteen hours on an eighteen-hour supply of oxygen. If they had been using it properly, they would have four more hours. Still they were about thirty minutes away from the summit, and I understood that there might not be enough "oxygen time" for them to descend to Camp IV.

————■————

About ten to fifteen feet from the top of the Hillary Step, Adams came upon Harris and Krakauer "yukking it up, just kind of laughing, celebrating, appearing not to be too concerned about anything," but Adams didn't stop to join in. "I didn't feel like getting into that kind of thing, so I moved to where the fixed ropes began at the Hillary Step." Adams was thinking about getting down, only about getting down. He'd had one delay after another throughout the day, slogging his way through slower climbers. Now he was in a position to lead the descent, and that was all right with him.

Clipping on to the fixed rope and preparing to rappel down the face of the Hillary Step, Adams peered over the edge, checking to see that the route was clear. "I look down," he said, "and I see three people coming up, and I'm thinking, 'Man, another delay!' and then I focus in on who's coming up: a Sherpa in the lead, then Makalu Gau, and then Scott Fischer, and, I'll tell you, I was amazed. I hadn't thought about Scott all day or where he was, and now he's here, and I can't believe it. I'm thinking this is a problem. He shouldn't be here."

As Adams was looking down, Fischer was looking up and advancing his jumar on the fixed rope. When he saw Adams, he yelled out to him, "Hey, Martin, you think you can climb Everest?" Adams said that he got the impression that Fischer thought he'd yet to get to the summit, that "he was encouraging me, trying to get my spirits up, like, 'Hey, bro, let's go do this together.'" Adams responded, "I already did!"

Seeing that the Sherpa and Makalu Gau above Fischer were moving slowly, Adams encouraged Fischer to try to move around them, to move onto a rocky rib that paralleled the fixed rope and free climb. "It would have been a bit technical, but I thought he could do it and pick up some time."

Fischer moved toward the rib, feeling out the alternative that Adams was trying to coax him to take, but, according to Adams, Fischer fell back into line. "Maybe he thought it was too exposed. I don't know. For whatever the reason, he stayed where he was. He probably made the right decision."

While Adams was trying to encourage Fischer to speed up his ascent, Boukreev descended past Harris and Krakauer and sat down on a rock immediately above Adams, and as he waited, he surveyed the sky, looking for some indication of where the weather was going. He noticed that some clouds had gathered, and a cold wind had picked up, but nothing indicated anything threatening.

———■———

On the summit, as Boukreev and Adams waited for Fischer at the Hillary Step, Beidleman was "very nervous and very anxious," he said. "I actually wanted to leave the summit much earlier with maybe Martin or Klev, but every time I got ready to stand up and go, it seemed like another person or another wave of people would come over the ridge, some including our members. I was very surprised that people kept coming. I thought they would have either turned around on their own or by somebody else. I didn't feel it was right for me to leave at that time until everybody had reached the summit. They were so close."❖

Between two-fifteen and two-thirty, the four Mountain Madness clients Adams and Boukreev had passed on their descent—Madsen, Fox, Gammelgaard, and Pittman—and Lopsang Jangbu Sherpa had made the summit. For Pittman the last several yards were among the most challenging of the day. Steering toward the aluminum tripod that marks the summit, the last of her oxygen drained from the third bottle she had collected at the South Summit. Presumably, she had been consuming at a higher than recommended flow rate. Fortunately, Lopsang Jangbu Sherpa saw her distress, retrieved the extra bottle he had carried in his pack from Camp IV, and tapped her into a new bottle.

Fischer had not swept any clients back to Camp IV during the day because he'd never made contact with any of them after Gammelgaard had parted from him early in the climb. By two-thirty, all the clients who had started the climb had made the top of the world. There were no more climbers to sweep, no place for the clients to go but down. But nobody moved off the summit until three-ten. There were forty minutes of celebration, picture-taking, tears, congratulations, and backslapping—and forty minutes less oxygen, forty minutes less daylight.

———————■———————

When, finally, Fischer cleared the top of the Hillary Step, Adams recalled, he wanted nothing more than to clip on and head down. But since Harris and Krakauer had arrived at the Hillary Step before he had, he asked them if they wanted to go down first. "With gratitude," Adams said, "they clipped on and went over the edge."

As Adams followed Harris's and Krakauer's progress down the Hillary Step, eager for them to clear the bottom so he could clip on, Boukreev, a little after two-thirty, had a conversation with Fischer.

I spoke with Scott while he was resting after climbing the Hillary Step. When I asked how he was feeling, he said he was tired, that the ascent had been difficult for him.

When I met Scott, my intuition was telling me that the most logical thing for me to do was to descend to Camp IV as quickly as possible, to stand by in case our descending climbers needed to be resupplied with oxygen, and also, to prepare hot tea and warm drinks.*

———————

*Boukreev assumed that all seven Sherpas who had been with the expedition at Camp IV had made an attempt on the summit. Fischer, at Camp IV, had given all the Sherpas the go-ahead to do just that. But, unbeknownst to Fischer and Boukreev, Lopsang Jangbu Sherpa had circumvented Fischer and told one of the Sherpas in his charge, Pemba Sherpa, that he wanted him to stay behind to receive incoming climbers as they returned to Camp IV.

Again, I felt confident of my strength and knew that if I descended rapidly, I could do this if necessary. From Camp IV I would have a clear view of the climbing route to the South Col and could observe developing problems.

This intuition I expressed to Scott, and he listened to my ideas. He saw our situation in the same way and we agreed that I should go down. Again, I surveyed the weather, and I saw no immediate cause for concern.

On the summit, too, as the Mountain Madness climbers lingered, there was little concern about the weather. Klev Schoening recalled, "When I was at the summit, there was a strong wind. I didn't feel it intensify, but I didn't see any evidence personally of snow or deteriorating weather."❖ Sandy Hill Pittman, likewise, was not concerned about the weather, but she was concerned about the hour. "I didn't sense any deteriorating weather. I felt the sense that we were late on the summit, not because I was told that we had a deadline on the summit, but because I was aware . . . from previous climbers' stories about when you should be off and on. And if I felt any anxiety up there, it was because we were late, but not because I saw any weather."❖

Lene Gammelgaard, however, saw something that had disturbed her. "Before I decided to go up over the Hillary Step, I noticed a whiteout coming from the valleys, and I saw the wind pick up over the summit."❖ Gammelgaard had witnessed the formative stages of a storm system that within a few hours would catch her and her climbing partners, vulnerable and exposed, at the most dangerous part of an Everest assault, the descent.

———■———

At the base of the Hillary Step, Adams resumed his descent along the cornice of the Southeast Ridge and, just before arriving at the South Summit, noticed someone slumped in the snow. "I'm on the traverse . . . and here's Krakauer laid out, hanging on to his ice ax, something of a self-belay. He's got the handle of his ax driven into the snow and he's holding on to the head, and I'm wondering what I'm going to do here, because neither one of us is clipped on to a fixed rope."*

Krakauer, like Pittman above him, had gone to the bottom of his canister. He was out of oxygen.

Immediately behind Adams was Boukreev. As Boukreev approached, he hustled Adams on, telling him, "Go, go, go." Boukreev didn't want Adams to delay. Klev Schoening, approaching a few moments later, recalled, "When I came across from the [Hillary] Step to the South Summit, Jon Krakauer was in distress there, and that kind of slowed me up. There was nothing I really could do to help him. I don't think I had the wherewithal to do that, but I wanted to stay there until I saw some action was being taken, because they [the Hall team] did have two guides on either side of him."❖

Fortunately for Krakauer, as with Pittman, someone from his expedition stepped in to address the problem. Mike Groom, who had summited at about the same time as the four Mountain Madness clients who had come up after Adams, Beidleman, and Klev Schoening, selflessly surrendered his canister to Krakauer. Because Krakauer observed that Groom "wasn't overly concerned about going without," he accepted the offer and in a matter of minutes made it to the South Summit where Hall's climbing Sherpas, as had Fischer's, had stashed a supply of oxygen. There, Krakauer "grabbed a new oxygen canister, screwed it onto my regulator, and headed down the mountain."†

——————■——————

While Krakauer was stuffing his third bottle of oxygen into his pack, Beidleman and the clients in his charge had begun their descent, and Beidleman recalled that already one of the clients was beginning to show signs of distress. "We got to the Hillary Step, and I was right behind Sandy. She seemed to

———————

*Krakauer had foundered just below the Hillary Step on that section of the route that had gone unfixed.
†See *Into Thin Air*, p. 188.

be the one most out of it at the time. Behind me were Charlotte, Tim, and then Lene. When we got to the Hillary Step, it's a real jungle of old ropes and pieces of tattered cord. Sandy was having [a] very difficult time even deciphering which cord was the one to hook into and how to negotiate the footsteps. I walked down to her. We tried to rappel her down, but the cords were too tangled by the wind, so we had to undo that and she hand 'rap'd' down with some assistance. She got down to the rest of the ridge, and I looked behind and it seemed as if the other people were making pretty good progress, so I wasn't too worried about them."❖

As Beidleman, Fox, Madsen, Pittman, and Gammelgaard approached the South Summit, they found Klev Schoening "sitting there."❖ Schoening, who had been testing discarded oxygen canisters to see if there was any extra to be had, remembered that Beidleman looked at him and said, "What the heck are you doing here? Get out of here."❖

"It was at that time," Schoening said, "that Neal . . . recognized the urgency of the hour and maybe the storm, and it was at that time that the fire was lit under me. And I think I left just about the time [Neal] got there."❖

———■———

Ten canisters of oxygen had been taken by the Sherpas onto the South Summit for Fischer's team. One each had been allocated for six clients, and one each for Beidleman and Fischer to be picked up on their descent. The remaining two, presumably, had been carried onto the mountain as the backup Boukreev had requested and that Fischer had agreed would be placed there for him.

Because they had been running late on the ascent, everyone except Beidleman had elected to pick up their third bottle on the ascent. Beidleman's third bottle he'd gotten from Boukreev at the Balcony earlier in the day, when Boukreev had given him the bottle he'd carried from Camp IV.

So, when Beidleman and the clients arrived at the South Summit, their cache of oxygen should have included three full canisters* and whatever partial canisters had been discarded when the climbers had changed bottles on the way up. But Beidleman recalled not finding what he expected. "There didn't seem to be too many left. There was one that was full, or practically full," and a few others, he added, that were partially full. "The full bottle, I believe at that time, went to Lene."❖

Beidleman took one of the partially full canisters that had been found, but it is unclear if any others were taken. At least two Mountain Madness clients, Charlotte Fox and Martin Adams, have said that they did not take any additional oxygen.

Adams recalled, "I got to the South Summit before the clients who had summited behind me, and I came down off the ridge to the small alcove where Neal and I had waited earlier that morning. Andy Harris was there going through this mound of oxygen canisters, maybe about twenty, looking to see what was available, I guess. I just went on. There wasn't any oxygen there with Martin Adams's name on it. I just kept on moving."

Just after leaving the South Summit, according to Adams, Boukreev passed him at a fast pace headed down the mountain. "I'm going down the ridge, doing fine, and Anatoli comes by, sizes me up, sees I'm doing okay and keeps on going. For me, it was business as usual, Anatoli's going by, and I had no problems with that."

About fifteen minutes after I left the South Summit, maybe somewhere around three-forty, I was on the fixed ropes, and the visibility began to deteriorate somewhat. The wind was blowing a light snow across the route, but I could still make my way with no serious concern, and I could clearly see Camp IV below.

When I got to the Balcony, I was surprised to find a climber who asked me about Rob Hall, wondering where he was. And I asked if he was okay. And he said, "Okay, but where is Rob Hall?" This man

---

*The two "safety" canisters for Boukreev that he'd not needed and had left behind and the "third" canister for Beidleman that he'd not collected, because he'd gotten his third from Boukreev at the Balcony.

was very cold, like frozen; he was hardly able to talk to me. And I told him I saw Rob Hall on the summit, that maybe in one or two hours he would come. I was worried about him and also for my clients, so I looked up the Southeast Ridge, and maybe at about 8,650 meters in the rocks I saw between the clouds someone coming down, and I thought, "Okay, everything is okay. I thought it might be Andy Harris, a guide from Rob Hall's expedition who can come and help his client."*

Boukreev continued his descent, constantly monitoring the weather. It was, he said, "Normal for Everest; not at that moment possible to say it was a serious problem, because I had a clear view of the climbing route."

---

*Boukreev had encountered Beck Weathers, a pathologist from Dallas, Texas, whom Hall had instructed not to advance any higher, because he had been having problems with his vision. When Boukreev encountered him, Weathers had been waiting for more than eight hours to be assisted down the mountain by an Adventure Consultants' expedition member.

CHAPTER 17

SNOWBLIND

According to Dr. Hunt, who was in Base Camp and had being getting sporadic radio reports from the mountain since 6:00 A.M., she had spoken with Fischer when he was on the summit (sometime around 3:45 P.M.) and he had reported that all the clients had made the top. Congratulating him and asking him how he was, she heard him report, "I'm so tired." Realizing how late it was to be on the summit and hearing Fischer's description of his condition, Hunt pushed the transmit button on her radio and said, "Get down the mountain."❖

Concerned about Fischer's condition, Hunt also spoke with Lopsang, and the two of them agreed to speak again at 6:00 P.M., but less than an hour after her radio contact, things changed dramatically. "Four-thirty that evening," according to Dr. Hunt, "the people from Rob Hall's camp came down here [Mountain Madness Base Camp] and said, 'We need to get some oxygen sent back up the mountain. We think one of your team members has collapsed at the Hillary Step and Rob Hall is with him.' . . . Rob Hall was sending messages to them [his

Base Camp] that 'I'm with this guy, and he's collapsed above the Hillary Step.' "❖

Immediately an effort was made to respond to the reported emergency, said Dr. Hunt. "We do everything we can to try to get oxygen sent up. One of the things is, we actually talked to Pemba and asked Pemba to keep trying to get ahold of Lopsang or anyone up the mountain and asked Pemba himself if he could go, and he said the weather was too bad, he didn't want to go."❖*

With no radio, Beidleman, who could conceivably have responded to the radio call and the reported emergency above him, continued his descent. "Somewhere just over the top [of the South Summit] and down the fixed ropes, I saw Charlotte standing over the top of Sandy with a big grin on her face. She was holding a needle in her hand, waving it to me. . . . I came over to her on the downhill side, and Charlotte told me that she had just given Sandy a dexamethasone shot and that Sandy looked pretty out of it at the time."❖

Dexamethasone is a steroid that decreases brain swelling and contributes to the reversal of effects of HACE. Each Mountain Madness client, in a medical kit provided by Dr. Hunt, had carried a syringe with an injectable dose onto the mountain, and Fox had been waving the empty syringe at Beidleman.

When Beidleman arrived on the scene, he said, he was "trying to figure out how to get her [Pittman] going,"❖ and he checked her oxygen gauge and discovered she had less than an hour's supply left. Seeing Gammelgaard come up behind him and recalling that she had picked up a new bottle on the South Summit, Beidleman asked Gammelgaard to swap cylinders with Pittman.

Gammelgaard gave up her canister, but not without some reservations. "I know at this point that this is dead serious. This is not funny, this is really serious. The worst thing is happening;

---

*Pemba Sherpa had been on previous Everest expeditions. In 1994 he had worked as a "kitchen boy" at Base Camp. He'd never been higher than Camp IV.

I know that . . . I'm the strongest, so I gave her my oxygen, which is basically very stupid, because you have two people who are out of it. But, if I have more than you have, and we are a team and you are in trouble . . . that's just the way it is."

At that point Gammelgaard said that the group was doing a good job, "the best they can helping each other and acting responsible. . . . Neal is doing the right things, the best things you can do. He is doing what I do, what Klev would do, what Tim would do." They were working as a team, not being led, according to Gammelgaard, but cooperating in their individual efforts to survive.

Beidleman had turned the regulator on Pittman's new cylinder, the fifth she'd gotten that day, up to a flow rate of three or three and a half because, according to Beidleman, "I wanted her to liven up pretty good." ❖ The gush of oxygen and the effects of the "dex," which can induce a mild euphoria, seemed to stimulate Pittman, who recalled, "Within fifteen minutes I felt pretty frisky again. I was renewed." ❖

On the move again, Beidleman got in front of Pittman on the fixed rope, and with Gammelgaard, Fox, and Madsen continued to descend.

Below, Adams had clipped off the fixed rope onto which Beidleman and the others had just clipped on. He was somewhere between the South Summit and the Balcony, and he was in trouble. "I'm going into these whiteout conditions and I couldn't see any footprints to follow, and my glacier glasses are starting to fog, so I took off my oxygen mask, because by doing that I could get my glasses to clear a bit. But, after a short while I went back to it, went down a bit more, and then realized I'd run out of oxygen."

Adams had exhausted his third bottle and did not have another to replace it. He'd honored the "three's the limit" rule; the only oxygen that was available to him was at Camp IV, more than six hundred vertical meters below.

"I just jettisoned my cylinder and kept heading down, trying to find the next set of fixed ropes, and I got a little disoriented, didn't know exactly which way to go, left or right around a crevasse that in my hypoxic state I couldn't remember from the ascent, so I just sat down, figuring I could make some sense out of it all if the visibility improved. I don't know how long it was, five minutes or thirty minutes or an hour, I couldn't tell you; I just sat there."

Adams had descended to just below the Balcony, and descending just above him was Jon Krakauer, moving slightly ahead of Mike Groom, one of Rob Hall's guides, and Yasuko Namba. Namba, an Adventure Consultants client, had summitted right behind the last of the Mountain Madness clients.

"So, I see these climbers coming down, and I think, 'Great! I'll just go down with them,' and Krakauer walks past me and I get up and ask Groom which way I've got to go, and he points me in the right direction, and I walk with him for a few minutes, and I ask him again which way do I need to go down, and he points me toward a couloir.* And Krakauer, right in front of me, hardly hesitates and he starts glissading† down on his rear in the fresh snow. And, I'm thinking that's a good idea, so I give him maybe fifteen yards, and I'm in there right behind him."‡

Adams was trying to shave minutes off his descent time, and he picked up quite a few. His "run," according to Adams, was as much as a hundred yards, maybe more.

Exactly at what time of day Adams hit the run-out of his glissade can only be a guess. Adams said that he was not wearing a watch on summit day. Below them, Adams remembered, the storm was abating and you could clearly see the way to Camp IV.

———■———

Boukreev estimates that he arrived at Camp IV somewhere around 5:00 P.M. As he approached the cluster of Mountain

---

*A couloir is an angled gully.
†A controlled slide that is done in a crouch, standing, or sitting.
‡ Jon Krakauer has not the same memory. He says that he "did no glissading whatsoever during the descent" and that, perhaps, Adams had mistaken Yasuko Namba for him. Adams insists it was Krakauer. Such are memories at high altitude.

Madness tents, he saw several Sherpas, including Lhakpa Galgen Sherpa, a climbing Sherpa from Henry Todd's Himalayan Guides, who was establishing a camp for Todd. Lhakpa and Boukreev exchanged a greeting, then Boukreev was met by Pemba Sherpa, who was carrying some hot tea. Boukreev thought that Pemba had made the attempt that day but had turned around and come back. Boukreev was not aware that Pemba had been in Camp IV all day.*

Anticipating that some other climbers would be descending immediately behind him, Boukreev asked Pemba to brew up some more tea, then headed toward the tent where he, Adams, Gammelgaard, and Schoening had settled in the night before, almost exactly twenty-four hours earlier. Curiously, Pemba mentioned nothing about the radio communication that Ingrid Hunt said had occurred around 4:30 P.M., when he'd been asked if he would take oxygen up the mountain, and as the evening wore on, nothing was ever said to Boukreev about the possibility of an emergency situation above the Hillary Step.

———————■———————

Radio communications between Dr. Hunt at Base Camp and Fischer and Lopsang on the mountain were problematic, and as the emergency went from serious to critical, Dr. Hunt was growing increasingly panicked. According to Dr. Hunt, "I would give a message to Ngima [Base Camp sirdar], and he would then in Nepali relate it to Gyalzen Sherpa [at Camp II] to Pemba [at Camp IV], and likewise when Pemba wanted to relay something—when anything was relayed down from the mountain, it would be through . . . Gyalzen, through Ngima, and then for me."❖

It had been Dr. Hunt's impression throughout summit day that she wasn't getting accurate or complete information from

---

*Two of the six climbing Sherpas from the Mountain Madness team did not summit. They turned around at the South Summit and had already returned to Camp IV.

Ngima Sherpa, that messages were being "augmented" to put the best spin on them. Compounding her problem was that communications seemed to be sporadic with Pemba. "I don't know why. . . ."❖

Frustrated with the quality and quantity of information she was getting from the Sherpas, Dr. Hunt shuttled back and forth between the Mountain Madness encampment and Rob Hall's because, according to Hunt, "Rob Hall's camp had better communications, so I was getting more information up there, but I was constantly talking on my radio to Ngima, saying, 'Any news? Any news?' "

Around five-fifteen, I think, maybe a short while later, I went to my tent, took off my crampons, pack, and overboots and zipped into my tent. My tent was positioned so I could see to the South Summit at 8,748 meters, but nothing was visible to me above 8,300 meters where the bottom of the storm cloud had settled, but I was still not worried, because this pattern was not unusual for that time of day, and often the clouds are blown off the mountain.

Boukreev had been in the tent maybe thirty to forty-five minutes, warming himself, observing the weather, and considering his options when Pemba came with a pot of hot tea.

I had been hoping that I wouldn't have to go back up, because, of course, it would be difficult, hard work after the climb, but I understood that the situation might not improve and no climbers were coming in, so I asked Pemba to prepare for me a thermos of hot tea and to bring me three bottles of oxygen.

In a few minutes Pemba brought me the hot tea and three bottles of oxygen and put them outside my tent, and I pulled them and my pack inside, where I packed everything and prepared to go out.

———■———

At 5:45 P.M., according to Dr. Hunt, she "learned that Lopsang and Scott were just below the South Summit; they were out of oxygen and Scott was very weak."❖ With that news the picture changed dramatically. She'd first been told by Rob Hall's team that a member of the Mountain Madness expedition was in trouble above the Hillary Step. In fact, the person in distress was Doug Hansen, one of Rob Hall's clients, the last climber to approach the summit that day.

Hansen had been a member of Hall's 1995 expedition to Everest and had been severely disappointed when Hall had turned his clients around on the South Summit. His return to the mountain in 1996 had been encouraged by Hall, who said he wanted Hansen to have another shot.

Before daylight on summit day, Hansen had been climbing in front of Lou Kasischke, who remembered coming up behind Hansen as he "stepped out of line." Hansen told Kasischke that "he was cold and he was going back." But something had obviously spurred him on, because a little after 4:00 P.M., as Fischer was departing the summit, Hansen was staggering toward the arms of Rob Hall, who shouldered him to the goal he'd encouraged him to reach for. Kasischke has since wondered why, after having seemed so definite about his decision, Hansen had continued for another ten hours. "I mean, Doug changed his mind. Now, why did he change his mind? I don't know. I've . . . speculated in some way that maybe Rob talked him into continuing."

The emerging picture, only pieces of which were visible to any one of the participants, was a nightmare. At 5:00 P.M. Rob Hall was with a client who had run out of oxygen above the Hillary Step. Lopsang had lingered behind Fischer to see that Hansen was safely under the control of Hall. He caught up with Fischer just above the Balcony, and Fischer, according to Lopsang, was in serious trouble, telling him, "I am very sick. . . . Lopsang, I am dead."❖

Unaware of the problems of Fischer and Hansen above, Boukreev understood that the Mountain Madness clients, none of whom had yet to appear, would soon be out of oxygen.

Sometime, about 6:00 P.M., I understood I needed to go up, so I began my preparations, and by six-thirty I was out of my tent getting into

Mountain Madness Everest Expedition members and Sherpas, 1996.
Expedition members, bottom row (left to right), Scott Fischer, Charlotte
Fox, Lene Gammelgaard (directly behind Fox); top row (left to right), Neal
Beidleman, Dale Kruse, Klev Schoening, Sandy Hill Pittman, Martin Adams,
Anatoli Boukreev, Tim Madsen (farther right wearing Mt. Everest knit cap),
and then Lopsang Jangbu Sherpa (wearing black baseball cap).
(Photo courtesy Anatoli Boukreev)

Mountain Madness Camp, Everest Base Camp.
(Photo © Anatoli Boukreev)

Camp IV on the South Col.
(Photo © Anatoli Boukreev)

Mount Everest as seen from Lhotse.
(Photo © Anatoli Boukreev)

Anatoli Boukreev approaches the base of the Hillary Step to fix rope, May 10, 1996.
(Photo © Neal Beidleman)

Anatoli Boukreev (left) and Martin Adams, with the national flag of Kazakhstan between them, on the summit of Mount Everest, May 10, 1996.
(Photo courtesy Anatoli Boukreev)

Klev Schoening approaches the summit of Mount Everest, May 10, 1996.
(Photo © Anatoli Boukreev)

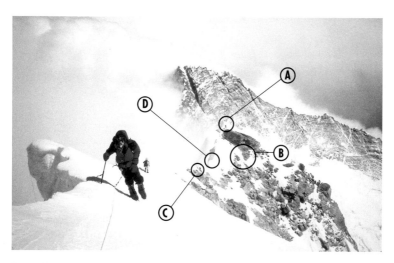

Doug Hansen (in red) of Adventure Consultants is approaching the summit of Everest. (A) South Summit; (B) rock alcove below South Summit, site of Mountain Madness and Adventure Consultants oxygen cache; (C) top of Hillary Step; (D) Krakauer foundered here on his descent and was assisted by Mike Groom. *(Photo © Neal Beidleman)*

Site of Camp IV at South Col, looking down from climbing route. (A) Tents, Camp IV; (B) site of Martin Adams/Jon Krakauer encounter; (C) Kangshung Face; (D) Pittman, Namba, Fox, and Madsen found here by Boukreev; (E) Beck Weathers collapsed here in the early morning hours of May 11, 1996.

(Photo © Anatoli Boukreev)

South Col, edge of Kangshung Face: Yasuko Namba in red climbing suit.
(Photo © Anatoli Boukreev)

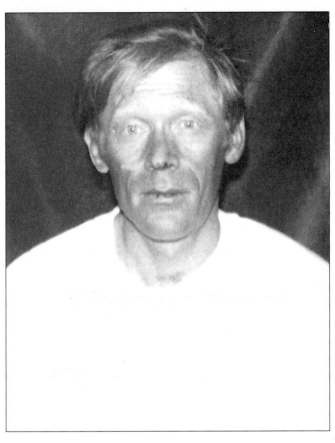

Anatoli Boukreev, USA visa photograph, taken shortly after his May 11, 1996, rescue efforts.

(Photo courtesy Anatoli Boukreev)

my crampons. The weather was deteriorating above me, but at the South Col, it still was okay, stronger and increasing wind, but okay.

Boukreev shouldered his pack containing three oxygen canisters, a mask, and regulator, and with an ice ax in one hand and a ski pole in the other, he headed back the same way he had come into Camp IV, to where the fixed ropes began at 8,200 meters. No more than ten to fifteen minutes away from his tent, the clouds that had been hovering above him dropped onto the South Col. Almost simultaneously, a lateral blow of snow propelled by winds of at least forty to fifty miles per hour began to pelt Boukreev, and the sky began to change from crayon gray to bedsheet white.

I realized then that my reserves might not be strong enough to handle the situation, so I began a flow of oxygen for myself. Looking behind me to see if I could keep a bearing on Camp IV, I could see that some people in Camp IV were flashing lights to try to guide the climbers who were still out, so I felt okay to continue my search. I moved onto some steep ice, understanding intuitively this was the way to the fixed ropes, but the poor visibility kept them hidden. I was using my ice ax on the ice, being careful, understanding that if I was too far off my course, I could slip and maybe fall down the face of Lhotse, and that would be the finish.

As Boukreev continued his desperate search for the fixed ropes that he thought would guide him to the clients above, his visibility problems were compounded when his glacier glasses, as had Martin Adams's during his descent, began to fog. When Boukreev would expel a breath, some of it would escape where his oxygen mask didn't cleanly seal with his face, and his relatively warmer expelled breath condensed on his glasses and immediately froze. He was literally climbing blind. Finally, to restore what little visibility there was, Boukreev removed his oxygen mask and continued his search. Sometimes just an upward step would cause him to lose sight of the lights being flashed at Camp IV. A step down would restore his visual contact. His life was tethered to a beam of light. To go any higher, to search any longer, he knew, was foolish. Dead, he wouldn't be able to help anyone; back at Camp IV, he thought, the climbers had perhaps come in, had somehow in an opening in the whiteout gotten by him and were back safe. If not, he could restore himself and make another attempt.

About thirty meters from the tents when I returned, my power was almost gone. I took off my pack, sat on it, and put my head into my hands, trying to think, trying to rest. I was trying to understand the situation of the climbers. "What is their situation, their condition?" I am considering this. The wind is driving snow into my back, but I am almost powerless to move. How long I was there, I don't remember. It is here that I start to lose track of time, because I am so tired, so exhausted.

When I was sitting there, someone I do not know approached me out of the darkness and snow, and he spoke with me as if he was a friend, but I did not recognize him. I thought maybe he was from the Taiwanese expedition or from Rob Hall's expedition, but I was not certain, and he asked me, "Do you need help?" And I said, "No. It is okay." And so he told me that he had to return to blinking the lights, and I told him I could make it to my tent. And after some time, I don't know how much, I found my tent, took off my pack and crampons, knocked the snow and ice off my boots, and without any power, went into the tent, but it was empty. Nobody had come. Nobody.

Boukreev was alone in his tent. A stone's throw away another climber, Lou Kasischke from the Rob Hall expedition, was also alone. His tentmates, Andy Harris, Beck Weathers, and Doug Hansen, had yet to return.

"I got back to camp about four-thirty or five," Kasischke said, "and I just collapsed in my sleeping bag from exhaustion. . . . I don't think I had a molecule of energy left in me. Later [I] awoke or regained consciousness . . . and it was a terrifying experience for me. Actually, it was the wind that woke me up. It was just pushing me around inside of my tent. It was actually getting under the floor of the tent, picking me right up in my sleeping bag and slamming me back down and pushing me around, and I regained consciousness and I couldn't see! . . . It was probably the worst moment of my life, because I was very confused. I couldn't figure out really even where I was, what time it was, what day it was, why I was alone and why I couldn't see, and it took me probably a couple of minutes to figure that out. Whoa, wait a minute, you're at high camp, you're snow-blind, and now the storm is in full force And I don't know what time it was. I tried to backtrack it a bit—and I'll tell you what happened next, but I'm figuring it's eight, nine o'clock. See my tentmates—nobody's there . . . This went on for hours. I was able to control my anxiety enough to know that I had to stick with my sleeping bag, that if I tried to go anyplace or do anything, that I was probably going to die . . . I couldn't figure out why I was alone. I was yelling for help, but I soon figured out nobody could hear anything. I mean, it was just like a hundred freight trains running on top of you, and I was screaming, but you know, a person five feet away couldn't hear anything."

CHAPTER 18

WALK OR CRAWL

After the run-out of his glissade, Adams picked up the last run of fixed ropes below the Balcony at about 8,350 meters and reached their terminus at 8,200 meters sometime after Boukreev had ended his first foray into the storm. During that course of rope he hadn't seen Krakauer or any other climbers. He was alone.

"I started out across the South Col and I'm moving along pretty well, and then I step into a narrow crevasse. I pulled myself out of that, and then the lights went out, because it had turned dark. And then, I went just a short distance more and fell into another crevasse, and that one was worse. My right leg and arm both went in, and they were dangling down, and I thought this may be it, and I was afraid to move. So, I surveyed my situation and I could see a solid patch of blue ice off to my right and above eye level, and I swung my ice ax that I had in my right hand and I got a purchase with my pick. Somehow I was able to leverage myself out, and I just picked myself up and continued on down."

As Adams pulled himself out of the second crevasse into

which he had fallen, his face was encrusted with snow and ice; his lips had turned a flat, morgue blue.

"Right after I start down again," Adams recalled, "I saw the light of a headlamp, and I walked up on somebody just sitting there about one hundred yards away from Camp IV. I'm wondering, 'Who is this guy?' and I'm thinking maybe he knows where the tents are, so I ask him: 'Where are the tents?' "

Adams had run into Jon Krakauer, but neither of them in their debilitated conditions recognized the other in the darkness. Adams remembers that in response to his question, "the guy"—Krakauer—pointed off to his right, and Adams responded, "Yeah, that's what I thought." Then he asked, "What are you doing here?"

Adams thought he had run into somebody from an expedition waiting to ascend and who had wandered out from Camp IV. So, he was particularly confused when "the guy" said, according to Adams, "Watch out. It's steeper here than it looks. Be careful. Go back to the tents and get a rope and some screws."*

"I'm thinking at that point," Adams said, "I've almost died coming down this mountain; this guy has been in camp all day doing nothing, gotten himself up a tree, and has the brass to tell me to go down, get some rope, and come back up to solve his problem! You gotta be kidding!" Adams had been descending without oxygen, operating only on instinct and experience. He was scrambling for survival.

Adams surveyed the slope of ice that he'd been warned about, but didn't see it as anything particularly dangerous. "It was a face-out situation," he said. "You needed to pay attention, but it wasn't a big deal, no more than a steep grade you'd see on a mountain pass in Colorado. You could see the bottom where it flattened out. There was no hazardous exposure."

Adams took two or three steps to move down the slope,

---

*Krakauer, thinking Adams was Andy Harris, a Rob Hall guide, was, according to Adams, "ordering me to render assistance."

tripped, pitched face and belly down onto the ice, and slid down onto the snow and shale surface of the South Col. "It was maybe a hundred feet," Adams remembered, "and I got up, turned around, and waved at 'the guy' and headed in what I thought was the direction of the tents, which by then had disappeared from view."

Above the Krakauer and Adams encounter, Madsen, Pittman, Beidleman, and Fox made it to 8,350 meters and the top of the last run of fixed ropes. Klev Schoening and Lene Gammelgaard, separated from the group at that point, were descending slightly ahead. Down the rope, Beidleman saw something blocking the route: "There was a body sitting facedown on the line, not really moving or moving very slowly."❖

Thinking at first that he'd come across Klev or Lene, with whom he didn't always have visual contact, he went in front of the slumped figure, looked more closely, and thought it was Lene who was down. He began to yell at her, to try to get her up and going, but she wasn't moving, so he jiggled her oxygen mask around, trying to get a response. Then, he realized it was not Lene Gammelgaard, but Yasuko Namba from Rob Hall's expedition.

"She was not moving whatsoever," Beidleman said, "most likely out of oxygen. I tried to talk to her to show her how to go down the line faster. After a few minutes of doing this, I realized she either didn't understand English or was incapable of doing what I was asking her to do. Again, I grabbed her harness and started sliding, standing, or rolling, depending on the terrain, down with her behind me. Several times her feet and crampons went through my [down] suit and into my back. She seemed to be capable of understanding what was going on, but was incapable of really physically helping the process much. . . .

"We eventually got down to the bottom of the fixed line after falling several times into crevasses that the lines went over. We had a hard time getting the Japanese woman to make the com-

mitment to go over the crevasses. She was a little scared. I believe Tim helped me several times in picking her up, throwing
her, pushing her, pulling her . . . over those crevasses."❖

Somewhere Namba had separated from Mike Groom, with
whom she'd been climbing earlier. Like Boukreev, Adams, and
Krakauer before him, Groom had encountered Beck Weathers
on the Balcony, where he was still waiting for help, almost literally frozen to the spot where Hall had told him to stay until
he could be assisted down.

Groom, when he observed Weathers's condition, tethered
him to his climbing harness and started him moving. As slow
as they were moving under the circumstances, Namba had apparently not been able to keep up and had been left behind.

———————■———————

Beidleman, at 8,200 meters and within approximately eight
hundred lateral meters of Camp IV, recalled that things went
to hell. "At the bottom of the line the storm had intensified.
The wind was blowing quite strong. Periodically you could see
a light back at Camp IV. I got one last fix on the direction and
then that was it. That was the last I saw of Camp IV."❖

Charlotte Fox also recalled that lights and the tents of Camp
IV were still visible when the climbers reached the bottom of
the fixed ropes. She and the other climbers who had summited
between two-fifteen and two-thirty had spent between forty and
fifty-five minutes on the summit before starting their descent.
At this juncture they could have used those minutes.

"It was dark," Beidleman has said. "It was blowing very hard.
It was snowing extremely hard. It was difficult to talk. All communication was by screaming, and usually only downwind. If
somebody were upwind, they may or may not have heard. I
don't recall even being able to turn my head much to try to
talk upwards. My headlight was still in my pack. I was unable to
get it out because I had grabbed the Japanese woman [Yasuko
Namba] by the arm and . . . we walked . . . arm in arm together.
There were two Sherpas with us at the time, and I believe that

Klev and Lene had left us, heading toward Camp IV in the direction they thought was correct."❖

Gammelgaard said that she had teamed up with Klev Schoening because she had confidence in him and the two of them had "the same way of being on the mountain. . . . And we just rush down as fast as possible. And I had been running out of oxygen, and Klev sort of stops me once in a while and forces me to take his oxygen, which I sort of refused, 'No! I don't need it,' but he could see how blue I was in the face for lack of oxygen."

At the terminus of the fixed ropes, according to Gammelgaard, she and Klev had been bearing to their right, "sort of agreeing upon, 'Okay, the camp must be over there.'. . . But then we see a huge mass of lights to the left and think, 'Okay, if so many people are over there, we'll join up with this group instead of going our own way.' And that's the wrong decision we find out later."

A "dogpile," as Beidleman would later call it, was forming up. Gammelgaard remembered it, including, "at the peak point . . . Beck Weathers, Yasuko Namba, Tim, Charlotte, Sandy, Neal, Klev, and I, and two or three Sherpas."❖ Beidleman remembered that Mike Groom was also a part of the group, but despite the presence of two guides there did not seem to be any clear leadership.

"It wasn't really clear that there was a leader versus a non-leader or followers at that point," Beidleman said, "because people were being buffeted around by the wind and walking based on whoever had a headlight in front of them. I tried to yell several times that we needed one leader and one headlight to follow, otherwise we would be wandering aimlessly. My intention was to not walk directly toward Camp IV, even though for one minute at the bottom of the fixed lines I knew the direction to it. . . . I had looked at the terrain from up above, before the storm came in, and made a decision that if the storm came, that the best thing to do would to be avoid the Lhotse Face and that precipice as much as possible."❖

Beidleman, when he could exert his direction on the pack, was herding the climbers away from the route by which Krakauer, Adams, and Boukreev before him had descended and toward the eastern side of the South Col. The descent there wasn't so steep and the climbers could avoid the possibility of walking off the face of Lhotse.

"I continued to walk with the Japanese woman on my arm," Beidleman said, "and, I believe, Sandy, Charlotte, and Tim behind. Mike Groom and Beck were somewhat in front of us. The two fastest people at the time were the two Sherpas, and they seemed to dart in front of us in many different directions, or at least changing directions. I tried to remember watching my feet, to stay on a side hill, not too great of a side hill, but a slight side hill, which would put us at the saddle of the South Col, near a high point, and at that point is where a rock, a very distinct rock band, crosses the Col. And I knew that once we found that rock, if we just turned right and wandered downhill within the rocks, we would either hit the camp . . . or all the trash right around. That was the plan or the tack that I thought was best at the time. Because of the wind and because people were being pushed forward and backwards and wandering around, and also because I could not travel to the front of the group, carrying the Japanese woman, and I didn't have a headlight out yet; it's my impression that we side-hilled too much. . . . Once we lost the side hill, I personally lost all orientation to what direction we were walking. There was nothing left to follow in terms of terrain.

"We wandered as a group for a while. I don't know how long. It seemed like quite a while. We were moving slowly. Different people would come to the front and fall behind, but we kept yelling, all of us, to stay together as a group. I felt very strongly that if any person made an attempt to find the camp by themselves or left the group, that either they would be extremely lucky and find the camp, but most likely be lost completely. At some point in this wandering, we most likely got turned around and got onto the Tibetan side of the South Col. Even though this may have been something that I understood in my mind at the time, my oxygen had run out a long time ago, everybody else was staggering around, and it just was extremely hard to think and to try to make sense out of the things that we saw, the direction of the wind or whatnot—it was like being inside of a milk bottle. The winds were blowing—I've asked people, trying to estimate, I don't know—anywhere from, on the low side, forty miles an hour up to maybe gusts of eighty or more. They were enough to knock us off of our feet many times. Finally, during this walking or at some time during this walking, maybe an hour's worth, I'm guessing, people were getting extremely cold, all faces were iced up. Maybe another headlamp went out, I don't recall. . . . We were on very difficult ice with rock sticking through. The dip in front of us was illuminated by the headlamp, it rose up a little bit, and I walked to the edge of the rise and looked over, and whether I actually saw something or sensed something, I just knew that was totally dangerous. There was no terrain like that on the South Col that we should be even close to, and I got very, very scared and came back to the group. I recall, with the help of Tim and Klev, yelling and screaming at people that we absolutely had to stay together, and I suggested or yelled or barked or ordered or whatever it was, that we huddle up and wait. I remembered from the night before that during the very bad storm, somewhere before ten o'clock, before we left, a similar storm had subsided and became very still. I was banking on the fact that if the storm did let up for just a minute, or we could see some stars or see the mountains, we could get our orientation and we could at least pick the direction that we wanted to go. I had no idea if we were looking at the Kangshung Face or the Lhotse Face or any other face up there.

"We did decide to huddle up. We got into a big dogpile with our backs to the wind. People laid on people's laps. We screamed at each other. We beat on each other's backs. We checked on each other. Everybody participated in a very heroic way to try to stay warm and to keep each other awake and warm. This continued for some period of time—I don't know how long. Time is very warped, but it must have been awhile because I was extremely cold pretty shortly after that. We were checking fingers. We were checking each other's consciousness. We just tried to keep moving. It was something of an experience that I've never really had before, being what I felt so close to falling asleep and never waking up. I had rushes of warmth come up and down through my body—whether it was hypothermia or hypoxia, I don't know—a combination of both. I just remember screaming into the wind, all of us yelling, moving, kicking, trying to stay alive. I kept looking at my watch . . . hoping that the weather would clear.

"At some point in the night, the winds did not subside, but the snow let up a couple times. Once, just enough, I looked up and I recall seeing vaguely some stars, and then it closed in again. That gave me a lot of hope and I recall talking to Tim and Klev that there were stars and that we could figure out what was going on. And we all started thinking in those terms and turning our minds onto what we could possibly gain by seeing stars or the mountains. Another time after that it cleared again, enough to look up. The wind was still howling, but I recall yelling myself that there was the Big Dipper and the North Star. Either Klev or Tim said, 'And yes, there's Everest.' I remember looking at it and being perplexed—not even knowing if it were Everest or Lhotse."❖

The dogpile had situated itself less than twenty meters from the Kangshung Face, about four hundred meters from Camp IV. In clear weather they could have made the camp in ten to fifteen minutes, but they were hopelessly lost, and the storm was not abating.

I don't know how long I was in the tent after I returned from my first attempt to find our climbers, but I was alternating between trying to restore my power, walking the camp perimeter and going out of the tent to observe the situation. Finally, I heard some noises and I zipped open the tent and it was Martin.* His face was covered with ice, and

---

*In the May 15, 1996, "debriefing" tapes (see Authors' Note), Adams recalled that he'd arrived at Camp IV about 9:00 P.M. In those same tapes Dr. Hunt says she got a radio communication saying Adams had arrived at 8:30 P.M.

he was not saying much, just groaning, and I asked him, "Martin, are you okay?" He said nothing. I took off his crampons, and I asked "Where is everybody?" but he didn't answer so well. I think maybe his face was frostbitten, and I helped him into the corner of the tent and into a sleeping bag, and I got one of the three oxygen bottles and put a mask to his face.

Then, I remember Pemba came to our tent with tea, because I think he saw Martin come. Martin drank a little, and I asked about the situation, but he could not help me with any information, so I asked Pemba, and he told me he had seen some lamps approaching the camp and was sure some people would soon be coming. So after about fifteen minutes of rest after the tea, I tried to go out again, but the wind was strong, rattling the tents, much worse than the night before we left for the summit. But outside, as I searched just beyond the tent, I could find nobody. At a distance I saw someone else looking out for climbers, somebody I think from Rob Hall's expedition. By now it was very dark, a true blizzard. I switched on my headlamp, but it was of no help, so I stepped back into the tent and discovered that Martin had collapsed into a sleep; he had nothing left.

In the dogpile, hope for a rescue was on the wane. Lene Gammelgaard recalled that she, Klev Schoening, Beidleman, and Madsen began to consider making a dash for Camp IV, but they couldn't agree on which way to run. Increasingly, she said, she had begun to place her bets on Schoening to get them out of there, because she perceived Beidleman as being totally lost. "I don't think Neal would have ever gotten back to camp if Klev had not been there. . . . He would have stayed with the clients because he didn't have a clue as to where he was."

Indeed, during a brief break in the storm, it was Schoening who got himself oriented and started insisting that he knew the way to camp. Beidleman remembered, "Klev, I believe, took the initiative and was absolutely positive—he had in his mind, he knew what direction camp was. He had figured it out. . . . We decided somehow—I don't recall the process—it was more of a mass-type standing. We tried to get everybody stood up. The Japanese woman was still hanging onto my arm, I recall. It was very hard for me to move or to look around. I tried to pull people up as well as everybody else around. About the only person that I recognized was Sandy because of the distinct color of her jacket. Everybody else was just bodies and voices. When we got up, we all started to move. There was one headlight—I don't know who had it on—who seemed to be moving in a direction forward. I tried to follow with the Japanese woman and somebody else under or behind my right arm—I don't know who it was. I kept asking Klev, 'Are you sure? Are you sure?' And he was positive. He seemed to be totally aware and understanding of which mountain was which and what direction we needed to go. It was in the opposite one that we had come. It was uphill and it just all of a sudden seemed to make sense to me, too. Somewhere along the way, the movement, the motion of people, split. There were people that could move and there were people that could not move. It was a choice at that time to stay or to make a break for it and hopefully find the camp."❖

According to Gammelgaard, Klev Schoening was unlike some of the others who were understandably in a "barely controlled panic." He was steady and realistic about the situation, she has said; his attitude was, "Okay, no panic, no fear, no disaster. What can we do about the situation?"

As he had in the rescue of Ngawang Topche Sherpa, Schoening had risen to the occasion, and his actions were definitely instrumental in keeping order and calm among everyone in the dogpile.

"We got everybody on their feet," Schoening remembered, "trying to walk in place, whatever it was, to get things moving. There were several people . . . that couldn't get up. . . . We stood up and tried to exercise everybody's legs to get them moving. And it was obvious that Charlotte and the Japanese woman, Sandy—were very immobile. They were able to stand, but walking unsupported was impossible. So we took people on our arms. My recollection was I had Charlotte initially and the Japanese woman, and quickly realized that there was no way because I was on my knees most of the time, just trying to get them back up. . . .

"I recall kind of juggling everybody around to try and see if we could try different combinations that worked. I had to leave the Japanese lady, and I believe at that time Tim then picked up Charlotte."❖

As Schoening tried to maneuver Fox and Namba into a position to walk, Beidleman wrestled with Pittman, trying to put an arm around her and get her to her feet, but she kept protesting that she couldn't walk. Beidleman, frustrated in his attempt to get her up and moving, yelled out, "Well, if you can't walk, then fucking crawl!"

Pittman recalled a similar scenario. "He [Beidleman] said, 'We've got to bolt for it now. This is our only chance. There's a break in the [weather], and if you can't walk, then crawl. Which I did. . . . I thought that sounded like a good idea, because I could crawl, but I couldn't walk. The wind was just knocking me down every time."❖

Pittman crawled after Beidleman and the others until they crested and went over a small rise and she lost sight of a headlamp that one of the climbers was wearing. She remembered, "I realized that my only hope was staying with somebody else, and so I saw another lamp and I yelled out and said, 'Hello, hello, hello,' and it was Tim."❖

Madsen, although he was as strong and able as any of the climbers who had decided to make a dash for Camp IV, had selflessly decided to stay with Charlotte Fox. "I had Charlotte on my arm, back, head, wherever, and I couldn't see where to go. And I also didn't have the strength to drag or carry her to camp. She refused to walk. So . . . we sat down for a second, and then I heard a moan about fifteen, twenty yards—about twenty feet behind us, which was the Japanese girl. So I went back and I grabbed her and brought her up to where Charlotte was. Also Mike [Groom] was still tethered to Beck [Weathers]. Beck was having a very hard time walking also. So I told Mike, since I presumed he was still functional, that he has to go to camp also and . . . get help. . . . The plan at this point was just to sit still and hope somebody would come back for us. There were five of us in the group once Sandy came back: myself, Sandy, Charlotte, the Japanese lady, and Beck. We tried to do the same thing which the bigger group did earlier, just stay huddled together, stay awake, and try to keep each other warm. The time of night I have no clue."❖

CHAPTER 19

THE RESCUE TRANSCRIPT

Gammelgaard remembered that initially she and Schoening led the attempt to find Camp IV. "Klev and I just sort of stick together. Neal is wandering a little bit here, a little bit there, and then he is sticking together eventually, too, and . . . I don't know where camp is at this point, but I say, 'Okay, I can as well trust Klev . . . it's as good a possibility as anything.' Then at a point I see light, and there I sort of take over and say to Klev, 'This is light from the camp. We have to turn left. It's there!' And we go there and it turns out it's Anatoli's headlamp."

Like all the returning climbers, Gammelgaard was teetering on the edge of total exhaustion, keeping upright out of the sheer exhilaration of having survived. Boukreev, she said, "looked at me, but we didn't have to speak. He just knew it was serious and he bent down to take off my crampons."

The events from that point, as remembered by Boukreev, were dictated to his coauthor, Weston DeWalt, within days after his arrival in the United States from Nepal. In the interest of maintaining his voice and the immediacy of the events he experienced, his words as spoken in English and without benefit

of an interpreter are presented here. They are interrupted only
for clarification.

Q: *What did you do when you saw them coming in?*

A: I saw exactly these lamps come and I saw Lene and Klev
come. And I saw them with lots of ice around the face,
impossible to see [oxygen] mask because is just ice. I
take off crampons of Lene and put outside of tent. I see
people was not able to do nothing, just I get crampon,
everything, and help for Lene and for Klev go inside by
crawl. And I saw what is happening, very serious. People
said . . .

Q: *Did you give them any oxygen?*

A: Yes, I gave some oxygen from like what is I have, three
bottles—one Martin, one Klev, one Lene. From tent.
And I give for people this, and this is situation. I understand I need to be ready. I began take my shoes, but it
is not so easy. Also I tried to find the shoes, I found the
shoes, take over my shoes, big shoes. It was before I was
without the shoes. And then was ready go out.

Boukreev had already given one of the three oxygen canisters
he'd received from Pemba to Martin Adams. The other two he
had given, one each, to Schoening and Gammelgaard. The
shoes for which he searched were his overboots, which he would
need to go back out into the storm.

Q: *So you put on your climbing boots again?*

A: Yes. Probably—I cannot say what time people come.
Now it is difficult to say. People talk like . . .

Q: *Twelve to twelve-thirty?*

A: I take my shoes and maybe I started go out. It is one
o'clock. I think maybe like eleven-thirty people come or
eleven o'clock. I was very slow because I was with Klev
Schoening, I spoke with people, I gave tea, I gave oxy-

gen, I gave sleeping bag, everything. There's lots of time, is like probably eleven-thirty the latest time clients come, I think, because now I tried to understand just for myself. I think like eleven to twelve o'clock. But I start go out exactly like around one o'clock.

Q: *What did you understand about the condition of the clients?*
A: Lene she say—Sandy is dying, maybe Charlotte also dying, and I think, "Okay, these people frozen, you need to hurry, maybe . . ."

Q: *She said Sandy and Charlotte were dying?*
A: Very close, like, "Sandy very close. Maybe if you will find, you will find her dead. And you need hurry." Also Klev understand—you need just make direction, no go up, just go, just cross this big square of South Col, and you will find people on the end, near of Kangshung Face. Not go up. I said, "How long time?" Probably fifteen minutes. I said, "Oh, very close, if people fifteen minutes, for me maybe five minutes or ten minutes." I ask, "For you or for me?" "Oh, for you it is maybe fifteen minutes." Okay, for me it is fifteen minutes.

Boukreev attempted to get from Schoening and from Gammelgaard directions on how to reach the climbers who had been left behind. With no landmarks to reference, no sighting point to walk toward, they were trying to guide a blind pilot to the field.

Q: *Did you ask for help from Neal?*
A: Neal go inside of tent with crampon. I get off his crampon, because I said, "Oh, he will cut this tent." And I get off his crampon. And he just collapse.

Q: *He's in his tent at this point?*
A: Just half of his body probably in tent, half of body outside of tent. And when I spoke with Lene, I said, "How

Neal?" And she say, "Maybe some problem with Neal." Mostly Lene, she was more talkative for this situation. Klev, I don't know what was situation, but Lene just talked. Maybe Klev have some problem with his head. And I go inside of tent, I tried to speak with Neal Beidleman, but he was very cold, impossible for him—no possible talk with him, and I understand. He began just use oxygen inside of tent.

Boukreev, on going to speak with Beidleman, found him half in, half out of his tent, his crampons still on. Concerned that his crampons could rip the tent fabric and expose him to the cold winds that were at times at hurricane force, Boukreev removed Beidleman's crampons and helped him into his tent. His condition was such that Beidleman could barely talk.

Q: *And then?*
A: I go again inside of my tent. Lene and Klev already in sleeping bag, and I check with her again to make sure I don't need go up. Lene and Klev told me, "You don't need go up. You need go just cross what is flat place." Lene told, "You don't need go up." Pemba go inside and he said, "Lopsang tell you, you need go up." Why, where, I need go up or I don't need go up? And I am responsible about life. I understand this—before, I hoped it is okay, these people have guides, people have Sherpas, people probably have some oxygen, it is okay, just not visibility. Now this situation, people just come, maybe people get frostbitten, and just all news come very quickly for me. I get this very upset very quickly. I get this power from upset.

Q: *Adrenaline?*
A: Yes, that is word.

Boukreev, in his first exchange with Klev Schoening, had been told that he didn't need to "go up" the mountain, but "across" the South Col. Given that the directions meant that the stranded climbers were considerably off the course of a normal descent, Boukreev wanted to check again what he'd heard.

As Boukreev was talking to Gammelgaard and Schoening, trying to get the best instructions possible, Pemba came to Boukreev's tent and said that Lopsang had returned to Camp IV with news that several hours earlier he'd had to leave Scott Fischer just below the Balcony. Out of oxygen, delirious, suffering from what appeared to be cerebral edema, Fischer had been unable to move without the assistance of Lopsang. Despite Lopsang's heroic efforts he'd not been able to get Fischer down. Desperate to get help for his friend, Lopsang wanted Boukreev to climb up to him, to take oxygen and hot tea to him. Boukreev was thoroughly confused by the conflicting bits and pieces of information that were coming at him through the climbers' hypoxic haze. Was Fischer with the clients? Were they in the same places? Where on the South Col did he need to go? Up or down or across? He was trying to sort it all out.

Q: *Did you speak with Lopsang?*
A: Pemba said Lopsang come and he spoke with us, and I jump out of tent and wondering where is Lopsang? I don't know. I go inside of tent where is Neal. Neal has collapse. And I help little bit him, and then outside of tent I heard some voice of Lopsang. He said, "Anatoli you need go up."

Q: *You don't see him? He's yelling at you from his tent?*
A: Yes, yes. Just—"Anatoli, you need go up." And I understand Scott is have difficult situation.

Q: *So what do you do then?*
A: I go again inside of tent and I said again, "Lene, Klev, I need go up or I need just cross this flat place?" They say, "You need just cross this flat place." "Scott is there?" I'm asking. "No," they say, "Scott not." So,

okay, now I am begin understand. Scott is up the mountain. Clients are down, different places.

Q: *So, is it after that that you go into the tent, to the Sherpas' tent, to get some oxygen?*

A: I went for Lopsang and say, "Lopsang, you need go together with me, some our clients probably died, we need carry our clients." And I didn't see him. He said again, "Anatoli, you need go up, Scott said he wait you, he respect you, he expect you help him like this, and you need carry oxygen and hot drink for him."

Q: *But you don't see him when you're having this conversation?*

A: Just at vestibule of tent, just I hear his voice. I think he need understand whole situation. "Lopsang, we need carry some clients, maybe fifteen minutes—are you able?" He said me again, "Anatoli, you need go up."

Q: *He doesn't answer, he just talks?*

A: Just talk directly what he have this idea inside of head, he didn't understand what I talk, he just heard my voice and told me just exactly what—all the same, repeat. And I need helping five people—I am one. I go inside of his tent, Sherpas' tent. I ask Pemba about oxygen. And I understand from second talk with Lene about Beck Weathers and Yasuko Namba. And I ask, "Okay, Pemba, you need to find for me oxygen. I will go for another tent, for Rob Hall's tent, maybe somebody will help me." And I go inside and maybe another camp—for Rob Hall's expedition, open one door. And I try, "Hey, somebody, can you help me?" No answer. I say, "Yasuko Namba, Beck Weathers, need helping—somebody—are you ready to help me?" No answer. Another tent, same. Another tent, same. And then I go inside—I saw some Sherpas' tents of Rob Hall. I open and somebody talk with me. And I say, "Yasuko Namba and Beck Weathers

need help. Some power from your expedition go together with me help for our clients." And I say, "Okay,
you need to be ready." And then I go Taiwan tents—
nobody. No answer.

Lopsang had made a promise to Scott Fischer when he had
to leave him behind. He'd told him, "Okay, please, you stay
here. I . . . leave you here. You stay here. I send some Sherpa
and oxygen and tea."❖ Groaning in pain, Fischer had told Lopsang, "You go down. You go down."❖ Leaving Fischer, Lopsang
had reassured him, "Please, Scott, you never walk anyway; you
stay here. I send some Sherpa and Anatoli. I send up oxygen
and tea."❖

Like Boukreev, Lopsang could see that the Mountain Madness Sherpas could not or would not go up the mountain. He
was counting on Boukreev, but Boukreev had reports of five
clients down, three of them with the Mountain Madness expedition. He couldn't do it all; he needed help, so he made a
quick round of the expeditions tented nearby: to the tents of
Rob Hall's clients, to the tents of Hall's Sherpas, to the tents of
the Taiwanese.

Rob Hall's expedition's members were either asleep, unable
or unwilling to lend support to Boukreev's effort. One of them,
Lou Kasischke, was totally incapacitated, still snowblind, still
alone in his tent. His tentmates, Andy Harris, Beck Weathers,
and Doug Hansen, as of 1:00 A.M., still had not returned to
Camp IV.

The failure of Boukreev to get assistance from the Rob Hall
expedition members at Camp IV was the second time that evening that a plea for help had gone unheeded. Mike Groom,
who had left Beck Weathers and Yasuko Namba behind in the
dogpile and returned with the Mountain Madness climbers,
Schoening, Gammelgaard, and Beidleman, had about an hour
earlier pleaded with various of the Adventure Consultants' team
members to attempt a rescue of their fellow climbers. He'd had
no better luck.

Likewise, from the Taiwanese, no assistance was offered. Nobody could or would help.

Q: *With no help, what do you do?*
A: I come back again to Pemba. "Pemba, do you have hot drink?" "I have hot drink." "Where is oxygen?" He says, "I didn't find oxygen." "How you didn't? I need oxygen, some bottles; clients need oxygen." He said, "All bottles empty." I tried to find oxygen also at this time. I hurry. I know somebody can die, and I hurry, hurry, hurry—check for bottle of oxygen—no I find—no. I go again inside of tents of our Sherpas. And I saw quiet. People just understood—maybe Anatoli wants us go out, but is dangerous—like quiet, stillness. And I say, "Lopsang, somebody need . . ."

Q: *Are you raising your voice with him?*
A: Yes, big strong wind outside, very cold, lots of problem come, and I upset with him in this situation.

Q: *What do you say to him?*
A: Nobody answer. Very quiet, like all people get collapse after hard work. I understand this very difficult.

Boukreev, when he discovered that Pemba could not supply him with any oxygen, was incredulous, angry, impatient, and desperate to get to the lost clients. Fifteen canisters of Poisk had been left at Camp IV before the assault bid. He'd gotten three canisters earlier. Somewhere, he reasoned, there were more, but Pemba was saying, "No oxygen."

Q: *So, you had no oxygen to take with you?*
A: Lene told me, maybe very bad situation with Sandy—you need hurry. Now I lose lots of time to try to find support of somebody who can help me. And now I didn't have oxygen, I have just my mask and reductor.

And inside of [Mountain Madness Sherpa] tent, nobody speak with me. And I saw Lopsang, and I saw he used oxygen. And for me this is little upset and I saw he used oxygen and he said many time, "I don't need oxygen," and just I take off his mask and get his bottle of oxygen. And I say, "I need this oxygen," and take this oxygen.

Q: *You took his oxygen?*
A: Yes, everything, and put in my pack.

Q: *Did he try to get it back?*
A: No, not answer. He just was very quiet. He don't like. I say, "Somebody need help and we need carry somebody." I was very hurried, just very fast. I get oxygen, I know I have some oxygen, I have some tea, and I have this oxygen together with mask, reductor, I didn't—I know, just off, and I think maybe I need hurry very soon—fifteen minutes, I try to find Sandy—what is happening with Sandy. And just I take this and I understand if I will try again to find support. And I run out. I get strong wind, no visibility, I begin keep my direction and go out.

Q: *So, you get the oxygen off Lopsang, you have the tea from Pemba, and you head out. So how do you decide which way?*
A: People say, not go to up. And I understand this. Actually, I remember what is—how it is South Col, plan of South Col. And I didn't get crampon, because I was very hurried and people said you don't need go up. I leave camp, just little walk, and just go direction from wind, I keep this direction and I cross the South Col, and I didn't see—I cannot see nothing, just my headlamp little bit just through white. And this is—I don't know, maybe fifteen minutes already. I was fifteen minutes, I saw watch, it is like began like fifteen minutes past one or twenty minutes past one. Now I began just saw this

watch because I began work, I began hurry. And I get fifteen minutes, just begin recognize just this big rock. And then after this rock began small part from right side and go down to Kangshung Face. And maybe thirty meters before, from this big rock, small rocks, and I didn't see nothing. And I didn't see nobody. I try go up, but without crampon, impossible. I think maybe I need little go up. And I think maybe these people get mistake. And I came back to camp.

Boukreev, walking with the wind to his back, had headed in the direction he thought Gammelgaard and Schoening had directed him, but in the elapsed time they said the trip would require, he had found no one. Thinking that Gammelgaard and Schoening had been mistaken in the description of where he could find the dogpile, he had headed in a direction that led him up the mountain. The route was too steep to be negotiated without crampons, and Boukreev returned to Camp IV, steering directly into the wind and blowing snow.

Q: *Did you go to Lene and Klev again?*

A: Yes, I look in the tent, I spoke with Lene and Klev. I said, "I didn't find nobody. Where is? I need maybe go up." People said, no. But I said I cross already—nobody, just rock finish—and people say probably you need to go down little bit. I said, "Okay, maybe it is small mistake, maybe I need go down little bit." I said, "Okay, I will try."

Q: *Did you go back to the Sherpas' tent at that point?*

A: It is probably all together like before two o'clock, the time now—before two o'clock. And I go out from my tent and I go inside of Neal's tent and spoke with Neal. Neal began just little speak. And he also talk me about Kangshung Face and how he go down. But when I saw Neal, I didn't ask about can you help me. For me, it is exactly—it is look like—like, I didn't ask Klev because Klev come and Klev cannot able, but I saw Neal and I saw his face. He just get terrible time and just frozen and shaking and just inside of tent he was very poor.

Q: *Did he ask you about Scott, or did you ask him about Scott?*
A: He didn't talk. He didn't talk nothing about Scott. I understand situation. I already understand. I try to find about various people—where is Sandy, her situation. And again then I go to tent of Sherpas. It is there quiet. Sherpas like clients get collapse. All Sherpas inside. And I go outside again for another tent, for Rob Hall expedition.

Q: *So you looked in the Sherpas' tent, and everybody's out of it?*
A: Out. And no possible. I saw the situation. I go again inside of Sherpas' tent from Rob Hall expedition and I ask somebody can help me. I said, "You need to go out together with me." This Sherpa try he say maybe to go out, and saw weather, and he said, "Okay." I saw he get out his pack. I said, "Okay, I go in my tent and I waited you." Maybe five minutes he will be ready. And then I go inside of my tent with Lene and Klev tent and little keep myself from wind and waited five minutes— nobody came. And then I just open my tent and try to go out—I saw the Sherpa come. And he said, "Actually, I don't like go out together with you because this situation, no other Sherpa go together with me, and also I don't like situation." I say, "Why you don't like?" He say, "No one other Sherpa come. Why I need go to risk? Just me and no one ready go together with me." I cannot say who is this Rob Hall Sherpa, but some Sherpa. And when I heard this, I understand. Again I run out, take my oxygen, and try to go out to find these people.

Q: *Did you try to find more oxygen or did you still have just the one canister you got from Lopsang?*

A: No. This is situation. Was very hurry. When next time I get close to same place, think, I saw some lamp, maybe Tim make this lamp. And I saw somebody make this light from headlamp. This is maybe after two o'clock. And I found the people. Very close together. I come and I say, "How are you?" and people was very slow, not able, just frozen voice, just very slow, somebody like Tim, very slow. Charlotte, she didn't able talk.

Returning to the same area that he had searched before, but staying on "the flat" and scanning the landscape, Boukreev spotted Tim Madsen's headlamp approximately thirty yards from where, on his previous trip, he'd diverted up the mountain.

Boukreev found Madsen, Pittman, and Fox huddled in a close circle; Yasuko Namba lying on the ground, appearing unconscious; Beck Weathers nowhere in sight. Tim Madsen has said that at some point Weathers had wandered away from the dogpile.

Q: *They're on their feet or . . . ?*

A: No, like sit down. Nobody, just like . . .

Q: *On their butts?*

A: The butts. But people have some packs and people sit down on them. And this situation—when I saw this situation, I take oxygen, I first time I open my tea . . .

Q: *You have one canister?*

A: I have one bottle of oxygen. I have one thermal bottle tea. And I give for tea, some cup. Charlotte, Sandy, and Tim. And then people drink tea. Just I saw the situation. I am one person and this is three people, and I saw Yasuko very close, maybe two meters from people. And I put mask for face of Sandy.

Q: *Was Sandy talking at all?*
A: No, nothing.

Q: *How was she behaving?*
A: Just little bit, just she is frozen. Just Tim can little talk.

Q: *Making any noises, Sandy?*
A: She can little talk. Sandy—for me, it was very difficult talk. Strong wind, I am tired. I cannot remember exactly about—but people, just Tim say, "Where is another people?" I said, "Just I am alone. Nobody can able to help." And just I have just one bottle of oxygen. And somebody can't come together with me. Sandy couldn't tell nothing. Charlotte, nothing, just frozen people. Very frozen, very small power. And Tim, very slow; he can little talk. I understand. And I understand these people not able without helping. I said, "Maybe somebody ready to go together with me." And Charlotte said, "Yes, maybe I like go." I said for Tim and Sandy, "Okay. This is one bottle of oxygen. You can share this oxygen. And, Charlotte, I take you." After one minute I take my pack again and I take Charlotte and we begin walk. I have some crampons now, and very strong wind just directly on our face. Impossible to see—nothing, just—I tried to help for Charlotte to stay on her feet.

Q: *Was it hard for her to stand?*
A: Yes. Just she can able little walk, but without me, no way. Just for me, very hard. Every time I tried to make this— equilibrium.

Q: *Her balance?*
A: Her balance—keep this balance. But very strong wind. And I understand, without my hands she will fall exactly.

Q: *Your right arm around her?*
A: Yes. She get her other [left] hand above my shoulder.

Q: *She's on your right side?*

A: Yes, and I hold to the left hand and we walk. And very
     strong wind for me. Actually I am frozen, she is frozen,
     she wasn't able talk very much, but very slow, step by
     step we go. But it is four hundred meters and step by
     step. Sometimes we stand, if I understand this is good
     place for make some rest, because another place, if I
     saw some stone little bit, I put Charlotte—little sit down.
     Because from ground it is very difficult to help her stand
     up, but from stones it is possible. And little, maybe
     three, four times, we made this stopping. Then I began
     recognize this place, some garbage . . .

Q: *Some empty oxygen canisters?*

A: Yes, very old bottles. My crampon is hitting metal, I can
     feel, and I understand is very short distance for camp,
     probably two hundred meters.

Q: *Is Charlotte trying to talk at all during this time?*

A: No, no. She just talk little—just she say "too hard" or
     something. Very hard for her. It take long time, more
     than for me when I go, maybe forty-five minutes. She
     just robot, walk like robot, I think. Me, too. We cross
     the South Col and I saw some lamps inside of tents,
     Pemba probably . . .

Q: *No blinking lights?*

A: No. This is around three o'clock probably already. And
     when I get to camp, maybe it is around three o'clock.
     And I get her [Charlotte Fox] out of her crampon, har-
     ness, everything, and she crawl inside of Neal's tent. And
     I ask Neal—he is much better; I saw the situation. He
     used oxygen, he just began grow up. And Neal, I said,
     "You need help for her." And I take mask from his face,
     put for her face because just like robot I work. And now
     again for this situation, I go for Sherpas' tent. This time

I ask again every tents to help me. I tell I saw this Yasuko
Namba . . .

Q: *You went again to Rob Hall's and the Taiwanese tents?*

A: Yes, and I ask again. I go, just I need relax, I work very
hard, and I use my time for little relax, for rest, go just
one tent, another tent, and tried again to help. Because
first time I was hurry. And then I ask some Sherpas of
Rob Hall, I talk about Yasuko Namba, and I come back,
I tried again talk with our Sherpas, with Pemba, with our
Sherpas, very quiet, like collapse people, didn't say noth-
ing. And I go inside of tent, also opposite of my tent is
Taiwan tent. I open some and ask—no, quiet. And then
I go inside of tent. I was very tired. It is three o'clock.
And also I ask Pemba, give some tea for Charlotte, and
I waited some tea and Pemba bring more tea for Char-
lotte and Neal, and then he bring some tea for me.

Q: *Are Lene and Klev asleep now?*

A: Lene also drink little tea and I tell her about Charlotte
and say, "Now, here's Sandy used oxygen and I have
now big problem with Yasuko Namba." Somebody, like
nobody help me. And it is very difficult for everybody.
Also I have not oxygen. And now people have one bottle
oxygen. Pemba couldn't find, didn't find, and I didn't
find oxygen.

Q: *Did you speak again with Pemba about oxygen?*

A: This is situation, just I waited little time—maybe somebody can be helping me—I checked all tent from Rob
Hall's and I waited. I was very tired and also I understand nobody can be responsible to help me. I go out
again and I go inside of tents of our Sherpas; I took
again just mask and some oxygen from another Sherpa,
put in my pack, and run out for my clients. And when
I get, it was around four o'clock probably. Maybe four-
fifteen, four-ten. Just begin light. Because in five o'clock

it started to get light. Five o'clock, possible to see, little bit.

And I went out and I found these people, Tim and Sandy, and they used oxygen maybe one hour already, maybe one hour. And people spoke with me. Sandy began spoke with me. And I ask, "How are you?" And people said, "Okay." And Sandy began talk with me and I understand. Now, it is much better for her.

Q: *What was she saying?*

A: I said, "How are you?" She said, "I am okay." I said, "What is happening with Yasuko?" because it is two meters. And I didn't ask people gave for her tea or people didn't. It is for me what I had, what I carried, I gave for tea. I didn't ask people gave her oxygen or tea because just one bottle, three people was together. And for me, this is very close situation. I will be very empty, without power. And for me, just I work like robot also. I take Sandy Pittman and same situation like Charlotte Fox.

Q: *You had another canister of O's?*

A: I give this for Tim.

Q: *What did Tim say?*

A: He just took mask and nothing. Also this situation, also I have carried some second bottle of tea, I think. I have very little drink; I gave some drink and we begin start walk. And probably around five o'clock it is begin light. Just no impossible to say sun come, but it is begin light and around probably I think like four-forty, four-forty-five we come. I was very tired, empty, and had just help for Tim, for Sandy, go inside of tent, ask again tea. And then I need rest already. And I say, "Pemba, I wait tea for me," and I go inside of my tent. Just I put Tim Madsen and Sandy inside of tent, help for people get out of crampons, like harness, everything, packs, help for people put inside of tent, closed, talked with Pemba, go inside of my tent, keep warm. Lene was near and she little talk about it. "Anatoli, you need rest. You need oxygen. Look for your face, you are very terrible." I say to her, "Okay, don't worry about me—what is happening now with Scott?" I think he get very difficult situation. Now all our clients in the tent, just without Scott. I think he have difficult situation. Now just problem with Scott. But I believe Scott is guide and maybe he can survive much better than these clients. And when Pemba come, we drink tea and I told Pemba now what is situation. Now I saw storm lose power and begin light. And we need send two Sherpas with oxygen to go up for Scott. And do you understand. And he say, "Yes, I understand." I say, "Try to talk with Lopsang and two Sherpas—we need to send for help, for Scott with oxygen." Try to find oxygen. I go inside of sleeping bag and drink little tea and just what I think about Scott—I understand this is problem, and I don't remember much from there, like two hours I slept.

Lene Gammelgaard, recalling Boukreev's return to their tent after shepherding Pittman and guiding Madsen, who was able to move under his own power, said, "I think about five o'clock in the morning I wake up, and he's back in, and it's light, and again no words. He's just sitting there and he's absolutely empty. There's nothing left in him. And I sort of think, perceive, whatever, understand that he's got Charlotte, Tim, and Sandy in, but I also have the feeling that he's been out there and not been able to do anything for Yasuko and the other one [Weathers] who was sitting out there. At this point I didn't know."

CHAPTER 20

THE LAST ATTEMPT

On the morning of May 11, the oxygen supply of Mountain Madness depleted, Neal Beidleman and the clients made the decision to retreat down the mountain. The few clients who needed oxygen on their descent were supplied by the IMAX/IWERKS expedition, which had generously come to their aid.

As Beidleman and the clients readied to descend, two Sherpas from the Mountain Madness expedition and a Sherpa from the Taiwanese expedition, carrying oxygen and hot tea, began to climb to just below the Balcony where Scott Fischer had bivouacked overnight with the Taiwanese climber Makalu Gau. Boukreev, not wanting to descend until he knew the condition of Fischer, spoke with Beidleman and told him he wanted to stay behind.

Rob Hall's team was in shambles. Radio reports from Rob Hall had continued through the night. He was immobile at the South Summit, freezing to death. Doug Hansen, who had been with Hall on the evening of May 10, was no longer with him and was presumed to be dead. Andy Harris had never returned to his tent. Beck Weathers and Yasuko Namba had been located by some of Hall's expedition members near the Kangshung Face, where Boukreev had discovered Madsen, Pittman, and Fox in the breaking hours of the day. Both of them, miraculously, had signs of life. John Taske, Jon Krakauer, Stuart Hutchison, and Mike Groom, according to Jon Krakauer, deliberated about what action to take and decided "to leave them where they lay," believing nothing could be done for them.

Just prior to the departure of the Mountain Madness Sherpas and the Taiwanese Sherpa who had gone up the mountain in search of Fischer and Gau, two Sherpas from Rob Hall's expedition had gone up in an attempt to rescue Rob Hall and any of their other climbers who might be found alive. Threatened by the weather, they turned back, never having found any of their missing climbers. At 6:20 P.M., Rob Hall radioed his Base Camp and was patched through to his wife in New Zealand. After sending his love and asking her not to worry, he signed off. They were the last words that were ever heard from him.

As Rob Hall spoke with his wife, Boukreev was again on the mountain, climbing to reach Scott Fischer. The Sherpas who had gone up in search of him had returned to Camp IV with Makalu Gau, whom they had been able to revive with hot tea and oxygen. Fischer they had discovered unconscious, but still breathing. At about 1:00 P.M. they had strapped an oxygen mask to his face and turned on a feed to a full bottle of oxygen.

I slept like two hours and after seven-thirty that morning Pemba came with tea. And I heard some Sherpas pass by our tent, and I ask Pemba, "What is the situation now? Somebody go to Scott or no?" And he gave some tea and he was just quiet. No answer. I said, "Scott needs help. Please send some Sherpas up." So, he went to the Sherpas' tent and he began to talk. And now I have no power. It would be for me a stupid idea to go again. I needed some recovery time.

At probably eight-thirty I took a look at our climbing route from yesterday, and I can see the storm has lost power. I see some Sherpas going up, and he says, "Okay, father of Lopsang started together with Tashi Sherpa," and I ask, "They carry oxygen?" and he tells me, "Yes."

And then I speak with Neal. "Okay, this is my position. I would like to stay here," and he says okay and he worked for the clients and took them down.

A strong wind had come up, and I kept myself inside the tent, but around one or two I went out, and I spoke with Todd Burleson and Pete Athans with Alpine Ascents (guides for a commercial expedition), who had come to Camp IV to help with getting climbers down from the trouble we had had. I asked them, "Do you know what is happening?" and they said some Sherpas had returned with Makalu Gau, so I went to the Taiwanese tents.

When I went into the tent, I saw this Makalu Gau, his face and hands all frostbitten, but he was talking a little bit, and I asked him, "Did you see Scott?" and he says, "Yes, we were together last night." And I had hopes that Scott could survive, but with this news I thought, "Scott is finished, dead already," and I got upset about this, but this news is only from the Taiwanese, so I want to talk with our Sherpas who went up.

I go inside the Sherpas' tent, and the father of Lopsang is crying with great sadness, and he says, "We cannot help." And he speak very small, very little bit of English. I don't understand. "What is happening?" And they said to me, "He died." And then I said, "Was he still breathing?" and they told me, "Yes, he's still breathing, but no more signs of life."

I asked, "Did you give him oxygen?" and they said, "Yes, we give oxygen," and I asked, "Did you give him some medicine?" and they said, "No." And now I understood, so I went outside the tent and talked with Todd Burleson and Pete Athans, and I asked, "Can you help me go up to help with Scott? People say he is still alive, like 8,350 meters."

Pete Athans, who spoke Nepali, understood the situation, and he said to me, "Actually I spoke with the Sherpas, and they said it's impossible to help Scott." And I said, "Why? Maybe we will try." He says, "But it is bad weather coming. Storm didn't finish. And people try to give him oxygen, but oxygen didn't help him." Todd Burleson was quiet, but Pete Athans talked with me. And he said, "Scott was, yes, able to breathe, but he wasn't able to drink tea, just people put his tea inside of his mouth, but he couldn't swallow."

And Pete Athans said, "Impossible. For this situation, impossible for him." I said, "But maybe, maybe some breathing, if he has some breathing, maybe oxygen will improve, and I go out again."

I went inside the tent again with Lopsang's father and asked him, "Can you say little more information? Did you give him no medicine? When you gave him new oxygen?" He said, "Oh, we gave him one bottle oxygen, put mask, and open oxygen."

And I said okay and got a radio from the Sherpas and radioed to Base Camp, and I spoke with Ingrid and asked her, "This is the situation, what do you advise?" And she is upset also and says to me, "Anatoli, try to help everything that is possible for you; please try to find some possibility." I said, "Okay, I will try everything that is possible, but what is your advice?" She said, "Okay, about medicine, do you have this small packet with the injections?" And I told her, "Yes, I have the injection." And she said for me to try it with Scott, and I promised her I would try everything.*

Then, I go to the Sherpas' tent, and see that Lopsang is using oxygen and some other Sherpas are using oxygen. And I said, "Okay, I need some oxygen. I need three bottles of oxygen and a thermal bottle of tea. Can you make it for me?" And people said, "Why you need?" I said, "I will go up." People say, "It is stupid idea."

So, I left the tent and then Lopsang's father came and began to speak with Pete Athans in Nepali, and Pete Athans came and said, "Anatoli, what do you want to do?" I said, "I will go up; I need oxygen; I need thermal bottles of tea." And Pete Athans tried to explain to me that it was a bad idea. He said, "Now the storm has gone down a little bit, and if you go now, you will get this storm again." I said to him, "This is what I need to do."

I knew from my experience; I explained to him my position. This situation with Scott was a slow process; maybe Scott, if he had oxygen, would possibly revive. Scott is just before the Balcony, and he has enough oxygen maybe until seven o'clock. I need some oxygen.

Pete is like the Sherpas, and I understand he thinks it is a stupid idea, but I get some oxygen. I ask for three, but get only two. I think

---

*Dr. Hunt has recalled that it was Rob Hall's expedition doctor with whom Boukreev actually spoke.

maybe it came from David Breashear's expedition, but I don't know for sure. I began to hurry; I began to prepare myself, but as I prepared, the wind began to come higher. It is just around four o'clock, maybe four-fifteen.

I took my pack and was leaving, and I saw Pete Athans outside of the tent, and I asked Pete Athans, "Maybe you will go up?" He said just, "No." And I said, "How many will try to help?" And just—he got sad, he just cried a little bit. He thinks there is no chance.

I just started from the tents and maybe 150 meters ahead, I saw a small moving point, somebody coming down to me, and I was very wondered. I thought it was like a phantom, a miracle, and I began to hurry. And in a short time I came up on this man, who was carrying his hands without gloves up in front of his body like a surrendering soldier. And I did not know then who this was, but now I understand it was Beck Weathers.*

I said, "Who are you?" He didn't speak or answer, and I asked him, "Did you see Scott?" And he said to me, "No one I saw. No one I saw. It is my last time in the mountains. I don't want to come back to these mountains. Never, never . . ." It was like crazy talk.

Just I think my head is broken, and I am thinking, "Anatoli, you need to be able to think if you go up again." And I yell back, "Burleson! Pete! Please help me!" And I asked them, "Can you help with this man? I will go. I will keep my time." And they tell me, "Don't worry, we will take care of him."

Everyone said it was stupid to go for Scott, but I saw this man survived, and this was a push for me. And I took a mask, everything, and I began to move with oxygen, without resting, and I climbed steadily, but darkness started to come, nightfall just began. And also a strong wind began with a blizzard and a difficult time.

And just around seven o'clock, five minutes past probably, I found Scott. Dark also, with a serious storm, and I saw him through the snow, again like a mirage. I saw the zipper of his down suit open, one hand without a mitten, frozen. I opened his face mask, and around the mask face it is frozen, but a different temperature, and

---

*Boukreev had not been told that Weathers earlier that day had been found alive, lying in the snow at the South Col.

under the mask it is like a blue color, like a big bruise. It is like not life in the face. I saw no breathing, just a clenched jaw.

I lose my last hope. I can do nothing. I can do nothing. I cannot stay with him.

It began to storm again, seven o'clock. Oxygen—I lose my last hope, because I thought when I started, "Oxygen will improve his life." If by now oxygen does not improve, no signs of life, no pulse or breathing. . . .

Very strong wind began, I am without power, without power. And for me, just what do I need to do? Actually, I understood this. If I found him like Beck Weathers, it would be possible to help him. He was revived. Like Beck Weathers revived, he would need help and possibly giving him this help, like oxygen, everything would be possible. It would be possible to help Scott. I understand there is no way for me. No way for him. What do I need to do?

And I saw his pack and I roped it around his face to keep away the birds. And with maybe four of five empty oxygen bottles around, I put them on his body to help cover. And just maybe seven-fifteen I started to go down fast. And I understand I lose power, I lose emotion. I can't say how it was. I was very sad.

Storm began, very strong, new blow of fresh snow with strong wind. And I began to use the ropes, and when I finish at like 8,200 meters, visibility is gone. Began just darkness, probably seven-forty, impossible to see. I have my headlamp. I used oxygen a little bit. Then I stopped oxygen because it is not helping my visibility, like two meters, three meters probably, impossible to see. And I found again Kangshung Face, same place, I think, near Yasuko Namba probably. I can see just two meters, but I understood. And then I go some more in a changed direction, and the snow on the ground is finished and I began to see some oxygen bottles. I turn back a little and go up a little, and I saw some tents.

I know these are not our tents, but next will be ours. When I found this place, I began to hear some voices. And I go without visibility, by the noise. And I come to the noise in a tent. I open. I see this man just alone by himself. I saw Beck Weathers, and I don't understand why he is alone, but I lose power, go for my tent, because I cannot help. Some sleeping bag I have. Just I crawl inside of my tent and go to sleep.

Returning to Camp IV, Boukreev descended in a storm just as severe as the one of the night before. Climbing alone, with no lights from Camp IV to guide him, he had used his intuition and his memory of the South Col to steer in what he thought was the correct direction. Coming across some discarded oxygen canisters enabled him to finally locate his camp.

As Boukreev searched through the tents at Camp IV, he heard some screams from one of the tents. Peering inside he found Beck Weathers, unattended by any of his teammates, writhing in pain. Exhausted, having narrowly escaped being lost in the storm, Boukreev had to leave Weathers to find his own tent where he collapsed, exhausted.

CHAPTER 21

MOUNTAIN MEDIA MADNESS

By the morning of May 12, hope for Rob Hall, Doug Hansen, and Andy Harris had been abandoned, and the remnants of the Adventure Consultants expedition began their descent to the safety of Base Camp. Beck Weathers and Makalu Gau, through the efforts of Todd Burleson, Pete Athans, Ed Viesturs, David Breashears, and members of other expeditions on the mountain, were evacuated to Camp I where a helicopter was able to land and fly them to Kathmandu.

As the Hall team members were descending, Beidleman and the Mountain Madness clients arrived in Base Camp where their plan was to rest, restore, and prepare for a trek to Syangboche where they would catch a helicopter and fly to Kathmandu. Up the mountain, Boukreev had gathered what he could of the Mountain Madness expedition gear and had begun his own descent, finally arriving on the evening of May 13.

Neal Beidleman, early in the morning of May 16, reported to Outside Online, "The team is going to be heading down to Pheriche very shortly, later this morning. . . . We're all hurting and healing . . . so we need to move down the mountain." Everest was over.

In the late morning of May 16, Beidleman and the Mountain Madness clients began their trek; later that evening Boukreev began a solo ascent of Lhotse.

As Fischer had promised Boukreev before Everest, he had packaged an expedition to Lhotse. He had signed on Fox, Madsen, and Pittman. Boukreev and Beidleman were to guide. Devastated by Fischer's death and remorseful over the death of Yasuko Namba, whom he had not been able to rescue, Boukreev wanted to go back to the mountains. At 5:46 P.M. on the evening of May 17, Boukreev, alone, summited Lhotse. From the top of the peak he stood and looked over to the summit of Everest and traced the route he and the other climbers had taken down. At the elevation of 8,350 meters his eyes stopped for a moment. That was as far as Scott Fischer had gotten; Boukreev had been unable to bring him home.

On May 22 the last of the Mountain Madness clients departed Kathmandu. Some had bandages covering their frostbite, but no one had suffered any damage that would result in amputations. Charlotte Fox was walking with a slight limp. Tim Madsen and Lene Gammelgaard had frostbitten fingers. These were our most "serious" cases. As for me, I was lucky. I had gotten away with slight frostbite on my hand, which in the upcoming days would cause me to lose the skin on my fingertips, and I also had some mild frostbite on my nose and lips. Truthfully, given what all of us had experienced, we got away lucky, with all of our fingers and toes—our lives.

Boukreev and Beidleman stayed behind in Kathmandu to settle the business of the expedition, and according to Boukreev, most of the responsibilities fell to Beidleman, for whom English came easier. After their ordeal on the mountain both men were physically and psychologically spent, eager to leave Kathmandu, to put the mountain behind them. Boukreev, particularly, was eager to get away from the press that had been on their backs since they had come off the mountain and holed up in the Yak and Yeti Hotel in Kathmandu.

The world seemed endlessly hungry for the story of what had happened. In my mountaineering career I had never seen so much interest in an event in the Himalaya. I wondered about this curiosity. What is it, this fascination with wrecks, wars, disasters, and catastrophes? I found it difficult to understand this.

Most of the expedition members and I tried to avoid the press. We wished to be among ourselves. For all of us it was as if the world were now painted in more vivid colors, and we were feeling life's simple pleasures with more clarity and meaning. For those of us who had been fortunate enough to come back alive, we were enjoying the moments of discovering life all over again.

On May 24, Neal and I managed to finish all of our business in Nepal. We bid farewell to the Sherpas, concluded our business with the Ministry of Tourism, and made it to the airport, where we both were beginning a journey to Denver, Colorado, where Neal would transfer to Aspen and I would be met by friends. As we boarded the plane, I think we both thought that for a while the events of May 10 would be behind us.

Boukreev and Beidleman had just settled into their seats on Thai Airlines, preparing for the first leg of their trip, which would take them to Bangkok and from there to Los Angeles and then on to Denver. As Boukreev was buckling in, one of the flight attendants approached and said that some friends had asked to see him before he took off.

I did not know who could be looking for me and made some joke with Neal about Interpol seeking the Russian felon. I went into the waiting lounge and was immediately met by two journalists with television cameras who asked many ridiculous questions about my condition and about the "meaning" of my Everest experience. For fifteen minutes I spoke with those people. Insignificant, I thought. Insignificant.

Boukreev was perplexed by the media interest and frustrated by the questions. What had happened on the mountain was a tragedy, impossible to explain in the few minutes he had to spend with the reporters. His first major encounter with the working press had been an inconvenience. In the weeks to come some of the encounters became incomprehensible.

Between Bangkok and Los Angeles I slept, but was troubled by many dreams. I kept going to the summit on the brink of my strength or being called upon to rescue stranded climbers without the power to reach them. The dreams, always with different stories, had the same themes. Climbers in trouble who were barely within the reach of my ability to get to them.

Finally arriving in Santa Fe, New Mexico, where he had been invited by a friend to rest and prepare for his fall return to the Himalaya, Boukreev slept most of the first several days he was in town, sometimes for as many as twenty hours straight, and the dreams continued.

The dreams did not stop with my arrival in Santa Fe, and my sleep was fitful. When I would awaken and have breakfast, I would be tired from my dreams and return to bed, where the dreams would begin again. Always I was searching, trying to find people. Then the phone would ring, and I would be awakened. Somehow, although I thought I had found some privacy, the press had located me in the United States.

The first journalist to find Boukreev was Peter Wilkinson, a contributing editor for *Men's Journal*, who called the morning of June 4 as Boukreev was having breakfast. Wilkinson explained to Boukreev that he wanted to do an on-the-spot interview and led with a couple of pointed questions. Boukreev, taken somewhat aback by the rapid-fire questions and having troubling fielding them with his limited English, covered the mouthpiece and asked for advice. "What am I to do? I don't know this person or what is his purpose."

Struggling to understand the questions, wanting to help Wilkinson, Boukreev continued with the interview and then gave up in frustration. His English was not good enough to keep up with the complexities of Wilkinson's questions.

I didn't want to remain private about these matters, because I understood this journalist was working hard and trying to understand the story from my professional perspective, but I wanted to be understood clearly.

Boukreev negotiated a plan, agreeing to continue the interview if a Russian interpreter could be brought to Wilkinson's office. Eager to get his interview, Wilkinson called back the next day, an interpreter on the line, and Boukreev tried again. Struggling as hard as he had the day before, but this time in his native language, Boukreev hung up the phone, exasperated. "They know nothing of the mountain. I speak better English than she speaks Russian!"

Looking at a faxed transcription of the interview Wilkinson sent him for review, Boukreev threw up his hands. "This is impossible! This is no good! No good!" His answers to the questions had become garbled in their translation. Wilkinson was told that the interview was unusable, with so many errors that Boukreev could not allow it to be used.

My retelling of the incident and my attempts to answer the questions aggravated my dreams, and I struggled to sleep without the story in my head.

Wilkinson faxed his questions to Boukreev and asked him to respond when he felt comfortable that he had understood them.

On the morning of June 7, I flew from Albuquerque to Seattle and went immediately to Jane Bromet's house and continued my work for Pete Wilkinson. On the next day, just before I was to go to a public memorial service for Scott, I faxed what I was able to do, incomplete as it was.

At the service, many people had come from all corners of the world to honor the memory of Scott. His family and friends were very kind to me even in their grief and thanked me for my efforts. I thanked them for their words, but it was difficult. I was devastated inside, disconnected from the reality of the memorial. I had done everything I could do, but I had been unable to save the lives of Scott and Yasuko Namba. For me this memory was difficult, and I stayed very much to myself on that day, having little desire to meet or talk with my many friends who were there.

The next day there was another service, a private one dedicated to remembering Scott. His parents and friends spoke intimately of his work and life, and like the day before, it was difficult for me. I found it very hard to sit and found myself pacing and looking at an exhibit of some of Scott's photographs. Scott and I were similar in many ways, different in others; we had our differences and misunderstandings, but I had much respect for him as a climber and as a man. In five years, perhaps even less, I thought, it may be that he will be remembered only by his family and closest friends, but I hoped that everything positive that he brought with him, that surrounded him, would live on in mountaineering. In his relationships with his fellow climbers and his clients, he brought an enthusiasm and an energy that captured people. He was perhaps more of a romantic than a businessman, and I appreciated that in him. His strength, love of life, and benevolence awoke something in me, and I hoped that in difficult times I could remember what he brought to climbing, that some of his ways could become more of a part of my own way of being.

To Boukreev's surprise and dismay, the memorial services for Scott Fischer did not bring any relief from the press. Several journalists attended, and Boukreev did his best to respond to their inquiries. *Life* and ABC's "Turning Point" asked for interviews, and Boukreev, making his best effort to make himself understood, spoke with them, hoping that what he could contribute would somehow answer the question that everyone was asking: What had happened? Boukreev had only pieces of the story; he was still struggling to understand for himself what had gone wrong.

Another interview in which he participated was with Jon Krak-auer, who was buttonholing expedition members to get their sto-ries. Boukreev, recalling the interview, said that he found it narrowly focused and that Krakauer had seemed frustrated by the limitations of his English. In an effort to better communicate his story to Krakauer, Boukreev gave him a photocopy of the an-swers he had offered to Pete Wilkinson's questions. In that copy was Boukreev's answer to a question that Wilkinson had asked about Boukreev's meeting with Scott Fischer above the Hillary Step as Scott was ascending, making his way to the summit:

> "Scott came up and we talked. Up to the summit he had about one-half or one hour to go. I don't know his speed. Scott was the boss and I felt he could make his decisions himself. He could stop and wait for clients or go on. What did I think? Scott was Scott. He was responsible for the expedition. He had great natural ability. He was very strong. No one feels very well at that altitude. He went on to the summit. I don't know. When I asked him how he felt, he said not very well, but it was okay. One had to know Scott. Everything was always okay with him. He was a strong climber, one of the strongest in America, therefore it was difficult to foresee the situation with Scott. I had to think of the clients, of the people, but I never thought that something could happen to Scott, and I talked to him about the situation with the clients mostly and I told him they all felt good. I asked him, with my concerns and in my position, what did he want me to do?—What did he say?—We discussed the need to have support below. We talked about my descent. He said that he considered it a good plan. That everything was good at that moment. My position was I felt that it would not be good if I stood around freezing, waiting. I would be more useful if I returned to Camp IV in order to be able to take oxygen up to returning climbers or to go help them if some became weak in the descent. If you are immobile at

that altitude, you lose strength in the cold, and then you are unable to do anything."

In late July, Boukreev obtained his copy of the Krakauer article and, coincidentally, on the same day Martin Adams arrived in Santa Fe to visit with Boukreev. They hadn't seen each other since Kathmandu. In the last hour of daylight on a summer evening, sitting on a patio around a large circular table with friends, Boukreev and Adams listened as the article was read aloud. When Krakauer referred to him, Boukreev leaned forward, trying to understand the words and their meaning: "Boukreev had returned to Camp IV at 4:30 P.M., before the brunt of the storm, having rushed down from the summit without waiting for clients—extremely questionable behavior for a guide."

Boukreev looked around the table, wondering if the people around him had heard the words as he had.

Scott authorized my going down, to be ready to go back up. This was the plan. It worked. I don't understand why he would write this.

As Krakauer's article continued, he implied that had Boukreev descended with clients, they might not have had the problems they did coming down, and that suggestion was devastating.

I had no clear idea that the weather was a potential problem until I was well down the mountain. My concern, as was Scott's, was that the climbers' oxygen supplies were going to run out. I did the job Scott wanted me to do. If I had been farther up the mountain when the full force of the storm hit, I think it is likely I would have died with the clients. I honestly do. I am not a superman. In that weather, we all could possibly have died.

Boukreev excused himself from the table and went into his friend's house to retrieve his Russian-English dictionary. When he returned, he thumbed through it, looking up words as the reading continued: "Boukreev's impatience on the descent more plausibly resulted from the fact that he wasn't using bottled oxygen and was relatively lightly dressed and therefore *had* to get down."

This time Boukreev said nothing when he left the table, but he returned within a few moments, some photographic prints in his hand. As he laid them on the table amongst the wine bottles, Martin Adams picked one up, one of him and Boukreev taken on the summit. "Toli," Adams said, "I don't need the pictures. You were as well dressed on the mountain as anyone I know. I'm the one who gave you the climbing suit." Taking a cigar out of his mouth, Adams shook his head. "This guy! This guy is so much smoke!" The picture that Adams had in his hand showed Boukreev in the climbing suit Adams had purchased as a gift for him when, just before the expedition, Adams had bought the exact same model for himself.

On the issue of Boukreev's climbing without oxygen, Boukreev was just as puzzled as he had been over the issue of how he was dressed.

I have climbed mountains for more than twenty-five years, and only once on an assault of an 8,000er did I ever use it. Never has it been a problem for me, and Scott approved my climbing without it.

As the article concluded, Krakauer offered a dramatic narrative describing how, just above Camp IV, he had encountered one of Rob Hall's guides, Andy Harris, and had a conversation with him about the danger of an icy slope that stood between them and the safety of their tents. Harris had slipped and fallen down the slope, Krakauer reported, and then had presumably walked off the face of Lhotse and vanished forever. Adams, listening quietly as the section was read, interrupted and spoke, a measure of cynicism in his voice. "That was me. That was me he saw above Camp IV, and I've told him that." In the weeks prior to Adams's coming to Santa Fe, Krakauer had called Adams and asked if it could have been Adams and not Andy Harris that Krakauer, on his descent, had encountered above Camp IV. Adams hung up and reread an interview that Krakauer had granted shortly after the disaster. Considering again Krakauer's physical description of events above Camp IV and drawing upon his own memory, Adams came to the conclusion that Krakauer had made a mistake. He called Krakauer back to say that he had become convinced that the person Krakauer had actually encountered above Camp IV had not been Andy Harris, that it had been him. When Krakauer seemed reluctant to accept Adams's conclusion, Adams said, "Let's make a bet. Ninety-nine to one. It was me." Krakauer, according to Adams, wanted more evidence and did not take the bet.

Boukreev was stunned and offended by the article, but more, he was baffled. What possible motive could Krakauer have for representing him as he had? Boukreev had given Krakauer a copy of the answers he had offered to Wilkinson, and in those responses was an explanation for his descent ahead of the clients. Had Boukreev misunderstood Krakauer's questions? Had Krakauer misunderstood him? Moreover, when Boukreev had been invited to the office of *Outside* in early June to discuss the potential use of some of his expedition photographs to illustrate Krakauer's article, he had provided the editorial department of *Outside* a copy of the same Wilkinson interview that he had given to Krakauer.

According to Boukreev, no one at *Outside* fact-checked with him the details of his discussion with Scott Fischer above the Hillary Step or the manner in which he was dressed on summit day. On July 31, Boukreev, with the help of friends, wrote a letter to Mark Bryant, the editor of *Outside*.

July 31, 1996

Mr. Mark Bryant, Editor
Outside
400 Market St.
Santa Fe, New Mexico 87501
USA

Dear Mr. Bryant:

I am writing you because I think Jon Krakauer's "Into Thin Air," which appeared in your September, 1996 issue, was unjustly critical of my decisions and actions on Mount Everest on May 10, 1996. While I have respect for Mr. Krakauer, share some of his opinions about high altitude guiding, and believe he did everything within his power to assist fellow climbers on that tragic day on Everest, I believe his lack of proximity to certain events and his limited experience at high altitude may have gotten in the way of his ability to objectively evaluate the events of summit day.

My decisions and actions were based upon more than twenty years of high-altitude climbing experience. In my career I have summited Mount Everest three times. I have twelve times summited mountains of over 8,000 meters. I have summited seven of the world's fourteen mountains over 8,000 meters in elevation, all of those without the use of supplementary oxygen. This experience, I can appreciate, is not response enough to the questions raised by Mr. Krakauer, so I offer the following details.

After fixing the ropes and breaking the trail to the summit, I stayed at the top of Everest from 1:07 P.M. until approximately 2:30 P.M., waiting for other climbers to summit. During that time only two [Mountain Madness] client climbers made the top. They were Klev Schoening, seen in the summit photograph (pages 46–47) taken by me, and Martin Adams, both of them from Scott Fischer's expedition. Concerned that others were not coming onto the summit and because I had no radio link to those below me, I began to wonder if there were difficulties down the mountain. I made the decision to descend.

Just below the summit I encountered Rob Hall, the expedition leader from New Zealand, who appeared to be in good shape. Then I passed four of Scott Fischer's client climbers and four of his expedition's Sherpas, all of whom were still ascending. They all appeared to be all right. Then, just above the Hillary Step, I saw and talked with Scott Fischer. He was tired and laboring, but said he was just a little slow. There was no apparent sign of difficulty, although now I have begun to suspect that his oxygen supply was, then, already depleted. I said to Scott that the ascent seemed to be going slowly and that I was concerned descending climbers could possibly run out of oxygen before their return to Camp IV. I explained I wanted to descend as quickly as possible to Camp IV in order to warm myself and gather a supply of hot drink and oxygen in the event I might need to go back up the mountain to assist descending climbers. Scott, as had Rob Hall immediately before him, said "OK" to this plan. I felt comfortable with the decision, knowing that four Sherpas, Neal Beidleman (like me, a guide), Rob Hall, and Scott Fischer would be bringing up the rear to sweep the clients to Camp IV. Understand, at this time there were no clear indications that the weather was going to change and deteriorate as rapidly as it did.

Given my decisions: (1) I was able to return to Camp IV by shortly after 5:00 P.M. (slowed by the advancing storm), gather supplies and oxygen, and by 6:00 P.M. begin my solo effort in the onset of a blizzard to locate straggling climbers; and (2) I was able, finally, to locate lost and huddled climbers, resupply them with oxygen, offer them warming tea, and provide them the physical support and strength necessary to get them to the safety of Camp IV.

Also, Mr. Krakauer raised a question about my climbing without oxygen and suggested that perhaps my effectiveness was compromised by that decision. In the history of my career, as I have detailed it above, it has been my practice to climb without supplementary oxygen. In my experience it is safer for me, once acclimatized, to climb without oxygen in order to avoid the sudden loss of acclimatization that occurs when supplementary oxygen supplies are depleted.

My particular physiology, my years of high-altitude climbing, my discipline, the commitment I make to proper acclimatization, and the knowledge I have of my own capacities have always made me comfortable with this choice. And, Scott Fischer was comfortable with that choice as well. He authorized me to climb without supplementary oxygen.

To this I would add: As a precautionary measure, in the

event that some extraordinary demand was placed upon me
on summit day, I was carrying one (1) bottle of
supplementary oxygen, a mask, and a reductor.* As I was
ascending, I was for a while climbing with Neal Beidleman.
At 8,500 meters, after monitoring my condition and feeling
that it was good, I elected to give my bottle of oxygen to
Neal, about whose personal supply I was concerned. Given
the power that Neal was able to sustain in his later efforts
to bring clients down the mountain, I feel it was the right
decision to have made.

Lastly, Mr. Krakauer raises a question about how I was
dressed on summit day, suggesting I was not adequately
protected from the elements. A review of summit day
photographs will show that I was clothed in the latest,
highest-quality high-altitude gear, comparable, if not better,
than that worn by the other members of our expedition.

In closing, I would like to say that since May 10, 1996,
Mr. Krakauer and I have had many opportunities to reflect
upon our respective experiences and memories. I have
considered what might have happened had I not made a
rapid descent. My opinion: Given the weather conditions
and the lack of visibility that developed, I think it likely I
would have died with the client climbers that, in the early
hours of May 11, I was able to find and bring to Camp IV,
or I would have had to have left them on the mountain to
go for help in Camp IV where, as was in the reality of
events that unfolded, there was nobody able or willing to
conduct rescue efforts.

I know Mr. Krakauer, like me, grieves and feels
profoundly the loss of our fellow climbers. We both wish
that events had unfolded in a very different way. What we
can do now is contribute to a clearer understanding of
what happened that day on Everest in the hope that the
lessons to be learned will reduce the risk for others who,

---

*Boukreev meant here "regulator."

like us, take on the challenge of the mountains. I extend
my hand to him and encourage that effort.

My personal regards,
Anatoli Nikoliavich Boukreev

One of *Outside*'s senior editors, Brad Wetzler, responded on
August 1, saying that the letter was too long to run in their
"Letters" section, but offered to edit Boukreev's response to
four hundred words to fit their format. Boukreev declined.

2 August 1996

Mr. Brad Wetzler
Outside
400 Market Street
Santa Fe, NM 87501

Dear Mr. Wetzler:

In considering your memo of 1 August (attached), asking
that I reduce my response to 400 words, I feel much the
same way Jon did when he was being besieged by the
media. What I have offered in response to Jon's allegations
is not "reducible to sound bites." It comes to this.

Jon's comments about my decision to descend were
written when he had on his desk the transcript of an
interview where I explained my decision and the fact that
Scott Fischer had approved it. This same interview was in
the hands of your editorial/fact-checking staff before the
September issue went to press. Certainly, Jon is entitled to
his own speculations, opinions, and analyses, but I have to
wonder, with contrary information at hand, why he didn't
bother to phone me and attempt to clarify matters. My
whereabouts were known; he had contact telephone and
fax numbers.

Jon's comments about the way I was dressed on summit day are clearly invalidated by a simple glance at photographs taken on summit day. I cannot imagine how this became an issue in his mind.

Jon's comments about my not using oxygen are equally as confounding. Anyone familiar with my climbing résumé, which I had provided to Jon, would know that it is my habit to climb without oxygen and that I have performed exceptionally without it. Too, as I mentioned in my letter of 31 July, I was authorized to climb without oxygen, because Scott Fischer was comfortable with my climbing history and capacities. I think my work and efforts on 10 and 11 May, 1996 are an endorsement of Scott's confidence.

When you consider the comments in their entirety, you wonder. With evidence on his desk that was either contrary to the allegation made or begging of their veracity, why weren't facts checked, calls made, clarifications sought?

In writing my letter of 31 July and in responding to your memo of 1 August, I in no way want to suggest that my actions or anyone else's on the mountain that day are above scrutiny. All of us, I know, have replayed the "what if" scenario a thousand times. What I do take issue with, as I've spelled it out, are analyses that have no basis in fact and innuendo.

If what was at issue here was the matter of a route map improperly drawn or an elevation improperly stated, I could live with the restriction of 400 words. But, more is at stake here, and I respectfully ask you to reconsider and run my letter in its entirety.

My personal regards,
Anatoli Boukreev

On August 2, Wetzler responded, offering again to edit Boukreev's original letter to help sharpen his "arguments" and to make it "probably" into a "more forceful piece of writing."

This time Wetzler offered a space of 350 words. Boukreev, again, declined.

5 August 1996
Mr. Brad Wetzler
Outside
400 Market Street
Santa Fe, NM 87501

Dear Mr. Wetzler:

Thank you for your letter of 2 August and your consideration of my request.

Your offer of an edit is generous, but there is no way in which I could possibly respond to Jon Krakauer in 350 words. The issues here are complex. They involve allegations which have no basis in fact, innuendo, matters of journalistic integrity and professionalism, expression of personal feeling, and my desire to encourage a fact-based analysis of events on Everest.

To edit my letter for the purposes of being argumentative or more forceful would be to dilute the details and compromise my intentions.

I appreciate your attention to this matter.

Anatoli Boukreev

Nine months later, in April of 1997, Jon Krakauer's book *Into Thin Air,* an expanded version of his earlier *Outside* article, appeared. Despite the extensive interviewing he had done after his original article, Krakauer's stance about Boukreev's role in the events on Everest had changed little. In the book, however, he quoted Boukreev's comments from the Wilkinson interview he had been provided in June 1996. "I stayed [on the summit] for about an hour. . . . It is very cold, naturally, it takes your strength. . . . My position was that I would not be good if I stood around freezing, waiting. I would be more useful if I returned to Camp Four in order to be able to take oxygen up to the returning climbers or to go up to help them if some became weak during the descent. . . . If you are immobile at that altitude, you lose strength in the cold, and then you are unable to do anything.''

Krakauer continues his narrative, saying that for "whatever reason, he raced down ahead of the group." As he had in his original article, Krakauer led readers to suspect that Boukreev had acted unilaterally, out of concern solely for his own well-being.

A comparison of Krakauer's quote to what Boukreev had said in his interview with Wilkinson (see page 212) reveals that Krakauer dropped out Boukreev's explanation for his early descent. "I asked him, with my concerns and in my position, what did he want me to do?—What did he say?—We discussed the need to have support below. We talked about my descent. He said that he considered it a good plan. That everything was good at that moment.''

Again, Boukreev was surprised at Krakauer's characterization of his descent, trying to fathom why Krakauer was ignoring the fact that he had not made an independent decision but had taken the action his expedition leader, Scott Fischer, had wanted. Boukreev was even more surprised after hearing about an interview that his coauthor, Weston DeWalt, had conducted in March 1997 with Jane Bromet, Fischer's publicist at the time of the tragedy and someone with whom Fischer had spoken about the details of expedition planning. The interview had gone in this way:

BROMET: You know there is something I want to tell you. I don't know if I should or not, but what happened with Anatoli going back up, that was, you know, one of the cards that got turned over; I mean, that was the plan.

DEWALT: What do you mean "the plan"?

BROMET: I mean Scott told me—you know, one of the sce-
            narios—that if there were problems coming down,
            Anatoli would make a rapid descent and come
            back up the mountain with oxygen, or whatever.

DEWALT: You're telling me that Scott told you this prior to
            the final assault?

BROMET: Yes, at Base Camp, yeah, several days before [I left
            Base Camp].

DEWALT: Just so I understand. Scott told you if they got into
            trouble, he would send Anatoli down to prepare
            to resupply the climbers coming down.

BROMET: Yes, that's what he told me.

DEWALT: When you were interviewed by Jon Krakauer, did
            you tell him this? Exactly what you told me?

BROMET: Yes.

On May 29, 1997, a review of Jon Krakauer's *Into Thin Air*
appeared in the *Wall Street Journal.* The highly regarded writer
and mountaineer Galen Rowell said of Krakauer's coverage of
Boukreev's role in the events on Everest:

> "Anatoli Boukreev comes off as an intransigent Russian
> guide who doesn't help clients and irresponsibly refuses to
> use supplementary oxygen. In this telling he emerges from
> the crisis more as an errant worker finally doing his job
> than as the mythical hero he would surely have become in
> a past era. While Mr. Krakauer slept and no other guide,
> client, or Sherpa could muster the strength and courage
> to leave camp, Mr. Boukreev made several solo forays into
> a blizzard in the dark at 26,000 feet to rescue three climb-
> ers near death. *Time* magazine failed to mention him in a
> three-page news story after a New York socialite implausibly
> wouldn't acknowledge that he saved her.
>
> "Mr. Boukreev is roundly criticized for descending far
> ahead of clients. Although Mr. Krakauer grants Mr. Bou-
> kreev certain strengths, he never paints the big picture of

one of the most amazing rescues in mountaineering history performed single-handedly a few hours after climbing Everest without oxygen by a man some describe as the Tiger Woods of Himalayan climbing. Mr. Boukreev has topped many of the world's highest peaks solo, in less than one day, in winter, and always without oxygen (because of his personal ethic). Having already done Everest twice, he foresaw problems with clients nearing camp, noted five other guides on the peak, and positioned himself to be rested and hydrated enough to respond to an emergency. His heroism was not a fluke.''

AFTERWORD

Scott Fischer, before departing for his 1996 Everest expedition, said to his office manager, Karen Dickinson, "Who knows what might happen up there?" And now we ask: What did happen up there?

Of the thirty-three climbers who ascended Mount Everest from its south side on May 10, 1996, only twenty-eight climbers returned. From the Mountain Madness expedition, Scott Fischer lost his life. From Rob Hall's Adventure Consultants expedition, Rob Hall, one of his guides, Andy Harris, and two of his clients, Doug Hansen and Yasuko Namba, lost their lives.

Three of the surviving climbers, Sandy Hill Pittman, Charlotte Fox, and Tim Madsen, narrowly escaped death; two of the survivors, Beck Weathers and Makalu Gau, suffered extensive frostbite and, later, the loss of extremities.

Lopsang Jangbu Sherpa's description* of Scott Fischer's condition in the evening hours of May 10 have strongly suggested

---

*Offered in the "debriefing" tapes recorded at the Everest Base Camp on May 15, 1996.

that Fischer had been stricken with HACE, high-altitude cerebral edema.* Whether or not Fisher had a pre-existing physical condition which contributed to his deterioration can only be a matter of speculation.

Fischer died approximately five hundred vertical meters above Camp IV. The heroic efforts of Lopsang, who struggled single handedly for more than five hours to get his friend and mentor down the mountain, have gone virtually unheralded.

Both Beidleman and Boukreev have wished they'd seen some definitive sign indicating serious distress on Fischer's part. Both have said that they would have made every attempt to turn him around if they'd had any idea of what was to come. Lopsang, after hearing of Fischer's death, blamed it entirely upon himself.†

Some pundits have looked for an explanation for Fischer's death in his personal history, mining his character as if a cause could be extracted from some flawed vein of his personality. Those explorations have done little more than denigrate a man whose life was no more complex than any of those who were on the mountain, or any of us who have chosen to write about the events of May 10, 1996. The "revelations" have contributed little to an understanding of what happened.

Fischer's deteriorating health, complicated apparently by a lack of oxgyen, the hour at which he was stricken, his position on the mountain, poor communications, the weather that arose and the conditions and abilities of his team members who could have offered help were, in combination, the factors that led to his death. To cite a specific cause would be to promote an om-

---

*HACE can strike anyone, anytime. Early in the expedition it struck Ngawang Topche Sherpa, one of the Mountain Madness Sherpas. All the efforts made to save his life, including his helicopter evacuation to a Kathmandu hospital, proved fruitless. In the month following his collapse at Camp II he died.

†With sadness it must be reported Lopsang Jangbu Sherpa never lived long enough to fully come to terms with the death of Scott Fischer. Less than four months after the death of his friend, Lopsang was killed in an avalanche while attached to an expedition on Lhotse.

niscience that only Gods, drunks, politicians, and dramatic writers can claim.

What is known is that one of the United States' most promising high-altitude guides died an early death. Several of the Mountain Madness climbers who signed up with Fischer, despite their individual problems with the expedition and how it was run, have said they would have made another climb with Fischer; that it should be remembered that they chose Fischer, it wasn't Fischer that had chosen them. Martin Adams said, "He was the rodeo king of high-altitude guides; we had our differences, but I trusted him; I would have gone with him again."

A year after Fischer's death, when you called his home and no one was there to answer the phone, you would hear his voice on the answering machine. When asked about this, his wife, Jeannie, said, "The kids like to call our number to hear their father's voice." The losses have been immense, and the full measure of the man is greatly missed.

As for the Mountain Madness clients who were imperiled in their descent and narrowly escaped with their lives, two factors seem to have significantly contributed: their delay in departing the summit and the problems encountered along the route of their descent, most notably the taking of valuable time to offer aid to Yasuko Namba, a Rob Hall client who had faltered on the fixed ropes and collapsed immediately above Camp IV. The time on the summit and the time lost while tending to the problems of Yasuko Namba had cost the Mountain Madness climbers more than an hour. At the bottom of the fixed ropes, at 8,200 meters, Camp IV (less than forty-five minutes away) had been visible for a moment and then the climbers were enveloped by the storm. Had they arrived an hour earlier, the situation could have developed very differently. Martin Adams said, "People mistakenly think it was the storm that caused the problem. It wasn't the storm that caused the problem; it was the time."

As for the deaths of Rob Hall, his guide Andy Harris, and Hall's two clients, Doug Hansen and Yasuko Namba, little light has been shed on their deaths by the surviving members of the

Adventure Consultants expedition. Why Hall was on the mountain so late with his client Doug Hansen, who it has been reported did not summit until after 4:00 P.M., has been a source of ongoing mystery. Jon Krakauer has speculated that his expedition leader may have been "playing chicken" with Scott Fischer, waiting to see who was "going to blink first and turn around," but by shortly after 3:00 P.M. Hall was aware that all of Fischer's clients had made the summit and Fischer was within tagging distance. If it had been a contest for Hall, the winner had been declared well before 4:00 P.M. Others, including members of Hall's expedition, have speculated that Hall's encouragement of Hansen to go for the summit had caused him to stretch his turn-around time well into the danger zone.

What happened to Harris and Hansen, also, can only be matters for speculation. Physical evidence, the discovery of Andy Harris's ice ax between the Hillary Step and the South Summit by members of the IMAX/IWERKS team that summited on May 23, have caused some to theorize that Harris had stopped his descent, headed back up the mountain to offer assistance to Hall (and perhaps Hansen), and had fallen off the mountain in the same exposed, unroped area where Jon Krakauer on his descent had foundered and Mike Groom had come to his aid.

As for Doug Hansen, all that is known is that Hall was with him above the Hillary Step, but was not with him when Hall bivouacked at the South Summit and was transmitting messages to his Base Camp. Somewhere between those two points Hansen had vanished.

The tragedy of Yasuko Namba's death is, perhaps, the most disturbing of all, but only because the evidence is so compelling that she, perhaps, could have survived. Struggling alone on the fixed ropes just above Camp IV, she had luckily been discovered by Neal Beidleman who, with the assistance of Tim Madsen, had managed to get her to the South Col. There, along with fellow expedition member Beck Weathers, she had huddled in the dogpile as the storm swirled around her. When Mike Groom, an Adventure Consultants guide, made his dash for Camp IV along with Beidleman, Schoening, and Gammelgaard, Namba, like Weathers, hadn't the strength to follow. Groom, when he found Camp IV, was unable to recruit members of his expedition for a rescue effort.

In Boukreev's forays into the storming black of the earliest hours of May 11, he'd brought what energy and oxygen he had to the situation. He'd asked for help from Rob Hall's expedition, but there wasn't any to be had. Neither he nor anyone else had enough power or reserves to deal with the problems of Namba. About his last crossing of the South Col, when he'd brought Pittman back to Camp IV, he's said, "I had my arms full with Sandy. I had no more energy left. If Tim had not been able to move under his own power, I would not have been able to help him. I think he would have died."

In the months since the deaths on Everest, much has been said and written about the events and personalities tangential to those losses, and it appears likely there will not be an end to those offerings anytime soon. There is an advantage to an open and ongoing debate, and the authors have contributed what they can to the discussions that should, most certainly, follow. As the debates continue, we would make the plea that questions be raised from the platform of known fact, not shouted from the dais of suspicion and rumor. The future of mountaineering, especially of commercially guided expeditions, can best be served by the truth.

EPILOGUE

THE RETURN TO EVEREST

In August 1996, Boukreev left the United States and returned to his family home in the Urals. Earlier in the summer, just after he attended memorial services for Scott Fischer, his mother had died.

I had endured enough of the controversy regarding Everest. I needed to make my peace at home, to visit my brothers and sisters and to mourn the loss of my mother. Finally, when I returned to my home in Kazakhstan, I was prepared to turn my face to the mountains. I felt unsuited for life anywhere else. I had committed myself to the 8,000-meter peaks I'd yet to climb, and I had to continue. It is a lonely and a strange life, inexplicable to some, but for me it is my home; it is my work.

Returning to Nepal, on September 25, 1996, Boukreev, alone, without the use of supplementary oxygen, summited Cho Oyu (8,201 meters) and on October 9 summited Shisha Pangma (North Summit) (8,008 meters).

During the fall climbing season, Boukreev stopped in Kathmandu to visit the offices of a friend, Ang Tshering Sherpa of Asian Trekking, where he was asked if he would consider consulting for an Indonesian team that was planning a spring assault on Mount Everest by the Southeast Ridge Route, the route that he had guided the year before for Scott Fischer. After much deliberation, Boukreev took on the role of lead climbing consultant.

The idea of leading an expedition to Everest was appealing for two reasons, because I had enormous unfinished emotional business on the mountain. For me it was important to return to the site of the terrible ordeal we had endured in the spring. Certain issues had become personally important. I wanted to somehow make a respectful burial of Scott's body and also of Yasuko Namba's body. What else can one do, when the best you could do in a bad situation was not enough to prevent some disaster?

With the Indonesians I was looking for the opportunity to work in a role that was congruent with the beliefs I have about climbing as a sport and a role that would allow me to make a living in the emerging commercial market of high-altitude mountaineering. I hoped I would be able to define and clarify this role as a coach and climbing team leader with the Indonesians.

Also, I have to admit my ego is as fragile as the next person's, and I felt fairly well maligned by the few voices that had captured the imagination of the American press. Had it not been for the support of European colleagues like Rolf Dujmovits and Reinhold Messner, I would have been depressed by the American perspective of what I had to offer my profession.

After meeting with Indonesian team organizers in Kathmandu in late November, I flew to Jakarta to meet with General Prabowo Subianto, the national coordinator of the expedition. In hard, graphic terms I laid out the prospect of success as a marginal expectation. In clear terms, I projected we had a 30 percent chance of summiting one individual. I also explained we had a fifty-fifty chance of losing someone on the mountain, odds that were unacceptable to me, personally. I suggested a year of training on progressively higher peaks. This suggestion was rejected out of hand.

I come from a tradition that promotes mountaineering as a reasonable sports endeavor, not as a game of Russian roulette; the death of a team member is always a failure that supersedes any summit success. There is an exponentially decreasing margin of safety for the amateur or even the well-conditioned amateur above eight thousand meters. I could not guarantee the safety of a group of men who had little or no mountaineering experience on the world's highest mountains. The Indonesians could buy the benefit of my experience, my advice, my services as lead climbing adviser, and as a member of a rescue team; but if they wanted the summit of Everest, they would have to take some responsibility for the hubris of this ambition with inexperienced men. General Prabowo assured me that his men were motivated, well conditioned, and they were committed to this objective even at the prospect of death. This was shocking in some way, but it was an honest response.

I outlined for myself a role that would give the Indonesians as much benefit from my experience as possible, but one that would still promote their independence. At the end we are each responsible for our ambition, and on Everest every bit of preparation you make will still leave you in short supply on summit day.

General Prabowo agreed the team would undertake training and conditioning before the expedition began. I knew we would need expedition consultants with excellent technical and high-altitude skill, who would function as advisers during training and acclimatization exercises and who could function as a rescue support team on summit day. The concept of a rescue team was important to me; I placed great emphasis on our role in this capacity. In my conversations with the general, I would not guarantee a summit success for any price.

I indicated I could not undertake the expedition if I was not given absolute control of the final summit-day decisions, and he had to accept the possibility that the condition of his men or conditions on the mountain would not allow us to proceed with a reasonably safe summit bid. I would make that decision. He also understood that the best rescue team cannot guarantee an effective rescue above eight thousand meters; but, if troubles arose, I was prepared to risk my life in this capacity. That was the basis of our deal.

Our training program would be to the point. During the coming winter, it would be possible to experience conditions of prolonged severe cold and wind, acclimatizing the team to six thousand meters. We would test endurance and mental discipline in the austere conditions we would confront on Everest. The training program would begin on December 15 in Nepal.

Thirty-four individuals, civilians with some climbing experience and military men who had no experience mountaineering but who were fit and disciplined, would make up the initial team. From this thirty-four, the best would be selected for the expedition. We would use health, endurance, ability, and attitude as our selection criteria. During this time the team would develop proficiency with the technical skills necessary to negotiate ropes and ladders and would practice basic mountaineering skills.

Communication was a huge problem last year, a problem I failed to completely appreciate until it was too late. Last year not only was the language barrier a source of personal frustration but the system of radio communication was not well thought out. Radios would be available for each team member this year. I recommended we have direct radio contact from Base Camp with support in Kathmandu. Also I requested we arrange for daily weather reports from the meteorological service at the Kathmandu airport. The military connection was helpful here, and these arrangements were made with the help of the Nepali Army in Kathmandu. Our expedition officer, Monty Sorongan, spoke English well. He would be the central contact in Kathmandu, coordinating communication between the mountain and the Kathmandu support service. English, it was agreed, would be our common language. With the climbing staff I wanted no misunderstandings, no omissions of opinion or impression between responsible parties because we had no common language.

As team leader, I wanted a solid, technically superior training staff, with a broad, deep experience in high-altitude rescue, and I wanted medical support at high altitude. I needed to be able to count on associates who could share my understanding and who would respect my impressions and opinions in critical situations. Likewise, I wanted the benefit of their expertise and some balance for my rather difficult personality. I looked for men with the same level of experience I wanted, men who could work on the mountain with or without oxygen; on whose strength and flexibility I could rely. I recruited the services of two respected Russian mountaineers, Vladamir Bashkirov and Dr. Evgeny Vinogradski. Forty-five-year-old Bashkirov, with more than fifteen years of experience in expedition organization to remote areas, and technical expertise on the great walls in the Pamirs and Caucasus, as well as six successful summit attempts on 8,000-meter peaks, two of those Everest, would be a great asset. He is a soft-spoken diplomat compared to me, with a good command of English. I would rely on his personable communication skills and good judgment throughout the expedition. He is a notable adventure cameraman and filmmaker in Russia. He would record the expedition on film for the Indonesians. Dr. Evgeny Vinogradski, fifty-year-old, seven-time champion climber in the Soviet Union with more than twenty-five years experience as a high-altitude climbing instructor and sports physician, would complete the instructor staff. Evgeny and I were on an '89 traverse of Kanchenjunga together. I count him a personal friend. His long history as an instructor and as a physician for athletes made him indispensable. His gentle good humor and steely calm in the worst situations is well known to me; the Old Eagle I call him. He has more than twenty 7,000-meter summits, and eight 8,000-meter summits to his credit; two of those are Everest, one as a personal guide on Everest.

Ang Tshering of Asian Trekking in Kathmandu provided all logistical support including the hiring of the Sherpa staff. We were fortunate to have the services of thirty-seven-year-old Apa Sherpa of Thami, seven-time summiter of Everest, as our sirdar and lead climbing Sherpa. The Sherpas would be accountable to Ang Tshering and to the Indonesian staff. They would provide the usual Base Camp support and would fix rope on the sections of the route above the Icefall, set up and supply camps up the mountain, and carry the extra oxygen we would need for team members on summit day. The division of labor would theoretically leave us free to deal with the climbing team or other difficult conditions on the route.

I left Jakarta for the United States on December 6. I had an appointment in the United States with doctors who would evaluate the damage to my face and eye, which had occurred in a bus accident in October.* Bashkirov and Vinogradski were left to supervise the training session on Paldor Peak in the Ganesh Himal, which began on December 15. Thirty-four climbers, half with no technical mountaineering skills, attempted Paldor (5,900 m); seventeen summited. They endured twenty-one days of slow acclimatization in the winter conditions of December in Nepal.

On January 10, expedition leaders Ang Tshering, Bashkirov, Vinogradski, and myself met in Kathmandu to coordinate plans and to begin team selection. Bashkirov and Vinogradski were not optimistic that more than the seventeen Paldor summiters would be in the final group for Everest. The groups had weeded out dramatically on Paldor.

We needed equipment. None of the men had satisfactory gear, and all expedition gear needed to be purchased as soon as possible. Arrangements were made for Monty Sorongan and Captain Rochadi, the military attaché, to fly to Salt Lake City, Utah, and attend an outdoor retailers show to meet with suppliers and fill our list. American companies such as Sierra Designs and Mountain Hardware were very helpful. They worked long and hard putting together our equipment orders in time for the expedition. Simone Moro of Italy helped expedition organizers purchase our One Sport boots. Not only did I want to avoid loss of life in this expedition, I wanted everyone to come home with feet and hands. Technical advances in clothing and footwear have made it far safer for the inexperienced to endure extreme temperatures. I saw what a difference good equipment could make last year. We were going to need every margin of safety for this group. Fortunately, expedition organizers were very cooperative and tried at every turn to follow our recommendations. Our gear was flown to Kathmandu with the help of the Thai Airlines cargo department, which now has a service to transport expedition equipment

---

*In late October 1996, after climbing Shisha Pangma, Boukreev was offered a ride on a Kazakh climbing team's bus traveling from Tashkent to his home in Almaty. It is presumed that the driver fell asleep at the wheel while driving late in the night. The bus sideswiped a transport truck, and the left side of the bus upon which Boukreev was sitting was sheared from the frame. The driver lost his left arm, and a young Kazakh climber sitting immediately in front of Boukreev was decapitated.

efficiently. It was shipped to arrive March 6; our departure date for Base Camp was March 12.

During January and February the entire thirty-four-member team went to Island Peak (6,189 m) for the second training exercise. Sixteen members summited, all of whom had summited Paldor. Team members spent twenty days in forty-below temperatures enduring strong winter winds. During three days and nights above six thousand meters in harsh conditions, team members were pushed to ascend and descend one thousand meters every day in less than five hours. It was the best we could do. Now I shake my head in disbelief: Paldor, Island Peak, Everest. I don't recommend this as a training program to anyone.

Back in Kathmandu, Bashkirov and Vinogradski made a list for Col Eadi. They rated the climbers by the criteria of speed, adjustment to altitude, general health, and attitude. They arranged the summiters in order of preference: one to sixteen. The military men, though inexperienced, were more focused, more disciplined, and showed greater motivation in difficult situations. Ten soldiers and six civilians were in the final group. We recommended a south-side summit attempt only; this idea was rejected by the Indonesians, who had hired Richard Pavlowski to head a north-side Everest team.* In the end, ten members would go with us to Everest Base Camp on the south side, and six would go to Tibet on the north with Richard. After Island Peak the teams had twenty-six days of rest. We would be the first team into the Khumbu. I wanted to be the first team on the mountain, the first to attempt the summit. I absolutely did not want to compete with other expeditions for the route on summit day.

The Russian helicopter lifted us out of the smog of Kathmandu toward Lukla on March 12. Ten members, three Russian climbing advisers, and sixteen Sherpas stepped onto the landing pad at Lukla (2,850 m). We were headed for Base Camp and the summit of the highest mountain on earth. What ambition!

I always return to Lukla with a feeling of relief. I love the mountains, it is here I am at home. You will not understand this com-

---

*An attempt from the north side was abandoned because of severe weather conditions.

punction unless you, too, have arrived in the early morning, dropped to some precipitous aerie by helicopter. Embraced by bony ribs of mountains jutting into the sky. Their jagged summits precisely articulated in the crystal air. You humbly apprehend in this majesty your smallness in the scheme of things. In seven days we would arrive in Base Camp. On that morning I knew as I always know, no matter what was before me, I was home, and this is the only life I am fit for.

There would be seventeen teams at Base Camp this year; I made a big effort to keep the group out of the usual Base Camp politics. There was a lot of brouhaha over who would fix the Icefall. The Sherpas from one or two expeditions fix the Icefall with ropes and ladders, and the expedition organizers get paid for their work. Colonialism dies hard. All the expeditions use this route, and the expedition leaders take the big money for use of the route from teams that don't contribute Sherpa help fixing the route. There was a brief lobby by the Pangboche Sherpa Cooperative to collect the big money this year. The competition for the ten to twenty thousand dollars is still too great. Henry Todd and Mal Duff pulled off the Icefall plum. Mal and a group of his Sherpas had hurriedly fixed the route we would use.

I foresee a time when the entire route to the summit of Everest will be fixed in advance by a team of climbing Sherpas. All expeditions will use this route and pay the Sherpas as contractors. The day will come when the Nepalis will control this mountain like the Americans control access to McKinley. But not without the machinations and protests of those who till now have benefited exorbitantly by the hard work of underpaid men.

Our team arrived at Base Camp on March 19. Due to the recent training sessions, we did not need acclimatization to this altitude. The Icefall was before us. This is always an important step in the psychological adjustment to the task of climbing Everest. It is jumping off into the unknown. The Icefall is predictably unstable. Each crossing is a gestalt in mastering your fear. Your attention is riveted to detail. For several hours you climb, continually crossing gaping crevasses on roped-together bridge ladders, winding ever up through the cascade of shifting blocks of ice the size of houses. On March 22 we ascended to Camp I with all members for one night of acclimatization. Our entire team did well. Though shaky at first on the route, by our second trip they were moving with confidence at a much faster pace.

That obstacle mastered, we settled into the routine of climb and rest that is acclimatization. After two days' rest, in Base Camp, on the twenty-sixth we ascended to Camp I at 6,000 meters, spent the night, and on the twenty-seventh ascended directly to Camp II at 6,500 meters. We stayed two nights in Camp II, making active acclimatization up to a height of 6,800 meters. On the twenty-ninth we descended to Base Camp. There were no health problems with any members or staff at this time. We rested at Base Camp for three days. Our third acclimatization exercise began on April 1. We ascended directly to Camp II in eight hours. There we spent two nights. April 4, we ascended to 7,000 meters and returned to Camp II. April 5 we rested in Camp II. On April 6 we ascended to Camp III at 7,300 meters. The fixed line to Camp III had been worked out by Apa and our team of Sherpas during the days of progressive acclimatization by team members. April 7 was a rest day for members at Camp III.

At this juncture the first problems in our organizational structure surfaced. The Sherpas were not under my control. They had been hired as support and we had agreed to certain duties: fixing line, establishing camps, and carrying supplies. Because we were the first on the mountain, there was a huge burden of work without the usual help of other expedition Sherpas. Apa was unhappy with me. Our Sherpas alone could not keep up with the work that needed to be done to keep the team moving steadily higher on the mountain. I understood the stress I was placing on Apa, but the limited skill and depth of experience in the Sherpa team was slowing our progress. I had fully intended to have our climbing team sleep at the South Col and ascend to a height of 8,200 meters in active acclimatization. I had also decided to establish a Camp V at 8,500 meters to deal with the possible problem of slow descent or bad weather. Due to the small mutiny now in the Sherpa contingent, I had to abandon this plan for the time being. As a compromise, I helped Apa with the route and fixed line from Camp III to the Yellow Band at 7,500 meters. April 8 we climbed with eight members to the level of the Yellow

Band and returned to Camp III. We spent the night, and April 9 we descended to Base Camp.

We began to see a difference in team members' performance and health. The altitude and effort had the effect of natural selection. The civilian climbers were less motivated and focused than the military climbers. In spite of their lack of experience, three were now obviously the stronger candidates for the summit team. They continued to move with relative ease and were tolerating the altitude without problem. They were still very motivated to succeed on the mountain. Descending, we noticed further deterioration in the performance of team members while our three strong members descended directly from Camp III to Base Camp with no obvious difficulty. The three men we had left were thirty-one-year-old Misirin Serjan, twenty-five-year-old Asmujiono Prajurit and twenty-nine-year-old Iwan Setiawan Letnan. Bashkirov, Vinogradski, and I felt with the deteriorating Sherpa support and the obvious differences in the physical condition and performance of team members, we were set on a summit team of three members, three climbing guides, and all Sherpa support that was healthy and capable.

We returned to Base Camp on April 9 for a week of rest. I firmly believe in low-altitude recuperation before a summit assault. I had team members descend to the forest village of Deboche at 3,770 meters for a full week of rest and recuperation. The green of the lush forest and the air saturated with oxygen restores the human psyche like nothing else. Here you completely escape the desolation of Base Camp, and after three weeks of effort in this icy wasteland your mind and body long for some relief.

I impressed on the military liaison officer, Captain Rochadi, the need to establish Camp V with two tents, ten bottles of O_2, and sleeping bags and mats. I expected him to negotiate with Apa and our team of Sherpas to accomplish this in the seven days of our absence. Apa is an extraordinary man, a hard worker, but he now had eight of sixteen men who were still fit to function. It is impossible for one man to take on the physical task necessary to promote the whole expedition's success. His previous experience had been as a member of other strong Sherpa teams, and here he had been left to hire men of his choice, and many were family or friends who could not accomplish their fair share of the work. In the end only eight of our sixteen Sherpas were able to assist us. This weak point in the organizational structure and ineffective control of the situation by the Indonesian team organizers was an ongoing threat to the effectiveness of our assault plan and our elaborate backup safety plans.

I blame no one here. I know from other expeditions, it takes years of repeated ascents and consistent monetary support to develop a team of Sherpas who can work together in equal strength and skill to assist an expedition.

The choices for us now were to line up with the other expeditions on the route or go up early and have the mountain to ourselves. After last year I had no intention of standing in line for a disaster. You have enough opportunity to face your own mistakes and shortcomings without taking on anyone else's. This manpower crisis worked itself out, but not optimally. Apa always tried, giving more of himself than he expected of others.

In Deboche, I left members for five days and traveled to Kathmandu to have a cracked filling in one of my teeth repaired. The ravages of time, I suppose, tell on us all. I had many things on my mind: the personal memories that haunted me; how I would function at altitude after the accident; and now this problem with my teeth. These were annoying drains on my energy.

The trip to Kathmandu was an unwelcome interruption of my concentration. I stupidly forgot my park permit and had to jump the fence in the middle of the night to get out of Sagarmatha National Park to catch the helicopter in Lukla. In Kathmandu I was quite fortunate to have the service of the American embassy dentist. I am grateful for his quick attention to my problem.

The team arrived rested and ready at Base Camp on April 21, and we gathered for a ceremony of prayer and supplication. The Indonesians always remembered their God, much like the Sherpas in their morning offerings to the mountain. I appreciate this respectfulness. The faces of team members and the summit group were serious and concentrated during our ceremony. The rest of the day was spent in private organization. It is a tense time, full of expectation. A meditative calm always comes over me, and I have an excitement for the challenge ahead.

I knew Camp V had not been established. Apa assured me it would be supplied as we ascended on summit day. We made arrangements with the Russian Lhotse team members for backup emergency support if necessary. They were now at Camp III acclimatizing. We would leave the second-choice summit team at Camp II with Sherpas for support at our next rung down the ladder. Bashkirov, Vinogradski, Apa, and I would carry radios on the assault. One or two of us would be with the team members at all times. We would have two Sherpas at the South Col with a radio, and radio contact with the Russians at Camp III and our team members at Camp II and Base Camp.

Weather reports from Kathmandu were encouraging. We were at the end of a small weather disturbance, but the five days ahead looked stable. *Stable,* you understand, is a relative term. At the summit of Mount Everest you are at the apex of long river valleys. The gorges become steeper with intervals of short flat plains of alluvium as the altitude increases. The increase in daytime temperatures condenses moisture in these valleys, and this moves naturally up the gorges to the summits of the mountains in the afternoons. You can always expect wind and some clouds around the summit in the afternoons. At eight thousand meters even these benign weather changes can be a challenge. We expected no malignant changes in the next few days, but the normal weather pattern would have to be respected. We knew we would be slow; Camp V at 8,500 meters was our answer to that unremediable problem.

At twelve midnight in the light of the full moon on April 22, three Russians and six Indonesians left the safety of Base Camp for our journey to the unknown. We ascended directly to Camp II. Our sturdy Indonesian team was moving well, six hours to Camp II with no problems. We rested that day, April 23, at Camp II. On April 24 we left the second summit team and Sherpas at Camp II. Bashkirov, Vinogradski, and I with Misirin, Asmujiono, and Iwan moved to Camp III. Team members were independent, they appeared strong, they needed no emotional reassurance or idle chatter for distraction. April 24, there were strong winds above on the South Col. We contacted Captain Rochadi at Base Camp. He contacted the weather service in Kathmandu, which reported that the winds did not indicate a serious weather change. The next two days the winds would likely be less fierce. We decided to keep all members at Camp III and the Sherpas would descend to Camp II. The decision on the Sherpas' movement was Apa's call. Apa reassured me he would see to establishing the emergency camp on our summit day. We rested April 24. Between 3 and 5 P.M. on April 25, all the team arrived at the South Col. The Indonesian members climbed to the South Col with oxygen. They appeared in good shape to us at the South Col. They were coherent, coordinated, and self-motivated.

During our summit bid, all Indonesian members would carry two bottles of oxygen, using it continuously at two liters per minute during the summit attempt. Our Sherpas would carry three extra bottles of oxygen for each team member. They would be using oxygen on the summit attempt as well. Conditions on the route were such that trail-breaking would be a huge energy expenditure. The snow was thigh-deep in some places and was knee-deep from 8,100 meters to 8,600 meters. Because we were the first expedition on the route, all ropes on the route would have to be fixed. Bashkirov, Vinogradski and I decided to carry two bottles of oxygen each for the ascent and requested that Apa have the Sherpas carry two additional bottles for each of us.

There were three reasons why I decided to use oxygen on this summit attempt. I have no dogmatic commitment to use or not to use oxygen. The big problem came in '96 when no one, not the guides or the clients, were able to function without the use of oxygen. That fact actually increased the potential for disaster.

The first reason I considered oxygen this year was my health. In 1996 I had successfully climbed three 8,000-meter peaks in the fall and winter of '96. I underwent a strenuous training program in January, February, and March. Before the 1997 season I had a serious accident, which left me with nagging concerns about my response to high altitude. My training program was completely different in the winter months before the expedition. I had several operations to recover from, and I spent a great deal of time organizing the details of this expedition. I did not feel I had the same reserve of power that I had going into the expedition of '96. The week before our ascent I had a tooth abcess and tooth extraction and I was recovering from the operation as we left for the summit.

The second reason evolved out of the expedition acclimitization program. I worked in '96 up to the South Col, fixing line without the use of oxygen for several days. This year, because of the manpower shortage with our Sherpa team, we were not able to spend the night of acclimitization at the South Col. I feel this is a crucial adjustment. This 24-hour period at 7,900 m without oxygen gives your body the opportunity to adapt to the stress of this altitude. It is not so important if you use oxygen to the summit, but generally I feel it is a very wise step in the acclimitization program. I was not able to spend the time at 7,900 m that would have reassured me that my body was functioning with its normal response to altitude.

The third reason, when we got to the South Col, we found the conditions on the route were very difficult. The snow was from two to three feet deep in places all along the route. I had only eight Sherpas functioning. I needed an emergency camp established. I could not ask the Sherpas to break trail and to carry heavy loads. Trailbreaking in these conditions is brutal work, exhausting work.

We had eight Sherpas at the South Col. Only Apa and Dawa would go with us to the summit, leaving the rest to shuttle supplies to the 8,500-meter emergency camp. Apa continued to reassure me that the supply of Camp V was under control and that I need not concern myself with this portion of the work. Bashkirov, Vinogradski, and I knew we would have to conserve oxygen, and we knew we would have to be ready to work without oxygen. The numbers simply did not add up. A bottle of oxygen will usually supply you at two liters per minute, which is a moderate flow, for six hours; at one liter it is double that. We had a lot of gear to get up the hill and a long trail to break in deep snow. I knew we were in for some hard work.

We left the South Col at twelve o'clock midnight on April 26. I began to use O_2 at one liter. I went to the lead and broke trail. I felt it was unfair to ask the Sherpas with their heavy loads to do this work. The trail was slow and difficult. Vinogradski and Bashkirov conserved their power and followed after with the Indonesians. By 8,300 meters I realized our speed was the same as last year. I was out ahead, Apa behind me. But the team was quite slow. I continued breaking trail until 8,600 meters. After nine hours of trudging through thigh-deep snow, I arrived at the South Summit fatigued.

Below me, Apa fixed line on the steep section of the route between 8,600 and 8,700 meters. This is the section just below and up to the South Summit. The entire team arrived at the South Summit at eleven in the morning. We discussed the situation with Apa. Apa suggested I go to the summit, breaking trail. I asked Apa for rope. He informed me we had no more rope. I was tired from trail-breaking. The effort you expend at this altitude is a brutal toll on ambition and physical condition. I did not feel strong enough to safely fix this section of route, piecing together fragments of old line. I was incredulous . . . where was the rope? Apa informed me he had used the last hundred meters of rope on a section of route that did not usually need rope. Because of the unstable snow I felt we needed to fix that section to secure our descent. The margins up here are this close. The shadows of problems you perceive down below, at this moment on summit day, become the consuming problems that predict your success or failure. You can bitch and moan now or you can deal with it. The dozens of conversations where I was reassured my equipment requirements would be covered evaporated.

Apa offered to go down and recover the line. I felt time was now of the essence. The clock was ticking and we had to go forward or go down. Apa, realizing this mistake regarding our supply of rope could compromise the whole effort of the expedition, did a brave thing. He went out and fixed the line with our remaining forty meters of rope and old pieces of rope exposed on the route from previous expeditions. I gratefully had a moment to recover. I began to notice a general improvement in my condition and power.

We understood from Dawa Sherpa when he arrived that we did now in fact have extra oxygen and a tent at 8,500 meters. Apa had pieced together line to the top of the Hillary Step. Our members so far were in fair shape. It was a little after 12:30 P.M. when Apa cleared the Hillary Step. The weather was holding, the emergency camp was set. Bashkirov, Vinogradski, and I decided to attempt the summit even though we would be very late in arriving, about three o'clock in the afternoon.

Misirin, while slow, was still functioning on his own. Asmujiono was moving well but now had the focus of a zombie, his consciousness somewhere deep inside. Iwan was slow and his coordination was beginning to falter; he was still functioning mentally. Misirin appeared overall in the best shape. Misirin, we thought, was the most likely to succeed. All the men had this highly focused determination. Each man wanted the opportunity to summit. I was in favor of going on with only one man, turning the others back. I allowed myself to be convinced we could postpone this crucial decision till above the Hillary Step. I assigned Asmujiono to Dr. Vinogradski because I felt his mental deterioration would be a critical factor, and I wanted a continuous medical assessment of his condition.

Bashkirov and Misirin went out first, then Iwan and me, and after, Asmujiono and Dr. Vinogradski. The ridge was quite different from last year; there was much snow and it was steeper. Iwan was moving slowly; he fell at one point, tenuously stopping on the old fixed rope. I began to show him how to use his ice ax properly on the ridge. Here I realized I was dealing with a man who had never seen snow until four months ago. We had expected the benefit of good ropes, which make an ice ax redundant in crossing an established trail on a ridge. Now here I was giving lessons on technique to this brave, determined young man as he struggled back onto the route. I can only wonder what this experience meant to these men. I am a sportsman; I will never think of the summit of a mountain as an achievement worth the sacrifice of a life. These soldiers were of a completely different mind-set. They were more committed to success than to life.

I focused on the task at hand as Iwan struggled back onto the ridge. We moved slowly on the ridge, and I came to the bottom of the Hillary Step. Here I confronted the body of a man.* He lay entangled in the ropes at the bottom of the Hillary Step, his crampons in the way as you ascend this last technical portion of the route. I could recognize no features. The conditions here are so harsh, I could only say for certain that his down suit was blue. I could not focus on this

---

*Boukreev had discovered the body of Bruce Herrod, a member of the South African Johannesburg *Sunday Times* Expedition, who had disappeared in 1996.

man, nor could any others of the climbing team. For this I am sorry. Respect is always due to the fallen. Yet here I was with the last flickering light of life of these three Indonesian men to guard. Our situation was far from stable.

I reached the top of the Hillary Step, Iwan and Asmujiono coming slowly behind me at the end of the ridge. I spoke with Bashkirov. We had to decide whether to turn the other climbers back and proceed only with Misirin. Apa and Dawa had gone on to the summit. Asmujiono climbed the Hillary Step. Vinogradski arrived at the top of the Hillary Step. He had tried to turn Iwan back, but he was now struggling up the Hillary Step. No one was willing to admit defeat. I was worried that these men were coming to the end of their power. It is one thing to go forward, another to get down. I knew they would have to move under their own power. We had come slowly to within one hundred meters of the summit. I gave this advice. I spoke with Iwan and Asmujiono. I recommended they stop and begin to go down. They refused.

We all moved off toward the summit. I went ahead and encountered Apa and Dawa thirty meters from the summit. I discussed my fears concerning the deteriorating condition of Asmujiono and Iwan. They were like zombies, unable to focus on anything but the summit. I wanted them to turn back while they were still functioning. We would very likely be using the camp at 8,500 meters. I wanted us to leave the summit as soon as possible. It was now three o'clock. It was very late. The weather was calm, but I could see thin clouds moving on the face of the mountain. The climbers were taking one step, resting one minute, and taking another step. They would be another thirty minutes at that rate. I arrived at the summit; thirty meters behind me were Misirin and Bashkirov. I watched as Misirin collapsed in the snow. Suddenly Asmujiono passed Misirin. He charged the summit, doggedly running in slow motion, to embrace the tripod of flags and poles that is the officially sanctioned summit of Mount Everest. He replaced his hat with his army beret and unfurled the flag of his country. Here I could only wonder.

The Indonesians had succeeded in this man's determination. This was enough, we were going down!

I reevaluated my physical resources; I was feeling well. I had no sense of being at the end of my power. I felt I had much left in reserve. Bashkirov and Vinogradski were strong and clear in their thinking. We were still making choices and directing the situation. Our Indonesian team was running on autopilot. We were on the brink of a dangerous situation.

I took photos of Asmujiono. It was three-thirty, very late. Bashkirov arrived at the summit. Apa returned to the summit. I sent him immediately down to set up the tent at Camp V. We spent only ten minutes at the summit. Vinogradski was approaching the summit, only meters away, and I ordered everyone down. Vinogradski turned and went to Iwan, who was about eighty meters from the summit poles. I reached Misirin, thirty meters from his goal. I knelt beside him, collapsed in the snow. I told Misirin he had achieved the summit. I was amazed to see him stand, collect his power, and begin the descent. We encountered Vinogradski and Iwan descending one hundred meters below the summit. It had been difficult to turn these men around, they had come so far, but now I insisted. Every minute was important. We would compromise our own plan for survival if we did not descend in the light of day.

We arrived at the South Summit at 5:00 P.M., moving painfully slowly over the old ropes that Apa had pieced together for the traverse. I came last, the members moving slowly ahead of me. Dawa Sherpa was waiting for us at the South Summit. Misirin fell several times descending the South Summit. Each time he would stagger up and continue. Iwan, using Vinogradski's oxygen, had disconnected himself from the rope and fell at the juncture of the fixed lines. If Vinogradski had not grabbed him and pulled him up onto the rope, he would have fallen more than one hundred meters. Asmujiono, moving well, descended with the Sherpas. I went to the lead of the group, using my headlamp to light the trail in the twilight. At seven-thirty all Indonesian members arrived with me at Camp V. Bashkirov and Vinogradski arrived about one hour later. Only the Indonesians were now using oxygen. I removed crampons from the members, moving them into the tent. The tent, missing two sections of the poles, functioned like a large bivy sack. We had a stove, pots, gas, a Karrimat, and two full bottles of oxygen in the tent. This was not my dream of an emergency camp. Six of us were in the tent. Already the temperature was dropping. Inside the tent it was far more hospitable than outside. No wind, thank God; Everest would be merciful to us that night. Apa wanted to descend with Dawa. I said he could go, that we would have radio contact in the morning.

Now began what Bashkirov in his diplomatic way describes as a dramatic night. Evgeny Vinogradski showed his true colors. He began immediately upon his arrival at Camp V to brew hot water and kept this up through the long night. Bashkirov and I alternated changing the oxygen mask on the three exhausted Indonesian summiters. We moved the mask between them, stretching the oxygen throughout the night. Left too long without the precious bottle, one would cry or pray. Bashkirov, Vinogradski, and I quietly worked in turns during the night. We made it by working together.*

The morning came with a splendid display of color, no wind. We emerged from the tent to spectacular views of Lhotse, Makalu, and Kanchenjunga to the east and south, and to the morning sun bathing the summit of Everest in a blinding glory of light. Now, with caution in the descent, we could survive. The tenuous victory of the summit would be a true victory when all our members walked into Base Camp.

We brewed one last round of water and gave everyone another drink. All members were collected psychologically. No one had frostbite. We were out of oxygen, but the Indonesians' acclimatization and the long night of weaning off the bottle had softened the bite of dependence. They were moving slowly, but they were moving. We knew Apa and the Sherpas at the South Col would be coming up to meet us. In the glorious light of morning with the world spread out below us, we began our descent. At the pleasure of Sagarmatha† we lived and descended now without injury or the burden of tragedy.

I now felt secure enough in the stability of the situation to deal

---

*Bashkirov and Vinogradski had stopped using oxygen while descending to Camp V. Boukreev stopped using it upon his arrival. During the night, Boukreev had said, "the advisers did not use oxygen. . . . This was not a problem for us. We were not expending energy. It was not a fiercely cold night; there was no wind."

†This is what the Nepalis call Mount Everest.

with my personal agenda on the mountain. I came to 8,400 meters and began to look for Scott's body. We had passed by only thirty meters away in the darkness during our ascent. I had searched then but to no avail. I carried a flag inscribed with farewells from Scott's wife and friends; I was to cover him. I hope Jeannie will know I did the best I could with this mission. I left the flag at the summit, as at that moment I was not sure with the shape of the team members and the task before us that I would be able to find Scott when descending. Now, the worst over, I needed to fulfill my commitment to bury Scott. I found him covered over almost completely by snow. I asked Evgeny to help me with this sad job. We covered him with snow and rocks, and we marked the place with the shaft of an ice ax that we found nearby. This last respect was for a man I feel was the best and brightest expression of the American persona. I think often of his brilliant smile and positive manner. I am a difficult man and I hope to remember him always by living a little more by his example. His flag is flying from the summit.

Evgeny and I arrived at noon at the South Col. Misirin, Iwan, and Asmujiono had been resupplied with oxygen at the Balcony. Here at the South Col they were convinced they had survived. We had tea and settled in to spend the night.

The morning of the twenty-eighth I went out across the Col to the edge close to the Kangshung Face where I had left Yasuko Namba in the terrible night last year. I found her partially covered with snow and ice. Her pack was now missing and the contents were scattered in the rocks and ice around her. I collected the small things for her family. Slowly I moved stones to cover her quiet, small body. I left as markers two ice axes I found in the rocks near her body. These small acts of respect are all I could offer her family and Scott's family in my great sorrow over their loss.

I think of how ready Iwan, Asmujiono, and Misirin were to die. I think how the families I know who have lost here someone they love are dealing with their sorrow. I know this success will only encourage other inexperienced individuals into the mountains. I wish with all my power there were other opportunities for me to make a living. I am a sportsman, and there are many objectives in the mountains I would like the opportunity to achieve. Like any man who has a skill,

I would like to explore the limits of my capability. It is too late for me to find another way to finance my personal objectives; yet, it is with great reservation that I work to bring inexperienced men and women into this world. It is harsh for me to say I will not be called a *guide,* to make a distinction that will absolve me of that terrible choice between another person's ambition and his or her life. Each person must bear the responsibility to risk his or her life. This distinction between *guide* and *consultant* is one I am sure will be mocked by some, yet it is the only protest I can make about the guarantee of success in these mountains. I can be a coach, an adviser, I will act as a rescue agent. I cannot guarantee success or safety for anyone from the crushing complexity of natural circumstance and physical debility that haunts you at high altitude. I accept that I may die in the mountains.

Misirin, Asmujiono, Iwan, Apa, Dawa, Bashkirov, Vinogradski, and I descended to the sweet embrace of victory. Many individuals contributed to this success; above all, we were lucky. The Indonesian expedition had an ending that does not burn in my heart.

POSTSCRIPT

After their success on Mount Everest, the Indonesian climbers and Boukreev, with the other Russian climbing consultants, returned to Kathmandu for a party of celebration and to conclude expedition business. In mid May, his work with the Indonesians completed, Boukreev and a friend flew again to Lukla to begin a return trek to Everest Base Camp, where Boukreev wanted to look at mountain and weather conditions for a possible Lhotse-Everest traverse: a summit of Lhotse, then a traverse to the summit of Everest.*

On the trekking trail just outside of Namche Bazaar, where

---

*The Lhotse-Everest traverse, which Boukreev wanted to attempt with Simone Moro of Italy, was aborted on May 26 after Boukreev and Moro had summited Lhotse along with eight members of a Russian team that included Vladimir Bashkirov. Bashkirov, a close personal friend who had been an adviser on the Boukreev-led Indonesian National Everest Expedition (1997), climbed without supplementary oxygen. After reaching the summit, Bashkirov collapsed, a victim of altitude sickness. Boukreev radioed the Russians' highest camp and asked them to bring oxygen up the mountain. Immediately, two Russians headed to the summit with emergency O's, but they arrived too late. Vladimir Bashkirov died on Lhotse.

the trail wound down steep hillsides covered with a blanket of rhododendron blossoms to a gorge of the Dudh Kosi, Boukreev encountered Dr. Ingrid Hunt, who had come to the Himalaya to place a bronze memorial plaque in honor of Scott Fischer. Boukreev and Hunt talked briefly, and Dr. Hunt said, tears in her eyes, that she intended never to return to the Himalaya.

Saying good-bye to Dr. Hunt, Boukreev continued on the trail toward Everest. He looked at every descending climber, hoping to find someone from a Japanese expedition that had abandoned Base Camp and their attempt to climb Everest. Boukreev had in Kathmandu some amulets and personal possessions that he had collected in the vicinity of Yasuko Namba's body after he had buried her in a cairn of stones. He wanted to send her personal things to her husband in Japan.

After a night in Pangboche, Boukreev and his friend departed early. Arriving in Gorak Shep about 3:00 P.M., they stopped for tea at a lodge in the growing shadow of the snow-covered pyramid of Pumori. In the courtyard of the lodge a Japanese man appeared, and he was asked if he might know of anyone who could take Yasuko Namba's possessions back to Tokyo and return them to her family. Understanding the question, the noted Japanese climber Muneo Nukita with whom Boukreev had been speaking motioned to a man standing about fifty yards away. It was Kenichi Namba, the husband of Yasuko Namba, who had come to Nepal with the hope of having his wife's body recovered from the South Col.

With Muneo Nukita acting as translator, Boukreev and Kenichi Namba shared a pot of tea and Boukreev tried, in halting, breaking English, to explain what had happened the year before. He apologized, saying repeatedly that he wished he'd been able to do more. As he spoke, tears ran down his cheeks. He said that he'd felt a personal sense of failure around Yasuko's death, because he'd not brought to her the aid that he'd brought to Charlotte Fox and Sandy Hill Pittman. He'd made assumptions; he'd hoped for help that never came. He was sorry.

Kenichi Namba listened quietly, intently, and when Boukreev could say no more, Kenichi Namba said in Japanese that he blamed no one, that his wife had been a mountaineer, that her ambition had been to climb Mount Everest and that she had succeeded. He thanked Boukreev for what help he could bring to the other climbers the year before; he thanked him for going where he could not, to cover his wife's body and spare her the vulnerability of exposure. For two hours longer they talked, and then, in the fading light of the day, Boukreev said good-bye and resumed his trek, to go again to the mountain.

IN MEMORY

Mountains have the power to call us into their realms and there, left forever, are our friends whose great souls were longing for the heights. Do not forget the mountaineers who have not returned from the summits.

ANATOLI BOUKREEV, 1997
Inscription written into *The Climb* for Ervand Ilinski, Coach, Army Sports Club, Almaty, Kazakhstan

On December 6, 1997, Anatoli Boukreev was honored as a recipient of the American Alpine Club's David A. Sowles Memorial Award. This award, one of the most prestigious that can be bestowed upon a mountaineer, is given only to climbers who have "distinguished themselves, with unselfish devotion, at personal risk, or at sacrifice of a major objective, in going to the assistance of fellow climbers." In Boukreev's case, the award was extended by unanimous decision of the award's granting committee, for Anatoli's "repeated, extraordinary efforts in searching for, then saving, the lives of three exhausted teammates trapped by a storm on the South Col of Mount Everest" and additionally for his "valiant attempt, at great personal risk, in going out into the renewed storm in one last-ditch effort to save his friend and expedition leader Scott Fischer."

The award was granted at the American Alpine Club's annual meeting in Seattle, Washington, and its announcement was met with sustained applause. Boukreev's peers, experienced and qualified high-altitude mountaineers, had for more than a year considered the circumstances of the May 10, 1996, Mount Everest tragedy and recognized Anatoli for his heroism.

Boukreev, who had departed the United States for Nepal a few weeks before the award presentation, asked that a brief note be read to the gathered audience of more than four hundred. In characteristic understatement, Boukreev offered a modest thanks: "I feel like the American Alpine Club has gone to great effort to understand a man from another culture."

Boukreev had gone to Nepal to rendezvous with Simone Moro, thirty, of Bergamo, Italy, one of that country's most respected high-altitude mountaineers. They were planning a winter ascent of Annapurna I (8,078 meters) by way of the South Face. Moro said that Anatoli was in good form when he arrived in Kathmandu, happy to be back in the Himalaya. Indeed, it was in the mountains that Anatoli was most at home, most himself. A few months prior to the Annapurna expedition he had responded to a Kazakh reporter who asked if he was ever afraid in the mountains, "Honestly, I do not experience fear in the mountains. On the contrary . . . I feel my shoulders straightening, squaring, like the birds as they straighten their wings. I enjoy the freedom and the altitude. It is only when I return to life below that I feel the world's weight on my shoulders."

Helicoptering on December 1 to the Annapurna Base Camp, Boukreev, Moro, and Dimitri Sobolev, a Kazakh cinematographer who was going to document the expedition, were cautiously optimistic about the expedition's chances for success. A heavy load of unconsolidated snow caused them to alter the planned assault route, but they were encouraged by the prospect of improving weather.

For three weeks, often breaking trail through chest-deep snow, Boukreev, Moro, and Sobolev labored to establish their Camp I at 5,200 meters. From there, it had been decided, they would fix ropes to the top of a ridge at just over 6,000 meters. Along that ridge they planned to traverse to the summit. It was a longer, more arduous route than the one they had originally chosen, but the thought was that they could reduce their exposure to the threat of avalanche by minimizing their time on Annapurna's slopes.

On December 25, 1997, Christmas Day, Boukreev, Moro, and Sobolev awoke at Camp I with the first light of the rising sun. Moro said that Anatoli was relaxed, telling jokes, and in high spirits. Throughout the morning the climbers fixed ropes, moving toward the ridgeline above them. At 12:27 P.M., Moro was at 5,950 meters. Below him Boukreev and Sobolev were advancing up a gully or couloir, Boukreev with a coil of rope over his shoulder, the rope with which they were going to fix the last fifty yards of the route to the ridge top.

Moro, just coming to a full standing position after bending to his rucksack, heard a loud, explosive sound and looked over his shoulder to see a house-sized block of ice coming toward him. A cornice, not visible from the climbing route below, had torn loose from the ridge above. In the three seconds before the leading edge of the avalanche hit him, Moro had only the time to look down the couloir and yell one word, "Anatoli!"

Boukreev, who was at approximately 5,650 meters, and Sobolev, who was just below him, looked toward the cry of warning and saw a wall of ice and snow cascading down. Moro said that Anatoli caught his eye, and in a calm, quick maneuver began to sidestep up the sloping walls of the gully in which he and Sobolev had been climbing.

Moro was swept down the mountain by the freight-train force of the avalanche, and it spewed him out just above the expedition's Camp I tent. Knocked unconscious, Simone was half-buried as the mass of the avalanche settled in a quaking shudder. When he came around several minutes later, Moro struggled to his feet and called for about twenty minutes into

the avalanche debris field, but there was no response from either Anatoli or Dimitri.

The palms of his hands shredded down to the tendons by
the friction from the fixed ropes, Simone went into the Camp
I tent to get a new pair of gloves, and then he began a tortur-
ously painful six-hour trek to the Annapurna Base Camp. Mer-
cifully, a Sherpa who had been given the option to abandon
the camp had remained behind. A helicopter was summoned,
and Simone was flown to Kathmandu for medical attention. Before going into surgery he made a phone call to the United
States.

The news reached Santa Fe, New Mexico, late on the evening
of December 26. It was received with a stunned disbelief. The
day before, Linda Wylie, Anatoli's girlfriend; Dyanna Taylor, a
cinematographer who had accompanied the 1978 women's expedition to Annapurna (where two climbers had lost their lives);
and I had celebrated Christmas by climbing Atalaya Mountain (a
modest trekking peak in northern New Mexico) in a blizzard. All
that day our thoughts and conversations had drifted toward Nepal and speculations about the day that Anatoli and Simone
would finally make their summit bid. We imagined they would
make their attempt as the full moon approached.

On December 28, Linda Wylie departed for Nepal to contribute what effort she could to a search that was being
launched for Anatoli and Dimitri. The hope was that, somehow,
they had been able to dig themselves out of the debris field and
make their way to the Camp I tent that had remained standing,
fully stocked with food, stoves, and the high-altitude clothing
that could keep them alive until rescuers arrived.

In the last days of December several attempts were made to
reach the site of the avalanche by helicopter, but cloudy
weather prevented a search team from getting anywhere near
Camp I. In the United States and Europe, press speculation
about the fate of the lost climbers was rampant. One of the
several phone calls I received was from a "fact checker" at *U.S.
News & World Report*, who asked if I might respond to the details

of a story they were planning to run about Anatoli's death. Surprised and expressing concern that the magazine would consider running a story before the fate of the two lost climbers was clearly established, I reluctantly agreed to comment on the accuracy of the story they were planning to run. Within a few lines of copy the reader said that Boukreev would "likely be best remembered as a villain in Jon Krakauer's best-selling *Into Thin Air*." With that I stopped the reader. "No, I think not. If Anatoli is dead, I believe he will be remembered as his peers saw him, a consummate mountaineer and a man of great courage."

On January 3, 1998, a team of Kazakh climbers, headed by Rinat Khaibullin, and some Sherpas were successfully airlifted to Camp I where they inspected the debris field and the tent where Anatoli had slept on Christmas Eve. The tent was as Simone Moro had left it: empty. Linda Wylie issued a statement from Kathmandu: "This is the end . . . there are no hopes of finding him alive."

I received the news at my home. Privately, I had held out hope that Dimitri and Anatoli would be found alive; that they would have been able to make it to their Camp I tent. The White Crow (Anatoli's nickname amongst his Kazakh friends who appreciated his uniqueness), if anyone, could survive I thought. I imagined that he would be found sitting cross-legged in his tent, sipping a freshly brewed cup of tea. I could envision the wry smile that would overtake his face when he asked his friend Rinat, "What took you so long?"

Hanging up the phone, I glanced to the wall behind my desk where for years a quote has been taped. The words are those of Andrey Tarkovsky, one of Russia's most highly respected film directors.

I am interested above all in the character who is capable of sacrificing himself and his way of life. . . . It is often absurd and impractical. And yet—or indeed for that very reason—the man who acts in this way brings about fundamental changes in people's lives and in the course of history.

Anatoli Nikoliavich Boukreev, in my experience, was one of those characters, and I am honored to have collaborated in his effort to tell his personal story. I have not the words to express how much Anatoli will be missed by me, his friends, those who climbed with him, those who loved him.

Dimitri Sobolev. Anatoli Boukreev. Not forgotten.

—G. Weston DeWalt, Black Mountain, North Carolina
May 10, 1998

EVEREST UPDATE: A RESPONSE TO JON KRAKAUER

"As a journalist, I understand you were faced with a problem:
. . . your opinion vs my statement of fact."

—ANATOLI BOUKREEV,
Head Climbing Guide, Mountain Madness expedition, personal letter
to Jon Krakauer, August 6, 1996

In the months immediately following the Everest tragedy Anatoli Boukreev and I met almost every day to discuss the book we were planning to write, this book. We often started early in the morning, so that Anatoli would have his afternoons free to train and to run in the Sangre de Cristo Mountains of northern New Mexico. On one of those mornings we sat at his kitchen table, between us a jar of Nepalese honey and a freshly baked loaf of bread. Waiting for the bread to cool, we drank a dark Russian tea and talked about the months ahead.

Anatoli was preparing to leave Santa Fe for attempts on Cho Oyu and Shisha Pangma, so we were discussing the book-related tasks each of us would be taking on in the weeks during which he would be gone. Reading from my notes, I ticked off the things Anatoli had agreed to do during his absence, and when I finished, I looked to him for a response. Slowly raising a mug of tea to his mouth, he looked at me, expressionless. Thinking I had gone too rapidly through the list and that he'd not understood my English, I read through it again a bit more slowly. For several seconds, never taking his eyes from mine, he sat rigid and quiet. Then, he relaxed, lowered his mug, leaned across the table, and said matter-of-factly, "If I come back, you will have this. If I don't, you must to do it."

Three times during our writing of *The Climb*, Anatoli departed Santa Fe for expeditions. Each time we agreed: I would finish anything that might be left undone if he did not return.

In late October 1997 *The Climb* was published, and almost immediately Anatoli and I began a book tour that St. Martin's Press had arranged. Most of our days began at 6:00 A.M. and ended at midnight. Anatoli chafed at the demands of the schedule because his training suffered, but he took on the job as he did the mountains he climbed, with rarely a complaint.

On the evening of Sunday, November 9, we arrived in Denver, road weary and hungry. At our hotel a fax was waiting, a note from a friend in New York who had sent a copy of a news clipping. Boukreev, curious, asked what the fax was about. I reminded him that the made-for-TV adaptation of Jon Krakauer's *Into Thin Air* was being aired that evening, that the article was a review of the movie.[*]

"It says what?" Anatoli asked. Putting my bag down, I read the review through. One paragraph he asked me to repeat.

" 'There are no dramatic inventions in this motion picture,' Sofronski[†] said. 'Every scene in this film came from Jon Krakauer's book. Jon came to the Austrian Alps with us and was an enormous help . . . and all through the rehearsals Jon was there to tell us how it was, how the climbers felt, what happens with no oxygen, etc. But every scene in the film is actual.' "

---

[*]Michael Starr, "Into Thin Air: Big Chill on Everest," *New York Post*, November 9, 1997.

[†]Bernard Sofronski was identified in the review as the movie's producer.

"Actual? It means [the] truth?" Anatoli asked.

"Yes."

"Actual? You think [the movie] is . . . actual?"

"Probably not."

"Why not?"

"I'm guessing. These things have a way of . . ."

"We'll watch, okay?"

"If that's what you want, but . . ."

"We'll watch," he said, insisting.

Later that evening, a room-service meal in front of us, Anatoli and I tuned to ABC, the network airing the film. With us was a friend of Anatoli's, Leo, a Russian who had become a successful businessman in Denver.

From almost the opening scene Boukreev was laughing. He pointed at details of climbing gear and repeated lines of the scripted dialogue in amused disbelief. Initially, Anatoli found the characterizations of members of the Mountain Madness team hilarious, and he struggled with Leo to find an English word to describe what he was seeing.

"A play?" Leo asked, thinking that's what Boukreev had in mind.

"No, not play," Anatoli answered.

"Drama?"

"No drama."

"Fiction?"

"Like fiction, but no."

"A cartoon?"

"Yes! Cartoon. That's the word. An Everest cartoon."

Each time the actor portraying Boukreev appeared on the screen, Anatoli laughed riotously. The made-for-TV Anatoli was imposing and belligerent, a cardboard-cutout malcontent. Boukreev said at one point, "Is like Cold War movie. They just need put on me fur cap with big red star."

As the movie progressed, the laughter stopped and Anatoli drew into himself. At one point he moved from a chair to sit on the end of his hotel bed. No more than two feet from the screen, he was totally absorbed as he watched the scenes depicting the struggles of lost climbers trying to find their way to Camp IV in a gathering storm. When a diminutive climber in a red climbing suit appeared in the action, Anatoli pointed to the screen and, speaking to no one in particular, said, "Yasuko."*

As he watched a scene that depicted his discovery of Scott Fischer's lifeless body, Anatoli's emotions almost overtook him. Leo and I exchanged glances, not knowing what to say. When the movie ended, Boukreev sat silently staring at the television, oblivious to the commercials that had filled the screen. Finally, he turned to Leo and me, a look of disgust on his face. "They have blood in their mouths with this story, like animals feeding on the dead," he said.†

Four days later Boukreev and I arrived in Seattle where we were to give a lecture at the REI flagship store. The lecture had been on Anatoli's mind for weeks. Seattle had been Scott Fischer's hometown; he was a local hero, a man missed on the streets. At a small copy shop where we were having some work done, a clerk recognized Boukreev and was effusive in his thanks for the last-ditch effort Anatoli had made to save Scott Fischer. Embarrassed by the attention, Anatoli, his eyes downcast, said simply, "Was my job."

The next evening, after the REI presentation, Boukreev received some news. Jim Wickwire, one of this country's most highly regarded mountaineers, privately informed Anatoli that a five-member committee of the American Alpine Club had unanimously decided to honor him with that organization's most prestigious award, an award for heroism. Boukreev was

---

*Yasuko Namba was a member of the Adventure Consultants expedition who lost her life on the South Col. Her lonely death was a subject that Anatoli often visited in our conversations together. She died "so close" Anatoli would say, meaning that her tent was no more than five hundred yards from where she perished. When Anatoli climbed Everest in 1997 with an Indonesian team, he took time on his descent to cover her body with stones. He told me, "Was for respect."

†A journalist for the *Detroit News* described the movie, *Into Thin Air: Death on Everest*, as "a morgue report overlaid with hoary music." Members of the mountaineering community were even less generous in their assessments.

taken by surprise and certainly didn't anticipate the reaction that would follow.

At midnight on the evening of November 14, 1997, I said good-bye to Anatoli in the lobby of our Seattle hotel. He was off to Nepal for a winter ascent of Annapurna I; I was returning home. We agreed we would see each other in the coming spring when he returned to Santa Fe. I never saw Anatoli again.

On December 6, 1997, I traveled to Seattle to attend the American Alpine Club's annual meeting, which was being held in the suburb of Bellevue. At a banquet that evening, Wickwire announced that Anatoli, Todd Burleson, and Peter "Pete" Athans had been named recipients of the David A. Sowles Memorial Award. All three were honored for their actions on Mount Everest in May 1996. Wickwire, who had chaired the award committee, said, "All three of this year's recipients are professional mountain guides and, as such, had to meet an even higher standard for this rare award."*

Wickwire, after the presentation, read a brief note that Boukreev had written before he departed the United States for Nepal. In it Anatoli thanked the American Alpine Club and said he appreciated the effort they had made to understand a man from another culture.

Two days after the award ceremony Jon Krakauer, who had also attended the American Alpine Club's annual meeting, wrote a rambling and accusatory letter to Jed Williamson, a former president of the organization and one of the five members of the David A. Sowles Memorial Award committee that had honored Boukreev. The letter, copies of which were sent to various members of the publishing and mountaineering communities and to journalists, was a catalog of indictments of Anatoli, me, and *The Climb.* Among the allegations:

---

*Later, Wickwire said, "We took into account all of the information that was readily available to us. . . . In Boukreev's case, this included his nonuse of oxygen as well as his quick descent ahead of the Mountain Madness clients." After their considerations, Wickwire said they had no difficulty in deciding that Boukreev was deserving of the award.

1. In writing *The Climb* Weston DeWalt did not attempt to interview Neal Beidleman (a guide with Boukreev on the Mountain Madness expedition).
2. Weston DeWalt "never contacted" or interviewed Ed Viesturs, a member of the IMAX expedition, who could have shed some light on the Everest story.
3. "Virtually every Sherpa on Everest in 1996 blames the entire tragedy on Boukreev."

Because Anatoli was by this time in Nepal at the Annapurna I Base Camp and out of communication, it fell to me to correspond with the recipients of Krakauer's letter. On December 16, 1997, I prepared and mailed a paragraph-by-paragraph response to the charges that had been made. A copy of that letter was sent to Krakauer.

To the allegation that I had not made an attempt to interview Neal Beidleman, I offered documentary proof and said that Krakauer's claim was "patently and provably" untrue, that prior to my submission of the manuscript for *The Climb:*

1. I had faxed Neal Beidleman a quote from the Everest Base Camp debriefing tape,* a quote in which he supported Anatoli's having descended ahead of the Mountain Madness clients.
2. In a phone conversation I had questioned Beidleman about the quote.
3. I had asked Beidleman, during our conversation, to participate in an on-the-record interview and he had declined.†

---

*This tape is described in the "Authors' Note" that appears in the first pages of this book. A partial transcript of the tape is reproduced in this edition of *The Climb.*

†I had explained to Beidleman that I was interested in discussing his memory of certain events on Everest (among them his time on the summit) and some of his comments on the Everest Base Camp debriefing tape recorded on May 15, 1996. Given the sensitivity and seriousness of the subjects I wanted to discuss, I asked him to go on the record, because, as a general rule, I try to avoid interviews that are off-the-record. I believe that the person being

To the charge that I "never contacted" or interviewed Ed Viesturs of the IMAX expedition, I offered: "It should be noted that Ed Viesturs graciously participated in an interview that I conducted in Salt Lake City, Utah, in January 1997. I have an audiotape and transcript of that interview. On pages 119–20* of *The Climb* I quote from that interview."

To the accusation that "virtually every Sherpa" blamed Boukreev for the Everest tragedy, I could only express wonder at the ridiculousness of such a claim, an expression that was echoed by the respected mountaineer and writer/photographer Galen Rowell.

A week before Anatoli's death Rowell wrote to Krakauer: "I've had a chance to read your recent letters about *The Climb*, which I have been asked to review.† . . . Being one of those rare writers who believes that actions speak louder than words, I'm trying to reconcile your statement 'that virtually every Sherpa on Everest in 1996 blames the entire tragedy on Boukreev' with the fact that every one of Boukreev's clients survived without major injuries while the clients who died or received major injuries were members of your party. Could you explain how Anatoli's shortcomings as a guide led to the survival of his clients, but to the deaths of your teammates?"‡

---

interviewed, unless he or she has a genuine reason to fear physical endangerment, should be accountable for his or her words.

*These page numbers refer to the St. Martin's Press hardcover edition, November 1997. Quotes from the interview with Viesturs appear on pp. 119–120 and p. 149 of this edition (St. Martin's Griffin trade paperback edition, July 1999). Future references to pages in *The Climb* will be to the pages of this edition.

†Galen Rowell was writing a review of *The Climb* for *The American Alpine Journal* when Krakauer contacted him to offer some critical commentary on the book. Rowell's review is reproduced here with his permission and that of the American Alpine Club.

‡In the spring of 1998, Rowell went to Nepal where he trekked to the Everest Base Camp. While walking through the Khumbu region and during his visit to the Everest Base Camp, he talked with more than thirty Sherpas, many of whom had been on Everest in May 1996. He has reported that he found no Sherpa who blamed the tragedy on Boukreev, nor any Sherpa who knew of anyone who did. He did find, he said, that the Sherpas had been deeply saddened by the news of Anatoli's and Dimitri Sobolev's deaths on Annapurna I on Christmas Day, 1997.

In February of 1998, mountaineers and friends from around the world gathered in Denver and in Boulder, Colorado, to hold a series of memorial services for Anatoli. At the services, Russian and Kazakh friends, including Rinat Khaibullin, who had headed a team that attempted to find Anatoli after the Annapurna I avalanche, remembered a strong and courageous climber who would not let the collapse of Soviet mountaineering thwart his desire to climb the high mountains. Scott Fischer's parents and one of his sisters attended. Their grace and compassion brought great comfort to those for whom the pain was barely bearable. Jack Robbins, an architect from Berkeley, remembered with deep emotion the patient Russian climber who, when Robbins was in his sixties, had guided him to the summit of Denali. Members of the Mountain Madness expedition, including Sandy Hill (Pittman), whose life Anatoli had saved on Everest, toasted a man whose spirit was greater than the power of the snows that had taken him away.

After the services, my expectation and that of most of Anatoli's friends was that the controversies of Everest, 1996, would subside. We hoped that decorum and objectivity would return to considerations of the tragedy, and that the American Alpine Club's evaluation and recognition of Anatoli's actions on Everest might temper Krakauer's accusations, which, it seemed to many of us, had in recent months become increasingly reckless and mean-spirited.

However, five months later, almost exactly two years to the date of the publication of Krakauer's *Outside* article, the Boukreev-Krakauer controversy was ignited again, this time by Steve Weinberg, Executive Editor of *The IRE Journal*, a highly regarded magazine for investigative reporters.

Writing for the July/August 1998 issue of the *Columbia Journalism Review*, in his article "Why Books Err So Often," Weinberg asked readers of *Into Thin Air* to consider: "If Krakauer's account [of Boukreev's actions] is accurate, some of the climbers in Boukreev's care would have suffered less if he had been more concerned and less macho. But if the account is exaggerated or plain wrong, it is a far greater error than simple factual inaccuracy, since it undermines a person's reputation."

Motivated by the importance of the issue raised by Weinberg, Dwight Garner, a senior editor for the on-line magazine *Salon*, wrote a feature article, "Coming Down," and posted it on the Internet.* The article, described somewhat ambitiously as offering "what really happened on Mount Everest that fatal May day two years ago," was reasonably objective and offered some interesting insights into the basic issues of the Boukreev-Krakauer controversy.†

After publication of Garner's article, Krakauer and I traded letters on *Salon's* Internet site, and at the conclusion of our exchange, which I thought had been exhaustive in its exploration of the issues, I imagined the controversy would quiet, that it would be left to others to sort out the issues that had been raised. However, that would prove not to be the case.

In November 1998, *Into Thin Air: The Illustrated Edition* was published with an extensive "Postscript." No less critical of Boukreev's 1996 performance as a guide on Everest than anything Krakauer had previously written, the "Postscript" did speak generously of Boukreev's prodigious skill as a high-altitude

---

*On the Web site www.salon.com.

†In his article Garner examined an issue that I considered no less important than the manner in which Krakauer had represented Boukreev's actions on Everest and one that I hoped would encourage a more careful reading of *Into Thin Air.* Garner pointed to the differing—"if not entirely irreconcilable"—accounts by Krakauer and Beck Weathers of what had happened when, during his descent, Krakauer had encountered Weathers, who was having trouble with his vision and was waiting for Rob Hall to help him down the mountain.

Garner says that, in his *Into Thin Air* account, Krakauer said that he had "implored" Weathers to come down to Camp IV with him and offered, "I'll be your eyes. I'll get you down, no problem." Garner then compares Krakauer's story with one that Weathers offered in a tape-recorded speech. Weathers, recalling his encounter with Krakauer, begins with his explaining the seriousness of his problem: "Jon, I don't think I can wait any longer. I think Rob's going to have to understand, but it's starting to go south on us. And I'm going to need somebody to act as my eyes. And it's not a big deal. We'll just go a little bit slow. . . . And Jon was clearly not happy with this idea. His body language and . . . his first reaction was to say, 'Beck, I'm not a guide.' "

climber and made a brief mention of his rescue of Mountain Madness climbers: "There is no question that Boukreev saved the lives of Sandy Pittman and Charlotte Fox, at considerable risk to his own safety—I have said as much on many occasions, in many places." Absent, however, was any mention that the American Alpine Club had honored Boukreev for his heroic actions on Everest.*

Overall, I found the "Postscript" disingenuous, an inglorious attempt, it seemed to me, to compensate for past lapses in authorial responsibility that I believe contributed to an erroneous understanding of Anatoli Boukreev's actions on Everest. Additionally, I thought that Krakauer's attempts to discredit *The Climb*—by repeating in the "Postscript" old complaints that had previously been addressed and resolved—seemed not to support but to undermine what appeared to be the primary purpose of the "Postscript": the defense of his integrity and that of *Into Thin Air*.

My first thought was to ignore the "Postscript." However, upon a second and third reading, I came to understand how committed Krakauer was to perpetuating the characterization of Boukreev that he'd constructed for his readers in *Into Thin Air*, a characterization that I believe was seriously flawed and grossly misleading. To ignore Krakauer, I realized, would be to betray a trust. I had promised Anatoli that I would do what needed to be done if one day he did not come home. A response, I thought, was necessary.

---

*Three months before publication of his "Postscript," Krakauer was quoted in Dwight Garner's *Salon* article as saying of Boukreev's rescue of Charlotte Fox and Sandy Hill Pittman, "He may have been fearless. But he was also pretty goddamn motivated," because, Krakauer said, "if Boukreev had been having tea when a lot of people died," it "wouldn't have looked so good." In that same article Garner quotes Krakauer as describing the members of the American Alpine Club, who honored Boukreev, as "elitists" who didn't like him very much.

A RESPONSE

"I believe that there are at least intersubjective criteria to tell if an interpretation is a bad one, in the very sense in which we are sure that . . . Marco Polo did not really see unicorns."

—UMBERTO ECO,
Serendipities: Language and Lunacy

The Boukreev-Krakauer controversy began with the publication of Krakauer's article "Into Thin Air," which appeared in the September 1996 issue of *Outside*.* In that article Krakauer criticized Boukreev's descent ahead of clients on summit day:

"Boukreev had returned to Camp Four at 4:30 P.M., before the brunt of the storm, having rushed down from the summit without waiting for clients—extremely questionable behavior for a guide." Krakauer went on to say that Boukreev's descent ahead of clients most "plausibly resulted from the fact that he [Boukreev] wasn't using bottled oxygen and was relatively lightly dressed and therefore *had* to get down quickly."†

On July 31, 1996, in response to the article, Boukreev wrote *Outside*. He explained, as he had to Krakauer when he was writing his article:

1. Scott Fischer had authorized his descent to Camp IV ahead of clients.
2. He and Fischer had agreed that the purpose of his descent was to prepare for the possibility that he might have to assist descending climbers.

In his letter to *Outside*, despite what he saw as critical omissions in Krakauer's article, Anatoli was moderate in tone

---

*The September issue, according to a former *Outside* employee, was fast-tracked, and it began to appear on newsstands as early as the last week of July 1996.

†Jon Krakauer, "Into Thin Air," *Outside*, September 1996.

and encouraging of an objective consideration of the Everest tragedy. He wrote: "I know Mr. Krakauer, like me, grieves and feels profoundly the loss of our fellow climbers. We both wish that events had unfolded in a very different way. What we can do now is contribute to a clearer understanding of what happened that day on Everest in the hope that the lessons to be learned will reduce the risk of others who, like us, take on the challenge of the mountains. I extend my hand to him and encourage that effort."

Krakauer's public response to Boukreev's letter* was virtually unrelenting in its criticism of the man and his actions. He complained that Boukreev was unrepentant and arrogant. He didn't acknowledge Boukreev's complaint that Krakauer, in his *Outside* article, had neglected to disclose Anatoli's explanation that his descent ahead of clients had been approved by Fischer.

After reading Krakauer's letter, Boukreev said, "For me, I don't understand this situation." Krakauer's stridency and his unwillingness to acknowledge Boukreev's explanation—that his descent ahead of clients had been authorized—puzzled Anatoli. He speculated, "What is purpose?"

For a year and a half, Jon Krakauer was arguably the primary source for the story of the Everest tragedy, and much of what was published about those events drew heavily upon his account, resulting in what the French sociologist Pierre Bourdieu has called the "circular circulation of information."† Krakauer's Everest reality, as he promoted it and the media repeated it, was becoming the public reality. Krakauer's portrait of Boukreev as a guide of "questionable behavior" was starting to hang permanently in the public mind.

Through it all, Boukreev was patient, knowing that eventually his side of the story would be heard. He worked hard on *The Climb*. He struggled with his English; he struggled with me, his

---

*An August 24, 1996, letter to the letters editor of Outside Online (www.outside.starwave.com), an on-line news and information source that had a cooperative relationship with *Outside*.

†Pierre Bourdieu, *On Television,* trans. Priscilla Parkhurst Ferguson (New York: The New Press, 1998).

coauthor; he tried to balance his climbing career against the demands of the book. He insisted on a book that did not attempt to place blame for the tragedy. The issues, he understood, were complex. The best he could do, he said, was to offer the events of Everest as he had experienced them.*

Finally, in late October 1997, *The Climb* was published, and a few weeks later Boukreev had his last encounter with Krakauer. The occasion was the Banff Mountain Book and Film Festival, where Anatoli and I had been asked to participate in a series of public panel discussions. One of those, on the subject of media and mountaineering, drew a huge crowd—in part, I suspect, because, in the year and a half since the Everest tragedy, Boukreev had rarely spoken publicly.†

For Boukreev, the event was of special importance. In August 1996, just after publication of Krakauer's *Outside* article, Anatoli had sat quietly in the audience of a panel discussion during which Krakauer had made several comments with which Boukreev had taken serious and personal issue. Anatoli's feeling was that Krakauer should have his platform, that a public forum was not the place for a confrontation between the two of them.‡

In his presentation** Boukreev argued passionately that greater care should be taken by journalists who comment on

---

*Boukreev felt that Krakauer, in both his *Outside* article and *Into Thin Air*, had focused much more critically on the Mountain Madness expedition than he had on his own Adventure Consultants expedition, and that, given Krakauer's proximity to his team, he might have offered more insight into the decisions and actions that had led to the tragic losses they had suffered.

†Boukreev's limited command of English often made it difficult for him to understand questions that were put to him from the audience, and he was often frustrated by his inability to clearly communicate the fullness of his thoughts in a language that was not his own.

‡In an August 6, 1996, letter to Krakauer (Russian to English translation), Boukreev encouraged Krakauer to meet with him and discuss their differences. He wrote, "I understand you are planning to be in Salt Lake City and have been invited to participate in the *Outside* magazine symposium on the subject of Everest. I am planning to attend and look forward to seeing you there. I hope that in the crush of things we will have an opportunity to sit down and talk."

**It was arranged that Linda Wylie, with whom Boukreev had been living in Santa Fe, New Mexico, would share a microphone with Anatoli and read his presentation to the audience.

the issues and activities of high-altitude mountaineering.* He let it be known that he had not been impressed with everything that had been written about the Everest tragedy of 1996. When it came time for the Q&A session, a feature of most of the panel discussions, Jon Krakauer was the first to take the audience's microphone. Offering no supportive evidence, Krakauer said he felt *The Climb* was "dishonest" and went on to say that Boukreev appeared to be discouraging a free press on Everest. The panel moderator asked if any of the panel's four members wanted to address Krakauer's comments. They all remained silent.

As the panel discussion drew to a close, David Roberts, like Krakauer a consulting editor for *Outside,* stood and assailed Boukreev, charging that *The Climb* was "self-serving."

Members of the audience and the panel were taken aback. Some audience members booed. The moderator intervened, and after a few moments civility returned to the auditorium. Later that evening, while Anatoli and I were having dinner with friends at a Banff pub, an officer of the Canadian Alpine Club came to our table and on behalf of Canadian mountaineers offered an apology for what had happened. "We don't do things like that up here," he said. An English mountaineer who had witnessed Krakauer's and Roberts's comments said with a wry smile that the whole thing seemed to him to have been "something of a cock-up." As we were finishing our dinner, Anatoli said, "Tragedy of Everest was enough tragedy." The disaster of May 1996, he thought, had been reduced to a side-show.†

---

*He referred to a specific situation that had greatly disturbed him, an Internet posting—immediately after his 1997 summit of Everest—of news that he had found a body at the base of the Hillary Step. Boukreev had not been able to positively identify the body—that of Bruce Herrod, a climber/photographer who had disappeared the year before. Boukreev had wanted to see if an identification of the body could be made and family members notified before news of his discovery appeared in the press.

†In his "Postscript" Krakauer has said that, immediately after the Banff Mountain Book and Film Festival debacle, he and Boukreev met briefly and that the two had "agreed to disagree" about certain issues. A witness to the Krakauer-Boukreev conversation, Linda Wylie, has said that Krakauer's interpretation of their meeting is, at best, questionable. Boukreev, she's said, had

THE ALLEGATIONS

"A person reproduces himself by what he has done."

—BORIS MIKHAILOV,
writer/photographer, *Unfinished Dissertation*

In his "Postscript" Krakauer repeats many of the complaints and allegations that he has made since publication of *The Climb* and to which Anatoli and I have previously responded in other forums. But because in his "Postscript" Krakauer at times neglected to share with his readers the responses and refutations that have in the past been offered to his charges, it will be necessary here to revisit some sites where these issues have been argued before. To those who have made a concerted effort to follow the Boukreev-Krakauer controversy I apologize for the repetition they will have to endure, but, I suggest, something is to be gained by retracing the trail.

THE "ERRORS"
In the opening salvo of his "Postscript" Krakauer attempts to undermine the reliability of *The Climb* by discussing the "errors" he says he called to the attention of St. Martin's Press, the majority of which he says were not corrected in the mass-market paperback edition, which appeared in July 1998.* In reality, the majority of what Krakauer specifically pointed to and labeled as "errors" were instances in the book with which he took issue for one reason or another. A careful consideration of Krakauer's comments was made both by St. Martin's Press and me, and we believe the mass-market paperback edition responsibly addressed his complaints.†

---

been surprised by Krakauer's aggressive outburst and the hostility of his comments. "It was Jon being Jon," Wylie said.

*St. Martin's Press Paperbacks edition, August 1998.

†Krakauer *was* correct when he called to the attention of St. Martin's Press that, in the initial printing of the hardcover edition of *The Climb*, Boukreev and I had misidentified the area in which Andy Harris's ice ax was found after the tragic events on Everest. Boukreev and I, after considering accounts of the IMAX expedition's having found both Andy Harris's and Doug *(cont.)*

INTERVIEWS

Krakauer, in his "Postscript," was critical of the fact that neither Anatoli nor I had interviewed some of the players in the Everest tragedy—such as Mike Groom from the Adventure Consultants' expedition—whom Krakauer deemed important to a telling of the Everest story. He made this complaint despite knowing that Anatoli, in deciding to coauthor *The Climb*, wanted not to offer a "codex catastrophical." Boukreev felt that to undertake anything suggesting a definitive explanation of the tragedy would be to "play God," and he wanted no part of such an undertaking. *The Climb* was to be a personal account.

Krakauer also makes an issue of our "failure" to interview two members of the Mountain Madness expedition: Neal Beidleman, a guide with Anatoli on the Mountain Madness expedition and Lopsang Jangbu Sherpa, Scott Fischer's climbing sirdar. The charge of "failure," which implies a lack of intention or effort, is more than curious.

As has been previously noted, on December 16 1997, about eight months before Krakauer wrote his "Postscript," I had informed him that I had asked Beidleman for an on-the-record interview and that Beidleman had declined to participate.

Krakauer's complaint that Lopsang Jangbu Sherpa was not interviewed for *The Climb* is one that he's made several times during the Boukreev-Krakauer controversy. A chronology:

December 8, 1997: Krakauer wrote a letter to Jed Williamson of the American Alpine Club and took issue with my "failure" to interview Lopsang Jangbu Sherpa.

December 16, 1997: In a letter to Jed Williamson (copy to Krakauer) I responded: "I was very tempted to attend the memorial services for Scott Fischer and interview Lopsang Jangbu Sherpa, but I chose not to intrude on his need to grieve the loss of his

---

Hansen's ice axes between the Hillary Step and the South Summit, had confused the location of where Hansen's was found with that of Andy Harris's. In all paperback editions of *The Climb*, a photo caption was deleted to correct what had been an honest and regrettable mistake.

friend. Lopsang, as you know, died a few months later, and the chance to interview him was lost."

August 7, 1998: Krakauer, in a letter to *Salon,* said: ". . . baffling was DeWalt's failure to interview Lopsang Jangbu Sherpa, Scott Fischer's head climbing Sherpa. . . . The reason for such conspicuous reportorial lapses can only be guessed at."

August 13, 1998: In a letter to *Salon* I responded to Krakauer's revived charge: "It was my plan, stated in writing to potential publishers of *The Climb,* that I would interview Lopsang in Nepal in the winter of 1997. As Krakauer knows, Lopsang was killed in an avalanche before I had the opportunity to do so."

August 14, 1998: Krakauer, in a letter to *Salon,* responded to my explanation: "I'm heartened to hear that DeWalt intended to interview him, and sorry that Lopsang's death precluded such an opportunity."

November 1998: In his "Postscript" to *Into Thin Air: The Illustrated Edition,* Krakauer says, "No less baffling was DeWalt's failure to contact Lopsang Jangbu Sherpa, Scott Fischer's head climbing Sherpa. Lopsang had one of the most pivotal and controversial roles in the disaster." . . . "The reasons for such conspicuous reportorial lapses can only be guessed at."

Krakauer's intention in begging questions to which he already had the answers, I think, need not be guessed at.

THE DEBRIEFING TAPES

In *The Climb* Boukreev and I drew heavily upon a tape recording made at Everest Base Camp on May 15, 1996, five days after the disaster. That tape, referred to in the recording as a "debriefing" tape, stands as an important contribution to the historical record and has contributed immeasurably to an understanding of some of the factors that led to the tragedy.*

In his "Postscript" Krakauer has charged that I didn't "corroborate" the quotes drawn from the debriefing tape that were

---

*Sandy Hill (Pittman), a Mountain Madness climber-client, recorded the debriefing and made a copy available to Boukreev.

utilized in *The Climb*. That charge has left me somewhat confused. To "corroborate" is to make certain or to confirm by evidence. My question: What is it that needs corroboration?

The participants in the taped debriefing agreed they would contribute the facts of the events on Everest as they knew them. Implied in that agreement was that each of them would speak truthfully. In choosing to use quotes from the debriefing tape, Boukreev and I assumed there was no need to verify the truth of the statements we chose to publish.

Krakauer also says that two Mountain Madness expedition members, Klev Schoening and Neal Beidleman, have complained to him that statements made by them on the "debriefing" tape and used in *The Climb* were "presented out of context" and "badly misconstrued." This claim I can only wonder about, because, prior to publication of the mass-market paperback edition of *The Climb* in July 1998, I communicated with both Beidleman and Schoening for the express purpose of discussing changes that might be made in *The Climb*. Neither of them challenged a specific detail in *The Climb* or suggested a change.*

Rather than examine each of the Beidleman and Schoening quotes as presented in *The Climb* and their context, a transcript of relevant sections of the debriefing tape has been included in this edition (see pp. 304–372).†

FACT-CHECKING

Krakauer in his "Postscript" disagrees with Boukreev's published claim in *The Climb* that *Outside* did not fact-check with Anatoli certain details of Krakauer's article "Into Thin Air" be-

---

*Additionally, Krakauer has reported in his "Postscript" a complaint from Beidleman that he found *The Climb* to be "dishonest." The charge is puzzling since Beidleman did not act upon my invitation to him, made prior to publication of the mass-market paperback edition, to submit changes he might want to see made in *The Climb*.

†Boukreev had approved publication of relevant sections of the transcribed Mountain Madness debriefing tape prior to publication of the St. Martin's Press hardcover edition, but the length it would add discouraged its inclusion.

fore it was published. Krakauer offers a rather lengthy explanation for why he believes that is not the case. If what Krakauer claims is true, I don't know how readers are to account for the errors that caught Anatoli's notice when he read through Krakauer's article. Among them, Krakauer's claim that Boukreev was "relatively lightly dressed on summit day." Photographs delivered to *Outside, prior* to publication of Krakauer's article, clearly show that Boukreev was adequately dressed for his ascent.

OXYGEN USE

"It doesn't bother me that some of our Sherpas and guides did not use oxygen. They had enough experience at altitude to know their limitations. These are exceptional people."

—CHARLOTTE FOX,
Mountain Madness climber-client, "A Time to Live, a Time to Die," *The American Alpine Journal, 1997*

"From my perspective, if Anatoli had done anything *different* that day . . . the outcome would have been different. I think that every single action he took that day was in the best interests of his clients. . . . Oxygen is fine, but when it runs out, you hit a wall."

—SANDY HILL (PITTMAN),
Mountain Madness climber-client, quoted in Dwight Garner, "Coming Down," *Salon*, August 3, 1998

"At a conservative flow rate of two liters per minute, each bottle [of oxygen] would last between five and six hours. By 4:00 or 5:00 P.M., everyone's gas would be gone. . . . The risk of dying would skyrocket."

—JON KRAKAUER,
Adventure Consultants climber-client,
Into Thin Air

Krakauer first criticized Boukreev's not having used oxygen on summit day in his *Outside* article and since then has consistently argued that Anatoli should have. Krakauer repeated this criticism particularly hard in his "Postscript," arguing that Boukreev's not having used oxygen "preordained" his "decision to leave his clients on the summit ridge and descend quickly." In an attempt to drive a finishing nail into his argument, Krakauer offered his readers an axiom: "Without supplemental oxygen, nobody—not even the strongest climbers in the world—can loiter on the frigid upper reaches of Everest."

The axiom Krakauer overlooked in building his case was: If you are climbing on the upper reaches of Everest with supplemental oxygen and you run out—*no matter who you are*—you can get into serious trouble, perhaps die, unless you get to a source of more oxygen.*

Boukreev's problem with Krakauer's criticism of his not having used oxygen on the final assault was Krakauer's continuing insistence on linking that fact to Boukreev's descent ahead of clients. Boukreev was perplexed by Krakauer's absolute refusal to consider that his descent—with Fischer's approval—had been predicated upon his understanding of the second axiom. The Mountain Madness climber-clients could run out of oxygen before they made it back to Camp IV. If they did, their risk of dying would skyrocket.†

Boukreev went down when he did on summit day, as he explained to Krakauer again and again, not because he was climbing without oxygen, but because the Mountain Madness climber-clients were.

---

*Boukreev, in his article "The Oxygen Illusion," published in *The American Alpine Journal*, 1997, talks extensively about the problems that can come to those who rely upon supplementary oxygen during high-altitude ascents.

†In an April 21, 1997, interview I conducted with Krakauer, he pooh-poohed this notion, saying, "Well, there was not an oxygen problem." This analysis of the prevailing situation is in sharp contrast to that offered by Ed Viesturs of the IMAX expedition, who, when he observed that Mountain Madness climbers were still going to the summit after 2:00 P.M., said, "So, kind of in my mind, I was thinking they're going to run out of oxygen—not only daylight, but they're going to run out of oxygen." (See *The Climb*, p. 149).

Boukreev and Fischer agreed before the expedition began that Anatoli—*if he were properly conditioned and acclimatized*—would guide without oxygen, and that agreement was made within this context: on summit day Fischer would provide three canisters (eighteen hours of oxygen) for each of his climber-clients. Those climbers, he planned, would depart Camp IV at twelve midnight on the morning of May 10, climb to the summit, and be back by 6:00 P.M. before the hard fall of night and before their oxygen supplies were exhausted. And, what would happen if things went awry? Fischer had made it known to Mountain Madness climber-clients and members of his staff that he had hired Boukreev for his ability to conduct rescues, to bring help (oxygen, hot drinks, physical assistance) to descending climbers if they needed it. If his clients weren't back at Camp IV by 6:00 P.M., Fischer would have the Boukreev card to play.*

What actually happened on May 10 when Scott Fischer arrived atop the Hillary Step at 2:35 P.M.? He saw only one of his climber-clients, Martin Adams, and Boukreev. Somewhere above him were five more climber-clients, his other guide, Neal Beidleman, and his climbing sirdar, Lopsang Jangbu Sherpa. The climber-clients and Beidleman, at that point, had approximately three and one-half hours of oxygen remaining *if* they had been adhering to the oxygen flow rates recommended before the climb.† Fischer had to be wondering, Where are they? When would they be making their descent?‡ What should he do?

When Fischer encountered Boukreev and Adams atop the

---

*Boukreev's power and strength as a high-altitude climber were well-known in the Himalaya. In 1995, Henry Todd, an English organizer of Everest expeditions, hired Boukreev as a guide because "if anything went wrong, I wanted a rope bullet up that hill." (Quoted by Paul Deegan in "Reviews," *High*, September 1998.)

†We now know that Neal Beidleman and at least one of the Mountain Madness clients had at times during the climb cranked their flow rates over what had been recommended.

‡In fact, Neal Beidleman and the five client-climbers, the last of whom summited at approximately 2:30 P.M., stayed on the summit until 3:10 P.M.

Hillary Step, Boukreev said to Fischer, "I'm going down with Martin." According to Adams, Fischer offered no objection, and as Fischer moved behind Adams to where Boukreev was standing, Adams prepared to go over the top of the Hillary Step and continue his descent. Boukreev has repeatedly explained that, at this point, he and Fischer had another conversation and they agreed that Anatoli should descend as quickly as possible to stand by at Camp IV. Boukreev and Fischer could appreciate, given the prevailing situation, that clients could run out of oxygen and get into trouble. If Fischer's climber-clients ran out of oxygen on the descent, where were they going to get more oxygen? He needed someone below at Camp IV.

Krakauer's dedication to discrediting Boukreev's explanation for his descent is, I believe, what motivated him in his "Postscript" to call to his readers' attention that "while doing research for his book, DeWalt instructed an assistant to call Peter Hackett, M.D., one of the world's foremost authorities on the debilitating effects of extreme altitude, in order to solicit the doctor's professional opinion about the oxygen-use issue. According to Dr. Hackett . . . he replied unequivocally that in his view it was dangerous and ill advised to guide Everest without using oxygen, even in the case of a climber as exceptionally strong as Boukreev. Significantly, after seeking out and receiving Hackett's opinion, DeWalt made no mention of it in *The Climb*."

In point of fact, during the interview with Dr. Hackett that Krakauer references, Dr. Hackett went a bit further in his comments than Krakauer has reported. He went on to say, "In his [Boukreev's] defense there is this school of thought that you're better off without oxygen because then you can't run out. I admit there is that school of thought. I don't agree with that. And there have been cases of where people have run out of oxygen and gotten into deep trouble."*

I can understand Krakauer would have appreciated my in-

---

*As did several climbers from both the Mountain Madness expedition and Krakauer's own Adventure Consultants expedition.

cluding Dr. Hackett's opinion—as presented by Krakauer—in
The Climb, but I don't think readers of the book were denied
anything by my not including it. Krakauer's critical opinion
about Boukreev's not having used oxygen, an echo of Dr. Hackett's, was offered in *The Climb.* In retrospect, I wish the statement—in its entirety—had been included. The example of Dr.
Hackett's ready willingness to acknowledge another school of
thought, even though he did not subscribe to it, might have
encouraged Krakauer to honor that the "standard" against
which he has been measuring Boukreev is not universally held.*

THE BROMET STATEMENT
In his "Postscript" Krakauer says that I "edited" a quote from
Jane Bromet and, as a result of having done so, did "wrongfully
suggest that Fischer had a predetermined plan in place for Boukreev to descend quickly after reaching the summit, leaving his
clients on the upper reaches of Everest." A review of the evidence, I think, will demonstrate that his allegation is not true.

Before the manuscript for *The Climb* went to the publisher, I
traveled to Seattle, Washington, to interview Jane Bromet, the
Mountain Madness publicist who had trekked into Everest Base
Camp with Scott Fischer and other members of the expedition,
arriving there on April 8, 1996.† My primary purpose in inter-

---

*In an August 7, 1998, letter to *Salon* I mentioned that Everest veteran
Reinhold Messner—reflecting upon the need to use oxygen as an Everest
guide—said, "I don't think there's a big difference between danger and not
danger, using or not using oxygen" (from a recorded speech given by Messner
on January 27, 1997). In calling this to the attention of readers my intention
was to point out that—on the occasion of his speech—Messner did not appear
to be in agreement with Krakauer's view that all Everest guides should use
supplementary oxygen. Krakauer, in his "Postscript," I think, came to an in-
appropriate conclusion as to the purpose of my comments. In no way did I
mean to imply that Messner was in agreement with each and every one of the
actions that Boukreev took on Everest in 1996. To this I would add that I
never heard Anatoli, privately or publicly, say that Messner had "endorsed"
his actions on Everest. What Boukreev did say in *The Climb* (p. 231) and in
various public forums was that he had gotten personal "support" from Messner.

†In addition to her role as publicist for Mountain Madness, Jane Bromet
was also working as a correspondent for Outside Online.

viewing her was to get background on the planning and promotion of the Mountain Madness expedition and to hear something of Jane's day-to-day observations of Everest Base Camp activity. The tape-recorded interview with Jane went on for more than two hours, and several times she ventured into topics that were not at all a part of my research agenda. More than once I was taken aback by her candor and openness. She seemed eager to talk, to tell all.

As the interview came to an end and I was preparing to leave her home, she took me by the arm and said, a nervous hesitancy in her voice, "You know there is something I want to tell you. I don't know if I should or not, but . . ."

Jane hesitated and it appeared that she might not continue, that whatever it was that she wanted to say was going to be swallowed and never spoken, but she continued, and I pursued the implications of what she revealed.

BROMET (continuing): . . . what happened with Anatoli going back up, that was, you know, one of the cards that got turned over; I mean, that was the plan.

DeWALT: What do you mean "the plan"?

BROMET: I mean Scott told me—you know, one of the scenarios—that if there were problems coming down, Anatoli would make a rapid descent and come back up the mountain with oxygen or, whatever.

DeWALT: You're telling me that Scott told you this prior to the final assault?

BROMET: Yes, at Base Camp, yeah, several days before.

DeWALT: Just so I understand. Scott told you if they got into trouble, he would send Anatoli down to prepare to resupply the climbers coming down.

BROMET: Yes, that's what he told me.

DeWALT: When you were interviewed by Jon Krakauer, did you tell him this? Exactly what you told me?

BROMET: Yes.

The next morning, unannounced, Jane showed up at my hotel where I was having coffee with my research associate, Terry LeMoncheck, who had come to Seattle to meet with Scott Fischer's wife.* Appearing somewhat distracted, Jane apologized for the intrusion and said she had come with a gift for Anatoli. From a sports bag she'd brought with her, she removed several pairs of trekking shoes. A sponsor, she said, would want Anatoli to have a pair. As we rummaged through the shoes, trying to guess what size Boukreev would wear, we talked. Jane said she'd been having some second thoughts about how forthcoming she'd been in our conversation the day before. Too, she said, she was concerned about how the public might respond to Krakauer's not having mentioned in *Into Thin Air* the information she had given him about Fischer's plan. "Jon is a friend, and I don't want to embarrass him," she explained.

Jane and I talked for twenty or thirty minutes, and I agreed that those of her comments that were unrelated to the events of the climb would not see print, but, I explained, it was difficult for me to ignore what I considered to be the importance of Fischer's conversation with her. If I saw fit, I was going with her statement. She did not protest.

On April 15, 1997, Bromet sent me an E-mail reiterating what she had told me in Seattle. "I know that information I gave you is vital to your story—the fact that Scott told me that it was his plan to have Anatoli go down ahead of the group." She went on to add that, if problems did arise with the climber-clients, Fischer wanted Boukreev in Camp IV "hydrated" and with "reserve energy" so that he could pull people off the mountain.

Two days later I spoke with Jane by phone. She wanted to make certain that I understood that she knew only what Fischer had told her, but nothing of what he had told Anatoli prior to summit day. I told her that, of course, I understood, and she went on to wonder aloud why Krakauer had not mentioned in *Into Thin Air* what she had told him, that Fischer had a plan in mind for Anatoli. She said about Krakauer, "I don't know why Jon didn't use it."

---

*Anatoli had dictated—for Scott Fischer's wife, Jeannie, and her children—a personal remembrance of Scott. It had just been translated into English and Anatoli had asked that it be delivered personally to Scott's family.

Before submitting the manuscript for *The Climb,* I read through Bromet's statement several times. I kept coming back to one specific exchange between the two of us.

DEWALT: You're telling me that Scott told you this prior to the final assault?

BROMET: Yes, at Base Camp, yeah, several days before.

What I had been looking for in my question to Jane was some clue as to where and when Fischer had made his comments to her. In responding, Jane had given me the where, but not the when. The where, I thought, was probably good enough to convey a sense of the timing of Fischer's comments. I knew—and had mentioned in the manuscript for *The Climb*—that Bromet, along with Fischer and other Mountain Madness expedition members, had arrived at the Everest Base Camp (EBC) on April 8, 1996, four weeks before the final assault. But, I thought, perhaps I could more closely fix the timing for readers.*

I went back through notes I'd made during conversations I'd had with Bromet, the transcript of my interview with her, and E-mails that she had sent me. In one of my notes I had recorded that Jane had remembered departing EBC about a week before the final assault. In an April 22, 1997, E-mail she had said, "I left base camp (EBC) approximately 10 days before summit assent [*sic*]." She said she was unable to come up with an exact date because she had been avoiding going back to her notes, wanting not to bring on a "tidal wave of memories."

Further on in that same E-mail message Jane said that her "days before" comment was referring to the days before she left EBC, but that she was not able to recall how many days before her departure Fischer had described his plan to her. She said, "Maybe it was seven days before," but it was impossible for her to peg an exact date.

Several, meaning more than two, but less than "many," is a

---

*I was not that concerned about specifying an exact date, because I felt that Fischer's statement to Bromet would not have been any less significant or relevant if it had been made on March 25 in Kathmandu or on April 2 during the trek to the Everest Base Camp.

useful word when one can't be specific, but Jane's use of it created problems for me in my effort to place Fischer's comments in the flow of events leading up to summit day. Using Jane's best recollections—that she'd left EBC between seven and ten days before the final assault and that Fischer had told her of his plan for Boukreev "maybe" seven days before that departure—I put Fischer's comments to Jane as happening somewhere between April 23 and 26.

Given the proximity of those dates to the date of the final assault which was on May 10, 1996, I felt comfortable in offering to readers of *The Climb:*

DeWALT: You're telling me that Scott told you this prior to the final assault?

BROMET: Yes, at Base Camp, yeah, several days before [the final assault on May 10, 1996].

The words added in brackets, by referencing the final assault, helped maintain a continuity with the preceding question and, I thought, fairly represented Jane's best estimates of when Fischer's comments to her had been made: fourteen to seventeen days prior to the final assault.

A few weeks before *The Climb* began to appear in bookstores, Bromet sent a letter to St. Martin's Press.* Its formal construction and wording struck me as odd, an extreme departure from her informal, off-the-cuff style. In the letter Bromet was critical of my use of her quote.† She felt, she said, that the quote was "grossly misleading" and that "too much credit was given" to the quote because Fischer had never mentioned his plan to anyone else but her. Frankly, Jane's attempt to distance herself from a statement she had willingly offered, that she had consid-

---

*This letter, dated October 8, 1997, was received after *The Climb* had been printed and shipped.

†Bromet explained in her letter that she had read the quote attributed to her in an advance copy of the manuscript that had somehow been obtained by a "third party."

ered "vital" to the Everest story, and whose implications she had clearly understood I found mysterious.

Three weeks after receiving Bromet's letter I received a fax from Krakauer. Quoting extensively from Bromet's letter, he complained about my inclusion of the Bromet quote in *The Climb.** My impression was that its publication had embarrassed as well as angered him.†

In his "Postscript" Krakauer used the Bromet letter as a platform from which to issue a fusillade of questionable arguments, an effort, I suspect, to diminish, if not to destroy, the possibility of the Boukreev-Fischer exchange during which Boukreev's descent was approved. Krakauer argued; I respond:

1. ". . . DeWalt chose to ignore the fact that the only evidence to support his conjecture about a predetermined plan was Bromet's recollection of a single conversation." (Krakauer, "Postscript," *Into Thin Air: The Illustrated Edition*)

My belief that Scott Fischer had a "plan" as Bromet put it, "a method for achieving an end" as the dictionary has it, is predicated upon Bromet's testimony and upon Scott Fischer's having told at least four people of whom I am aware that one of the primary reasons he hired Anatoli was to bring aid to climbers in the event of problems during the expedition.

---

*There had been no suggestion in Bromet's letter that Krakauer had been sent a copy.

†On April 4, 1997, I had faxed a copy of Bromet's statement to *Outside*. Because I felt that the magazine had, before publication of Krakauer's article, neglected to check with Anatoli certain details of his descent on summit day, I asked in my fax, "Was anyone at *Outside* aware, at any point before Jon's article went to press, that there was information at hand that would have clarified the issue around Boukreev's descent?" (I got no answer to my inquiry.) Shortly after my communication with *Outside,* Krakauer phoned my home office. Enraged, he said he would "draw my guns" if I went public with the Bromet statement.

2. ". . . it would be wrong to assume that Fischer's comments indicated that he had anything resembling an actual plan in place." (Krakauer, "Postscript," *Into Thin Air: The Illustrated Edition*)

I have never argued that Fischer had a plan "in place," but I have never doubted that he had one in mind. His statement to Bromet is more than ample proof. What Fischer did have *in place* was Boukreev, who was able and prepared at Camp IV where, it turned out, he was needed.

3. "Before *The Climb* was published, Bromet sent a letter to DeWalt and his editors at St. Martin's complaining that DeWalt had edited her quote in a way that significantly changed its meaning." (Krakauer, "Postscript," *Into Thin Air: The Illustrated Edition*)

Bromet, in her October 8, 1997, letter, *never* said that I misquoted her. What she did say was that the bracketed words that had been added—"the final assault on May 10, 1996"—would mislead readers into thinking that Fischer's conversation with her had taken place in the days immediately preceding the final assault. She went on in her letter to recall what she had not been able to remember previously—that she had left Everest Base Camp "weeks before the climb."

Considering her most recent recollection as to when she had departed EBC, St. Martin's Press and I discussed the matter, and we decided to remove the bracketed words "the final assault on May 10, 1996" from Bromet's statement and replace them with words that better reflected the reality of her situation at the Everest Base Camp as she was now representing it. The question became: What words? Bromet, in her letter, had not provided an exact date for either her departure from EBC or the date of her conversation with Fischer.

I looked to the pages of *The Climb* to consider the more than a dozen references to Bromet that had been included, thinking there might be a way within the text—before the reader got to the "Mountain Media Madness" chapter where Bromet's statement was included—to add a sentence or two to indicate her general recollection as to when she had departed EBC.

Examining the text, I discovered something I had overlooked when, in the last days of manuscript preparation, I had struggled with how to time Fischer's comments to Bromet. I noted a sentence in *The Climb* (p. 91) that referred to Bromet's having departed EBC by the early morning of April 23, 1996 (in Nepal), late afternoon of April 22 (in Seattle).* I was dismayed that I had overlooked this reference to Bromet's return to Seattle when trying to figure the date she had left EBC, because, had I noted it, it would have raised a flag. Despite her reluctance to revisit the events of Everest, I would have encouraged Jane to reconsider her guesses at when she had returned to Seattle.

As dismayed as I remain at having overlooked the reference to Jane's Everest Base Camp departure, I see one benefit in my having done so. Krakauer, in his "Postscript," suggests that I might have had some ulterior motive in my choice of words to bracket in the Bromet quote, that I may have attempted to mislead readers. I suggest, if I had chosen the words to bracket so as to purposely misrepresent the timing of Fischer's comments, it's hard to imagine that I would have left in *The Climb* a reference that would have so clearly betrayed the dark intention Krakauer thinks I might have had.

My annotation of the exchange between Bromet and myself with which Jane had taken issue was revised to read:

DEWALT: You're telling me that Scott told you this prior to the final assault?

BROMET: Yes, at Base Camp, yeah, several days before [I left Base Camp].

---

*Going back to my notes, I determined that I had inferred this date by examining dispatches that Bromet had filed on Outside Online.

The new annotation—"[I left Base Camp]"—makes Jane's statement consistent with the fact that she had departed Everest Base Camp for Seattle by April 22. This change was made in the third printing of the hardcover edition of *The Climb* and was included in all of its subsequent printings as well as in all printings of the paperback editions that have followed it.

4. "As Bromet stated in her letter to DeWalt, the edited version of her quote that appears in *The Climb* is 'absolutely wrong!' " (Krakauer, "Postscript," *Into Thin Air: The Illustrated Edition*)

In Jane Bromet's letter to St. Martin's Press of October 8, 1997, she complained about the addition of the bracketed words "the final assault on May 10, 1996." She said, "The way in which this was put into words implies that this conversation was immediately preceding the climb (a few days). This is absolutely wrong!" What Krakauer did in his "Postscript" was to pirate Bromet's expression ("absolutely wrong!") to suggest that my original annotation of Jane's statement had, in Krakauer's words, "significantly changed its meaning." In fact, it did not change the "meaning" of either what Scott had said to Jane *or* what Jane had said to me. It changed only the timing of Scott's comments to Jane. The fact remains: Scott Fischer told Jane Bromet he had a "plan" for Boukreev to descend ahead of climber-clients.

On November 14, 1997, five weeks after I had received the letter she had written to St. Martin's Press, I saw Jane Bromet in Seattle in the REI meeting room where Anatoli and I were preparing to give a lecture. She came out of the assembling crowd, and we talked for a while. She was apologetic about the letter that she'd sent and asked me if I had been upset. She offered, "You understand why I had to write the letter? No hard feelings?" Thanking her for coming, I said, "None, absolutely none. I understand Jon is a friend. I understand." Jane did not respond, but smiled and turned to take a seat in the front row of the audience. Despite other demands on her schedule, Bromet stayed for Anatoli's and my presentation, contributed to the Q&A session that followed, and was at all times supportive of Anatoli.

For Jane Bromet's courage in stepping forward I have always been grateful. From the moment she offered me her statement I have understood, as she did, that it was "vital" to the story, and it was for that reason I included it in *The Climb*.

THE IN-CAMP SHERPA ARGUMENT

In his "Postscript" Krakauer quotes David Breashears of the IMAX expedition as questioning Boukreev's descent ahead of Mountain Madness climber-clients and wondering why Boukreev would have needed to descend to "make tea," given that "there were Sherpas waiting at the South Col" for that purpose.* It may be that Breashears, when he made his statement, was not aware that on summit day Boukreev believed that no Sherpas—nor any other expedition personnel—were at Mountain Madness's Camp IV (see p. 154, *The Climb*). Boukreev knew that Scott Fischer had given all seven of the expedition's climbing Sherpas permission to make a summit attempt. Boukreev thought they had all headed to the top. What he did not know at that time was what Krakauer revealed later in *Into Thin Air:* "In the end, Lopsang went behind Fischer's back and ordered one Sherpa, his cousin 'Big' Pemba, to remain behind."†

---

*Breashears, to his credit, has taken the high road in his consideration of Boukreev's actions on Everest. When he and Boukreev were interviewed together on CNN's *Larry King Live,* he said, "I've read most things, and it's hard for me to second-guess a situation I wasn't in."

†On summit day, when climbers above Camp IV began to run into trouble, Pemba Sherpa was contacted from the Everest Base Camp and was asked to go up the mountain with oxygen to help climbers who were in trouble. Pemba declined, saying that the weather was too threatening.

DESCENT AHEAD OF CLIENTS

"I knew that Anatoli had gone down. I had no problem
with that. I knew that it would have been nice for him to
stay, but at the same time it wouldn't have necessarily facilitated our descent any better. I wasn't aware of his instructions to go down immediately from Scott, but after
hearing that, I support that. I think that's a very good idea,
and, in fact, had he not gone down, his efforts at the bottom collecting people wouldn't have been possible."

—NEAL BEIDLEMAN,
Mountain Madness guide,
Mountain Madness Everest debriefing, May 15, 1996

I began formally interviewing Anatoli in the first days of June
1996, within four weeks of the tragedy on Everest and approximately eight weeks before Jon Krakauer's *Outside* article began
appearing on newsstands. During that interval, on at least three
different occasions, I asked Anatoli to walk me through the se-
quence of events that had led to his descending ahead of clients
on summit day. His answer, consistent from one telling to the
next: above the Hillary Step, as Scott Fischer was ascending and
Anatoli was preparing to descend, Anatoli and Scott agreed that
Anatoli should descend as quickly as possible to Camp IV, their
highest-altitude camp, and stand by to assist climber-clients if
they were late returning and needed assistance.

Since in his *Outside* article Krakauer had chosen not to in-
clude Boukreev's explanation that his descent ahead of clients
had been authorized, and since Boukreev had immediately
questioned Krakauer's omission of it, both Anatoli and I were
curious as to how Krakauer—in his forthcoming book, *Into Thin
Air*—would relate the events above the Hillary Step where
Fischer had authorized Boukreev's descent.

When I purchased a copy of the newly published *Into Thin
Air*, I read:

"After we [Krakauer and Fischer] exchanged pleasantries, he
[Fischer] spoke briefly with Martin Adams and Anatoli Bou-

kreev, who were standing just above Harris and me, waiting to descend the [Hillary] Step. 'Hey, Martin,' Fischer bantered through his oxygen mask, trying to affect a jocular tone. 'Do you think you can summit Mount Everest?'

" 'Hey, Scott,' Adams replied, sounding annoyed that Fischer hadn't offered any congratulations, 'I just did.'

"Next Fischer had a few words with Boukreev. As Adams remembered the conversation, Boukreev told him, 'I am going down with Martin.' Then Fischer plodded slowly on toward the summit, while Harris, Boukreev, Adams, and I turned to rappel down the Step."*

The account didn't ring true. I read again the transcripts of the several interviews I had conducted with Martin Adams, a Mountain Madness climber-client. I read again the transcripts of the interviews I had conducted with Anatoli. I called Martin Adams. It was a lengthy conversation. According to Adams:

1. The exchange between Martin Adams and Scott Fischer ("Hey, Martin, do you think you can summit Mount Everest?") had not occurred in Krakauer's presence, but as Adams was peering over the edge of the Hillary Step and while Fischer was climbing up. Krakauer had been out of earshot and had not heard the conversation (see pp. 152–153, *The Climb*).

2. Boukreev, yes, had told Fischer he was going down with Adams, but Krakauer had not heard that comment.

3. Neither Adams nor Krakauer were privy to whatever conversations Boukreev and Fischer might have had after Boukreev's "I am going down with Martin" comment because, as Krakauer and Andy Harris were rappelling down the Hillary Step, Adams was peering over the edge watching their progress.

On April 21, 1997, I spoke with Jon Krakauer. At first, he was reluctant to talk openly and said, "This stuff I'm telling you— I have some problem talking to you because you're not just a

---

*The construction of this scene—the placement of characters and the timing of its action—virtually precluded the possibility that Boukreev could have had the conversation with Fischer during which his descent ahead of clients had been authorized, the conversation that, as in his *Outside* article, Krakauer failed to mention to his readers.

journalist; you're Anatoli's attorney." When he got it straight that I wasn't an attorney, Krakauer relaxed somewhat and I went immediately to my primary interest, Krakauer's presence above the Hillary Step and the events to which he had actually been a witness.

Initially, Krakauer claimed to have been a witness to Anatoli's first encounter with Fischer when Anatoli had told Fischer he was going down with Martin Adams. Krakauer told me, "There were five people present for that. Scott and Andy Harris are dead. Anatoli, Martin Adams, and I all heard this conversation." Later, after I told Krakauer that Adams had said that Krakauer had not been present when Boukreev made that comment, Krakauer moved away from his position and said, "What I do know is what Martin told me, and that's how I reported it."*

As to the second conversation, during which Fischer had approved Anatoli's descent, I asked Krakauer if he knew "for a fact" that the conversation had not happened as Boukreev had reported it. Krakauer said he felt it hadn't happened as Boukreev had represented it. Then he offered, "I could be wrong about that. I'm not—I didn't—I was there. I left the Step before Anatoli. Now Scott himself—I thought their conversation had ended by that point. Maybe I'm wrong. I wasn't there."

CONCLUSION

"I do think it's inexcusable that the paperback edition of *Into Thin Air* ignores the charges in Boukreev's book. There is a dispute here, and how are readers supposed to know the truth?"

—STEVE WEINBERG, author of "Why Books Err So Often," *Columbia Journalism Review,* July/August, 1998, quoted in Dwight Garner's "Coming Down," *Salon,* August 3, 1998

---

*Despite the fact that more than a year earlier Krakauer had said that he'd reported what Martin Adams had told him, he wrote a letter to *Salon* (August 14, 1998) and said, ". . . this is what I know to be true about the conversation between Fischer and Boukreev atop the Hillary Step: Andy Harris, *(cont).*

In his "Postscript," in defense of his decision not to acknowledge in *Into Thin Air* Boukreev's explanation that Fischer had authorized his descent, Krakauer says that he "found many of Boukreev's recollections to be singularly unreliable." I have heard Krakauer offer this excuse before. Eight months prior to Anatoli's death, during a phone conversation I had with him, Krakauer said he had transcripts of interviews with Anatoli in which Boukreev had offered "conflicting testimony," one time saying that Fischer had okayed his descent, another time saying that Fischer had told Anatoli to go down.

Because I knew the limitations of Anatoli's English and had, by the time of my conversation with Krakauer, spent more than two hundred hours in conversation with Anatoli, I could readily understand the possibility of his making those statements but not seeing any arguable difference between the two. On more than one occasion, in going through the events above the Hillary Step, Boukreev explained to me. "Fischer says, 'Okay, go down.'" In that expression, as I understood it then and do now, was an agreement and an order. In effect, "Yeah, Anatoli. Okay. Go down."

I suggested to Krakauer that a possible explanation for the "conflicting testimony," as he had called it, was Anatoli's poor command of English. Krakauer responded, "The language problem admittedly is a real problem here. Anatoli is at a huge disadvantage. His English isn't perfect, and that's a problem." With agreement on that fact, I told Krakauer that I wanted to "take a look at the interviews," thinking I could share them with Anatoli and give him an opportunity to address Krakauer's questions, but those transcripts were never shared with me or with Anatoli, who was then very much alive and willing to respond.

And, what of Fischer's conversation with Bromet in which Fischer described a plan for Anatoli's descent ahead of clients

---

Martin Adams, Boukreev, and I were waiting together above the [Hillary] step when Fischer arrived on his way to the summit. Both Adams and I—the only witnesses to that conversation who are still alive—recalled the conversation in exactly the same way . . ."

in the event that Fischer perceived potential difficulties for his clients? Krakauer offers in his "Postscript" the promise of "compelling evidence" that no such plan ever existed. The evidence?

Krakauer says that no climbers in the Mountain Madness expedition, including Boukreev, were aware that Fischer had a plan,* suggesting, it seems, that a plan only becomes a plan when someone other than its creator becomes aware of it. If that is the suggestion, I don't buy it.

I have no doubt, based upon Bromet's statement and Fischer's acknowledged purpose for hiring Anatoli, that Fischer had a plan in mind and that atop the Hillary Step, given the lateness of the hour and the fact that his clients were sucking on a limited supply of oxygen, he put his plan into action. Krakauer's attempt at semantic snooker, suggesting that because there was not a plan "in place," there was no plan at all, is no credit to his credentials as a journalist.

> "I don't know why he descended alone from the South Summit, ahead of everybody else, abandoning his clients; as I said in my article, I can only speculate."
>
> —JON KRAKAUER
> Memo to: Mark Bryant and Brad Wetzler, *Outside;* et al.
> August 5, 1996

> "So, do I wish I had portrayed Boukreev differently in writing this book? No, I don't think so."
>
> —JON KRAKAUER
> "Postscript," *Into Thin Air: The Illustrated Edition,*
> November 1998

---

*Boukreev has never said that he knew of Fischer's plan in advance of summit day. In fact, on p. 138 of *The Climb* he explains that just above the Balcony he waited on the fixed ropes for Fischer to appear: "I was unsure about many details. About the general plan, yes, I understood, but things were changing." Boukreev, seeing that the expedition's progress was slower than had been projected, wanted to know what Fischer had in mind. It wasn't until just above the Hillary Step that he connected with Fischer and found out.

Krakauer's choice to ignore, absolutely and entirely, Boukreev's explanation that Scott Fischer had approved his descent *and* Scott Fischer's conversation with Bromet in which he offered that he had in mind a plan to have Anatoli descend ahead of clients is, in my opinion, indefensible. If Jon Krakauer had reason to question Boukreev's veracity, he had the pages of *Into Thin Air* in which to make and prove his case while Anatoli was still alive. Instead, he chose not to publish information that I think was critical to an understanding of the Everest tragedy. He showcased his judgments instead of allowing his readers to consider all of the available evidence.

—G. Weston DeWalt, London/Los Angeles
April 1999

A REVIEW FROM *THE AMERICAN ALPINE JOURNAL*

After all that has been written about the 1996 Everest tragedy, why should we care to read yet another account? The media avalanched us with an unprecedented depth of raw facts, yet left us with the escalating controversy that drew head guide Anatoli Boukreev of Kazakhstan to publish his side of the story with a co-writer, G. Weston DeWalt. In *The Climb*, Boukreev describes how he single-handedly performed one of the most amazing rescues in Himalayan history a few hours after climbing Everest without oxygen.

Depending on your source, Boukreev was either the villain or the hero of the unfortunate events on Everest. Just a month after *The Climb* was published in November 1997, he died in an avalanche on a winter ascent of the South Face of Annapurna. When DeWalt was called for a national news quote, he learned that they planned to say Boukreev would be best remembered as the villain of Jon Krakauer's bestseller, *Into Thin Air*. DeWalt cautioned that the American Alpine Club had just given Boukreev a major award for heroism and would be remembered by his peers as one of the greatest Himalayan mountaineers of all time.

When Boukreev disappeared on Annapurna, his newly published book and AAC award were fanning the flames of controversy to new heights. *The New York Times* included the following in a report of Boukreev's death: "Krakauer accuses Boukreev . . . of compromising his clients' safety to achieve his own ambitions . . . and endangered them by making the exhausting climb without the aid of bottled oxygen. . . . However, Krakauer credits Boukreev with bravely saving the lives of two [*sic*] climbers." Here is the controversy reduced to a sound bite.

The Climb presents a much-needed breath of fresh air, written from a guide's point of view, that dissipates some of the intriguing thin air surrounding the media-created search for blame. We learn, for example, that every one of Boukreev's clients survived the tragedy without major injuries, while those who did die or incurred major injuries were members of Krakauer's party. The leaders of both teams, Scott Fischer and Rob Hall, also did not live to tell their story.

The question of why these two competing leaders stayed so high so long, pushing clients toward the summit beyond a reasonable turnaround time, is never directly answered. Between the lines, however, the spotlight shines on those who have asked for it most forcefully. The extreme pressure Fischer and Hall felt to get the most positive free ink in *Outside* that would lure more high-dollar clients comes across as clearly as if the words were penned in blood. The reader senses that the presence of an *Outside* journalist as a client on the most fatal commercial Everest venture was no coincidence.

Far from trying "to achieve his own ambitions" that day, Boukreev fixed the Hillary Step for clients after Sherpas failed to do so, foresaw problems with clients nearing camp too late, noted five other guides on the peak, and descended to the South Col to be rested and hydrated enough to respond to an emergency. Boukreev now had climbed Everest three times without oxygen. His high-altitude performance, often alone and in extreme conditions, was unparalleled. He had climbed Manaslu in winter, Dhaulagiri in 17 hours, Makalu in 46 hours, and had traversed all four 8,000-meter summits of Kanchenjunga in a single push, to select just a few here. When he learned that climbers were lost in a blizzard in the dark, he made several solo forays late into the night to rescue three people near death. No other client, guide or Sherpa could muster the necessary strength and courage to accompany Boukreev as he went from tent to tent, asking for help.

Late the next day, Boukreev climbed alone back up to 8,350 meters on the slim chance he could save Scott Fischer, last seen by Sherpas lying comatose in the snow. Meanwhile, *Time* magazine was preparing a sensational three-page story about the tragedy, based on satellite phone and fax reports from the mountain, that failed even to mention Boukreev's name.

On May 16, after just two days' rest in the Western Cwm, as helicopters, Sherpas and other expeditions helped evacuate the survivors, Boukreev set off to solo Lhotse in the record time of 21 hours, climbing on a permit Fischer had obtained to guide the peak after Everest. Had Fischer survived unscathed, he almost certainly would have passed on Lhotse and accompanied his clients back to Kathmandu.

In *The Climb*, Boukreev reveals his thoughts as a professional guide, but holds the iron curtain over his own persona. With classic Russian reticence, he doesn't brag, mention his degree in physics, or apologize for actions on the mountain that others judged to be self-centered and uncaring. He counters a strong rebuke from Scott Fischer by saying that it had not been made clear to him that "chatting and keeping the clients pleased by focusing on their personal happiness" was equally important to focusing on the details that would bring safety and success. Unlike Krakauer, he is afraid to admit human failings that could help endear him to his audience and his climbing companions. He lets down his armor only far enough to admit to sometimes being a difficult person.

Even with DeWalt's impassioned prose and editing of Boukreev's transcribed interviews, *The Climb* fails to sustain the superb narrative quality that brought *Into Thin Air* to the pinnacle of literary success atop the *New York Times* bestseller list. But while it lacks the carefully choreographed structure and characterizations that make *Into Thin Air* impossible to put down, it forces the reader to think, rather than to accept armchair answers passively.

Boukreev avoids Krakauer's penchant for focusing on the idiosyncrasies of his companions by simply accepting fellow climbers at face value for who they are on the mountain. He succeeds without more complete characterizations because most readers already are very familiar with the players and the basic setting from *Into Thin Air* and a plethora of media stories.

Writing about a person invariably honors them or devalues them. Both Boukreev and DeWalt err on the side of honoring those attempting Everest, while Krakauer draws his reader toward tabloid-style assumptions that erase heroism from the Himalaya as surely as modern journalism erases greatness from the presidency.

A vastly experienced guide told me over dinner that he loved *Into Thin Air* and felt somewhat chagrined never to have paused to question its conclusions until he read Boukreev speaking his own language, thinking his own thoughts. He strongly related to the behind-the-scenes guide talk and the dilemma of being a nice guy attending to a client's every need versus nursing that person up into the Death Zone, where their survival would be dependent on their ability to keep going under their own power. DeWalt includes an especially fascinating three-page, first-person account of client Lou Kasischke's inner thoughts as he made an agonizing personal decision to turn around on the summit day.

The media circus surrounding the Everest tragedy appears to be a postmodern American phenomena. Single tragedies have claimed the lives of more climbers in the Himalaya many times before, but not Americans, not clients paying up to $65,000 each, not with daily reports on the Internet, not with a journalist climbing on assignment, and not with a broadcast phone call from a dying man to his wife. Thus the regrettable deaths of five climbers on Everest on May 10 degenerated from a real-live tragedy involving heroism and compassion into a veritable O.J. trial in which no participant is left unscathed. With *Outside* indirectly pulling media strings (as live television influenced Judge Ito's court), it is little wonder that justice and dignity took a backseat to the entertainment value of the sufferings of well-intentioned climbers. To much of the public, high-altitude mountaineering itself has been on trial. It is to this end that *The Climb* may have its most lasting significance.

Motivations are all important. If, as Krakauer suggests, the people who now climb Everest (graciously including himself) do it for questionable reasons, then our avocation is indeed in trouble. As Eric Shipton wrote in 1938 after several attempts on the mountain, "The ascent of Everest, like any other human endeavor, is only to be judged by the spirit in which it is attempted. . . . Let us climb peaks . . . not because others have failed, nor because the summits stand 28,000 feet above the sea, nor in patriotic fervor for the honor of a nation, nor for cheap publicity. . . . Let us not attack them with an army, announcing on the wireless to a sensation-loving world the news of our departure and the progress of our subsequent advance."

The mass appeal of the 1996 Everest story relates to the clear violation of every one of Shipton's tenets of more than a half-century ago in a new era in which blame is God.

—Galen Rowell, copyright © 1998

MOUNTAIN MADNESS EVEREST DEBRIEFING: A TRANSCRIPT

A NOTE TO READERS

The following is a partial transcript of the Mountain Madness debriefing that was tape-recorded on May 15, 1996, five days after the tragic events that claimed the life of their expedition leader, Scott Fischer, and the lives of Rob Hall, Doug Hansen, Andy Harris, and Yasuko Namba of the Adventure Consultants Guided Expedition. Included in this transcript are comments and discussions relating to the tragedy and its aftermath. Other commentary—relating to interests in the tape-recording of the debriefing and to the disposition of that recording—have been excluded to protect the privacy of the participants in the debriefing.

Those who participated in the debriefing were Neal Beidleman, expedition guide; Anatoli Boukreev, head climbing guide; Lopsang Jangbu Sherpa, climbing sirdar; Dr. Ingrid Hunt, Everest Base Camp manager and expedition doctor; and six of the expedition's eight climber-clients: Martin Adams, Lene Gammelgaard, Tim Madsen, Sandy Hill (Pittman), Klev Schoening, and Pete Schoening. Absent were Dale Kruse, who had not made a summit attempt and had departed Everest Base Camp, and Charlotte Fox. Fox had been airlifted from Everest Base Camp and taken to Kathmandu to get medical attention for frostbite.

SANDY: All right, the tape is rolling. We've got plenty of tape, so . . .

INGRID: Am I supposed to go first?

SANDY: I don't think so.

KLEV: We're just going to ramble, up and down, forward and back . . .

NEAL: Yeah, but we do need to find a starting place that makes sense.

KLEV: Sure.

TIM: One question that Ingrid wanted to try to establish was when Scott left camp [Camp IV], so why don't we start there?

SANDY: I think, actually, Camp IV, leaving in the morning, and the scene leaving that morning, might be a logical place to start. Camp III doesn't seem to be particularly relevant—or is it?

NEAL: Well, to me, there's a couple of facts that would make sense, and those can be added quickly in terms of, you know, my—again, as a perception but somewhat fact about Scott [Fischer]. It's my perception, but I believe it's a fact, that he was very tired walking.

SANDY: From Camp III to Camp IV?

NEAL: Yeah, and that establishes something.

KLEV: Why do you think he was tired?

TIM: He did not walk from Camp III to Camp IV with oxygen.

KLEV: Why'd he do that? Anybody know? Was it a conservation thing or a personal challenge?

NEAL: I think it was bullheadedness, myself. But, see again, now we're kind of in the gray area. Do we put information like that on the tape or not?

MARTIN: No, I think it should simply be facts.

SANDY: Well, it's a fact.

MARTIN: Scott went from [Camp] III to [Camp] IV without oxygen, period. Whatever else transpired, let somebody else interpret it—if it becomes a question.

NEAL: Well, Martin, you have a pretty good feel for this. Why don't we start with you simply because you're probably the most directed and you'll give us a really good pattern or a pro forma on how to do it. Is that okay?

MARTIN: Personally, I don't mind discussing it. On the recorder, I have reservations about that. I am perfectly willing to sit here. If I disagree with something and I know that I'm correct, I'll disagree. But I do not want to give my interpretation on the tape as to what transpired, for legal reasons. I've got too much to lose. Sorry. I would like to hear you discuss it. If I think something is out of line or wrong and I know it's wrong, I'd like to have the opportunity to correct it, for the record, but I don't want to be the record.

NEAL: Do we abandon the tape and just go with notes?

MARTIN: I think that's a wise decision.

KLEV: I would object to that, personally.

MARTIN: I think the tape's going to get you into trouble, if there is trouble. Because people are going to interpret every little thing you say or don't say, any way they like.

INGRID: I think you're much more likely to get the whole story on the tape.

MARTIN: I think, as far as getting the correct story, that may be correct, but—

INGRID: Then we'll have to do it some other time, because I want as much of the whole story as I can get.

KLEV: I'm filled with questions, personally. I've been in litigation. I recognize your concern. I'm putting that behind me in this case. This is an exceptional situation, and personally I'm willing to take that risk. I recognize everything you're saying, Martin.

MARTIN: Well, fine.

KLEV: Well, why shouldn't I?

MARTIN: So, let someone else do it.

KLEV: Oh, you mean as far as moderate?

MARTIN: That's correct.

KLEV: Yeah, well, I nominate Neal as moderator.

MARTIN: I think the most important thing is to get Lopsang's and Anatoli's interpretation.

LENE: Yeah, I think that's true. They've been there.

MARTIN: I think we should start there and let them go and—

SANDY: Rather than chronological? Just start at the crisis?

MARTIN: Sounds reasonable to me.

SANDY: Can we go through—why don't we go through quickly the—

MARTIN: The chronology?

KLEV: I think Martin can explain himself. He's already indicated that he's ready and willing to do that.

MARTIN: I'm willing to participate. I don't want to—

SANDY: Let's just go through leaving the tent in the morning, the order we left in, who left with who, who saw who going where and approximate times at key landmarks on the mountain. Let's get ourselves to the summit in about—

MARTIN: Five minutes.

SANDY: —five or ten minutes and then let's go on from there, because that's what really matters. Okay? Does that sound like a plan?

MARTIN: Yeah.

SANDY: Okay, so we woke up at ten o'clock [10:00 P.M., May 9, 1996].

NEAL: First, Sherpas. It was exactly ten o'clock when they started rumbling around.

SANDY: You gotta speak up, Neal.

NEAL: Oh, is the tape running?

SANDY: Yeah.

NEAL: Oh, Okay. This is Neal. Ten o'clock exactly is when I heard the first Sherpa rumbling around, and approximately fifteen minutes or so after that we had a pot of tea from the Sherpas. We spent the next hour and fifteen minutes organizing ourselves, and at approximately 11:30 [P.M.] we piled out of the tents. That process probably took ten or fifteen minutes, and, with the intention of leaving at twelve o'clock, put our crampons on. I remember helping Tim with his crampons quite a bit; and Charlotte. I didn't see who left before them, but I did tell Charlotte to leave at approximately 12:00, 12:10 [A.M.].

SANDY: I left first. I left camp first with Lopsang.

NEAL: At what time?

SANDY: I don't know what time it was, but Scott said, "Is anybody ready? Because, Lopsang is, and, if anybody is ready, they should go with him." And, Rob Hall's* people were about an hour ahead of us on the hill already. You could see their headlamps up there, and so Lopsang and I took off, and I would say we were at least ten minutes ahead of the pack. Would you say that is correct?

NEAL: Okay.

KLEV: I have a question for Lopsang. The night before, what time had been arranged for you, for you, Lopsang, to leave?

LOPSANG: Twelve o'clock [midnight].

KLEV: Twelve o'clock. You were supposed to leave with the members?

LOPSANG: Yeah, with members.

KLEV: You were supposed to leave with—

NEAL: Were there any Sherpas from our group that were supposed to leave at ten o'clock to go fix ropes?

LOPSANG: No.

KLEV: Who was going to fix ropes?

LOPSANG: Fixed ropes already other people to making.† And after so

_____

*Rob Hall was the leader of the Adventure Consultants expedition.
†Here Lopsang appears to be referring to a Montenegrin (Yugoslavian) expedition that had reported fixing some ropes above Camp IV on May 9, 1996, before abandoning their summit attempt.

he like—[UI]*—and Anatoli and Neal fix, because I am going to pass while they're there. I'm also sick and vomit.†

KLEV: You were sick and vomiting and you were unable to go earlier?

LOPSANG: And, no, I decide go to with member. Last camp, also, I'm sick, so I wait—[UI]—and after, so I'm going to summit, so all members summit, after I wait for Scott and so I waiting—

SANDY: So—but there was no assignment earlier in the day for you to leave early to fix ropes?

LOPSANG: So, I have all fix—[UI]—I carry, but I fix every year. So, I fixing rope; every year where I'm making.

KLEV: How were those ropes to get in front of Rob Hall? He left an hour before us. How were we supposed to get those fixed ropes in front of Rob Hall? Were there arrangements with our other Sherpas in light of your illness?

LOPSANG: Before, so already making so first times of the other group, trying get making ropes, and they are not gain summit. They come back South Summit to come back.

KLEV: Did anybody follow that?

TIM: He says Sherpas from Rob Hall's group were going to fix the lower mountain?

LOPSANG: Yeah, so they're going to first—they're going to Rob Hall Sherpa going to pass first back, already making rope before other Sherpa. So, the other group try to pass summit and South Summit to up, not gain, come back. And South Summit to after Neal and Anatoli

---

*While the recording of the debriefing was of fairly good quality, it is often difficult to understand Lopsang Jangbu Sherpa. His command of English was limited. The symbol [UI] will be used in those places where his comments were unintelligible and in a few other places in the transcript where the spoken words of participants were not readily understandable.

†Boukreev often speculated that Lopsang's sickness was due primarily to his having broken his acclimatization routine when he had helicoptered to Kathmandu with his uncle, Ngawang Topche Sherpa, who was suffering from an altitude-related illness to which he would later succumb.

fixing rope. I carry ropes up, and last camp I give to Neal and Neal carry rope up.*

NEAL: And, what time did you reach the summit Lopsang? Do you know? Did you look at your watch?

LOPSANG: So, we reach summit half past one [1:00 P.M].

SANDY: Half past one?

LOPSANG: Yeah.—No?

NEAL: No, I reached the summit at 1:25 or 1:28 [P.M.] and you were at least two hours after me.

LOPSANG: Yeah, 1:25, so—[UI].

ANATOLI: One o'clock I was on summit. Maybe seven minutes past one o'clock I was on summit. And then—

LOPSANG: And so, after I come back—[UI]—so you know South Summit—[UI]—all summit after Rob Hall and Doug [Hansen] also summit—[UI]—after all summit, after I come back, because, so, there rope, so my ice ax to keep rope, and after, so all come down, and my ice ax take out and I come down.†

---

*On a couple of occasions before his tragic death by avalanche on September 25, 1996, Lopsang explained: (1) a guide from a Montenegrin expedition that had made a summit attempt on May 9, 1996, had told him that his team had fixed some ropes as they climbed toward the South Summit, where they abandoned their attempt; (2) Rob Hall's Adventure Consultants expedition left forty-five minutes before the Mountain Madness expedition, and if any ropes needed fixing, it was their responsibility to do it; (3) his sickness was not due to not having been using supplementary oxygen or to his having assisted Sandy Hill (Pittman) for a brief time, but it did interfere with his capacity to fix ropes when it was discovered that neither the Montenegrin nor the Adventure Consultants expeditions had fixed ropes ahead of the Mountain Madness team; and (4) Neal Beidleman and Anatoli Boukreev should have been more aggressive in their efforts to fix ropes.

†Lopsang Jangbu Sherpa summited somewhere in the vicinity of 2:30 P.M. and waited on the summit until approximately 3:40 P.M. when Scott Fischer finally arrived. Approximately fifteen minutes later they began their descent; Fischer first and then Lopsang. Just below the summit Lopsang stopped to retrieve his ice ax where, on his ascent, he had anchored it in the snow to fix a length of rope for ascending climbers. On his descent Lopsang noticed that Rob Hall, who had summitted around 2:30 P.M., had come off the summit and was assisting an exhausted Doug Hansen, one of Hall's clients, up the rope that Lopsang had fixed to his ice ax. Lopsang, wanting to make certain that Hall and Hansen would be secure on their descent, waited by his ice ax in

KLEV: I have a question for Neal and Anatoli. This is Klev. What was the arrangement for fixing lines ahead of the group and in conjunction with Rob Hall? What was—

ANATOLI: I heard from—I am Anatoli Boukreev—I heard from Scott Fischer about this plan: start at twelve o'clock; I need to be with group and see group; Neal will, with some Sherpas, will fix line—what I heard from Scott, exactly. And, what is your questions?

LENE: I heard specifically—this is Lene—I heard specifically that Scott said that the lines would be fixed in advance so that the members should at no point wait.

SANDY: I also heard that the lines were all to be fixed by our Sherpa and by Rob Hall's Sherpa in advance, and that they were going to leave at ten o'clock; we were going to leave at midnight, because Scott was laughing and telling me that he thought I should leave with the Sherpa since I was so slow.

KLEV: This is Klev. I concur with Sandy. That was my understanding of what was supposed to transpire.

NEAL: This is Neal. That's also my understanding of what was to happen.

SANDY: What time—should we talk about what time everybody reached—I guess the key landmarks don't matter, but the summit. You were on the summit first, Neal?

LENE: That's one thing that I would like to say.

SANDY: Okay.

---

subzero temperatures until the two climbers made the summit and returned (somewhere between 4:15 and 4:30 P.M.). Lopsang would not catch up to Fischer until approximately 5:45 P.M. by which time Fischer was in serious trouble.

Why Rob Hall encouraged Doug Hansen to continue his ascent remains one of the most perplexing questions of the Everest tragedy. An experienced and respected guide whose penchant for going by the book was well-known, he broke one of his cardinal rules by not turning Hansen around. What may have motivated such a careful and responsible guide to shelve his better judgment has been a matter of endless speculation. What is known is that the decision to take Hansen to the summit directly impacted the subsequent decisions of Lopsang Jangbu Sherpa and Andy Harris, one of Hall's guides, drawing their attention from other problems that were developing on the mountain.

LENE: This is Lene. The night we arrived at the South Col, it was blowing heavily, and it kept on blowing until some point in the evening. And I had doubts in me, and I know there were some people in our tent talking about it. "Are we going to climb or are we not going to climb?" Because, I don't personally think it's a wise thing to start out climbing after a big storm, because it's not a good sign. It's not a good sign that you'll have stable weather. And, at a certain point, I think it was ten o'clock that night, Scott talked to Rob Hall, and I got the understanding that they agreed that both teams were going to leave together.

KLEV: This is Klev. At that time the wind had totally subsided.

LENE: Right.

KLEV: At ten o'clock [10:00 P.M., May 9, 1996].

LENE: Yes.

KLEV: By ten o'clock.

NEAL: Before ten o'clock.

LENE: Yes.

KLEV: Sometime earlier than that in—I've got a question about the oxygen and how much oxygen was stocked on the mountain, and maybe, Lopsang, you could start. How much oxygen was at Southeast Ridge?

LOPSANG: So—

NEAL: Let's start at Camp IV.

KLEV: Or, Camp IV, sure. How much oxygen was at Camp IV before members arrived?

LOPSANG: The Sherpa carry twenty-one oxygen bottle up.

KLEV: They carried twenty-one? On summit day are you talking about? Or before members arrived?

LOPSANG: So, summit day, they carry up—[UI].

KLEV: Do you understand?

LENE: How many oxygen bottles were at the South Col to begin with?

LOPSANG: South Col to carry [to the] summit?

LENE: No, just in the South Col to begin with.

KLEV: Before members arrive, before we go up, before summit day.

LOPSANG: Sixty-two, sixty-two bottle.

KLEV: How many big bottles? How many small?

LOPSANG: Nine big bottle.

KLEV: Nine big bottles for sleeping on—

LOPSANG: Yeah, and small—umm—

KLEV: It would be the difference. Okay.

NEAL: This is Neal. The original plan was to have eleven bottles at Camp III and later a bottle was found on the lines that was asked to be brought down to Camp III, so we would have eleven and a half, or basically twelve bottles at Camp III. The original plan called for either sixty—I believe sixty-nine bottles—I can look in my notes—at Camp IV. We were not concerned that the number was sixty-two, because the sixty-nine number included Pete and Dale's oxygen supply.* That included a contingency night waiting at the South Col, sleeping on half a bottle a night for each person. So, with the number of bottles that Lopsang told us, sixty-two to sixty-five, I can't remember the number exactly—told to us before—we felt comfortable that was more than we had originally anticipated.

KLEV: Then, Lopsang, how many were carried up and where were they put?

LOPSANG: Our Sherpa carry twenty-one bottles.

KLEV: Twenty-one bottles were carried onto the mountain?

LOPSANG: Yeah.

NEAL: And, how many of those are used by Sherpa?

LOPSANG: The Sherpa used two—[UI].

KLEV: How many Sherpas did we have on the mountain?

---

*Pete Schoening and Dale Kruse were Mountain Madness climber-clients who did not climb on summit day, May 10, 1996.

LOPSANG: Six Sherpa.*

KLEV: Six Sherpa counting yourself?

LOPSANG: But, I no use. I carry one bottle, so I give to—[UI]—at the summit.[†]

SANDY: Can you tell us the names of the Sherpa that were climbing that day?

LOPSANG: We have six Sherpa. One, I am Lopsang Sherpa, and Tashi Tshering Sherpa, Ngawang Tenzing Sherpa, Ngawang Sya Kya Sherpa, Tenzing Sherpa, and Ngawang Dorje Sherpa, and all—Ngawang Tenzing Sherpa and Ngawang Sya Kya Sherpa is near Hillary Step—[UI]—going back, because Ngawang Tenzing Sherpa is a little sick and going back.

KLEV: One Sherpa went back because he was sick.

LOPSANG: Two Sherpa.

KLEV: Two Sherpa went back?

LOPSANG: One Sherpa back and—[UI].

KLEV: So, we had four?

NEAL: Where did they turn around?

LOPSANG: And, we had four Sherpas summit: Lopsang Sherpa, Tashi Tshering Sherpa, Tenzing Sherpa, and Tashi Tshering Sherpa.[‡]

NEAL: And, where did the two Sherpa turn around?

LOPSANG: Two Sherpa going to—[UI].

NEAL: Yes, they turned around though where? How high?

---

*As has been noted (see p. 154, *The Climb*), Fischer had authorized all seven Sherpas who had climbed to Camp IV to make a summit bid. Unbeknownst to Fischer and other Mountain Madness expedition members on summit day, Lopsang had ordered one Sherpa, Pemba Sherpa, to remain at Camp IV during the final assault.

[†]Here, Lopsang appears to be noting that at 8,820 meters, just below the summit, he gave the full canister of oxygen that he had been carrying to Sandy Hill (Pittman).

[‡]Lopsang repeats Tashi Tshering Sherpa as one of those who made the summit. The fourth summiting Sherpa, it is believed, was Ngawang Dorje Sherpa.

LOPSANG: Uh—[UI].

SANDY: Around 8,800 meters?

TIM: South Summit.

LOPSANG: 8,800 meters—South Summit.

NEAL: I thought that your father, Ngawang [Sya Kya] Sherpa, turned around somewhere lower down by the Southeast Ridge.

LENE: No, I saw him at the South Summit.

LOPSANG: [UI].

NEAL: Okay, and then we had one Sherpa that stayed at the South Col, Pemba Sherpa. Right?

LOPSANG: Pemba Sherpa.

KLEV: I'm still confused. Of those six Sherpa, who was on oxygen? How many used oxygen, how many Sherpa?

LOPSANG: They use, uh, twelve oxygen.

KLEV: Two were on oxygen?

LOPSANG: Twelve. Twelve.

SANDY and INGRID (simultaneously): Twelve bottles?

LOPSANG: Five Sherpa use oxygen—ten oxygen.

KLEV: Five Sherpas used oxygen. You were the only Sherpa that did not use oxygen.

LOPSANG: I no use oxygen.

KLEV: Why did you not use oxygen?

LOPSANG: Because I climbing so many times, so—three—now this is my fourth time—before three time without oxygen. I use oxygen, but more vomit—[UI]—and after so I'm—[UI]—with oxygen.

INGRID: Does that mean you tried oxygen on this trip, but it made you vomit?

LOPSANG: Yes, before many, before '93, I had climb. Never use oxygen.

SANDY: He started vomiting with oxygen.

INGRID: Oh, on other trips you've tried oxygen and you think it made you sick?

LOPSANG: Yeah, I used oxygen, so I'm vomit; I'm no—[UI]—a headache. I climb with oxygen.

KLEV: Did you use any oxygen here?

LOPSANG: No.

KLEV: You didn't.

NEAL: But, some in the tent, yes?

LOPSANG: Tent, so they give to oxygen bottle, but now empty, but no oxygen.

KLEV: After summit day?

LOPSANG: No.

KLEV: Night before summit, you were given oxygen, empty oxygen bottle?

LOPSANG: No oxygen. And so I carry extra one bottle oxygen up, so Sherpa, all the Sherpa not coming, and so send the oxygen please. I give—[UI]—summit.

KLEV: Okay, so twenty-one bottles were put on the mountain by Sherpa—

LOPSANG: Yeah.

KLEV: And where—?

LOPSANG: Sherpa and members—

NEAL: No, but twelve of those bottles are used by the Sherpa themselves.

LENE: Maybe, because everybody carried oxygen, and I think that the Sherpas also carried their own oxygen, but—

LOPSANG: Members, extra two with Sherpa, two is members—the Sherpa carry four bottle oxygen.

KLEV: Sherpas all carried four bottles of oxygen—

LOPSANG: Yeah.

KLEV: And every member carried two bottles of oxygen. Is that accurate for Neal and Anatoli also?

ANATOLI: Not Anatoli. I didn't use oxygen. I carry one bottle extra and I give for Neal when Neal work forward to fix lines. I gave him one my bottle extra.

KLEV: Anatoli, why weren't you using oxygen?

ANATOLI: My point about this. I have big experience with oxygen. If you use oxygen, it is very dangerous when oxygen finish. I afraid about this. I felt I can work without oxygen. If I will use oxygen and oxygen will finish, it will be much more difficult. Because it is physiology. You need use oxygen full-time. I afraid about this weather because I talk with Scott Fischer about this weather. Was not sure about weather will be very good. And, my point, not climb with this date. But Rob Hall have big experience, much bigger than my experience, and—

KLEV: Have you ever used oxygen, Anatoli?

ANATOLI: Where?

KLEV: Have you ever used it anywhere? Have you ever used it?

ANATOLI: Yes, in traverse of Kanchenjunga, for summit of Kanchenjunga I use oxygen.* And this is very—you can see this with difficult weather, you need—for me, very important to this ability—what I did. If I will use oxygen, then oxygen will finish, it is more difficult to work. Very hard. Because it is body ready to oxygen; oxygen finish and you stop. Like what we saw with Scott.

KLEV: Had Scott ever used oxygen before?

NEAL: Yes, he had. He climbed Lhotse with it, and I believe his first two trips to Everest were oxygen trips.

ANATOLI: But, for work without oxygen, you need experience. Is very— you need, not like first time go without oxygen. You need to have big experience about this. If you have this, it is okay. If you have not this, it is not okay. Also, for security, if you some get sickness, you need extra bottles. I was not sure about how many bottles extra Sherpa have

---

*In 1989 Boukreev was as a member of a Russian national team that successfully traversed the summits of Kanchenjunga. Boukreev, at the insistence of his coach, used supplementary oxygen.

for members. And for me it was a question. Now for Lopsang. Lopsang, how many Sherpas have extra for members—bottles?*

LOPSANG: Ten bottles.

ANATOLI: Ten bottles.

KLEV: There were six Sherpas, and they all have two bottles—they all had four bottles, excuse me—

LOPSANG: Five Sherpa carry extra bottle, ten bottle, and I carry one bottle.

KLEV: Because you were carrying fixed ropes also.

LOPSANG: Yeah, all carry—[UI].

KLEV: Did somebody follow that totally?

INGRID: Yeah.

SANDY: Yeah.

TIM: So, there was eleven bottles, would be extra for people to use?

KLEV: Eleven bottles that the Sherpas were carrying.

LOPSANG: Carry—[UI].

KLEV: Okay, then where did you put those? Where were those put?

LOPSANG: So we give to South Summit—

KLEV: South Summit?

LOPSANG: Yeah.

---

*Boukreev knew that the climbing Sherpas were to carry one bottle to the South Summit for each of the climber-clients and that a reserve of oxygen was to be on the mountain for him, but he was unsure how many bottles of oxygen were actually delivered.

SANDY: You deposited them on the South Summit? They were left on the ground at the South Summit?*

LOPSANG [UI]—but I not carry them down—[UI].

KLEV: I didn't understand that.

TIM: He didn't bring the extra empty bottles down.

KLEV: Oh, yes.

LOPSANG: So I not can because I have Scott—[UI]—I tell to [Scott], "Please we go to Camp IV." He [Scott] say, "I'm not going to Camp IV, I'm—[UI]."

SANDY: He's jumping ahead.

ANATOLI: Excuse me. How many bottles Scott have oxygen?

LOPSANG: He had three bottles please, yeah.

ANATOLI: Three.

---

*The plan had been for the Mountain Madness Sherpas to deposit—at the South Summit—ten bottles of oxygen. From that supply, each of the six Mountain Madness climber-clients on the final assault, Neal Beidleman, and Scott Fischer were to take one bottle on their descent. The additional two bottles, it is assumed, were the bottles that Fischer had agreed he would make available to Boukreev in the event he needed them on summit day (see p. 52, *The Climb*).

Like Mountain Madness, Rob Hall's Adventure Consultants expedition was to have extra oxygen bottles cached at the South Summit for its climbers. How many bottles of oxygen remained at the South Summit as members of the Adventure Consultants team began their descent remains a question to this day. Mike Groom, one of Rob Hall's guides, and Jon Krakauer, one of Hall's climber-clients, have offered different figures in their published accounts of their expedition's summit attempt. Krakauer has said that "at least six" bottles remained when he, Andy Harris, Mike Groom, and Yasuko Namba, another climber-client, arrived at the South Col. Mike Groom has said that he distributed "full" bottles of oxygen to Harris, Namba, and Krakauer, took one for himself, and that two full bottles were taken from the cache by Ang Dorje Sherpa and Ngawang Norbu Sherpa, two of Rob Hall's climbing Sherpas who had descended ahead of Hall and Doug Hansen. If there were no more than six bottles of Adventure Consultants oxygen at the South Col when that expedition began its descent and if Groom's account of how that oxygen was parceled out is accurate, that means that no bottles of Adventure Consultants oxygen remained when Hall (and perhaps Hansen) reached the South Summit. However, it should be noted that Jon Krakauer has said in *Into Thin Air* that Rob Hall, upon his arrival at the South Summit, "had possession of two full oxygen canisters."

KLEV: How many?

LOPSANG: He had two bottles before.

KLEV: Two bottles—

LOPSANG: And, so one Sherpa give to him and Sherpa going to pass—[UI]—

ANATOLI: In summit he go with oxygen?

LOPSANG: Yeah, with oxygen.

KLEV: And at South Summit he passed a Sherpa that gave him another bottle?

LOPSANG: Yeah.

KLEV: So he had the two he carried up and then a Sherpa gave him a third one?

LOPSANG: Yeah.

SANDY: And what was the flow rate? Do we know? Does anybody—I mean, did he mention it or did you see it?

LOPSANG: He's very sick.

SANDY: Yes, but what number was the flow of his oxygen? Did you see it?

LOPSANG: No, we don't see. So, we have all full oxygen bottle—[UI]—one hundred fifteen, one hundred twenty—[UI].

KLEV: I wanted to jump back—this is Klev—to the fixing of the lines again, because there was some mention that, from either Anatoli or Lopsang, I've forgotten now, that it was Neal's responsibility to be up there, and I personally followed Neal—

[GAP ON RECORDING]*

KLEV:—have any indication, make any indication to me that he was

---

*On the audiotape of the debriefing that was provided to Boukreev, there are occasional breaks in continuity. Boukreev recalled that at certain times during the taping, if someone wanted to go off the record, the taping would be halted. Boukreev was unable to determine, in listening to the audiotape, whether a break in continuity was intentional or due to recording or copying procedures. Whenever a break in continuity was noted, the transcriber inserted "[GAP ON RECORDING]."

supposed to be up there. So I'm a little confused there, and think there's some clarification in order.

NEAL: It was not my understanding that I was to fix lines. It was my understanding from Scott that I was to be in the middle of the pack and try to organize and help as many people as possible, just continue up the mountain. The reason that I started fixing lines from basically taking the initiative to move forward and to get into position to fix lines from the Southeast Ridge was that I looked at my watch at that time and it seemed that we were very slow based on the cutoff times that Rob Hall had recommended. They weren't stringent, but it just seemed that we were behind and that there was no organization up front. From the Southeast Ridge, I remember yelling back to people to hurry up and not wait too long. I followed Lopsang and Ang Dorje, a Sherpa from the Rob Hall expedition, up over the first little bulge. Klev was behind me. We made a new trail off to the left which was a little safer, broke through some deep snow up to a bench. Lopsang was there; he was very sick and vomiting. From there I took three ropes? from? two ropes? two long ropes?

LOPSANG: [UI].

NEAL: Ah, I took two ropes from Lopsang, a very long white polypropylene rope and maybe sixty meters of 7 mil. Perlon rope. And I don't recall—did I take an oxygen bottle from you or no? Yes? No. I did not there. We continued up. Ang Dorje fixed, but we climbed some more. Ang Dorje fixed one rope. After that I took out the long white polypropylene rope and fixed another long pitch and dug out the remaining ropes to the South Summit. I arrived there, according to my watch, at exactly 9:58 [A.M.]. I remember looking because Rob's cutoff time was about ten o'clock at the South Summit, that I recall. And I thought, boy, we're getting late, and was very antsy. Martin followed me up to the South Summit. He was the second person there, probably trailing me by, I'm guessing, a half an hour. I was on the South Summit for roughly one hour, and then moved down below the South Summit behind the rock where everybody sat to watch the traverse. I was there for approximately forty-five minutes. I recall looking around at the Sherpas that were there and none of our Sherpas were there and Ang Dorje was either tired, sick, or didn't want to fix. I looked at Anatoli—

KLEV: To fix across the—

NEAL: To fix to the summit. I looked at Anatoli and thought we better get going. I yelled at Andy Harris, a guide from Rob Hall's expedition, if he would help.* We [Beidleman and Boukreev] took the Perlon rope that I had, unfurled it, and Anatoli and I started across the ridge.

KLEV: This is Klev. You made some references to turnaround times, and I'm wondering what kind of discussions you and Scott and Anatoli had in regard to those?

NEAL: The discussions that I had with Scott was that I was to be in the middle of the pack, and I thought Anatoli would be up in front, fixing ropes, which he did from the South Summit on, and Scott was to be sweep. And Scott would make all the hard decisions about who could continue and who had to turn around, as a function of his leadership role, and I wasn't comfortable telling somebody on the expedition at that point that they had to turn around when they may have thought they had a chance to continue on. So, I just pushed forward, knowing that, at least from the position I was in, I felt comfortable getting down. I didn't think it was too late. I knew I could move fast and essentially felt that the responsibility for turning people around was behind me and not at me. Either I could push the route forward or I could stay there as a tollgate and turn people around. If Anatoli and I had not gone forward, no one would have made the summit; everybody would have been stacked up at the South Col and that would have been the end of the game anyway.

[GAP ON RECORDING]

LENE: My personal way of being in this group has all the way been trust yourself, trust yourself, trust yourself, because I haven't heard anything about this. Then—and I have a question to the guides, and that is: Everybody, before we even started out toward the summit bid, leaving the South Col, was talking about that Lopsang was extremely sick. Who the hell is responsible for keeping a Sherpa off the mountain who's vomiting, maybe because of altitude, instead of sending him on the mountain? I don't understand that. I would never have done that.

SANDY: With all this discussion, we've not said anything about Scott's

---

*Andy Harris passed on assisting Beidleman; instead, he proceeded up the mountain with Jon Krakauer, a climber-client with the Adventure Consultants expedition, who had become concerned about his dwindling oxygen supply. (See "Mountain Madness Everest Debriefing," p. 324 and *The Climb*, p. 147.)

whereabouts. Did anybody—up to the chronology that we've got to this point—did anybody see Scott?

LENE: No.

TIM: Halfway up the first fixed line, above the Southeast Ridge—this is Tim—I stopped and I looked back because everybody was stacked up there and nobody was moving. And, I made a count of approximately thirty people who were coming up, and I was curious where Scott was, so I did look around for him, and I thought I saw him maybe about the same spot where Lopsang was sitting and was sick earlier.

SANDY: Lopsang, did you climb with Scott? Before the summit? Before the summit, not after the summit. But, before the summit?

ANATOLI: No.

SANDY: Did you climb with Scott or did you see Scott?

LOPSANG: No.

ANATOLI: No, he was very behind I think. I tried to see him, but I didn't saw him. I didn't see him also. And very I understand, uh, Scott, because very difficult to make exactly plan. Sometime situation tell for you what you need to do. And very difficult to make sure plan about who will fix line, what is time, because it is depended of weather, depended how you feel, necessary discuss about. I, many time, I try to stop and wait [for] Scott and make some questions for him because for me, also, I didn't understand many things on this last attempt. And, maybe he get some sickness; it is also possible. Also he believe for Neal, for me, we can to do this with Neal. With Neal—I met Neal before, when he go forward to fix line, after 8,500 meters.— The last time when I saw Scott come. Scott felt—his look was okay, not questions, little behind of group, but I don't understand he— maybe he felt not so very well.*—And, then Neal go forward; we little discuss with him. Neal said he will go with Ang Dorje, the sirdar of Rob Hall expedition, and he go to fix line, and he work with oxygen. I have some extra bottle, so I gave him if he will need for hard job. And South Summit, we get probably—what is time, Neal?

---

*Boukreev, here, is referring to his encounter with Fischer above the Hillary Step, as Boukreev was descending from the summit and Fischer was heading up the mountain.

NEAL: South Summit I arrived at ten o'clock [10:00 A.M., May 10, 1996].

ANATOLI: And I didn't see [fixed ropes], because, before also, Scott told me maybe Sherpas will fix line; it is not difficult. But I didn't see nothing, [no] initiative from nobody. I told Neal, "You will belay me and I go to forwards." Then I saw some two guides from Rob Hall expedition go behind me with long rope.

NEAL: Actually, one was a guide, Anatoli. Andy Harris [was a guide], and the other [was] a client, Jon Krakauer.

ANATOLI: Yeah, but strong climbers, I think.

NEAL: Yes.

ANATOLI: And very simple way, we didn't fix line, because I think behind somebody will make this simple, and I go for difficult place and we make this very fast, I think, not so difficult, not so long time, we make very fast. And after Hillary Step is one also little steep place, but with crampon, with ice ax, not so difficult. Our ropes is finished. We go to summit and—

NEAL: Actually, from there, Anatoli, I stopped and got the rope from Jon Krakauer, because I wanted to fix that section because of the wind.

ANATOLI: [Wind] began.

NEAL: Yes, Andy [Harris] and Jon [Krakauer] asked if they could go around me because their oxygen was low.* I said, "Fine." I uncoiled the rope. It was very long, maybe a hundred meters. Martin was below me. I asked Martin if he would help me pay out the rope and tie the end to [an] anchor, which he did. I started up. I made it maybe twenty or thirty feet, until the rope caught in the rocks. I had to come back a little bit and wait. Martin finally helped me untangle the rope from the rock. I continued up to a snow stake, tied off the rope. There, the remaining forty or fifty meters, I walked up further to fix. I didn't find another anchor. We didn't have anchors with us because we thought that the Sherpas would. It didn't appear to be my job earlier

---

*Andy Harris and Jon Krakauer of the Adventure Consultants expedition, like Beidleman, Fischer, and the Mountain Madness climber-clients, had been allocated three canisters (approximately eighteen hours) of oxygen for their summit bid. At this encounter with Beidleman—around noon—Harris and Krakauer had been climbing for more than twelve and one-half hours.

to think about bringing anchors as well. I got to the end of the rope and I didn't want to leave my ice ax because it was still steep and I wanted to self-arrest. I threw the end of the rope off the remaining forty meters into Tibet so no one would grab the rope and think it was fixed and pull up. And then I continued up to the summit and arrived there about 1:25 to 1:30 [P.M.].

SANDY: Should we just state everybody's summit times? What they think?

ANATOLI: Maybe seven minutes past of one o'clock I make summit.

SANDY: Anatoli was seven minutes past one o'clock. I think I was 2:15 [P.M.].

NEAL: I was 1:25 to 1:30 [P.M.].

LENE: I think around 2:30 [P.M.].

SANDY: Lene around 2:30 [P.M.] on the summit.

MARTIN: I was with Neal. I don't know what time it was.

SANDY: Martin was with Neal.

KLEV: This is Klev. I was approximately a half hour behind Neal.

INGRID: I'd say about two o'clock.

TIM: This is Tim. I think Tim and Charlotte summited about 2:20, 2:25 [P.M.].

SANDY: You were ahead of me, so either I'm wrong or—

TIM: Well, within five minutes of each other.

SANDY: You guys were ten minutes ahead of me.

TIM: Between 2:15 and 2:30 [P.M.] is when I think the four of us put it.

SANDY: Yeah, and, Lopsang, what time did you get on the summit?

LOPSANG: Same.

SANDY: We were at the same time.

LOPSANG: Same time—[UI].

TIM: You were ahead of us.

LENE: I always thought we were very close together at that point; that's true, yeah.

LOPSANG: Summit to come back, so I'm 4:30 [P.M.]—

LENE: Yeah.

KLEV: This is Klev. I'm maybe fifteen minutes behind Neal—correction. —I have a question for Anatoli: What time did you leave Camp IV?

ANATOLI: From Camp IV?

KLEV: Yes.

ANATOLI: Twelve o'clock.

KLEV: And who did you climb with, Anatoli, from Camp IV to Southeast Ridge?

ANATOLI: Martin first time; then he go—

KLEV: You climbed with Martin from Camp IV to Southeast Ridge?

ANATOLI: Yes.

LENE: And I saw Anatoli. He was sometimes behind me, sometimes in front of me.

ANATOLI: I saw people—very stability—[UI].

KLEV: How about if we talk a little about radios and radio placement?

SANDY: That's a good idea.

KLEV: Where they were and who had 'em?

SANDY: Who had a radio? Did you have a radio?

KLEV: Lopsang, did you have a radio?

LOPSANG: Yeah, a small one.

INGRID: A small yellow one.

KLEV: What color?

LOPSANG: Yellow.

SANDY: You had my—one of my small yellow radios.

LOPSANG: Yeah, yeah—[UI]—only Scott had one.

KLEV: Scott had one of the small yellow radios?

SANDY: And Scott had a small yellow radio.

KLEV: And you had one?

INGRID: How did you?—

LOPSANG: I give you?—[UI]

SANDY: Yeah.

INGRID: How did you talk to Pemba?

LENE: Did any of the other guides have a radio or any arrangements for radio contact with the expedition leader?

NEAL: I did not. Originally, Scott and I were going to split the radios, but no specific arrangement was made for me to have the radio. We were going to have a radio at the front of the pack and the back of the pack, and we assumed Lopsang would be at the front and Scott at the back. When I passed Lopsang, at the altitude and under the circumstances, it didn't occur to me to grab the radio.

INGRID: So, Lopsang, you had a black radio and a yellow radio?

LOPSANG: Yes—[UI].

INGRID: And when I talked to you on the summit, you were talking on the black—?

LOPSANG: Yeah, black one.

SANDY: And only Sherpa had black radios?

LOPSANG: What I had—other Sherpa had—[UI].

SANDY: You had no radio, Anatoli?

ANATOLI: No.

INGRID: You had the only black radio that could communicate with the other camps?*—Okay.

---

*Dr. Ingrid Hunt was confirming with Lopsang that he had been carrying a black radio that was tuned to the frequency being used by those Sherpas at Camp IV, Camp II, and at the Everest Base Camp. The "small yellow" radios previously mentioned did not have the capacity of the black radios and were not used to communicate with the Everest Base Camp on summit day.

KLEV: Jumping back to the protection. Lopsang, you carried some fixed ropes. Did you have any ice-screws or any slings or any—?

LOPSANG: Every year we carry only rope and we find some other rope and other rope we—

KLEV: You and other Sherpas carry only rope? No ice-screws, slings, or—protection?

ANATOLI: For this route, Klev, we don't need ice-screws—

LOPSANG: Ice-screws we don't need to go up.

ANATOLI: Never people like—I talk with Rob Hall—never people used ice-screws.

KLEV: Never need ice-screws—

LOPSANG: So, we carry—

KLEV: Neal, did you think that the "Sherps" had some?

NEAL: Well, I was—I didn't know. I just assumed that they would—they know the route and would take care of whatever equipment necessary to fix the route.

KLEV: Uh-huh.

NEAL: And that does vary, not only from year to year, but what time within the expedition season you go up. If other groups have gone before you, much of the route may be fixed. If only an individual or two, or nobody has gone before, then there's more fixing required. So it was my understanding that the Sherpas would figure out who had been where and what needed to be fixed, and bring the appropriate equipment.

LENE: And, you're saying, Lopsang, that all the other years, when you have summited Everest, nobody brings snow stakes, only rope?

LOPSANG: Yeah, every year we carry only rope. And, after, so we find some snow stakes up. This year so we carry no snow stakes and ice screw, because so the other people there. We no need rope, so we all fixing rope, already. —[UI]—So, already fix rope. They tell them we are. So, we ask, so, already fix rope.

KLEV: Did anybody understand that?

LENE: Who told you that the route was already fixed to the summit?

LOPSANG: Which group that come back? South Summit? May ninth?

ANATOLI: Maybe Yugoslavian climbed. Also, I heard somebody climbed [to the] South Summit.

SANDY: Yugoslavians said that the ropes were fixed to the summit already?

LENE: South Summit.

LOPSANG: Yugoslavian guide tell to me so—[UI] already fix rope; you no need anything.

LENE: Okay.

LOPSANG: And, so we carry one hundred fifty meter rope more up, and I give to two rope Neal, and I taking so after we have problem, some problem. I keep one rope extra my bag insides and after, so Scott need many rope to come down.

SANDY: All right. So, we left the summit and—who saw Scott on the summit?

TIM: I saw him about—Charlotte, Neal, and I, we left the summit about the same time. I don't know what time it was.* And I think we saw Scott within five minutes of the summit.†

NEAL: Walking down—five minutes, yeah. That's about five minutes for him going up.

SANDY: Right. I saw him at the same time.

TIM: He was between the Hillary Step and the summit.

SANDY: Right. That's when I saw him, too, and I gave him a high five or a thumbs-up. And it was five minutes from the summit for me but perhaps thirty minutes from the summit for him. Is that accurate? Is that anybody else's experience?

LENE: I saw Scott on the summit, coming down, and I gave him a hug, and he congratulated me and I said—

---

*Neal Beidleman has since reported that he and the four Mountain Madness climber-clients on the summit with him began their descent at 3:10 P.M.

†Fischer topped the Hillary Step at approximately 2:35 P.M. He made the summit a little over an hour later, at approximately 3:40 P.M.

SANDY: You saw him when you were coming down or when he was coming down?

LENE: When I was coming down, and I said, "I'm tired," and he told me, "I am very tired." And then, I went on, because I knew I didn't want to be alone on that mountain, so I followed Charlotte, Tim, and Neal pretty close.

KLEV: I'm going to estimate I saw Scott at approximately 2:30, just above the Hillary Step. Does that coincide—?

SANDY: That would make sense.

ANATOLI: Yes, I also—

SANDY: Two-thirty; if I summited at 2:15 [P.M.] and came down then, yeah.

ANATOLI: I met Scott when was before Hillary Step, before go down this fixed line.

KLEV: My recollection was that Scott had a mask on. He had an oxygen mask on.

ANATOLI: Yeah, but—

KLEV: Whether he had oxygen in his tank or not, I can't say.

LENE: What was it that Scott told you when you met him? Because he told you something, me something, and then you something different.

ANATOLI: First time I met Rob Hall—I saw Rob Hall a little forward than Scott, maybe twenty minutes or fifteen minutes; I don't remember. And, I talked with Rob Hall how he feel. He said, "Okay, not so big problem." He said me, "Thank you very much for fix lines." I ask, "Maybe you need helping for summit?" He said not. Then I met Scott Fischer also. Scott was little slow and with mask—I think with mask—but I don't know [whether] he use oxygen or not because the mask protect from wind. And, also, little [I] talk with Scott. I talk with Scott how he feel. He said, "Okay, I feel tired." Maybe little sickness; he don't understand. I ask him about plan go down, because I come back from summit, began strong wind, very cold. I spent more than one hour on summit. It was very cold, and my point keep myself in maybe—[UI]—and wait, and I ask Scott about what we will do. He said, "Is not problem now; we have time for go down, exactly very soon to summit." What our plan he tell me, "You need go down and save yourself in South Col and prepare tea." And, I thought about this; it is good plan because somebody we need to have some reserve, because I didn't see Sherpa. Sherpa, for Sherpa go to summit, tired, used oxygen. If oxygen will finish, will be some difficult time. And I don't understand about Sherpa who in South Col, how this people strong, and we talk little bit, like fifteen minutes or ten minutes with Scott about this. And then I go down to South Col. What I—*

KLEV: On the summit—this is Klev—I personally did not see any threatening weather. And I know that Neal mentioned to me that he, after the fact, that he did. You just mentioned that you some kind of weather pattern coming in.

ANATOLI: What?

KLEV: You saw some kind of weather coming in from the summit? Did you see bad weather coming in?

ANATOLI: Strong wind began. Because it was—before it was little white and sun, and began strong wind and cold wind. I felt what I felt.

KLEV: When I was at the summit, there was a strong wind. I didn't feel

---

*After the Everest tragedy, in conversations with his coauthor Weston DeWalt, Boukreev described Fischer as being tired, but not apparently ill. Perhaps, Boukreev speculated, Fischer was already beginning to fail but was not consciously aware of the seriousness of whatever it was that overtook him. In their exchange above the Hillary Step, Boukreev told Fischer that the clients on the summit all looked good, but he expressed concern that, given the cold and the dwindling oxygen, there could be problems. Fischer said he felt that things were "okay" at that moment, that he would be on the summit soon and that, if things went well on the descent, it was possible that the Mountain Madness climbers could make Camp IV before dark. However, given the delays to that point and the hour of the day, Boukreev said that he and Fischer decided that the best place for him was in Camp IV where, if the climber-clients were further delayed or ran into trouble, Boukreev could be ready to offer assistance to those above him. Boukreev, because he had already considered the value of that option and decided that it was the best course of action for him to take, was pleased that he and Fischer saw things similarly.

When his descent ahead of clients was made an issue in the media, Boukreev revisited Fischer's and his decision to consider if there might have been a better course of action for them to have taken. Boukreev concluded that, given what they both knew at the moment of their meeting at the Hiliary Step, they had made the right decision. Had he known, he said, that Fischer was ill and that Lopsang Jangbu Sherpa's attention would be drawn to members of Rob Hall's expedition, certainly, he would not have made a rapid descent.

it intensify, but I didn't see any evidence personally of snow or deteriorating weather.

SANDY: I agree. I didn't sense any deteriorating weather. I felt a sense that we were late on the summit—

KLEV: Yes.

SANDY:—not because I was told that we had a deadline on the summit, but because I was aware of it from previous climbers' stories about when you should be off and on. And, if I felt any anxiety up there, it was because we were late, but not because I saw any weather.

LENE: This is Lene. Before I decided to go up over the Hillary Step, I noticed a whiteout coming from the valleys and I saw the wind pick up over the summit.

ANATOLI: Little bit, maybe little bit. It is difficult to feel. But when I asked somebody, maybe— How many time, Klev, you spent for summit—on summit?

KLEV: You're asking me how much time I spent?

ANATOLI: Yeah.

KLEV: I think I spent about twenty, twenty-five minutes there.

ANATOLI: Yeah, because I was longer, and I felt this.

KLEV: Yes, you were there much longer than I was.

ANATOLI: More than one hour.

KLEV: Yes.

ANATOLI: And I felt this began strong wind. Not so—Very difficult to say that it will be bad weather. Little, like intuition. Little began wind and cold. I ask somebody to make picture. Nobody have initiative to make many pictures because it was cold. Very cold.

KLEV: So, Anatoli, Scott asked you at the summit, when you saw him, to beeline it to camp and start making tea. My question for Lopsang is, who was left in camp of the Sherpas?

LOPSANG: Pemba Sherpa.

KLEV: Pemba? One Sherpa. Pemba was left in camp.

LOPSANG: Yeah.

KLEV: And what were his instructions? What was he supposed to do there?

LOPSANG: Making tea, uh—

SANDY: Can you pause just a second while I change tapes?

SANDY: This is tape number two, Everest debriefing, May fifteenth, 1996.

SANDY: The last question was, What was the responsibility of the Sherpa that was left at Base Camp—I mean at the South Col—and was he aware—?

LOPSANG: Pemba Sherpa.

SANDY: His name was Pemba.

INGRID: Is he considered a climbing Sherpa? So, he was someone who could go to the summit? Has that kind of experience or whatever?

LOPSANG: Yeah, he had the experience climbing with—[UI]—so, we need—[UI].

INGRID: So you left a strong Sherpa at the South Col?

LOPSANG: And, we keep to South Col.

INGRID: Okay.

ANATOLI: Pemba, what has Pemba climb before? This your brother—

LOPSANG: He climbing Everest six times.

ANATOLI: Six times?

LOPSANG: Not going to summit; he no pass.

ANATOLI: Who make tea, yeah?

LOPSANG: He climbing with me Kanchenjunga, 8,300 meter—[UI]—Japanese—[UI].

ANATOLI: He have experience?—[UI].

LOPSANG: [UI].

ANATOLI: But he look like—

LOPSANG: Climbing ten or eleven mountain. Same age. Looks very young, but same age. And he making tea and hot water. So two Sherpa come back and he tell to Pemba and you and Pemba going to have some member.

KLEV: This is Klev. Did Pemba have a radio?

LOPSANG: Yeah. He had a radio.

KLEV: He had one of the black Base Camp radios?

LOPSANG: Yeah. Black radio. Camp IV.

SANDY: Let's talk about the chronology of the descent. Martin led the descent for the group, right? Or, Anatoli?

ANATOLI: Began, yes. First time I pass Martin and I began to go down for fix line because I afraid this is very old rope who make to like two people and began strong wind with snow. What I felt maybe between 8,700–8,500 meters.

SANDY: Is where the storm began?

ANATOLI: Yes. Yes.

SANDY: What is the landmark there?

ANATOLI: Visibility lose.

SANDY: What's the landmark? Below the Southeast Ridge?

KLEV: Halfway between the South Summit and the Southeast Ridge maybe?

SANDY: Is where we—

LENE: It's sort of where the descent starts with the sort of slab snow, rock slab, old fixed ropes. Yeah.

SANDY: And you led the descent?

ANATOLI: Yes, and I made Camp IV—thirty minutes, maybe five o'clock, maybe thirty minutes past of five.

SANDY: And, it's storming but visible.

ANATOLI: Yes. Began storm, not visibility, and I saw—Pemba give me tea. We talk little bit, I saw some Sherpa come from Camp III, another expedition to Camp IV, and I drink little bit, little rest and then I saw nobody, very slow, nobody come, began snowstorm. I ask Pemba. I didn't see Sherpas.* I think I didn't understand about plan of Sherpas. And I didn't see Sherpas. I ask Pemba about oxygen. I took three bottle of oxygen and go up again, try to find fixed line, because began dark and nobody go down.

TIM: Did you find the fixed line when we went back up?

ANATOLI: Began very strong wind and I have mistake, little go left, strong, hard ice. I didn't found nothing. Somebody in Base Camp† I ask somebody who made light for people, and I saw this and little saw our Camp IV and try to find fixed line, and spent maybe like three and a half hour for this, but without success. Was terrible wind and also I little tired. I took mask, oxygen, and try go up. This help me, but not visibility, dangerous, possible go South Face, and I come back; maybe, forty-seven minutes past nine I was in tent again. I spent so this time to try to find somebody.

KLEV: What time did you get down, Martin?

MARTIN: About nine.

INGRID: The first we heard that Martin was down was 8:30 [P.M.].

LENE: There's been a lot—

ANATOLI: No. No. Maybe after one hour Martin come.‡

MALE SPEAKER NOT RECOGNIZABLE: I thought it was six.

ANATOLI: Maybe thirty minutes past ten.

INGRID: No. It was dark. It was well dark at that time, so it has to be past seven, and I remember asking, when I got back up to Rob Hall's camp, asking the two women who had come down here to—I think they were coming down to get me—what time that was when they

---

*Upon arriving at Camp IV and running into Pemba, Boukreev was not aware that Pemba had been in camp throughout the summit day. He thought Pemba had made an attempt on the summit and had then turned back. Neither was he aware that two other Sherpas were at Camp IV, Mountain Madness climbing Sherpas who, after reaching the South Summit, had returned to Camp IV and gone to their tent.

†Here Boukreev was referring to Camp IV, not the Everest Base Camp.

‡During Boukreev's first attempt to locate stranded Mountain Madness climbers, he's said that he started to lose track of time (see p. 168, *The Climb*). After reviewing this transcript, he said that he still felt his timing of Adams's arrival was reasonably accurate, but that, because he had not specifically noted the time, he was prepared to accept Adams's own recollection.

came down because that was the same time that we got the radio call, and they were keeping records of things and they said that was about eight to eight-thirty.

ANATOLI: No possible.

INGRID: That's when we got the message that Martin had gotten in.

NEAL: Ingrid, can you tell us who was up there on the radio and how the messages got taken up to you?

INGRID: Yeah, I can. The difficulty was that the only people carrying radios on the mountain were Nepalis.* And so it was very difficult for me to give a message to Gyalzen† to give to Pemba to give to Lopsang to give to a member in English. I was not confident that any message—any English message—would get through. So I used Ngima.‡ I would give a message to Ngima and he would then in Nepali relate it to Gyalzen Sherpa, to Pemba to whoever, and likewise when Pemba wanted to relay something—when anything was relayed down from the mountain it would be through Pemba through Gyalzen, through Ngima, and then for me. And Ngima was very inconsistent in what he told me. I was either here at Rob Hall's camp, because Rob Hall's camp had better communications, so I was getting more information up there, but I was constantly talking on my radio to Ngima, saying, "Any news? Any news?" And every time I heard a Nepali conversation going on I would try to understand what I could and then call Ngima and say, "Any news?" But to give you an example of how accurate this was, when at one point at 10:46 [P.M.] on that summit day I called Ngima and said I heard a Nepali conversation and called Ngima and said, "What's the news?" he said, "Nothing." And, I said, "Well, who are you talking to?" and he said, "Oh, I was talking to Pemba." He said that Scott, Lopsang, and Makalu, and three Taiwanese Sherpas and one New Zealand Sherpa were near the South Col. And I said, "You know, Ngima, that's news I want to know. You have to tell me things like that." And then, subsequently, at 1:00 A.M. [May 11, 1996], Ngima again spoke with Gyalzen who reported recently speaking with

---

*Dr. Hunt is referring to the black radios that Fischer had provided for the expedition, the radios operating on the Everest Base Camp frequency (see pp. 60–61, *The Climb*).

†Gyalzen Sherpa, who had been the cook at Camp II during the expedition, was stationed at Camp II on summit day.

‡Ngima (Neema) Sherpa was the Everest Base Camp sirdar for the Mountain Madness expedition (see p. 44, *The Climb*).

Lopsang, who had still had not arrived at Camp IV and reported that Lopsang was "coughing and in bad condition." And, I was at Rob Hall's camp at that time. I raced down here. I was able to understand that in Nepali, that he was coughing and in bad condition, so I raced down here hoping I could get them while they were on the phone,* and Ngima doesn't—nobody thinks that, [with] a sick person [at hand], we should probably get some medical advice;[they apparently don't think] we have a doctor at Base Camp. —By the time I got down here the connection is gone and we don't hear from anyone for six hours. So that was the nature of the radio communication. And I really recorded pretty much every call that we got for the whole ascent, like starting on the day you guys left. And the last time I actually talked with Scott, before the summit, was on the eighth [May 8, 1996], and that was the 8:00 A.M. radio call. And I would like to go through this at some point. Should I go though this now?

SANDY: Yeah.

LENE: Why not?

INGRID: Okay; 8:00 A.M.—on the eighth [May 8, 1996]—I spoke with Scott. He stated that everyone was doing fine and the team was heading up to Camp III. There had been some talk of leaving earlier, but the wind was bad and there was a later morning than you all expected as I understood it. From 12:00 to 4:00 P.M. I made numerous radio calls between myself and Gyalzen, who is the Sherpa working at Camp II. Gyalzen reported talking to Scott and he was relaying messages. I tried to get ahold of Scott, but was unsuccessful. Gyalzen said he was climbing and Scott reported by the late afternoon, maybe 4:00 P.M., everyone was at Camp III and everyone especially, quote: "Charlotte and Tim were doing well." That was the last I heard until the ninth [May 9, 1996], and on that day I attempted to call the team as usual in predetermined radio times—8:00 A.M., 12:00 P.M., and 6:00 P.M.— but received no answer. Again, received messages from Gyalzen at times directly and at times though Ngima. Messages received state that all the climbers reached Camp IV between 4:00 and 5:00 P.M. with Sandy, Scott, and Neal maybe a little bit later, bringing up the rear. Reports continually said, you know, I got the feeling that Scott was saying, "Just tell Ingrid we're okay. Just tell Ingrid we're okay." Be-

---

*There were no satellite phones being used by Mountain Madness climbers or Sherpas on summit day, so it is assumed, here, that Dr. Hunt was referring to a radio, not a phone.

cause the reports kept on saying, "All the climbers are doing well. All the climbers are doing well." Well, that may be, you know, the message that got augmented as it came down the hill because they knew that's what I wanted to hear. In the evening Ngima talked directly with Scott. My radio was open and with me at that time, but perhaps because I was working in the communication tent or elsewhere at Base Camp, the communication wasn't well. I did not receive that communication. I didn't hear that communication. I asked Ngima about it, checked the battery on my radio, confirmed that it was well charged. I changed radios with Ngima at any rate. Ngima told me that Scott said that everyone was doing well. I specifically, certainly did not hear anything about Lopsang being sick and not being able to go up and fix lines early. I didn't hear anything about Scott being sick. Likewise, just to go back a second: The night that you all spent at Camp II, that Scott spent down here after he brought Dale down, I had many people saying he was sick for five days. I had no indication that he was sick. He was just—

PETE: Joking around, had a beer—

INGRID: He was Scott.

PETE:—wanted Dale to have a beer.

INGRID: You know, he typically left. He gave me a big pinch on the butt à la Scott, you know, just like the way Scott always is. I had no indication that he was sick.

LENE: Who had been saying that he had been sick for five days?

INGRID: Martin said that.

ANATOLI: No sick from high altitude, I think. Just after Camp IV.

INGRID: Okay, 8:00 A.M., then on that—6:00 A.M. on the summit day, there was a call between the Sherpa in South Col, which is Pemba, and Gyalzen and Ngima report that all climbers doing well and approaching the South Summit, so, obviously, again, there is some real discrepancy here. That's the first report we got that you are approaching the South Summit at 6:00 A.M. and that was six hours before you all really did.* The night before, Scott had told Ngima to tell me that we'll have an 8:00 A.M. call the following day, so at 8:00 A.M. I tried to

---

*Neal Beidleman has reported that he arrived at the South Summit at 9:58 A.M.

reach Scott and wasn't surprised that I couldn't reach him because I knew he was climbing. Then, again, I received the report at 8:00 A.M. that all climbers had reached the South Summit. Then I didn't get any messages at all, and I was going back and forth to Rob Hall's tent to see what information they had. I was probably up there from 1:30 to 2:30 [P.M.] definitely and at maybe 2:20 [P.M.] they got their call from Rob that Rob was up there and everybody had summited except that Doug was just coming up to the summit.* I came down here to see if we had any news, and so at 2:30 [P.M.] I was down here, and Ngima said he spoke with Lopsang and that all the members had summited. About three o'clock I spoke briefly with Scott. He said all the members had summited. I congratulated him. He said, "I'm so tired." I said, "Get down the mountain."† Lopsang was on the radio again. I agreed with Lopsang to talk at 6:00 P.M. [At] 4:30 that evening, the people from Rob Hall's camp came down here and said, "We need to get some oxygen sent back up the mountain. We think one of your team members has collapsed at the Hillary Step and Rob Hall is with him." Because, Rob Hall was sending messages to them that "I'm with this guy," he kept saying, "and he's collapsed above the Hillary Step." So we, you know, do everything we can to try to get oxygen sent up. One of the things is, we actually talked to Pemba and asked Pemba to keep trying to get hold of Lopsang or anyone up the mountain and asked Pemba himself if he could go, and he said the weather was too bad, [that] he didn't want to. At 5:45 [P.M.] we learned that Lopsang and Scott were just below the South Summit. They were out of oxygen and Scott was very weak.‡ Again, this was a message. I pressed Ngima to get some information. I got the message and I immediately think: I have to talk to him; I have to give him some advice; I have to tell them [the Sherpas with the radios] to give Scott some messages. And we couldn't hear from anyone until—uh— and we try and try and try to get to Gyalzen to get to Pemba to get

---

*Doug Hansen, it has been reported, did not summit until after 4:00 P.M.

†Fischer's transmission was made from the summit around 3:45 P.M. (see p. 160, *The Climb*). Because Fischer's transmission from the summit was made on Lopsang's black radio and because Fischer had not been in direct communication with the Everest Base Camp after the morning of May 8, some have speculated that his radio may not have been functioning properly.

‡Lopsang has said that Fischer was not out of oxygen (see "Mountain Madness Everest Debriefing," p. 343), that he'd picked up a third, full bottle at the South Summit, but for some reason, after he made the summit, he was unwilling or unable to draw upon that supply.

to anyone up there. So, from 5:45 [P.M.] to 10:45 [P.M.], I know that Scott is up there, weak without oxygen. I don't know why we have such sporadic communication with Pemba. He knows there's an emergency going on with Scott and Rob Hall, but cannot contact them. [At] 10:46 [P.M.], as I said, we get a message from Pemba that the whole crew, Lopsang and Scott and Makalu and three Taiwanese Sherpas and one New Zealand Sherpa are near the South Col and Pemba actually says, "We're flashing lights with Lopsang. We've had our headlights flashing, and we're now making a lot of noise with oxygen bottles to try to attract them here." Meanwhile, I've learned at Rob Hall's camp that there is a complete whiteout up there, so I am not sure, like, how Lopsang is flashing lights at people, but I wonder if this—again—they were trying to give me some hope or something.

SANDY: Were you flashing lights?

LOPSANG: Light?—[UI]—So, we not see a way.

ANATOLI: Very strong wind and it's impossible.

LOPSANG: Windy, and it's snow, all ice, and so we need so oxygen, and we need light, please, call to up, but we don't—

INGRID: Did you see Pemba flash lights?

ANATOLI: Somebody from Rob Hall made very strong light. Impossible to see headlamp. It is like milk with snow, strong wind. I go up. It's impossible.

INGRID: So, uhhh—

LENE: This kind of light can have been anybody on the mountain, because there's been twenty people who can—you know—

INGRID: Absolutely, yeah. So why I was told that Lopsang and Scott were flashing their lights and near the camp, I'm not sure; 1:00 A.M.—

LOPSANG: [UI]—I have opened radio—[UI]—Anatoli already go to bring oxygen and tea bring going already up—[UI]—waiting.

INGRID: You were waiting?

LOPSANG: Yeah.

INGRID: I see.

LOPSANG: So we were waiting, then after so no coming. Also, Scott not walking.—[UI]—[Scott is saying], "I need helicopter. I never walking go down." [UI]—[I] tell you [Scott], "We going to Camp IV, please, please. I have rope. You no dead. I play rope." And, he say, "I'm not go. I need helicopter." [UI].

SANDY: Lopsang, where exactly did you stop with Scott?

LOPSANG: So, you know that pass to going up—[UI]—one hundred meter up.

SANDY: And you made the full descent with Scott, right, from—?

LOPSANG: Yeah, so I have rope, many rope to bring down.

SANDY: From the summit, you walked the whole way from the summit to there with Scott?

LOPSANG: [UI]—so summit to I send Scott first.

SANDY: And you had Scott tied on a line because he was weak?

LOPSANG: After, so, last camp—[UI]—I have rope, many rope. He not walking, so—[UI]—to play ski, like this.

KLEV: He was going to glissade?

LOPSANG: Yeah, and go to other route.

LENE: Yeah. Going the wrong way.*

LOPSANG: People are going this way. Anybody this way. Easy down.

SANDY: But, was he playing when he said, "I'm going to go this way and ski"?

LOPSANG: Yeah. So, he going like this, so that time, so he think it's easy go like this, walking—[UI].

KLEV: Tim, you saw Scott glissading somewhere. Where was that?

TIM: That was right—South Summit.

LOPSANG: South Summit, I see.

---

*At approximately 8,650 meters Fischer had come to some fixed lines that required some complex rope work. Tired and failing—and without Lopsang who had been delayed just below the summit—Fischer opted to glissade (slide on his butt) down a snow slope that terminated about a hundred meters off the route he should have taken.

TIM: Yeah, from the top of the first fixed line, above the Southeast Ridge where it goes into rocks.

LOPSANG: He goes down and I play rope, rope him up and up and after so last camp go together many rope, many rope to come down I play down eight hour, but—

SANDY: Was he being funny? Did he think it was fun?

LOPSANG: He say, "Tell her I am very sick. I am—[UI] sick." [UI]—not all gone. [UI]—I took out ice, and my glove took out—[UI]—make him hot, make him hot, but not—

INGRID: So after he ran out of oxygen, did he drop his oxygen bottle? He put it down?

LOPSANG: [UI]—maybe fifty pressure, have pressure oxygen. But he no use.

SANDY: He took it off?

LOPSANG: No. [Scott said,] "Lopsang, I am dead. I am jumping, going to Camp II, jumping; [UI]—please catch and quick rope to fix here."

KLEV: And where was that when you tied a rope to him?

LOPSANG: Last camp.

KLEV: Last camp?

NEAL: Which is called the Southeast Ridge.

KLEV: Southeast Ridge?

LOPSANG: Yeah. So people coming this way, he going—[UI]—ski that way.

SANDY: But, was he laughing? Did he think this was funny?

LOPSANG: No laughing.

SANDY: He wasn't laughing.

LOPSANG: No laughing.

SANDY: He knew he was sick?

LOPSANG: [Lopsang imitates Fischer groaning and saying,] "I'm sick."

SANDY: Okay, so he wasn't being crazy.

LOPSANG: That time I checking oxygen pressure, but he said—

KLEV: He had five pounds of pressure, but he took his mask off?

LOPSANG: Yeah, no use.

KLEV: He didn't want it.

LOPSANG: And, I give to summit, so I give a tea, juice. I give juice. And, please, you go to pass. You are very tired, sick. I come to last, because—[UI]—maybe ten meters rope, so I—[UI]—my ice ax. And, so all people come down, and so Rob, also Doug [Hansen] also summit; after I come back and my ice ax take out, and so I am come quickly, and Rob guide tell me, "Please, Lopsang, you going to Hillary Step. I give to you five hundred dollars. You give to please oxygen. Take up, please," he tell me.* But I tell you [Harris], "Sorry, my member Scott is sick. I have him. I am going to pass. I am not going to back. I come to pass." After I come down, so Scott going this way, play ski wrong way, go down. All member going the other way. After I am going to pass, so I have rope take out—[UI]—Rob led down and take up. And, after, so, that time—[UI]—"Lopsang, I no need rope. I am never walking, so I am jumping," he [Scott] tell me, "I am very sick. I am jumping, Lopsang." [Lopsang imitates Fischer groaning in pain.] "I am jumping," he tell me. I tell [Scott], "Please, no problem. I have you. I have rope, and I fix rope and have many rope and we together coming slow, slow, slow come down." So, two minute come down; then another minute rest. Fifteen minute come down, and so ten-minute rest. After come down, down, so I have two battery, all battery please, and we don't see—[UI]—and you stay and I'll come down—[UI]—He [Fischer] say, "I never walking out." [UI]—[I say,] "Please, we going to Camp IV. Now, Camp IV only twenty minute." [Lopsang seems to suggest that Scott responded], "Because—maybe, one hour or more." I tell to [Scott], "Maybe ten minute, twenty minute," I tell him. But, he [said], "I not walking. I need helicopter." But, night came, very windy and snow; we cannot see any way. This way—road—this way; this way we no see anything— yeah. And, so I tell [Scott], "Okay, please, you stay here; I make you little hole. You stay here. I send some Sherpa and oxygen and tea." [Lopsang imitates quaking voice of Fischer.] "Okay, you go down.

---

*Andy Harris, a guide for Rob Hall's Adventure Consultants expedition, offered Lopsang five hundred U.S. dollars to take oxygen to Rob Hall and Doug Hansen, who were atop the Hillary Step.

You go down. You go down. You go down." I stay together for one hour together, and—[UI]—and to anything I do [Lopsang imitates Scott shivering as he speaks] "You go down. You go down," he tell me. And after, so, I am also very cold, and I—[UI]—[say to Scott], "Okay, please, Scott, please you never walk anyway. You stay here. I send some Sherpa and Anatoli. I send up oxygen and tea." But, morning, I send two Sherpa, oxygen and tea, soup, but he is already gone. What can do? I give to—[UI]—to Makalu and Scott only—[UI]—but Makalu not dead. Scott dead.

SANDY: When did Makalu* join?

LOPSANG: Makalu and he two Sherpa, I—

SANDY: When did Makalu come with you?

LOPSANG: Makalu, saw after, after—

SANDY: He saw you after you'd already—[UI]—the hole?

LOPSANG: After, so I bring Scott down, down, down. After, so, Makalu also coming—[UI].

KLEV: Makalu by himself?

LOPSANG: Yeah, he had two Sherpa.

KLEV: He has two Sherpas?

LOPSANG: He had two Sherpa, and after he also no can and two Sherpa gone—[UI]—And after, so I keep together.

LENE: Were Scott and Makalu in the hole together?

LOPSANG: Yeah. When Makalu gets me, his head put here. [UI]—So, I have so only Scott. And, after, so Makalu—[UI]—[I tell Scott and Makalu,] "Okay, you—[UI]—stay here; I send some Sherpa and Anatoli; I send oxygen and tea." But, morning I send Sherpa and oxygen, tea—

LENE: Yeah.

LOPSANG:—but Makalu is not dead. Scott is dead. What can do? So—[UI]—He stay like this. [I had told Scott,] "You never walk anyway.

---

*"Makalu" Gau Ming-Ho was the leader of the Taiwanese National Expedition, an ill-fated effort that had already claimed the life of Chen Yu-Nan, a fellow expedition member.

You stay. No problem. I send strong Sherpa. My father send up, my father and Tashi." But, he's, Makalu—[UI]—Scott, all jacket take out and glove throw anyway, like this. And, after, then, two Sherpas use oxygen full pressure, three hour using, and—[UI]—but nothing. Gone. What? We try. So very bad weather that day.

ANATOLI: Very, very, very, very bad.

LOPSANG: That day, so there—[UI]—Many people dead. [UI].

KLEV: Did you and Anatoli talk on radio that night?

ANATOLI: I have not radio contact. I think Pemba and—

LOPSANG: Yeah, he had no radio, but I listen—

INGRID: But, you were in communication with Pemba who had a radio?

LOPSANG: I listen, so they are tell to Anatoli: three oxygen bottle and tea bring up, already gone. Pemba in the Base Camp [Camp IV] contact Camp II contact and I listen. So, but I have—[UI]—new radio—but this one—[UI]—not can, not can.*

LENE: Ah, you couldn't change the battery.

LOPSANG: Not can, so I change battery.

INGRID: Well, the next communication I got was at one o'clock [1:00 A.M., May 11, 1996]. Yeah, I think I told you that at one o'clock Ngima spoke with Gyalzen, who reported speaking with Lopsang, who was in bad condition and coughing, and at 1:35 [A.M.] Ngima again speaks with Gyalzen, who has reported he has heard from Camp IV. Four members have arrived. Lene is one of them. They will get back with to us with other names—

[GAP ON RECORDING]

INGRID: —Camp IV at three o'clock [3:00 A.M.] we heard from Stuart [Dr. Stuart Hutchison, a climber-client] from the New Zealand team that he found two of our climbers, Anatoli, who was lying on the ground per Scott's—and Lopsang and had returned them to our

---

*Lopsang appears to be suggesting that his black radio—with which he could communicate with other Mountain Madness Sherpas—was sometimes not operating and that he overheard traffic between Pemba at Camp IV and Gyalzen at Camp II indicating Boukreev had left Camp IV with three bottles of oxygen and hot tea.

camp. At 5:00 A.M. New Zealand team heard from Rob Hall on the South Summit.

SANDY: We should go back and say that 3:00 A.M. they heard that Anatoli and Lopsang were on the ground couldn't possibly be factual because we know that they were in other places at the time.

INGRID: Okay. And from then to 7:15 [A.M.] numerous attempts to reach [by radio] Camp IV. At that time we had gotten the South African expedition, who did have contact with their Camp IV, to go and try to give their radios to one of you or to see what was up in our camp. Ian [Woodall]* made an attempt to find the camp, couldn't, came back. We scoured the base camps here [Everest Base Camp] to see if any of the climbers or Sherpas had a more precise location for where our camp was in relation to other camps. We sort of found some information. We gave that back to the South African team just as they were about to send one of their climbers out to try to find our camp again. We heard from Camp II, that heard from Camp IV, that everyone was in Camp IV except for Scott.

SANDY: At 5:00 A.M.?

INGRID: No, at 8:00 A.M. That's when we heard from Gyalzen. At 9:20 [A.M.] we heard—this is via again Rob Hall's communication system. We learned that two Taiwanese Sherpa were leaving to find Makalu. [At] 9:50 A.M. we heard that three Sherpa from the New Zealand expedition were leaving to rescue Rob Hall. At that time Bruce [Herrod] from the South African team† and Neal‡ from the New Zealand

---

*Ian Woodall was the leader of the South African, Johannesburg *Sunday Times* expedition.

†Bruce Herrod was expedition photographer and deputy leader of the Johannesburg *Sunday Times* expedition. On May 25, 1996, he made his own attempt on Mount Everest, and at 5:15 P.M. he radioed to say that he had made the summit. After that radio call nothing was heard from Herrod again. He never returned to Camp IV. Not until nearly a year later was his fate known. On April 27, 1997, Boukreev was leading an Indonesian national team to the summit of Everest. As he reached the base of the Hillary Step, he discovered the body of Bruce Herrod fouled in the fixed ropes. (see pp. 245–246, *The Climb*).

‡There was no "Neal" or "Neil" on the New Zealand Adventure Consultants expedition. Likely, Dr. Hunt is referring to Neil Laughton of the Himalayan Guides Commercial Expedition led by Henry Todd of Edinburgh, Scotland. Brigitte Muir, a member of Todd's expedition who was with Laughton on the South Col on the evening of May 10, says that Laughton, "from the United Kingdom," had been radioed by Henry Todd and asked to do a

team were making rounds at Camp IV to try to determine the extent of personal injury. The rest is just news on the descent, which is not that important right now.

TIM: Lopsang, what time did you get to Camp IV?

LOPSANG: I don't see, but people tell that three o'clock.

SANDY: You think you got to Camp IV at three o'clock?

LOPSANG: Yeah, the other people tell—[UI].

LENE: Yeah, because I remember Lopsang coming in. I think you brought something hot to drink.

LOPSANG: No.

LENE: No?

LOPSANG: No.

LENE: When you came in and then you—

LOPSANG: I coming—[UI]—your tent—

LENE: Exactly, and you told me that Scott was sleeping at Camp I, at the Southeast Ridge.

LOPSANG: Yeah.

LENE: Yeah, and it must have been around, I think, three o'clock—

LOPSANG: And, I tell to Anatoli also, "Please, Anatoli, you go up. Scott tell you, Anatoli, to come up."* Yeah.

LENE: That's right.

LOPSANG: You see my face. All ice.

LENE: I saw you Lopsang. I saw you.

TIM: So when you got to Camp IV, Anatoli was out—or was in the process of looking for the rest of us?

"head count" of survivors. Source: Brigitte Muir, *The Wind in My Hair* (Ringwood, Victoria, Australia: Penguin Books Australia Ltd., 1998).

*Lopsang had struggled for several hours in his attempt to get Fischer off the mountain. He wanted Boukreev to go up for Fischer. Boukreev, who was consumed by his continuing efforts to rescue climber-clients, explained his situation to Lopsang and asked Lopsang if some Sherpas could be motivated to go up.

ANATOLI: What?

TIM: When Lopsang got to Camp IV, you had already started the process of looking for us—no? Yes?

ANATOLI: Yes.

SANDY: How did you learn that we were missing?

ANATOLI: What?

SANDY: How did you learn that we were missing? Or did you just see that we weren't there?

ANATOLI: How I found you?

SANDY: No, how did you decide that we were missing? Did somebody tell you that we were out?

ANATOLI: Nobody. Not information. What I told: Between six and ten o'clock [6:00 P.M. and 10:00 P.M, May 10, 1996] I tried go up. It was stupid idea I understand, because no visibility, possible fall crevasse or get some wrong way and go [off the Kangshung Face], and difficult. I come back with oxygen. And then Martin come, maybe I think ten, ten-thirty he come. I was very glad. I ask him. He didn't see never nobody. He didn't see. And go up again. It was wrong. Much better wait and see light. I tried to see some light of headlamp. I was ready with crampon, with shoes with everything, with oxygen, three bottle of oxygen [in] our tent. And then, probably one o'clock [1:00 A.M., May 11, 1996], Neal, who was together with people, come with Klev, with Lene, and people say me, "Tolya, Sandy and Charlotte and Tim stayed and need helping. Maybe like for you, like fifteen minutes." But, it was more longer way, go flat. First time I go I tried; I was very near. First time, [I missed finding them by] maybe like thirty meters, but I didn't see nothing. Weather like began snowstorms, very strong wind, very cold and with snow. And, I tried to find them. I maybe go up, but Klev said [to] me, "You don't need crampon." And, I wasn't; I hadn't crampon, and I get decision came back ask Klev maybe he made a wrong decision. I need crampon. I need go up little bit. I come back again. It was like intuition, without eyes, to find [Camp IV]. Also, spend some time. I don't know how long, maybe between two and three o'clock I was again in camp and ask people where I can to get you, our group. And people told me, "Tolya, flat, just flat, go China side. You will see." And to this little tired; I didn't sleep. I spend no rest because between my start to attempt of summit without rest. I need helping. And I tried to go to Sherpas again, Pemba. Pemba give me a little drink with tea. In this I talked with Lopsang about [and said], "We need to go to help for people, because people I understand very well. It is more than fifteen hours, three bottles [oxygen] finish. Without oxygen, people use oxygen, people cannot move; cannot struggle; hard for life." It was exactly [as I remember it] for me. And I go inside of Himalayan Hotel [tent housing Sherpas]. I understand Sherpa very tired after attempt, but I understood some four people or five people climb summit, but somebody didn't climb.* I like to find some fresh power to help myself to carry, because for me only carry somebody it is also difficult in South Col. And I saw Sherpa sleep and used oxygen, sleep, without power, because it is difficult, difficult for me, difficult for Sherpa. I understand it is very well. It is big risky also for life. Sherpa not responsible about this. Is guide responsible. But I saw also Neal; without fresh power it is impossible for him. He made very good job. Because I believe for Neal; Neal will come and I will know which way and I go to help for people. And Neal made this deal; it is very important. If Neal didn't made this, impossible for me to help for people. Very important thing. And he was without power; he used oxygen; he get very cold, very long time I understand it is necessary. For me it is also. I have big experience for high altitude, but fifteen hours without rest or more than twenty-four hours we spent. In three o'clock it was more than twenty-four hours without rest. In high altitude it is somebody just can to survive this. And I understand also Sherpa cannot go up.

SANDY: Yeah.

ANATOLI: "Maybe somebody?" I ask Pemba. Pemba said, "I try to find fresh power." I ask everybody.†

SANDY: But, Pemba said no?

ANATOLI: Pemba didn't said nothing. I think I ask; he didn't answer. I ask Lopsang—maybe Lopsang strong, but he said he get sickness.

---

*Boukreev, by this point in the developing crisis, had discovered that some of the Mountain Madness Sherpas who had made a summit attempt that day had turned around before the summit. Boukreev thought they might have a reserve of strength to assist him in his rescue efforts.

†In addition to going to the tent housing the Mountain Madness Sherpas, Anatoli went to the tents of the Adventure Consultants expedition and to those of the Taiwanese National Expedition. He could find no one who was willing or able to assist him in his rescue efforts.

He told me, "You need go to Scott, directly up." But, for me, I understand Scott need helping, but I believe he is strong; he can— Many people survive one night without camp and near of summit of Everest. I know this. And, I believe for people need helping much more than Scott. It is my experience. And I told Lopsang about. Maybe somebody can to help me go for people, but because I afraid about people very much. Somebody, like Lene, told me Sandy died, near to died without moving, without everything, without—also go up to Scott, spend some power. I have some Sherpas from last year expedition who have power like Lhakpa [Galgen Sherpa] from Himalayan Guides and spent to go up.* It is impossible. Sherpa, if you have dangerous, Sherpa don't like go up. It is exactly. It is normal in the Himalaya. It is work for guides. And, this my decision: go to help for people.† Second time also I have tea. I have oxygen and without—I try to find, I understand maybe you have a regulator mask or you have not, and I took. I tried to find extra; it is also time. I spend some time to this. But I was hurry. I try to find mask, regulator, and complete—go to give for you. [I] ask Lopsang. I found this mask, regulator, and fresh new bottle of oxygen and go along. I tried also to [recruit] somebody from another camp, like from Rob Hall, maybe some Sherpas, but nobody. And then, I go directly again this way I made and I saw this light from Tim maybe, somebody voice, saw my light, maybe Tim. Tim felt much better than Charlotte and you [Sandy Hill (Pittman)]. And, I saw like four people, this woman, Japanese woman also together with you.‡ And, I found you. And I saw like four people, this woman, Japanese woman [Yasuko Namba]. Maybe it is—I don't—3:30 [A.M.] probably. I am not sure. Maybe three o'clock. I didn't see. It is not so important for me. I give oxygen for you. Charlotte took and carry for camp, for our tent. Also, I spent some time. I spend Charlotte, put in the tent.

---

*Boukreev was suggesting that if he had stronger Sherpas on the Mountain Madness team—like Lhakpa Galgen Sherpa with whom he climbed the year before—he might have found a Sherpa willing to go with him.

†With Scott Fischer stranded on the mountain and with the climber-clients stranded at the South Col, Boukreev had to make a painful decision. He felt that Fischer, a highly experienced, high-altitude mountaineer, would fare better in the situation at hand, that the climber-clients had to be his immediate priority.

‡Boukreev has said that during his forays onto the South Col in the early-morning hours of May 11, 1996, he had seen only four climbers: Sandy Hill (Pittman), Charlotte Fox, Tim Madsen, and Yasuko Namba. He'd heard there was another climber stranded, Beck Weathers (a climber-client of Rob Hall's), but did not come across Weathers.

Neal began work with Charlotte, help for Charlotte, get oxygen, get warm, gave warm. I also—Lopsang, Pemba also. Pemba prepare just tea. Because it [the storm] was strong, not visibility, and I saw the situation. Tim told me about this one from Rob Hall expedition, one member [Yasuko Namba] from Rob Hall expedition. I try to find some Sherpa from Rob Hall. I found some Sherpa, Lhakpa [Chhiri Sherpa], from Rob Hall expedition. I told [him] about Japanese woman need help. It is possible to helping? Spend like one hour, give some oxygen, tea and possible to help for this member. I didn't know about this woman. I think maybe member, and so our camp it is very close. Everybody [members of Rob Hall's expedition] I understand heard about this [Yasuko Namba's situation]. I tried also found some Sherpas [Mountain Madness or Taiwanese] who can help me again, but again I tried ask Lopsang about to help. Nobody go. I took again tea, again oxygen, and made this way. I found you [Sandy Hill (Pittman)] and get another bottle oxygen for Tim. Tim was enough strong to go without me and we got with you, Sandy, and we get to camp, maybe near of five o'clock, maybe few minutes past of five, I think, and begin visibility. Just between four and five [o'clock] snowstorm go down. Begin visibility. I spend you to Neal again; Neal began work with you in tent. And this I told [talked] again with Sherpa, with Pemba. We need because Pemba didn't sleep. Pemba work very hard, but just in camp. He afraid about his life. I understand. It is exactly. And, I ask [said to] Pemba, "Pemba, now I empty. I cannot go with oxygen, without oxygen. I didn't sleep two night. It is impossible for me. But now it possible. Five o'clock; we need to send two Sherpa with oxygen for Scott. Pemba, please tell somebody; ask." He said— he was quiet. He didn't answer, because he understood maybe nobody can. Is hard work, after summit of Everest, again go up. And then, I tried to get some warm for myself. I go directly for Lene. [Participants laugh and Boukreev joins in.] Not for Lene, but near of Lene sleeping bag, and I slept like two hours again. And before I also send Pemba with tea near tent. And I slept like maybe two hours. In two hours, I again ask Pemba about, "Did [you send] some Sherpas for Scott with oxygen?" He said, "No, nobody cannot." And maybe just nine or ten o'clock, somebody go up with oxygen, your [Lopsang's] father and Tashi. But I was—

LOPSANG: [UI].

ANATOLI: It is impossible, Lopsang. I spent very big power, without rest, like thirty-five hours.

LOPSANG: Yeah, so I am coming through the all together night with Scott, and because I come down to Camp IV.

ANATOLI: I understand.

LOPSANG: I thinking, so all members are [at] Camp IV, but I not thinking—

ANATOLI: I told you exactly—

LOPSANG: And so I am so crazy, very some crazy. So I see my friend Scott, and I get up and so he tell me, "I need Anatoli send up." And so I come down. So I think that all member right at Camp IV, good; only Scott up. But after, so I am come down so I—[UI]—and after, so just morning. I have some member some day. Pemba tells me. Also night, Anatoli maybe at camp, give to tea, will make it hot, he tell me. And, so I think, so, Anatoli strong; he use oxygen; he going to up. I think after morning, so I ask other Sherpa, "Anatoli's going up?" No. And, so then after I tell two Sherpa who going, two strong Sherpa, I give ten thousand, ten thousand Nepali rupee I give to. Please Scott take down. But, two Sherpa going up. No life.

KLEV: I have a question for Neal. We heard that Anatoli's instructions from Scott were to save himself and go to camp and make tea, make ready for members. Did you have any instructions directly from Scott?

NEAL: I did not. When I passed Scott, [I] just said, "Hi, how's it going?" I gave him a slap on the back. I was somewhat preoccupied because I had just tried to orchestrate everybody getting off the summit. I'd been screaming at Charlotte and kept telling Lene, no more pictures, let's go, and Sandy had been there a little bit and tried to get them to come behind me. I was more interested in looking up the hill and making sure that everybody was coming as quickly as they could. I knew that Scott was close. We've climbed together before. I had a pretty strong bond with him, and just a look from him and one from me, I think, indicated what had to be done, and that was okay. He was close, tag the summit and get the hell out of there. And, I figured he would catch us very shortly on the way down. I wasn't worried about him at the time.

SANDY: Neal, maybe you should give a quick bit about your experience on the descent, because you sort of led the band of the four of us.

NEAL: This is my interpretation of how we came down. We started off at the summit and still pretty euphoric for the first part of the snow.

Obviously everybody made it to the summit and was very happy, and we were still seeing people coming up that were celebrating in their triumph, so the seriousness of it, I don't think, [had] set in with everybody. All the people—but, I was very, very nervous and very anxious. I actually wanted to leave the summit much earlier with maybe Martin or Klev, but every time I got ready to stand up and go, it seemed like another person or another wave of people would come over the ridge, some including our members. I was very surprised that people kept coming. I thought that they would have either turned around on their own or by somebody else. I didn't feel it was right for me to leave at that time, until everybody had reached the summit. They were so close. I knew Anatoli had gone down. I had no problem with that. I knew that it would have been nice for him to stay, but at the same time it wouldn't have necessarily facilitated our descent any better. I wasn't aware of his instructions to go down immediately from Scott, but, after hearing that, I support that. I think that's a very good idea, and in fact, had he not gone down, his efforts at the bottom collecting people wouldn't have been possible. So, anyway, we got to the Hillary Step, and I was right behind Sandy. She seemed to be the one most out of it at the time. Behind me were Charlotte, Tim, and then Lene. When we got to the Hillary Step, it's a real jungle of old ropes and pieces of tattered cord. Sandy was having [a] very difficult time even deciphering which cord was the one to hook into and how to negotiate the footsteps. I walked down to her. We tried to rappel her down, but the cords were too tangled by the wind, so we had to undo that and she hand "rap'd" down with some assistance. She got down to the rest of the ridge, and I looked behind and it seemed as if the other people were making pretty good progress, so I wasn't too worried about them. At the rock just below the South Summit, Klev was sitting there. He had been testing oxygen bottles. There didn't seem to be too many left. There was one that was full, or practically full, I was aware of, and then a couple others that had somewhere between three to five.* Klev, that was my recollection. I knew that I was close

---

*Why there were not more full bottles available is something that puzzled Boukreev when, as he was working on *The Climb*, he considered Lopsang's statements about how many bottles had been delivered to the South Col. Lopsang had been clear. Ten bottles of oxygen—not counting the one that Lopsang had taken up the mountain and given to Sandy Hill (Pittman) just below the summit—were taken to the South Summit. While several—if not all—of the Mountain Madness climber-clients had retrieved a bottle on their way to the summit—as opposed to on their descent as had been planned—

to or out of oxygen at the time, as well as some of the other members. Maybe Klev can help me with some of the arrangements that we had on bottles for different people. It's somewhat of a blur to me. I was pretty out of it at the time, myself, but I do recall taking one bottle myself that had a pressure of either three or five, and then the other bottle that I was still breathing on had the opposite, either three or five, I can't remember. The full bottle, I believe at that time, went to Lene—

LENE: Yes, it did.

NEAL: —and the other people were still coming and Klev was there. Charlotte came by and passed and walked to the South Summit, and it's my recollection that Tim also did, so they were on their way. I was screaming at Sandy to get going and she also did. Lene I believe followed me. I'm not exactly aware of when Klev left, whether he was behind me or in front of me.

KLEV: I'll jump in. When I came across from the [Hillary] Step to the South Summit, Jon Krakauer was in distress there, and that kind of slowed me up. I think I was— There was nothing I could really do to help him. I don't think I had the wherewithal to do that, but I wanted to stay there until I saw some action was being taken, because they did have two guides on either side of him.* When Neal arrived at the South Summit, he looked at me and said, "What the heck are you doing here? Get out of here." It was at that time that Neal—he'd recognized the urgency of the hour and maybe the storm—and it was at that time that the fire was lit under me. And I think I left just about the time you got there. You really motivated me to get down.

SANDY: I'm going to have to change the tape, but I'm going to listen to what's on it first.

---

no less than three full bottles should have remained cached at the South Summit as the Mountain Madness team made its descent. One of the bottles would have been Neal Beidleman's third bottle, which he'd not needed, as Boukreev had given him a third bottle in the vicinity of the Balcony as they were ascending. The other two, presumably, were there as Boukreev's reserve. What happened to the Mountain Madness oxygen remains a mystery.

*Rob Hall's two guides, Andy Harris and Mike Groom, were on either side of Jon Krakauer, who would, ultimately, be the only Adventure Consultants client-climber to both summit and survive. Doug Hansen and Yasuko Namba perished on their descent from the summit.

NEAL: —his suits are for a hundred dollars or a hundred thousand dollars, that's beside the point. These questions—

SANDY: This is tape three, Everest debriefing, May fifteenth, 1996. We were at the point in the last tape where Neal was talking about his descent and speaking sort of generally for—

LENE: Please don't speak for me.

SANDY: —for the descent—at least the four of us—right? Neal, Tim, Charlotte, and me.

NEAL: Excuse me. I'd like to explore that comment. What does that mean?

LENE: I said, "Please don't speak for me." Because, she said she was generally speaking for us and I said, "Please don't speak for me."

SANDY: I said the four of us, and I articulated it was Tim, Charlotte, because you guys, you and Klev, sort of descended in a slightly different pattern than we did, but, anyway, Neal was, in the last tape, talking about his descent, and I am willing to let him speak for us until he misspeaks. Are you?—Okay—Neal?

NEAL: Okay, yeah. I am just thinking about something here that's very upsetting. Anyway, I don't quite remember where I was, somewhere around the South Summit, in the last tape. The focus that I had at that particular point was on Sandy. I thought that she was the one that was having the most difficulties, as I think I indicated. When I left the South Summit or the rock below the South Summit, somewhere just over the top and down the fixed ropes, I saw Charlotte standing over the top of Sandy with a big grin on her face. She was holding a needle in her hand, waving it to me. I don't recall where the other people were at that time exactly, other than what I said previously about when I thought they left the South Summit. I came over to her on the downhill side, and Charlotte told me that she had just given Sandy a dexamethasone shot and that Sandy looked pretty out of it at the time.* We were trying to figure out how to get her going. Two things happened, and I don't recall the order in which they happened. Maybe somebody can help me. The two things were that, number one, I realized that we had to motivate pretty heavily on

---

*Sandy Hill (Pittman) has since explained that she had asked Charlotte Fox to give her an injection.

Sandy. I got in front of her, clipped on the rope. This was at the point where if you go out skier's left, if you will, you can slide down the fixed lines. I grabbed Sandy's harness and started her down and told her a process that I had used before many times, pretty successfully, which was that I would start her down. I would slide down the rope on my butt, somewhere between ten to fifty feet, depending on the steepness of the hill, and then she was just to basically slide on her butt, out of control if necessary. The snow that she built up in her feet against my back would stop her and we could start over. And, if she didn't have enough strength to start that process, then I would continue grabbing her harness and pulling her down. The other thing that happened, and again, I can't recall the order in which this happened, was that we looked at her oxygen tank and the pressure was getting down there somewhere, maybe ten megapascals. I knew that Lene had just gotten a fresh bottle of oxygen, and I asked if she would switch bottles with Sandy, since she could move a lot faster and make it down. Lene agreed to that and we did. Again, I can't remember if that occurred before Sandy started sliding or if it happened a little bit further down. Does anybody recall?

SANDY: I don't recall where it was.

TIM: I think it happened approximately the same spot that Charlotte gave Sandy the shot.

NEAL: All at one time?

TIM: Yes.

LENE: Yeah, because I was right behind them—[UI].

SANDY: I'd buy that, because within fifteen minutes I felt pretty frisky again. I was renewed.

NEAL: We turned, or I turned the oxygen bottle up to three or three and a half on Sandy because I wanted her to liven up pretty good. She followed me down in the fashion I described earlier to the bottom of the upper set of fixed lines, the bottom one being the most complicated with a little bit of a traverse. I had to grab her and yank her several times off to the skier's right to get her to the flat. Once she got to that point, you have to walk without a line, but she seemed to be more alert and conscious, and I recall reaching into her pack and turning the flow rate down slightly so that she would have enough oxygen to make it down. Near the bottom of the fixed line Lene passed me on my left looking down. She looked like she was doing okay. I wasn't too worried about her at the time. She looked like she understood the urgency of the matter and was going fast. Above me Tim and Charlotte were coming down. They looked under control, and I wasn't too worried about them at the time. We all walked as a group, carefully, down the very exposed, unroped section between the two fixed lines, basically to the Southeast Summit. On the Southeast Summit, Klev was just ready to leave, and I believe, with Lene. They had pointed down a slightly different variation to get to the top of the line, which actually ended some, maybe, fifteen to twenty meters from the Southeast Summit. Instead of traversing over to the rocks, a very scary process, the new snow allowed us just to skate straight down the middle, I believe.

KLEV: Excuse me. This is Klev. Are you talking about below the Southeast Ridge?

NEAL: Yes, from the Southeast Ridge down.

KLEV: From the Southeast Ridge down, Lene and I stayed on what I believed were the original fixed ropes that we used coming up.

LENE: Yes.

KLEV: Yes, Lene?

LENE: Yes. That is why Neal is saying that. Instead of sort of traversing over the rocks to start with, we just sort of went right through the snow because it was so deep, it slowed us down.

KLEV: Okay, yes.

NEAL: On my descent, somewhere near or somewhere, I believe, below the upper set of fixed ropes, the bottle of oxygen that I had that had a pressure of three or five ran out. I went for a while with no oxygen at all and just was starting to stumble myself. I ran into Tashi Sherpa and asked him to switch the hose from one bottle to the other. I am not sure if he took the old bottle out or not. I could have been carrying two bottles still at that point. I know that I only had a very small pressure left and asked him to turn it to the smallest setting, which was, I believe, half a liter a minute. I continued down. We organized ourself a little bit at the Southeast Summit, excluding Klev and Lene, who had descended just prior to me arriving there. Tim and Charlotte looked pretty good. In fact, I remember Charlotte preparing herself a little bit. She had reached into her pack and maybe even gotten something to eat or a headlamp. I don't exactly recall what it was, but both of them looked pretty good. Sandy was still doing okay but moving slowly at the time.

KLEV: Approximate time? Do you have a guess what time that was? I'm curious what time we—

SANDY: It was near dark.

NEAL: Yeah, at that time I—

TIM: Six [6:00 P.M.].

LENE: I know we left about six o'clock. Klev, when we headed down, it was about six o'clock.

NEAL: I wasn't looking at my watch. My impression was that the valley floor was basically dark or very close to dark and that we were traveling only in the light of the fact that we were up very high on the mountain, alpenglow through the storm. It was snowing at the time but not extremely windy. We could see—I could recall seeing an occasional light flicker down near Base Camp through snow and mist. I knew that we were close, but still had a lot of time to go. I was still very worried about getting down, but having made it off of the most exposed section, the upper part towards the South Summit, I was feeling a little bit confident and that we were moving pretty well. Same process on the next set of fixed lines. Slid on my butt down; people behind me followed; seemed to do pretty well. I recall about that time seeing quite a ways below me two men tethered together. As we found out later, that would be—

SANDY: Beck Weathers.

NEAL: —Beck Weathers in front and Mike somebody-or-another [Mike Groom], the guide for Rob Hall, behind. They were moving very slowly, but I recognized the jacket eventually on the guide and figured he was in good shape and under control. At the bottom of the second set of fixed lines there is several hundred meters vertical of some difficult descent on shale, which was snow-covered at the time. Occasionally a track could be found, but we were following the path or following the figures ahead of us in general terms. Again, some of the people behind lagged just a little bit and I recall waiting several times. Klev and Lene were ahead. They were figures; they were dark objects walking. I don't recall exactly how—what distance they were at the time. Eventually, we got to the final ledges which lead you to the top of the very first fixed line if you're coming up, clipped onto that, waited for a while, and watched as Tim, Charlotte, and Sandy followed down behind. Again, they seemed to be doing pretty well. I started down the line and somewhere, maybe a third of the way down the line, there was a body sitting, facing down, on the line, not really moving, or moving very, very slowly. I got to this point and there were other people around, possibly Beck Weathers and Mike, the guide. It could have been Lene and Klev. I wasn't sure, but I recall going in front of the person on the line and I thought it was Lene. I yelled at her several times. I moved her [oxygen] mask around or whatnot and realized it was not Lene. I recognized the woman as the Japanese woman from Rob Hall's group [Yasuko Namba]. She was not moving whatsoever, most likely out of oxygen. I tried to talk to her, to show her how to go down the line faster. After a few minutes of doing this, I realized that she either didn't understand English or was incapable of doing what I was asking her to do. Again, I grabbed her harness and started sliding, standing, rolling, depending on the terrain, down with her behind me. Several times her feet and her crampons went through my suit and into my back. She seemed to be capable of understanding what was going on, but was incapable of really, physically helping the process much. Sometime after we started, Tim and Charlotte came behind. We were in a larger group now—maybe even two of the Sherpas—I don't recall the faces. Tim offered assistance I recall. I remember hearing his voice. We eventually got down to the bottom of the fixed line after falling several times into crevasses that the lines went over. We had a hard time getting the Japanese woman to make the commitment to go over the crevasses. She was a little scared. I believe Tim helped me several times in picking her up, throwing her, pushing her, pulling her, something to that effect, over some of those crevasses. At the bottom of the line the storm had intensified. The wind was blowing quite strong. Periodically you could see a light back at Camp IV. I got one last fix on the direction and then that was it. That was the last I saw of Camp IV. It was dark. It was blowing very hard. It was snowing extremely hard. It was difficult to talk. All communication was by screaming, and usually only downwind. If somebody were upwind, they may or may not have heard. I don't recall even being able to turn my head much to try to talk upwards. My headlight was still in my pack. I was unable to get it out because I had grabbed the Japanese woman by the arm and she—we walked, staggered, arm in arm together. There were two Sherpas with us at the time, and I believe that Klev and Lene had left us, heading towards Camp IV in the direction they thought was correct. The distance that they were in front of us was probably not very far, but under the condition—

[GAP ON RECORDING]

KLEV: Once Lene and I connected with your group—you, Tim, Charlotte—we absolutely stayed with you because we had a couple Sherpas that we were putting our faith and our confidence in to lead us to camp.

NEAL: That's correct, Klev, but wasn't it—I recall vaguely that your group, or the group that I was in, had walked some distance after the fixed line and then we saw you come from our right or below and come back to us. So I'm assuming that you had left towards Camp IV in a direction, and again, this may only have been thirty seconds or a minute.

KLEV: Lene and I were ahead of you guys. I believe we came down maybe a different set of fixed ropes. And we came down maybe two or three hundred yards to the right, skier's right, of you. When we reached the end of the fixed ropes, then we realized that we had one broken headlamp and we made an immediate traverse to join you.

NEAL: Okay, that seems accurate, because it was—it seemed very shortly after we started walking that you two joined us.

KLEV: Let me back up. It could be very well that we did come down the same fixed ropes. However, we were so far ahead of you, and you guys, immediately, when you got to the end of the fixed ropes, started to the skier's left. That's where our divergence came from. Tim, I see you shaking your head. Or, nodding your head. That's what you believe happened? That is probably more than likely what happened.

NEAL: Okay. It wasn't really clear that there was a leader versus a non-leader or followers at that point, because people were being buffeted by the wind around and walking based on whoever had a headlight in front of them. I tried to yell several times that we needed one leader and one headlight to follow, otherwise we would be wandering aimlessly. My intention was to not walk directly towards Camp IV, even though for one minute at the bottom of the fixed lines I knew the direction to it, because of the fact that the rope gave a line that I could follow. What I wanted to do was side-hill on the left a bit. I had looked at the terrain from up above, before the storm came in, and made a decision that if the storm came, that the best thing to do would be to avoid the Lhotse Face and that precipice as much as possible. I'd heard of people falling off there before. I'd been warned by friends who had climbed to be very, very careful of getting sucked down into that gully, because once you get into the gully and you lose the side hill, it's very easy to think you're walking on the flat but in fact you're walking right towards the edge of the cliff. So I continued to walk with the Japanese woman on my arm and, I believe, Sandy, Charlotte, and Tim behind. Mike Groom and Beck were somewhat in front of us. The two fastest people at the time were the two Sherpas, and they seemed to dart in front of us in many different directions, or at least changing directions. I tried to remember, watching my feet, to stay on a side hill, not too great of a side hill but a slight side hill which would put us at the saddle of the South Col, near a high point, and at that point is where a rock, a very distinct rock band, crosses the [South] Col. And, I knew that once we found that rock, if we just turned right and wandered downhill within the rocks, we would either hit the camp or the Geneva Spur or the fixed ropes coming up to it or all the trash right around. That was the plan or the tack that I thought was best at the time. Because of the wind and because people were being pushed forward and backwards and wandering around and also because I could not travel to the front of the group, carrying the Japanese woman, and I didn't have a headlight out yet, it's my impression that we side-hilled too much to the point where we were on the crest of the ridge and the side hill went away. Once we lost the side hill, I personally lost all orientation to what direction we were walking. There was nothing left to follow in terms of terrain. We wandered as a group for a while. I don't know how long. It seemed like quite a while. We were moving slowly. Different people would come to the front and fall behind, but we kept yelling, all of us, to stay together as a group. I felt very strongly that if any person made an attempt to find the camp by themselves or left the group, that either they would be extremely lucky and find the camp, but most likely be lost completely. At some point in this wandering, we most likely got turned around and got onto the Tibetan side of the South Col. Even though this may have been something I understood in my mind at the time, my oxygen had well run out a long time ago, everybody else was staggering around, and it just was extremely hard to think and to try to make sense out of the things that we saw, the direction of the wind or whatnot. It was like being inside of a milk bottle. The winds were blowing. I've asked people, trying to estimate [the wind speed].

I don't know; [it was] anywhere from, on the low side, forty miles an hour up to maybe gusts of eighty [mph] or more. They were enough to knock us off our feet many times. Finally, during this walking or at some time during this walking, maybe an hour's worth I'm guessing, people were getting extremely cold. All faces were iced up. Maybe another headlamp went out. I don't recall. There weren't very many following us, or with our group. I recall seeing a small dip in the ground. We were on very difficult ice with rock sticking through. The dip in front of us was illuminated by the headlamp. It rose up a little bit and I walked to the edge of the rise and looked over, and whether I actually saw something or sensed something, I just knew that was totally dangerous. There was no terrain like that on the South Col that we should be even close to, and I got very, very scared and came back to the group. I recall, with the help of Tim and Klev, yelling and screaming at people that we absolutely had to stay together and I suggested or yelled or barked or ordered or whatever it was that we huddle up and wait. I remembered from the night before that during the very bad storm somewhere before ten o'clock, before we left, a similar storm had subsided and became very still. I was banking on the fact that, if the storm did let up for just a minute or [if] we could see some stars or see the mountains, we could get our orientation and we could at least pick the direction that we wanted to go. I had no idea if we were looking at the Kangshung Face or the Lhotse Face or any other face up there. We did decide to huddle up. We got into a big dogpile with our backs to the wind. People laid on people's laps. We screamed at each other. We beat on each other's backs. We checked on each other. Everybody participated in a very heroic way to try to stay warm and to keep each other awake and warm. This continued for some period of time I don't know how long. Time is very warped, but it must have been awhile, because I was extremely cold pretty shortly after that. We were checking our fingers. We were checking each other's consciousness. We just tried to keep moving. It was something of an experience that I've never really had before, being what I felt so close to falling asleep and never waking up. I had rushes of warmth come up and down through my body. Whether it was hypothermia or hypoxia I don't know, a combination of both. I just remember screaming into the wind, all of us yelling, moving, kicking, trying to stay alive. I kept looking at my watch. I thought I saw times. I can't really say that I knew what I was looking at. I was just looking at my watch, hoping that the weather would clear. At some point in the night, the winds did not subside, but the snow let up a couple times. Once, just enough. I looked up and I recall seeing vaguely some stars and then it closed in again. That gave me a lot of hope and I recall talking to Tim and Klev that there were stars and that we could figure what was going on, and we all started thinking in those terms and turning our minds onto what we could possibly gain by seeing stars or the mountain. Another time, after that, it cleared again, enough to look up. The wind was still howling, but I recall yelling myself that there was the Big Dipper and the North Star. Either Klev or Tim said, "And, yes, there's Everest." I remember looking at it and being perplexed, not even knowing if it were Everest or Lhotse. But, Klev, I believe, took the initiative and was absolutely positive. He had in his mind; he knew what direction camp was. He had figured it out with that bit of information. We decided somehow. I don't recall the process. It was more of a mass-type standing. We tried to get everybody stood up. The Japanese woman was still hanging on to my arm I recall. It was very hard for me to move or to look around. I tried to pull people up as well as everybody else around. About the only person that I recognized was Sandy because of the distinct color of her jacket. Everybody else was just bodies and voices. When we got up, we all started to move. There was one headlight—I don't know who had it on—who seemed to be moving in a direction forward. I tried to follow with the Japanese woman and somebody else under or behind my right arm; I don't know who it was. I kept asking Klev, "Are you sure? Are you sure?" And, he was positive. He seemed to be totally aware and understanding of which mountain was which and what direction that we needed to go. It was in the opposite one that we had come. It was uphill and it just all of a sudden seemed to make sense to me too. Somewhere along the way, the movement, the motion of people, split. There were people that could move and there were people that could not move. It was a choice at that time to stay or to make a break for it and hopefully find the camp. Whether this is just my perception or whether it's something that I felt as—

KLEV: I'd like to jump in a little bit—back up maybe to where we broke the huddle when we had our bearings. We had our bearings, and we discussed, Tim and Neal and I, that it was time to move, and it took some time like you were saying. We got everybody on their feet, trying to walk in place, whatever it was, to get things moving. There were several people that, like Neal said, couldn't get up. We also had in our huddle—I don't know that it was mentioned—Beck [Weathers] and Mike [Groom].

UNIDENTIFIED MALE VOICE: And two Sherpa.

KLEV: And two Sherpa. Who was it?

SANDY: Tashi and Ngawang Dorje.—This tape is going to run out in about two seconds.

SANDY: All right, this is Everest debriefing tape four, May fifteenth, 1996.

KLEV: I think I had jumped in there just to correct from the point where we broke the huddle on. We stood up and tried to exercise everybody's legs to get them moving. And it was obvious that Charlotte and the Japanese woman, Sandy, were very immobile. They were able to stand, but walking unsupported was impossible. So we took people on our arms. My recollection was I had Charlotte initially and the Japanese woman, and quickly realized that there was no way, because I was on my knees most of the time, just trying to get them back up. And then—I wish Tim was here.*

NEAL: Stop the story.

SANDY: Stop it.

[GAP ON RECORDING]

KLEV: So, [on] our first attempt to get people on their feet, we had various people on our arms, went a few feet, and then I recall kind of juggling everybody around to try and see if we could try different combinations that worked. I had to leave the Japanese lady, and I believe at that time Tim then picked up Charlotte. Lene and I got teamed up.

NEAL: I went to Sandy. Your gloves were off—somehow—you were pleading with me to put your gloves back on. I tried to put my arm around you and pull you along and you said that you can't walk. I remember telling you if you can't walk that you needed to crawl. And then somewhere close to that, in my account, Klev and I and possibly Tim—I don't recall Tim—Klev and I had this conversation that—

KLEV: Lene was there.

LENE: I was there.

---

*At this point in the debriefing Tim Madsen is not present.

NEAL: That either we were going to go and make it and send help, or—

KLEV: Huddle up or something.

NEAL: Or huddle back up or it wasn't going to happen. There was a pretty intense fear and high adrenaline at that time because of the clearing, and I think at that time we decided that we would go. And we stumbled, got up, stumbled, ran, walked, whatever we did, up this hill, and sometime, not too far over the hill, we were fortunate to see a flicker of a headlight in the distance, and we ran toward it, and it was Anatoli and one other person—I don't know who—just outside of our tents.

LENE: Pemba.

NEAL: We all fell in front of the tents. Anatoli helped us with our crampons off and directed us, shoved us, pushed us, into different tents.

KLEV: By that time we had walked a thousand, twelve hundred feet, into the wind, and I think we were snowblind.

NEAL: Frozen thick and solid.

KLEV: We were totally snowblind. Lene, you were not?

LENE: I don't think I was snowblind, and I wasn't filled with fear or adrenaline. I was at no point convinced that we were going to die or anything.

KLEV: I recall—I want to give Tim some credit here, because I saw him at least twice, maybe three times, put Sandy's gloves back on. For some reason [Klev laughs], Sandy, you were obsessed with taking those things off. I think you owe Tim—

SANDY: Those [brand name deleted] gloves don't work very well.

KLEV: It sounds like Neal put them on a few times. I think those guys saved your fingers, for sure, in my mind.

NEAL: Well, sorry to indicate that I thought everybody ran with fear and adrenaline. [Klev laughs.] I did. I didn't realize that Lene was totally under control.

LENE: I was totally under control within myself, Neal.

NEAL: I'm glad.

LENE: I am, too.

SANDY: Neal's recollection of what happened is also mine. I share that. He said, "We've got to bolt for it now. This is our only chance. There's a break in the wind and if you can't walk, then crawl." Which I did.

KLEV: I don't believe there was a break in the wind. It was the visibility. We had a break in the visibility.

SANDY: Not the wind. I'm sorry; the visibility. And I actually did crawl. I thought that sounded like a good idea, because I could crawl, but I couldn't walk. The wind was just knocking me down every time. And I do remember there was like this—there was a figure that darted off by itself without a headlamp, and I don't know who that was, but it could have been Beck at that point.

INGRID: The man with the mandolin?*

SANDY: No, it wasn't the man with the mandolin. It was before I got delusional. But, anyway, I crawled and I did manage to follow the group for a while, but then, when they crested a hill, I lost sight of that lamp and realized that my only hope was staying with somebody else, and so I saw another lamp and I yelled out, and said, "Hello, hello, hello." And, Tim didn't know who it was. He hello'd back and eventually I rejoined Tim and Charlotte and the three of us huddled together.

TIM: What happened was, I had Charlotte on my arm, back, head, wherever, and I couldn't see where to go. And I also didn't have the strength to drag or carry her to camp. She refused to walk. So, I decided—so we sat down for a second and then I heard a moan about fifteen, twenty yards, about twenty feet behind us, which was the Japanese girl. So I went back and I grabbed her and brought her up to where Charlotte was. Also Mike was still tethered to Beck. Beck was having a very hard time walking also. So, I told Mike, since I presumed he was still functional, that he has go to camp also and come back and get help.† That was probably the dark figure that Sandy made

---

*Prior to the debriefing session, Sandy Hill (Pittman) had recounted that, while she was in the "dogpile," she had been hallucinating, and in one of her hallucinations she had seen a man playing a mandolin.

†Mike Groom has said that, alone, he headed into the darkness and a heavy gale that lashed him with high-velocity ice particles. "I had no idea where I was going," he remembered. Wandering for what seemed like hours and edging into a warm lethargy that belied the reality of his critically low and falling

reference to. The plan at this point was just to sit still and hope some-body would come back for us. There was five of us in the group once Sandy came back: myself, Sandy, Charlotte, the Japanese lady, and Beck [Weathers].* We tried to do the same thing which the bigger group did earlier, just stay huddled together, stay awake, and try to keep each other warm. The time of night I have no clue, but what did eventually happen was word was gotten to Anatoli and after a try or two, he did find where we were sitting, and as he recalled, he picked up Charlotte, gave an oxygen bottle to Sandy, hauled Charlotte back, and then sometime later made a second trip with tea and an-other oxygen bottle where he grabbed Sandy, hauled her back, and I followed. And that's—I believe I was the last member into Camp IV.

KLEV: Neal, how far from camp did you think we were? In our original huddle?

NEAL: When it cleared, how far did I think we were?

KLEV: No, I mean how far do you think we walked, ultimately, reality? How far were we from camp?

NEAL: I would say four hundred meters. And I think that was con-firmed the next day by people that went out and found our gear where it was strewn, and the Japanese woman.

TIM: I know when the first time Toli came and found us he mentioned that he thought it was a twenty- or thirty-minute walk. Which didn't

---

body temperature, he got a glimpse of Camp IV in a momentary break in the weather. Stumbling into Camp IV, he passed one tent and stopped at the next. It was the tent of Stuart Hutchison and Jon Krakauer, climber-clients and members of his expedition. Through the door of their tent he blurted out a slurry of frozen words that he hoped would convey the urgency of the situation and the location of those stranded at the South Col. He's recalled, "Whatever I said, I hoped I gave some accurate directions and instructions to help find Beck, Yasuko, and the others. I was convinced that as a result of whatever conversations took place between us, rescuers would be rounded up to help me get Beck and Yasuko back into camp." Now, Groom says, it's his understanding that Hutchison went out into the storm, but that the ferocity of the blizzard prevented a rescue effort. Source: Michael Groom, *Sheer Will* (Milsons Point, NSW, Australia: Random House Pty. Ltd., 1997).

*Weathers, prior to Boukreev's discovery of the "dogpile" on the South Col, had apparently wandered away from the group because, as has previously been mentioned, Boukreev found only four climbers on the South Col during his early-morning rescue efforts.

instill a whole lot of hope in me, but as it turned out, it wasn't that far.

SANDY: It didn't seem like it was that far at all. I don't think that, even assisted, I was up for a twenty- or thirty-minute walk. It seemed more like it was a ten-minute walk at the most.*

TIM: I think the difference was the path that we took. His was a lot longer than ours.

NEAL: Also, as part of the next morning confirmation, four hundred meters was the estimate given by some of the people that went out to the packs. Also another estimate of ten to fifteen meters from the edge of the Kangshung Face was given.

[BRIEF DISCUSSION ABOUT DISPOSITION OF DEBRIEFING TAPE—DELETED]

SANDY: —but the next day Anatoli went up to find Scott.

INGRID: Well, the first thing that happened was the Sherpas went up to find Scott.

SANDY: And do you know that fact? Do you have radio?

INGRID: Yeah. Well, I have the radio call was that they left between— they left around 9:50 [A.M.].

NEAL: I personally saw Ngawang [Sya Kya Sherpa] and Tashi. Ngawang, Old Ngawang [Lopsang's father], came up to me and slapped his chest and said, "I carry oxygen. I go look for Scott." And I wished him well and looked up the hill myself. There appeared to be two other people somewhere above the hard ice, maybe right at that bottom of the first fixed lines at that time. And I assumed that they were the other two Sherpa. I'd heard that they had been sent out to go help.[†]

INGRID: Did you give them any instructions before they left?

_____

*Boukreev did not have the same recollection. When reviewing the debriefing tapes, he recalled that the return to Camp IV with Sandy Hill (Pittman) had taken longer than ten minutes.
[†]Two of Rob Hall's climbing Sherpas, Ang Dorje Sherpa (climbing sirdar), and Lhakpa Chirri Sherpa, whom Boukreev had tried to recruit for a rescue of Yasuko Namba, made a valiant but unsuccessful attempt to climb to Rob Hall and rescue him.

NEAL: No, it seemed pretty clear to me that they would go up and do the best job that they could. They had oxygen. Their goal was to go find Scott and bring him down.

INGRID: And the report we got from the Taiwanese Sherpas—it was about four o'clock that afternoon—was that Makalu was back, that they had found Makalu and that Scott—they first said he was dead. And there was a lot of people could not believe that at Base Camp, that Makalu would survive and Scott wouldn't. And so, the Sherpas were further questioned, and they said, "Well, yes, he was breathing." And at that point Anatoli had already decided to go up, I believe, and Caroline,* the doctor from Rob Hall's camp, talked to Anatoli over the radio and gave him instructions. Anatoli can give his account now of what happened when he went up to find Scott for the second time.

ANATOLI: The next day, after our attempt and after terrible night, when I know some our Sherpa go up with oxygen, I like to see the situation. And, from my experience, I saw our members, and I saw this is, will be everything okay, not big deal. I afraid just about Scott, because, actually, I believe for his power, for his experience, he can survive this night, maybe little frostbited, but with down jacket with One Sport, I know this many examples people survived this without big frostbited. And our Sherpa go up with oxygen and I saw the situation. And, somebody ask about me, helping to go down.† But my decision, it was [to stay] in Camp IV and wait this situation about Scott. And I am sorry for Klev. Klev ask me helping, but I said I talked with Neal little bit, and I think is most important wait, because for me, I was sure. Scott maybe have some—maybe he tired—but he can survive this.

SANDY: The next morning—the weather—let's just ask about [that]. Can you mention what the weather was the next morning and day?

ANATOLI: Weather, it was like not so bad. It is okay. Look like good visibility, not very strong wind. It was windy, but not very strong, like cold. Just cold. Maybe I felt like this cold. And when members left, all members left, I saw the situation. I saw somebody go up, somebody

---

*Dr. Caroline Mackenzie, Everest Base Camp doctor for the Adventure Consultants expedition.

†Klev Schoening, who was having some difficulty with his vision, asked Boukreev to help assist him down the mountain, but Boukreev, after checking with Neal Beidleman, said that he would be remaining at Camp IV to await word on Scott Fischer's condition.

go down face of Everest, this couloir where fixed line above fixed line, yellow fixed line. And I saw the situation. I slept like few hours and eating, little rest, and I felt before in morning I felt like empty, not go up, not go down. But then members left, I little rested. I felt much better and I waited this result from Sherpas. Maybe in one o'clock or two o'clock I have not information. Maybe Lopsang have contact. I don't know. I just waited. Also I talk with Todd Burleson and Pete Athans* about this situation. These people was ready to help me and we talked about this situation, about crazy situation, and he [Scott] depended of people. But Scott just alone. He is strong with experience, and we waited result from Sherpas. Afternoon, I saw somebody go down. It was Tashi [Sherpa], more stronger than father of Lopsang. He was much stronger, and somebody, also, Todd Burleson told me [about] Makalu [Gau], one Taiwanese man, came back. He survived this night together with Scott. I can talk with this man. I talked with this man. He said, "Oh"—but he was very; is very difficult situation, frostbited and cannot say too much, but he told, "Oh, Scott didn't sleep; talked all night; keep power; great person." [This is] what I understood from this man.

INGRID: I'm sorry. I'm not sure I understood. Makalu, he told you that Scott was talking to him all night?

ANATOLI: All night, yeah. And this is—I believe Scott, maybe, get some problem, but he will survive. And when I talked with Tashi and Lopsang and Lopsang's father and these people told me he didn't walk. They found him at the rock, at the steps, and he without moving, without anything what is possible. I understood this from Sherpas. He gets like cerebral edema; he didn't talk; he have problem; but he—maybe it possible to help him. And began three o'clock [3:00 P.M., May 11, 1996], began snow, wind again, and I prepare oxygen, tea, and I prepared for my trip to go up again. But all people told me, Toli, it is impossible for you to help him, because Sherpa told he is—he have cerebral, like cerebral edema and impossible to help him. I saw the situation, and I like to see from my eyes about this situation. And, I took oxygen, two bottles. It was difficult to find because our

---

*Todd Burleson was the leader and a guide for the Alpine Ascents International Guided Expedition. Pete Athans was one of Burleson's guides. These two climbers, as was Boukreev, were honored when, in December 1997, the American Alpine Club bestowed upon them the David A. Sowles Memorial Award for their heroism on Everest.

oxygen gone. I saw Sherpas tent. I found these bottles. Sherpas use oxygen. I took this oxygen from Sherpas. No so easy. [Boukreev laughs.] And also Sherpas don't like if I go up because he said impossible. They was right. I get Scott too late. And when I spent two hours to go up with oxygen. After yellow ropes, after white ropes, maybe like two hundred, between 8,200, 8,300 [meters] I found his body. Without—what is possible to say for English—without . . . ?

INGRID: Signs of life?

ANATOLI: Signs of life. His eyes like closed and go down. I tried to open; impossible, frozen. Color, all face like frozen. Down jacket open; one hand from down jacket, without down jacket, without down suit. All hand without mitts. And down jacket also open and oxygen finished. Time, seven o'clock [7:00 P.M.], just same time when I get Scott, begin very strong wind. And, very fast and with snow, and I lose all visibility. I began little keep his body, because impossible. I saw this. I have little experience with this, and I saw impossible for me to move his body to life. And just put his pack in his body, put oxygen, ropes, little packed his body what I can. And also began dark, and I was hurry. I go down very fast. I take his ice ax, little things from his self for his family, and go down very fast. Visibility gone after fixed line, incredible time, like last night again. Without eyes [and] without visibility, I tried to find our camp [Camp IV]. It was very difficult. Sherpas slept; didn't help me; nobody.

KLEV: The Sherpa slipped? A Sherpa was with you?

INGRID: The Sherpas slept and didn't put a light out for him.

KLEV: Oh, *slept.* I'm sorry.

ANATOLI: Not light. Just before when I go up, also, I believe I can to help for Scott because I saw this one guy from Rob Hall expedition came back; he survived this night. He lose maybe hands, like half of hand, he survived this night.*

KLEV: That was Beck?

INGRID: Yes.

ANATOLI: Before, when I go up, I ask him [Beck Weathers], "Did he

---

*Boukreev is describing his encounter with Beck Weathers just beyond the perimeter of Camp IV on the afternoon of May 11, as Boukreev headed up the mountain for Scott Fischer (see p. 203, *The Climb*).

see [Scott]." But, he [Weathers] understood nothing. Like he—he
was very crazy, and I hope I can help for Scott, but this man just made
voice and this voice I heard it. Is like my intuition helped me to find
camp in the night.* And also very, very cold. I get very cold, very tired.
So is my night at the South Col, but I survived it. It is no problem.
And, what I can say about this?

---

*Boukreev, here, is describing how Beck Weathers's screams of pain at
Camp IV helped him find his way back to the Mountain Madness tents after
he'd gotten lost in the storm that hit during his last-ditch attempt to save Scott
Fischer (see p. 205, *The Climb*).

Visit **www.panmacmillan.com** to read more about all our books and to buy them. You will also find features, author interviews and news of any author events, and you can sign up for e-newsletters so that you're always first to hear about our new releases.